THE BROTHERS

THE
BROTHERS

JOHN FOSTER DULLES, ALLEN DULLES,
AND THEIR SECRET WORLD WAR

STEPHEN KINZER

TIMES BOOKS
HENRY HOLT AND COMPANY NEW YORK

Times Books
Henry Holt and Company, LLC
Publishers since 1866
175 Fifth Avenue
New York, New York 10010

Henry Holt® is a registered trademark of
Henry Holt and Company, LLC.

Library of Congress Cataloging-in-Publication Data
Kinzer, Stephen.
The brothers : John Foster Dulles, Allen Dulles, and their secret world war /
Stephen Kinzer. — First Edition.
    pages cm
Includes bibliographical references and index.
ISBN 978-0-8050-9497-8 (hardcover)—ISBN 978-1-4299-5352-8 (electronic
book)   1. Dulles, John Foster, 1888–1959.   2. Dulles, Allen, 1893–
1969.   3. United States—Foreign relations—1953–1961.   4. Statesmen—United
States—Biography.   5. Spies—United States—Biography.   6. Cabinet officers—
United States—Biography.   7. United States. Central Intelligence Agency—Officials
and employees—Biography.   8. Intelligence service—United States—History—20th
century.   I. Title.
E748.D868K56 2013
327.12730092'2—dc23   2013007718

First Edition 2013

Designed by Kelly S. Too

Printed in the United States of America

1   3   5   7   9   10   8   6   4   2

That inscrutable thing is chiefly what I hate; and be the white whale agent, or be the white whale principal, I will wreak that hate upon him.

—Captain Ahab in *Moby-Dick*,
by Herman Melville

CONTENTS

THE BROTHERS

INTRODUCTION

When John Foster Dulles died on May 24, 1959, a bereft nation mourned more intensely than it had since the death of Franklin Roosevelt fourteen years before. Thousands lined up outside the National Cathedral in Washington to pass by his bier. Dignitaries from around the world, led by Chancellor Konrad Adenauer of West Germany and President Chiang Kai-shek of Taiwan, came to the funeral. It was broadcast live on the ABC and CBS television networks. Many who watched agreed that the world had lost, as President Eisenhower said in his eulogy, "one of the truly great men of our time."

Two months later, Eisenhower signed an executive order decreeing that in tribute to this towering figure, the new super-airport being built at Chantilly, Virginia, would be named Dulles International.

Enthusiasm for this idea waned after Eisenhower left the White House in 1961. The new president, John F. Kennedy, did not want to name an ultra-modern piece of America's future after a crusty Cold War militant. As the airport neared completion, the chairman of the Federal Aviation Authority announced that it would be named Chantilly International. He left open the possibility that a terminal might be named for Dulles.

That sent partisans into action. One of them was Dulles's brother, Allen, who had run the Central Intelligence Agency for nearly a decade. Pressure on Kennedy grew, and he finally relented. On November 17, 1962, with both Eisenhower and Allen Dulles watching, he presided over the official opening of Dulles International Airport.

"How appropriate it is that this should be named after Secretary Dulles," Kennedy said in his speech. "He was a member of an extraordinary family: his brother, Allen Dulles, who served in a great many administrations, stretching back, I believe, to President Hoover, all the way to this one; John Foster Dulles, who at the age of 19 was, rather strangely, the secretary to the Chinese delegation to The Hague, and who served nearly every Presidential administration from that time forward to his death in 1959; their uncle, who was secretary of state, Mr. Lansing; their grandfather, who was secretary of state, Mr. Foster. I know of few families and certainly few contemporaries who rendered more distinguished and dedicated service to their country."

Then, in what became a newsreel clip seen around the world, Kennedy pulled back a curtain and unveiled the airport's symbolic centerpiece: a larger-than-life bust of John Foster Dulles. It was on a pedestal overlooking an evocative reflecting pool at the center of the airport that the architect, Eero Saarinen, hoped would calm travelers' turbulent spirits.

Half a century after Dulles's death stunned Americans, few remember him. Many associate his name with an airport and nothing more. Even his bust has disappeared.

During renovations in the 1990s, the reflecting pool at Dulles International Airport was filled. The bust was removed. When the renovation was complete, it did not reappear. No one seemed to notice.

After several fruitless inquiries, I finally tracked down the bust. A woman who works for the Metropolitan Washington Airports Authority arranged for me to view it. It stands in a private conference room opposite Baggage Claim Carousel #3. Beside it are plaques thanking the Airports Authority for sponsoring local golf tournaments. Dulles looks big-eyed and oddly diffident, anything but heroic.

Dedicated by the president of the United States while the world watched, now shunted into a little-used room opposite baggage claim, this bust reflects what history has done to the Dulles brothers.

A biography published three years after John Foster Dulles died asserted that "he provoked an extraordinary mixture of veneration and hatred during his lifetime, and since his death, in spite of a surge of emotion in his favor towards the end, his memory has remained contentious and intriguing." That memory faded quickly. In 1971 a journalist wrote that although the Dulles name had not been completely forgotten, "certainly most of the *éclat* had gone out of it."

John Foster Dulles was, as one biographer wrote, "a secretary of state so powerful and implacable that no government in what was then fervently referred to as the Free World would have dared to make a decision of international importance without first getting his nod of approval." Another biographer called his brother, Allen, "the greatest intelligence officer who ever lived."

"Do you realize my responsibilities?" Allen asked his sister when he was at the peak of his power. "I have to send people out to get killed. Who else in this country in peacetime has the right to do that?"

These uniquely powerful brothers set in motion many of the processes that shape today's world. Understanding who they were, and what they did, is a key to uncovering the obscured roots of upheaval in Asia, Africa, and Latin America.

A book tracing these roots could not have been written in an earlier era. Only long after the Dulles brothers died did the full consequences of their actions become clear. They may have believed that the countries in which they intervened would quickly become stable, prosperous, and free. More often, the opposite happened. Some of the countries they targeted have never recovered. Nor has the world.

This story is rich with lessons for the modern era. It is about exceptionalism, the view that the United States is inherently more moral and farther-seeing than other countries and therefore may behave in ways that others should not. It also addresses the belief that because of its immense power, the United States can not only topple governments but guide the course of history.

To these widely held convictions, the Dulles brothers added two others, both bred into them over many years. One was missionary Christianity, which tells believers that they understand eternal truths and have an obligation to convert the unenlightened. Alongside it was the presumption that protecting the right of large American corporations to operate freely in the world is good for everyone.

The story of the Dulles brothers is the story of America. It illuminates and helps explain the modern history of the United States and the world.

PART I

TWO BROTHERS

1

UNMENTIONABLE HAPPENINGS

Early every summer morning in the first years of the twentieth century, two small boys awoke as dawn broke over Lake Ontario. Their day began with a cold bath, the only kind their father allowed. After breakfast, they gathered with the rest of their family on the front porch for a Bible reading, sang a hymn or two, and knelt as their father led them in prayer. Their duty done, they raced to the shore, where their grandfather and uncle were waiting to take them out to stalk the wily smallmouth bass.

Never have a couple of catboats on any lake held three such generations. The old man with billowing sideburns had been America's thirty-second secretary of state. His son-in-law was on his way to becoming the forty-second. As for the two boys, they would ultimately outshine both of their illustrious fishing partners. The elder, John Foster Dulles, would become the fifty-second secretary of state and a commanding force in world politics. His brother, Allen, would also grow up to shape the fate of nations, but in secret ways no one could then imagine. Later in life he came to believe that his interest in espionage was shaped in part by the experience of "finding the fish, hooking the fish and playing the fish, [working] to draw him in and tire him until he's almost glad to be caught in the net."

Those morning fishing trips through the lakes and rivers of upstate New York, and the afternoons and evenings that followed, were a cascade of lessons in American history and global politics. They influenced the boys in ways they could not yet begin to fathom, making them part of the swirl of forces that would shape the United States when, half a century later, it entered its period of greatest prosperity but also most terrifying dread.

"Here in delightful surroundings we indulged ourselves not only in fishing, sailing and tennis, but in never-ending discussions on the great world issues which our country was then growing up to face," Allen later wrote. "These discussions were naturally given a certain weight and authority by the voice of a former secretary of state and a secretary-of-state-to-be. We children were at first the listeners and the learners, but as we grew up we became vigorous participants in international debates."

The first American member of this extraordinary Scots-Irish family, Joseph Dulles, fled Ireland in 1778 to escape anti-Protestant repression, made his way to South Carolina, and became a prosperous, slave-owning planter. His family was pious and inclined to the clergy. One of his sons, Joseph Heatly Dulles, served as an officer of three Presbyterian churches in Philadelphia. That officer's son, John Welsh Dulles, "a delicate boy," went to Yale to study medicine but felt called to missionary work instead. At the age of twenty-six he set off to preach the gospel in India, famously traveling for 132 days aboard a tempest-tossed ship to reach Madras. Five years later, health problems forced him to return home to Philadelphia, where he took a job directing missionary campaigns for the American Sunday School Union. He wrote a religious manual for Union soldiers in the Civil War, traveled in the Holy Land, and published two books with strongly Christian themes, *Life in India* and *The Ride Through Palestine*.

Two of John Welsh Dulles's three sons followed him into the clergy. Reverend Joseph H. Dulles III directed the library of Princeton Theological Seminary for nearly half a century. His brother Reverend Allen Macy Dulles was a preacher and theologian whose two sons became secretary of state and director of central intelligence.

One of the most cosmopolitan young American women of her generation, Edith Foster, met Allen Macy Dulles in 1881, when both were touring Paris. Edith, just eighteen, was living a Gilded Age fairy tale. Her extravagantly bewhiskered father was John Watson Foster, an eminent lawyer, diplomat, and pillar of the Republican Party. Foster had a fascination with children, and after his only son and one of his daughters died in childhood, he lavished attention on the two daughters who survived. He took Edith and her younger sister, Eleanor, with him when he was named minister to Mexico, and the family lived there for seven years. Then they moved to St. Petersburg, where Foster was minister to the court of Czar Alexander II, emancipator of the Russian serfs. The girls grew up in elegant diplomatic circles, riding horseback in Mexico City's Chapultepec Park, dancing at grand balls with Russian princes, and touring European capitals alongside their doting father. Edith's blossoming romance with Reverend Dulles was interrupted when her father was named minister to Spain. For the next year and a half the young clergyman waited patiently while she enjoyed life among Spanish aristocrats, making a special friend of the *infanta*. When the family returned home in the summer of 1885, Edith found her suitor as ardent as ever. They were married the following January.

The couple settled in Watertown, a haven for New York millionaires on the shore of Lake Ontario, where Reverend Dulles was pastor of the First Presbyterian Church. When Edith became pregnant, she moved to Washington for a few months to enjoy the comfort of her father's three-story mansion. On February 25, 1888, she gave birth there to her first child and named him after her father: John Foster Dulles. Five years later, on April 7, 1893, came a second son, Allen Welsh Dulles. There were also three girls, and all developed a strong sense of family solidarity.

The boys grew up swimming, sailing, hunting, and fishing, but neither was especially strong or athletic. Foster, as the older brother was called then and throughout his life, survived a severe fever as an infant and at the age of thirteen caught typhus, nearly died, and for many months was too weak to walk and had to be carried wherever he went. Allen, whom the family called Allie, was born with a clubfoot, which was then considered a source of shame, but was operated on secretly as soon as doctors considered him old enough and came to walk almost normally.

Religiosity permeated the Dulles household. Morning rituals were only part of their piety. Each Sunday the boys attended three church services, carrying pencil and paper so they could take notes on their father's sermons. Afterward the family would discuss and analyze them. On many evenings they gathered for religious reading: stories about missionaries, articles from the *Herald & Presbyter*, and devotional classics like *Pilgrim's Progress* and *Paradise Lost*. Home life was shaped by contests to see who could recite the longest Bible passage, and by singing hymns.

Foster, whose favorite hymn was "Work for the Night Is Coming," felt the impact of this environment most deeply. According to his mother's diary, by the age of two he was fascinated with prayers and "always says Amen very heartily"; at four he was a fully attentive Sunday School pupil; at five he displayed a "lovely devotional spirit"; and he celebrated turning seven by memorizing seven psalms.

Missionaries on home leave were frequent guests at the Dulles household. Many told captivating stories of their efforts to convert unbelievers in lands from Syria to China. Their commitment to spreading the Gospel was held up as fulfillment of a divine ideal.

"We did not think of these people in terms of foreign policy, but we did grow to understand the life, the poverty, the superstitions, and the eager hopefulness of those with whom the missionaries dealt," the boys' younger sister Eleanor later wrote. "Foster gained much from these contacts, some of which he renewed in later life. . . . There was something unique that left an indelible mark on all of us—not only a deep faith in central religious truths, but also a sense of the obligation of such a faith toward each other and toward those distant people who were striving to gain new light and freedom."

Edith considered her boys too special to be left to public schools, and arranged for them to be given extra tutoring from live-in governesses and at a private academy. When Foster was fifteen, she took him on a grand tour of Europe; Allie joined them later. She did much to open their eyes to the world's possibilities. For all her influence, though, most of what they learned as they grew up came from two formidable men.

Reverend Dulles was a vigorous Presbyterian and a product of missionary tradition. He was austere and demanding, but also scholarly, wise, and devoted to his family. His fervent belief in Christianity, and in the need for missionary work to spread its essential truths, blended easily into a conviction that America's destiny was to go forth and raise up the world's benighted masses.

"Its strengths, I think, lie in the feeling that you are given a certain task to perform," one member of the Dulles clan later wrote of this Calvinist approach to life. "Its weakness lies in the reverse of that, that you may make the mistake of feeling that you are God's spokesman."

The other towering figure of the Dulles brothers' youth, "Grandfather Foster," gave them a quite different but strikingly complementary set of interests, perspectives, and values. During summers on Lake Ontario as the nineteenth century turned into the twentieth, and later at his manse in Washington, he mesmerized them with tales from his tumultuous life: moving westward, clearing land, subduing nature and hostile natives, starting a business, joining with ambitious men, and finding a path to wealth and power. He had lived a classic pioneer life in the age of manifest destiny, embodying the archetypal story of a brave man who sets off to tame wild lands and illuminate dark places. America was to him a nation blessed by Providence, powerful to the point of invincibility, whose people were destined to spread, civilize, and command. He transmitted this belief to his grandsons. From him they also learned how profitable it can be to ingratiate oneself with men of wealth and influence.

"Grandfather Foster" grew up on the Indiana frontier, became editor of his hometown newspaper, and used it to promote the Republican Party. His diplomatic posts were rewards for helping to elect Presidents Ulysses S. Grant, Rutherford B. Hayes, and James A. Garfield. In 1892 another Republican president, Benjamin Harrison, appointed him secretary of state. He served just eight months because Harrison failed to win re-election.

History remembers John Watson Foster's brief term as secretary of state for a singular accomplishment. In 1893 he helped direct the overthrow of the Hawaiian monarchy. President Harrison had discreetly encouraged white settlers in Hawaii to rebel against Queen Liliuokalani, and when they did, Secretary of State Foster endorsed the landing of American troops at Honolulu to support them. The settlers proclaimed themselves Hawaii's new government, the United States quickly recognized their regime, and the monarchy was no more.

"The native inhabitants had proved themselves incapable of maintaining a respectable and responsible government," Foster later wrote, "and lacked the energy or will to improve the advantages which Providence had given them."

This made John Watson Foster the first American secretary of state to participate in the overthrow of a foreign government. Others would follow—including, more than a half century later, his grandson.

After leaving office, "Grandfather Foster" considered returning to his Indiana law practice, but after hearing another Indiana lawyer recount a long legal battle over a hog, he decided to stay in Washington. He set out not to become a lawyer like others, but to invent a new profession: broker for corporations seeking favors in Washington and chances to expand abroad. It was an idea that fit the era. American farmers and manufacturers had so effectively mastered the techniques of mass production that they were producing far more than the United States could consume. They needed foreign markets to fend off ruin. Many also coveted resources from overseas. This required a muscular, assertive foreign policy that would force weaker countries to trade with Americans on terms Americans considered fair. With a career of diplomatic service behind him, capped by a term as secretary of state, and with deep ties to the Republican Party, John Watson Foster was ideally placed to help these American businesses. Corporations hired him to promote their interests in Washington and in foreign capitals. He was counsel to several foreign legations. The White House sent him on diplomatic missions. He negotiated trade agreements with eight countries and brokered a treaty with Britain and Russia regulating fur seal hunting in the Bering Sea.

This visionary protolobbyist thrived on his ability to shape American foreign policy to the benefit of well-paying clients. Both of his grandsons would do the same.

In order to be near his daughter and her boys, "Grandfather Foster" bought a home at Henderson Harbor, near Watertown. Soon afterward, another eminent figure entered their remarkable family. Edith's sister, Eleanor, married a dapper lawyer and diplomat named Robert Lansing, whose family had deep roots in Watertown. Lansing and "Grandfather Foster" had many interests in common, among them fishing, Washington intrigue, and global politics. The old man welcomed Lansing into the clan, and the boys came to adore their "Uncle Bert." This was the foursome that set out onto the choppy waters of Lake Ontario every summer morning.

"Grandfather Foster" was infatuated with the boys and decided that spending summers with them was not enough. He arranged to "borrow" them for the winter months at his red brick mansion near Dupont Circle in Washington. There they lived amid exotic art objects from China and other faraway lands, studied under private tutors, and were attended by liveried servants directed by a majordomo one member of the clan remembered as "Madison, the graying colored butler." Best of all, they had the chance to sit through dinners with a dazzling parade of America's political and business mandarins.

Foster was first "borrowed" when he was just five years old, and soon after arriving made his first visit to the White House, as a guest at a birthday party for one of President Harrison's grandchildren. Allie began his visits a few years later. During their childhood and early teens, both brothers came to feel at ease in the most rarefied circles. They dined with ambassadors, senators, cabinet secretaries, Supreme Court justices, and other grand figures including William Howard Taft, Theodore Roosevelt, Grover Cleveland, William McKinley, Andrew Carnegie, and Woodrow Wilson. Although they were too young to join dinner-table discussions of world events, they paid close attention. From these long evenings they absorbed not only the precepts, ideas, and perceptions that shaped America's ruling class, but also its style, vocabulary, and attitudes.

"The women with their sequins and plumes and the men with their decorations and sashes were dashing and romantic," their sister Eleanor later recalled. "Altogether, the teas and dinners had a dignity and graciousness that make modern cocktail parties seem chaotic by comparison."

Even at this early stage of life, Allie showed extraordinary curiosity about other people. In Watertown he had made a hobby of observing his father's habits and making notes about them. He was only seven years old when his grandfather "borrowed" him for the first time, but he was fascinated by the lively debate that shaped dinner conversations. After the guests departed, the future spymaster would sit in his bedroom and write reports of what he had heard, summarizing the opinions of the statesmen whose company he had just left and seeking to analyze their characters.

"I was an avid listener," he later recalled.

During that first winter in Washington, Allie developed a fascination with the Boer War, and he poured out his passion in a six-thousand-word essay asserting that "the Boers want peace but England has to have the gold and so she goes around fighting all the little countries." His grandfather was so impressed that he paid to have the essay privately printed, complete with spelling errors, and Allie became a published author at the age of eight. His older brother was unimpressed, sniffing that Allie's anticolonial ideas were "wrong-headed and infantile."

That view may have been correct, but in pronouncing it, Foster showed a judgmental harshness that never softened. From early childhood he was solemn, disciplined, and reserved, but also sharply self-righteous. He never lost his temper or complained, but disdained those who fell short of his standards. Memorizing long Bible passages—he could recite the book of John by heart—was one of his favorite pastimes.

Already the two brothers were developing markedly different personalities. Foster was hardworking, narrowly focused, socially inept, and serious beyond his years. His sister Eleanor saw him "more like a second father than a brother." Allie was outgoing and amiable, but prone to explosions of temper. "His intensity of rage, his emotion when he objected to something, was often overwhelming," Eleanor wrote.

The passage of time deepened these differences. Foster's trademarks were a dark hat and umbrella, Allie's a rakish mustache and pipe. Foster became rich and powerful, but remained nearly friendless and often seemed ill at ease. Allie developed into a witty raconteur whose genial manner could beguile almost anyone. He was, as one biographer put it, "the romantic and adventurous member of the family" but also "a much darker, more ruthless and unscrupulous man than his brother."

Two of the boys' three sisters lived their lives away from the limelight—Margaret married a clergyman, Nataline became a nurse—but the third, Eleanor, was as formidable a character as they were. She was nearsighted almost to the point of blindness, but her upbringing made her a hardy swimmer and nearly as good a hunter and angler as either of her brothers. Though hardly a rebel, she was a free thinker who quietly rejected much of her family's Christian piety, had lesbian encounters while an undergraduate at Bryn Mawr, wore silk stockings, cut her hair short, smoked in public, and was even known to swear. Later she earned a doctorate from Harvard, traveled extensively in Europe, Latin America, and South Asia, taught economics, helped run the Social Security system, attended the Bretton Woods conference that reorganized the world economy after World War II, held a variety of diplomatic posts, and wrote a dozen books with titles like *The French Franc 1914–1928*. Her intellect was comparable to that of either of her brothers. Had attitudes toward women been different during her lifetime, she might have risen to outshine them both.

In the autumn of 1904, when Foster was sixteen, he entered the all-male environment of Princeton, his father's alma mater, which had been founded by Presbyterians and was considered a kind of country-club seminary. He was uncomfortable at first, partly due to an outburst of self-hatred fueled by what the family biographer Leonard Mosley called "an emotion of a kind he had never experienced before."

He developed a schoolboy "crush," for he was only sixteen, on one of his fellow students, a wild-eyed rebel two years older than himself. The feeling was more than returned. It was an exhilarating experience until the moment when he discovered from his adored older partner that male relationships can also have their physical side. To a young man who had, so far, only embarrassedly bussed a girl at a party, it was a devastating and shocking revelation of what he knew from his Bible to be a shame and a sin. He conveyed this sense of degradation with such effect that the fellow student walked out of his room and left the college.

At the end of his junior year, Foster was given an opportunity few college students could imagine. The imperial government of China, which "Grandfather Foster" represented in Washington, hired the former secretary of state to advise its delegation to the Second Hague Peace Conference in the Netherlands, and he took his grandson along as secretary. The conference was part of an ambitious effort, promoted by President Theodore Roosevelt and Czar Nicholas II of Russia, to establish global rules that would reduce the danger of war. History assigns it only modest importance, but for nineteen-year-old John Foster Dulles it was a breathtaking introduction to the world of high-level diplomacy and international law. He was able to watch statesmen from dozens of countries ply their trade, with his grandfather at hand to interpret their aims, motives, and tactics.

By the time he returned to Princeton, Foster had decided he would not become a preacher, as those closest to him had expected, but a "Christian lawyer." This "nearly broke my mother's heart," he later confessed.

Not every student at Princeton during those years dreamed of life in the political and economic elite. One young man who graduated in 1907, a year ahead of Foster, chose a radically different path. He was a Nebraskan named Howard Baskerville, like Foster the son and grandson of clergymen but moved by another sort of idealism. Neither Washington nor Wall Street appealed to him. Upon graduation he took a mission job as a schoolteacher in Iran. When he arrived, he found the country in the throes of revolution. He passionately supported the embattled democratic movement and, when it seemed about to be crushed by foreign-backed royalists, recruited a band of young fighters to defend it. On April 20, 1909, he was killed in battle, becoming the first and only American martyr to the cause of Iranian democracy. The news shocked Princeton. There is no record of how Foster reacted—he had already graduated—but the two young men's life choices reflected much about both of them. They also foreshadowed a fateful clash. Howard Baskerville died defending parliamentary democracy in Iran; forty-four years later, Foster and his brother would help crush it.

Foster graduated second in the class of 1908 with a degree in philosophy. His thesis, entitled "The Theory of Judgment," won him a year's scholarship at the Sorbonne in Paris, where he studied under the philosopher and Nobel laureate Henri Bergson. Upon his return to the United States, he enrolled at George Washington University Law School, which he chose so he could live with "Grandfather Foster." He finished the three-year course in two years. When not in class or studying, he worked as an assistant to his grandfather.

During these years, Foster sharpened his ambition. He saw how effectively "Grandfather Foster" used an insider's knowledge of politics and diplomacy to promote the interests of corporate clients with global ambitions. This, he decided, was the career he wanted.

Allie arrived at Princeton two years after Foster graduated. Their dramatically different campus experiences reflected the psychic gap that separated them all their lives. Allie plunged into a sparkling world of clubs, parties, and girls. This drove his father to distraction and set off angry arguments whenever he returned home. Allie's practice of last-minute cramming for exams always seemed to work, though, and like his brother he graduated with distinction. His thesis won him a cash prize of five hundred dollars, which he used to book passage to India, where through a Princeton connection he had found a job teaching English. It was his first step out from under his family's long protective wing.

Among the many girls Allie dated while at Princeton was a dainty, fragile one named Janet Avery, whose family lived in Auburn, New York, where Reverend Dulles had moved to teach at Auburn Theological Seminary. Allie found Janet staid and boring, and quickly moved on. Soon afterward, Janet became the object of his older brother's affection. The traits that led Allie to drop her—steadiness, down-to-earth practicality, conventional attitudes, lack of frivolity—were just the ones Foster admired. With typical precision, he made a date to take her canoeing on the same day his bar exam was scheduled in Buffalo; if he felt confident he had passed, he would propose. The exam went well. A few hours later, while paddling, Foster asked Janet to marry him. She accepted immediately.

As Foster had guessed, he passed the bar exam easily. At his grandfather's suggestion he applied for a position at Sullivan & Cromwell, the country's most eminent corporate law firm. His credentials were impressive: an outstanding academic record at Princeton, graduate study at the Sorbonne, a precocious understanding of international law, some command of French, German, and Spanish, and even a summer of behind-the-scenes work at a major diplomatic conference. The partners at Sullivan & Cromwell were unimpressed. They rarely hired anyone who had not graduated from an Ivy League law school.

Foster, however, was better connected than most applicants rejected by Sullivan & Cromwell. He turned to his grandfather, who had known Algernon Sullivan, the firm's late co-founder, and was willing to use that connection to appeal to the surviving co-founder, William Nelson Cromwell. "Isn't the memory of an old association enough to give this young man a chance?" he asked Cromwell in a letter.

Cromwell understood that when a former secretary of state recommends his grandson for a job, a law firm that relies on Washington connections should pay heed. He overruled his partners, and in the autumn of 1911 Foster joined Sullivan & Cromwell as a clerk. His starting salary was $12.50 per week, which his grandfather generously supplemented. From his new office at 48 Wall Street—the firm occupied the nineteenth and twentieth floors of the Bank of New York Building—he could see the portico of Federal Hall, where President George Washington was inaugurated in 1789.

"Just you wait!" he wrote to Janet upon learning that he had been hired. "In a year or two, I'll be hiring young men myself. I'll be a partner, too."

The two were married in Auburn on June 26, 1912. Foster was twenty-four and Janet had just turned twenty-one. If she did not already realize that work would always be the center of his life, it became clear during their honeymoon in the Catskills. He had contracted a severe case of malaria while on a Sullivan & Cromwell mission to British Guiana—his assignment was to persuade its government to allow duty-free imports of American flour—and the combination of its effects and those of the quinine he took as treatment left him barely able to walk. A nurse accompanied them throughout their honeymoon. Nonetheless their marriage began splendidly, and they remained devoted to each other. Half a century later, after Foster's death, she was told that a forthcoming book would portray him "warts and all."

"What warts?" she asked. "Foster was perfect."

By the time Foster joined Sullivan & Cromwell, it had already become a unique repository of power and influence. Enormous fortunes were accumulated in the United States during the last decades of the nineteenth century. Many of the men who accumulated them used Sullivan & Cromwell as their link to Washington and the world.

Algernon Sullivan and William Nelson Cromwell founded their law firm in 1879 to pursue a new business art: bringing investors and enterprises together to create giant corporations. Sullivan & Cromwell played an important role in the development of modern capitalism by helping to organize what its official history calls "some of America's greatest industrial, commercial, and financial enterprises." In 1882 it created Edison General Electric Company. Seven years later, with the financier J. P. Morgan as its client, it wove twenty-one steelmakers into the National Tube Company and then, in 1891, merged National Tube with seven other companies to create U.S. Steel, capitalized at more than one billion dollars, an astounding sum at that time. The railroad magnate E. H. Harriman, whom President Theodore Roosevelt had denounced as a "malefactor of great wealth" and "enemy of the Republic," hired the firm to wage two of his legendary proxy wars, one to take over the Illinois Central Railroad and another to fend off angry shareholders at the Wells Fargo bank. It won the first with tactics that a New York newspaper called "one of those ruthless exercises of the power of sheer millions," and the second with complex maneuvers that, according to a book about the firm, amounted to "deceit, bribery, and trickery [that] was all legal."

Soon afterward, working on behalf of French investors who were facing ruin after their effort to build a canal across Panama collapsed, Sullivan & Cromwell achieved a unique triumph in global politics. Through a masterful lobbying campaign, its endlessly resourceful managing partner, William Nelson Cromwell, persuaded the United States Congress to reverse its decision to build a canal across Nicaragua and to pay his French clients $40 million for their land in Panama instead. Then he helped engineer a revolution that pulled the province of Panama away from Colombia and established it as an independent country, led by a clique willing to show its gratitude by allowing construction of a canal on terms favorable to the United States. One newspaper called him "the man whose masterful mind, whetted on the grindstone of corporate cunning, conceived and carried out the rape of the Isthmus."

Clients favored Sullivan & Cromwell because its partners, as Cromwell later put it, had "come to know, and be in a position to influence, a considerable number of public men in political life, in financial circles, and on the press, and all these influences and relations were of great and sometimes decisive utility." Sullivan & Cromwell thrived at the point where Washington politics intersected with global business. John Foster Dulles worked at this intersection for nearly forty years.

His first clients were an early taste of the Sullivan & Cromwell mix: investors in Brazilian railroads, Peruvian mines, and Cuban banks. After war broke out in Europe, he traveled there to promote the interests of other clients, including Merck & Co., the American Cotton Oil Company, and the Holland America Line. All were pleased with the young man's work.

Allie was also setting out on the path that would define his future. Soon after graduating from Princeton in 1914, he departed for Ewing Christian College in central India. On the way he stopped in Paris, which for him, as for many of his class of Americans, would become almost a second home. He ran with a crowd of Princeton men who were enjoying the good life there, and although he later recalled reading about the assassination of Archduke Franz Ferdinand during his stay, his most vivid recollection was of the Grand Prix at Longchamp, a highlight of the thoroughbred racing season and a social event of the first order.

Aboard the steamship that took him from France to India, Allie read and was captivated by *Kim*, Rudyard Kipling's classic novel about the "great game" of big-power conflicts and the clandestine maneuvers that shape them. Its hero is an Irish orphan who is reared as a Hindu in the teeming bazaars of Lahore, learns eternal truths from a Tibetan lama, and finally becomes a secret agent for the British, who are described as "the sort to oversee justice" because "they know the land and the customs of the land." In the book, Kim is told that "from time to time, God causes men to be born—and thou art one of them—who have a lust to go ahead at the risk of their lives and discover news. Today it may be of far-off things, tomorrow of some hidden mountain, and the next day of some nearby man who has done a foolishness against the State. . . . He must go alone— alone and at the peril of his head."

Kim is about the glory of empire and the nasty things that must sometimes be done in secret to defend it. In an introduction to a later edition, the critic and activist Edward Said called it "a master work of imperialism." To Allie it was beyond inspirational. He never parted with his copy. It was on his bedside table when he died.

During his stay in India, Allie developed a lifelong taste for servants; afterward, his sister Eleanor wrote, "there was hardly a time when he didn't have someone to fetch and carry for him." He also explored ancient ruins, studied Hindi and Sanskrit, and even heard a reading by the mystic poet Rabindranath Tagore. The anticolonial movement intrigued him, and after attending several subversive meetings, he was invited to the home of an activist leader, the lawyer Motilal Nehru. There he met Nehru's two children, Jawaharlal, who was just back from Cambridge and would become India's first prime minister, and his teenage sister, Vijaya, an even more passionate advocate of independence, who would become a diplomat and the first female president of the United Nations General Assembly.

Allie completed his year of teaching at Ewing Christian College and was invited to stay, but much of the world was at war and he wanted to be closer to the action. He could not return home across the Atlantic because German submarine attacks had made the passage too dangerous. So in the spring of 1915 he set off eastward, taking steamers and trains on a leisurely trip that included stops in Singapore, Hong Kong, Canton, Peking, Shanghai, and Tokyo. American diplomats welcomed him at each stop, and he was invited to several formal receptions. He understood why.

"It is a great thing to have had illustrious relatives," he wrote in a letter home.

The homeland to which Allie returned at the age of twenty-two, after circumnavigating the globe, was much changed from the one he had left fourteen months earlier. America's complacency had been shaken by news of war in Europe, driven home most terrifyingly by the torpedoing of the liner *Lusitania* with the loss of nearly 1,200 lives, including those of 128 Americans. President Woodrow Wilson, who had been Foster's favorite professor at Princeton, differed with his secretary of state, William

Jennings Bryan, on how to respond to Germany's attack on the *Lusitania*, and their dispute led Bryan to resign. In his place Wilson appointed Bryan's deputy, Robert Lansing, the mustachioed Anglophile who was also Foster and Allie's beloved "Uncle Bert."

The boys had grown up with a grandfather who had been secretary of state, and now "Uncle Bert" had been elevated to that post. This gave them closer connections to the inner circle of American power than any pair of young siblings in the country.

Foster had already made use of these connections to secure a job at Sullivan & Cromwell and was building a lucrative career there. Allie had not yet decided what he wished to do with his life. Indirectly, the sinking of the *Lusitania* set him on the path toward espionage and covert action. It led to his "Uncle Bert" becoming secretary of state, which gave him a strong new tie to Washington's most exclusive elite—and his first glimpse of the clandestine world.

Much of the outrage that erupted in the United States after the *Lusitania* attack was based on the belief that she was a defenseless passenger liner, although Germany charged that she was engaged in a secret mission to supply weapons to Britain in violation of the U.S. Neutrality Act. This outrage contributed to the American decision to enter World War I two years later. Only a handful of people knew that Germany's charge was actually correct. One of them was Secretary of State Lansing.

Few in Washington had ever paid much attention to collecting intelligence about other countries, either because they believed the United States did not need it or because of the notion that, as a previous secretary of state, Henry Stimson, memorably put it, "gentlemen do not read each other's mail." One of the few American officials who had promoted intelligence gathering was John Watson Foster, who in 1892–93 had begun the practice of assigning military attachés to American legations and embassies, and had dispatched agents to European cities to "examine the military libraries, bookstores, and publishers' lists in order to give early notice of any new or important publications or inventions or improvements in arms." He also established a Military Intelligence Division in his office, staffed by an army officer and a clerk, to analyze their reports. When Robert Lansing became secretary of state a generation later, the division had more than doubled in size—to three officers and two clerks. With war on the horizon, Lansing moved decisively to expand it. By 1918 it had more than twelve hundred employees who systematically analyzed intelligence from diplomats, military officers, the Secret Service, the Justice Department, and the Postal Inspection Service. Some of these employees also conducted what Lansing called "investigations of a highly confidential character."

So it was that two of Allie's beloved relatives, "Grandfather Foster" and "Uncle Bert," laid the foundation of the American intelligence network he would one day direct.

Of all that Lansing did to steer Allie toward a career in covert action, nothing had more effect than introducing him to Captain Alex Gaunt, a suave and elegant British agent based in Washington during World War I. The two older men spent weekends at Lansing's estate at Henderson Harbor and attended football games in New York. Often "Uncle Bert" brought Allie along. In this close company, Gaunt spoke candidly about his work, which included hiring Pinkerton detectives to monitor American ports and sending agents to infiltrate groups he suspected of anti-British leanings. Allie was transfixed.

"He thought Gaunt was one of the most exciting men he had ever met," according to one account. "He made up his mind that one of these days, he would become an intelligence operative just like him."

With that ultimate goal in mind, Allie took the foreign service examination in 1916. He passed, joined the State Department, and set off on a decade-long career as a diplomat.

His first post was Vienna, capital of the dying Austro-Hungarian Empire. He had the lowest rank in the foreign service: secretary of embassy class five. A few months after arriving, he and Minister Frederic Penfield represented the United States at the funeral of Emperor Franz Joseph, who had ascended to the throne sixty-eight years earlier following the revolutions of 1848. Mechanized war was raging across Europe. As Allie stood in mourning dress at Saint Stephen's Cathedral on November 30, 1916, he could not have avoided the sense that an era was ending and a new one, full of unknown possibilities and terrors, was about to dawn.

In the spring of 1917, as the United States prepared to declare war on Germany and Austria-Hungary, Allie was transferred to the Swiss capital, Bern. Because Switzerland was neutral, it had become a magnet for exiles, agents, and revolutionaries from across Europe and beyond. When Allie asked his new boss what his responsibilities would be, the answer came like a gift from Heaven—or, perhaps, from "Uncle Bert."

"I guess the best thing for you to do is to take charge of intelligence," he was told. "Keep your eyes open. This place is swarming with spies. And write me a weekly report."

The war years gave Allie his first chance to plunge into the netherworld where he would spend much of his life. Though not yet twenty-five, he became a genuine spymaster, spending his days and nights with a polyglot carousel of Serbian, Croatian, Montenegrin, Albanian, Ukrainian, Lithuanian, Czech, Bulgarian, Polish, Romanian, Hungarian, German, and Russian plotters. Often, like other foreign agents, he worked from the ornate lobby and dining room of the Bellevue Palace Hotel, surrounded by baroque elegance that posed a surreal contrast to the hellish trench warfare being waged not far away. He also had a small apartment where he could, as he wrote to Foster, "entertain all the strange characters whom one can hardly meet in a hotel or a restaurant." His results were impressive: a stream of detailed reports about German troop movements, planned attacks, and even the location of a secret factory where Zeppelin bombers were being manufactured.

"The Department finds these dispatches of the highest value, and considers that they show not only careful labor in preparation but also exceptional intelligence in the drawing of conclusions," his superiors wrote in a commendation.

While he was doing such impressive work, Allie also found time to enjoy Bern, which unlike other European capitals remained lively during the war years. He joined a fun-loving circle of expatriates who filled their days with tennis, golf, and hiking, and partied their nights away with balls, formal dinners, and jazz concerts at the Bellevue Palace. By one account he also "made the most of the area's recreational facilities, including the attractive young ladies from the staid local community, from refugee families, and from among the pool of Swiss girls who flocked to the embassies to work as secretaries, stenographers, and clerks." When tennis balls became hard to find, he delighted his friends by arranging for Foster, through friends in the State Department, to send him a dozen in each week's diplomatic pouch.

In one letter home Allie reported that his life as a secret agent was full of "unmentionable happenings" and "incidents of more than usual interest." Years later, two of them came to light.

Allie was preparing for a date on a Friday afternoon—according to one version he was meeting "two blonde and spectacularly buxom Swiss twin sisters who had agreed to a weekend rendezvous at a country inn"—when he received a telephone call from a Russian exile who said he had an urgent message to deliver to the United States, and insisted they meet that night. With his mind focused on the forthcoming weekend, Allie brushed him off. Years afterward he learned that the caller was Lenin, and that the reason Lenin never called back was that the next day he boarded his sealed train to St. Petersburg and set off to change the course of history.

"Here the first chance—if in fact it was a chance—to start talking to the Communist leaders was lost," Allie later admitted.

Around the same time, Allie was informed by British officers that a young Czech woman he was dating, who worked with him at the American legation and had access to his code room, was passing information to Austrian agents. They had decided she must be liquidated, and he understood it as a necessity of wartime counterespionage. One night he took her to dinner and then, instead of squiring her home, delivered her to two British agents who were waiting in front of the fourteenth-century Nydegg Church. She was never heard from again.

By the time the Dulles brothers' first great patron, John Watson Foster, died in 1917, "Uncle Bert" was secretary of state and had become their new one. He subsidized Allie's freewheeling lifestyle in Bern with a private stipend, and also gave Foster his first chance to intervene in the politics of a foreign nation.

A pro-American regime in Cuba, led by the Conservative Party, was seeking to hold power after losing an election, and followers of the victorious Liberals rose up in protest. Violence threatened the interests of thirteen Sullivan & Cromwell clients, owners of sugar mills, railways, and mines who had $170 million—the equivalent of $42 billion in the early twenty-first century—invested in Cuba. They turned to the firm for protection. Foster took the case and traveled immediately to Washington. The next morning he had breakfast with "Uncle Bert." By his own account he "suggested that the Navy Department send two fast destroyers—one for the northern coast and one for the southern coast of the portion of Cuba controlled by revolutionaries." Lansing agreed, and the warships were dispatched that afternoon. Marines landed and spread into the countryside to repress protests, beginning what would be a five-year occupation. Liberals realized the futility of resistance and called off their uprising.

This was the first foreign intervention in which Foster played a role. It showed him how easy it can be for a rich and powerful country, guided by the wishes of its wealthiest corporations, to impose its will on a poor and weak one.

"Uncle Bert" was impressed with his nephew's understanding of how American power can be used abroad. A few months later, he gave the young man another mission. One of his projects as war drew near was to cleanse Central America of German influence and confiscate the property of German immigrants who lived there. He decided to send an envoy on a secret trip to Costa Rica, Nicaragua, and Panama to enlist the support of their leaders—and who better than his twenty-nine-year-old nephew? Sullivan & Cromwell had played a key role in creating the Republic of Panama and building the Panama Canal, and it was legal counsel to the Panamanian regime. Questions about the conflict of interest inherent in sending a private lawyer on a diplomatic mission to a region where his clients had deep financial interests—and where one of the governments with which he was to negotiate was also his client—were subsumed by family ties, and Foster was duly appointed.

Costa Rica at this time was ruled by the most brutal dictator in its modern history, General Federico Tinoco, who had seized power in a coup promoted by the United Fruit Company, a Sullivan & Cromwell client, and whose family was deeply in debt to United Fruit. Foster found him a willing partner and urged the State Department to reward his "sincere friendliness" by recognizing his government; President Wilson, who took a dimmer view of generals who deposed democratic governments, declined to do so. At his next stop, Nicaragua, Foster worked equally well with General Emiliano Chamorro, a pliant dictator whose Conservative Party the United States had helped place in power after engineering the overthrow of a Liberal regime that had tried to borrow money from European rather than American banks. In Panama he persuaded the regime to declare war on Germany by suggesting that if it did not, the United States might start taking a new tax out of the $250,000 it paid Panama each year to rent the Canal Zone.

By the time Foster returned from Central America, the United States had finally entered World War I. He took a leave from the firm and sought to enlist for military service, but poor eyesight, an affliction in the Dulles family, kept him out. "Uncle Bert" arranged for him to be given the rank of captain and made legal adviser to the new War Trade Board, which was tasked with turning American factories into efficient suppliers of war matériel. While in Washington he met and impressed one of the era's best-known financiers, Bernard Baruch, who was working on another war-related commission. Baruch had made a fortune speculating in sugar while still in his twenties and had become one of the wealthiest and most influential deal makers on Wall Street. Foster found in him a mentor, role model, and soul mate. Later he would give Foster a decisive boost toward the top level of international diplomacy.

While working at the War Trade Board, Foster also recruited new clients for Sullivan & Cromwell and nourished existing ones. He secured lucrative government contracts for the Aetna Explosives Company, and arranged for the German-owned Mumm Champagne Company to avoid seizure by the U.S. government through a sham stock sale to American investors. Already he had become comfortable tending simultaneously to the interests of the United States and those of Sullivan & Cromwell clients.

The armistice ending World War I took effect at the eleventh hour of the eleventh day in the eleventh month of 1918. Less than a week later, on Sunday morning, November 17, Foster and his wife were arriving for a service at Washington Presbyterian Church when a friend gave him startling news: President Wilson had decided he would personally head the American delegation to the peace conference in Paris, where the post-war world was to be designed. No president of the United States had ever left the country while in office—except for Theodore Roosevelt's trip to Panama and two American territories, the Panama Canal Zone and Puerto Rico—so this was momentous. The next day, as Wilson was announcing his decision, Foster visited "Uncle Bert" at the State Department and asked to be named part of the delegation. The prestige of this assignment, he realized, would be an ideal capstone to his wartime experience and add diplomatic luster to his growing reputation.

Foster found his uncle, who had hoped to head the American delegation himself, deeply distressed by Wilson's decision. He not only believed that his mastery of craft would be more useful in Paris than Wilson's naive idealism, but also imagined that if he could return home covered with the glory of having helped reshape the world, he might use it to propel himself to the Democratic presidential nomination in 1920. Wilson, however, not only rejected Lansing's appeal to head the American delegation but was offended by it. He could not leave his secretary of state behind, but their tiff left "Uncle Bert" unable to ask permission to bring Foster.

This news naturally disappointed the young man, but a few days later he found another route to Paris. Wilson chose Bernard Baruch to be one of his counselors at the talks, and when Foster asked to come along as his assistant, Baruch agreed. He booked passage on the liner *George Washington* and passed much of the trip playing bridge in a foursome that included the assistant secretary of the navy, Franklin Roosevelt, who was also on his way to the peace conference.

Foster's nine months in Paris were even more rewarding than he had hoped. Baruch became the American delegate to the Reparations Commission, which was charged with deciding what punishments should be meted out to Germany. Foster threw himself into the commission's work, mastering arcane details of debt financing that would prove invaluable to his banking clients. His European counterparts were young men of equal ambition and talent, among them John Maynard Keynes, who would soon begin revolutionizing economic theory, and Jean Monnet, one of the visionaries who, a generation later, would lay the foundation for what became the European Union.

In between negotiating sessions, Foster concentrated on expanding his already impressive network of international contacts. On some days he lunched with foreign dignitaries like the president of Brazil, whose railroad network Sullivan & Cromwell was then reorganizing. Other days, he invited influential American politicians like George Sheldon, a financier who had helped direct William Howard Taft's presidential campaign and was treasurer of the Republican Party in New York. One night he hosted four guests: his uncle Secretary of State Lansing; his boss, the legal genius William Nelson Cromwell; Foreign Minister Lou Tsen-Tsiang of China; and the American ambassador to France, William Graves Sharp, whose son would later join Sullivan & Cromwell. In a letter to his wife, he reported that the dinner had cost him the remarkable sum of $110.

"Still," he added, "it was worth it, don't you think?"

An event of such global significance as the Paris peace conference naturally attracted Allie as well. He arrived from Bern, having managed to win a post on the Boundary Commission, whose job was to draw new borders in Europe, and installed himself at the Hotel Crillon along with the rest of the American delegation. Following a predilection that would mark his life, he quickly sought female company. He found what he wanted at Le Sphinx, an elegant brothel in Montparnasse where the air was redolent of rose perfume, lush fabrics covered the walls, and nude women sat at an elaborate art deco bar. It was one of several lavish houses that became legendary in Paris and far beyond during the 1920s. They attracted an array of sensualists, among them the writers Lawrence Durrell, Ernest Hemingway, Marcel Proust, and Henry Miller; film stars including Humphrey Bogart, Cary Grant, and Marlene Dietrich (women were welcome); artists like Pablo Picasso and Alberto Giacometti; and even the Prince of Wales, later King Edward VIII. All pursued what one chronicler of the age called "an art of living fueled by desire and eccentricity [in] a world where money and class put moral judgments in abeyance."

For Allie, a visit to Le Sphinx satisfied more than just his well-developed sexual appetite. It also gave him a chance to mix with a new kind of elite and to observe people's behavior at moments free of inhibition. By day he watched statesmen grapple with great questions of war, peace, and the fate of nations. By night he saw some of the same people, plus a diverse parade of others, in far looser circumstances. It was food for the mind.

And for the heart as well. According to Allie's future boss General Walter Bedell Smith, also a patron of Le Sphinx, he became attached to a woman who worked there and rented an apartment for her nearby. By one account she became pregnant and Allie wished to marry her, but Foster brought him to his senses and sent the expectant mother a sum of money to forget the relationship.

Their sister Eleanor was also in France. She had asked "Uncle Bert" to find her a useful position in the post-war relief effort, but he dismissed her, saying that the only way a woman could contribute would be by knitting socks. Infuriated, she paid her own way to Europe and went to work for a Quaker relief group that was building homes for refugees along the Marne River. Every week or two she would turn up at the Crillon for dinner and a hot bath, then return to her work in the devastated countryside.

"Thousands of fine young men were buried in their blood, covered with rubble and mud," she wrote afterward. "I felt sick and lost among the ghosts of broken bones, the shards of warfare and its desolation."

This was a grand chance for the three siblings to throw themselves into the heart of world events while still young—Foster was thirty, Allie twenty-five, and Eleanor just twenty-three. The only member of the clan who did not thrive in Paris was "Uncle Bert." President Wilson pointedly ignored his advice, relying instead on his own instincts and the counsel of his ubiquitous alter ego, "Colonel" Edward House. He spent more time with Allie and Foster, who idolized him from Princeton days, than with his secretary of state.

Present and future leaders of nearly a dozen countries came to Paris to promote their causes. One of them would later duel with the Dulles brothers for the fate of his people.

The twenty-eight-year-old Vietnamese nationalist who would later be known as Ho Chi Minh had already seen much of the world. He had visited India, Africa, the Middle East, Europe, and even the United States, where he worked briefly as a pastry chef at the Parker House Hotel in Boston. The end of the Great War found him in France, which ruled his native Vietnam as a colony. There he became an anticolonial agitator. Soon after the peace conference convened, he published a broadside demanding for Vietnam "the sacred right of all people for self-determination." He had several thousand copies printed, distributed them widely—the text set off riots when it reached Saigon—and on a June morning in 1919 carried one to the Hotel Crillon, where he hoped to present it to Wilson. By one account he even rented a morning suit for the occasion. He was unable to see Wilson, but delivered his pamphlet to Colonel House, and received a note acknowledging its receipt. As far as is known, neither of the Dulles brothers was aware of him.

Wilson argued ceaselessly for the principle of self-determination. He defined the term as meaning that "national aspirations must be respected," that no people should be "selfishly exploited," and that all must be "dominated and governed only by their own consent." His application of this principle, however, was highly selective. He believed that self-determination was the right of people who lived in the collapsing Ottoman and Austro-Hungarian empires, but not those who lived in overseas colonies. That excluded the Vietnamese, so the conference ended with Ho Chi Minh empty-handed. A year later he became a founding member of the French Communist Party. He then made his way to Moscow, joined the Comintern, and set out to wage revolutionary war against the overlords of the world—among them, three decades later, the Dulles brothers.

Wilson's double standard set off four other explosions of anger from subject peoples. All broke out within a few months of one another in the spring of 1919: a revolution against British rule in Egypt, an anti-Japanese uprising in Korea, the opening campaign of Gandhi's epic resistance movement in India, and a wave of protest by anti-imperialists in China, which the independence leader Sun Yat-sen attributed to their anger at "how completely they had been deceived by the Great Powers' advocacy of self-determination."

By refusing to confront nationalist demands that were emerging in these and other countries, the Western leaders who gathered in Paris laid the groundwork for decades of upheaval. Their determination to preserve their dominions far outweighed their commitment to the abstract principle of self-determination. This was as true for Wilson as for the others.

"If the United States delegation had agreed to examine the status of the French colonies, a colossally pernicious Pandora's box would have been opened, and a principal edict of diplomacy violated, having to do with those living in glass houses," the historian David Andelman wrote in his account of the peace conference. "After all, who were the Americans to cast stones when they had their own possessions—from the Philippines to the Caribbean? If the peace conference were open to the issue of places like [Vietnam], why not Hawaii or Puerto Rico for that matter?"

There is no hint that Foster or Allie ever regretted the failure of delegates in Paris to address the aspirations of colonized nations. They did, however, come to rue some of the other decisions embodied in the final treaty, which was signed at Versailles on June 28, 1919. Foster feared the consequences of crushing Germany with demands for exorbitant reparations, but the victorious European powers insisted that the Germans must suffer for their role in starting the war. Allie helped award the disputed Sudetenland, populated mainly by German-speakers, to the new nation of Czechoslovakia, and later admitted that his Boundary Commission had turned Czechoslovakia into "a banana lying across the face of Europe."

Fourteen years later, the Nazis would rise to power in part by exploiting German anger at these two fiats.

The Paris conference was a global coming-out party for a triumphant America. Wilson's delegation numbered in the hundreds, far more than had ever represented the United States anywhere. Europe gave him a tumultuous reception, and, without hesitating, he reached to assume the mantle of global leadership. It was the destiny of the United States, he declared in a speech before departing, "to carry liberty and justice and the principles of humanity" to the world's less civilized peoples, and to "convert them to the principles of America."

One or the other of the Dulles brothers was involved in almost every important matter that came before the peace conference. They gained Wilson's confidence and met many of the titans who would shape world politics over the next half century. Allie wrote home that the experience was "one of thrilling interest and opportunity" that gave him "a rare chance to get a glimpse into world politics." For Foster it was that and more: a decisive push toward wealth and power.

This was also the first chance in several years that the two brothers managed to spend time together. They had been living on different continents and maintained only sporadic contact, but in Paris they occupied adjoining rooms at the Crillon and enjoyed long hours of conversation. They came to realize how similarly they viewed the world. The intimate connection that would define their later lives—and shape the fate of nations—grew from a deep mutual trust and sympathy that they developed for the first time as adults in Paris. Opposites in personality, they were in perfect accord politically and philosophically.

During their months in Paris, Foster and Allie fell fully under the spell of Woodrow Wilson. He influenced them every bit as much as their father and "Grandfather Foster" had during their childhood. Foster had sat at Wilson's feet in college—he later said that the chance to take his courses was "the major benefit I got from Princeton"—and like many Americans, he and his brother were thrilled by Wilson's meteoric rise from campus to the White House. In Paris they came to know him well. He was the quintessential missionary diplomat: cool, pontifical, sternly moralistic, and certain that he was acting as an instrument of divine will. Both brothers took his example deeply to heart.

Wilson's idealism had a strong pro-business aspect. When preaching his internationalist gospel, he often described it in commercial rather than idealistic terms. "Our industrial fortunes are tied up with the industrial fortunes of the rest of the world," he declared in one speech. "I am looking after the industrial interests of the United States." This principle—that American engagement with the world is good for American business—fit perfectly with what the Dulles brothers had already come to believe.

A strong strain of paternalism also shaped Wilson's worldview. He was a product of Southern gentility, admired the Ku Klux Klan, and considered segregation "not humiliating but a benefit." As president he ordered both the federal bureaucracy and the Washington transit system segregated. He hosted the premiere of the film *The Birth of a Nation* at the White House and lamented afterward that its portrayal of black men as violent simians "is all so terribly true." During his eight years in office he sent American troops to intervene in more countries than any previous president: Cuba, Haiti, the Dominican Republic, Mexico, Nicaragua, and even, in the turbulent period following the Bolshevik Revolution, the Soviet Union.

Presidents had ordered interventions before, but Wilson's were different because of the reason he repeatedly gave: he wanted to bring democracy to oppressed people. This was a radically new concept. Past American leaders had taken the opposite view, that darker-skinned people were incapable of self-government and needed to be ruled by others—a view summarized by the first American military commander in Cuba, General William Shafter, when he pronounced Cubans "no more fit for self-government than gunpowder is for hell." Wilson thought otherwise. "When properly directed," he asserted, "there is no people not fitted to self-government."

The Dulles brothers were products of the same missionary ethos that shaped Wilson. His example strengthened their conviction that there is nothing intrinsically wrong—and indeed, much that is admirable—in American intervention abroad.

The overwhelming emotion that drove the Paris conference was fear of what Wilson called "the poison of Bolshevism." Secretary Lansing described Communism as "the most hideous and monstrous thing that the human mind has ever conceived," supported only by "the criminal, the depraved, and the mentally unfit."

His nephews enthusiastically agreed. This was a natural reaction from men devoted to defending the existing order. Not every capitalist at the Paris talks, however, saw the ideological threat so simply. No less a pillar of conservatism than Herbert Hoover, who was advising President Wilson on food relief issues, urged the president to recognize Bolshevism's "true social ends" and roots in "grievous injustices to the lowest classes in all the countries that have been affected," and to "rap our own reactionaries for their destruction of social betterment and thereby their stimulation of Bolshevism." No such thoughts clouded the mind of either Dulles brother.

Once home from the peace conference, Wilson did all he could to combat the poison he saw emanating from Russia. Using the newly passed Sedition Act, he endorsed the deportation of supposed subversives, and after several anarchist bombs exploded and police uncovered a plot to mail others to wealthy industrialists and bankers, he authorized Attorney General A. Mitchell Palmer to launch the first of what would become two years of raids that led to the arrest of thousands of immigrants and the deportation of hundreds. No less than twenty-five times in 1919 and 1920, Wilson deployed the United States Army to suppress "labor unrest" or "racial unrest." Americans were in the grip of their first great Red Scare, set off in part by Palmer's prediction to Congress that radicals would "on a certain day . . . rise up and destroy the government at one fell swoop." They never did, but many Americans were seized by the fear of a new, unknown, diffuse but evidently horrific enemy.

The Dulles brothers returned from Paris with newly burnished reputations. Foster in particular had made a powerful debut on the world stage. By impressing influential Europeans and becoming a confidant of President Wilson, he showed his boss, William Nelson Cromwell, how fully he had learned to thrive in those lucrative thickets where business, politics, and diplomacy overlap. Soon after he returned to work in New York—and let it be known that another firm had offered him a job—Cromwell made him a partner. Some of his work was domestic, like merging a group of oil drillers and refiners into the corporation that became Amoco. More was international. His clients owned mines in Chile and Peru, sugar plantations in Cuba, utilities in Panama, oil wells in Colombia, banks in France, and paint factories in Italy and Russia. Two of his specialties were organizing overseas-loan syndicates for New York banks and helping utility companies take control of utilities in foreign countries.

Foster also took a ghostwriting assignment from his mentor Bernard Baruch, who like many of Wilson's friends and admirers was disturbed by the runaway success of a 1919 book attacking the Versailles treaty, *The Economic Consequences of the Peace*, by John Maynard Keynes. The book warned that the treaty's reparations section, which Foster had drafted and Baruch presented as his own, exposed Europe to "the menace of inflationism." Baruch resolved to reply. His book, ponderously titled *The Making of the Reparation and Economic Sections of the Treaty*, argued that reparations clauses were "vital to the interest of the American people and even more vital to world stability." Foster did most of the writing and editing, for which Baruch paid him ten thousand dollars.

Soon after the United States resumed diplomatic relations with Germany, the State Department assigned Allen—he had stopped calling himself "Allie," even in letters to his parents—to the American legation in Berlin. He arrived at the beginning of 1920 and witnessed the early days of the Weimar Republic and the right-wing Kapp Putsch that sought to destroy it. "Uncle Bert" had resigned his post as secretary of state by then, but both brothers had established their reputations and no longer needed a patron.

Three months after taking up his post in Berlin, shortly after celebrating his twenty-seventh birthday, Allen took a vacation and returned to his childhood home in upstate New York. On one of his first weekends there, he attended a party at a posh resort and met a green-eyed blonde named Martha Clover Todd, the daughter of a language professor at Columbia University. He proposed to her a week later, and on August 3, 1920, they were married.

It was not a happy match. Clover was sensitive, delicately balanced, and prone to fits of melancholy. Her philandering, workaholic husband, who once wrote to her suggesting that she ask friends for advice on "how to live with a queer duck like me," proved unwilling or unable to give her the emotional support she needed. He had a fierce temper and often ranted at her. She would respond by curling her body into the fetal position and then, when he was finished, silently leaving the house to wander, sometimes for hours. They contemplated divorce several times, but remained together until his death nearly fifty years later.

Rather than send Allen back to Berlin after his holiday, the State Department posted him to Constantinople, the capital of the defeated Ottoman Empire. He and Clover spent their first year together in a two-story house overlooking the Bosphorus. In 1922, with Clover pregnant and desolate over distressing news from home—her older brother had committed suicide—they returned to the United States. On the day they departed, Allen received a cable informing him that he had been promoted, and that instead of returning to Constantinople he was to settle in Washington as chief of the State Department's division of Near Eastern affairs. Over the next four years, he shuttled between Washington and the Levant, cultivating figures like King Faisal of Iraq, King Abdullah of Transjordan, Kemal Atatürk of Turkey, and even T. E. Lawrence, whom he knew from the Paris peace conference.

Meeting with remarkable men was not all that Allen did during his years in the Middle East. The State Department was actively promoting American oil interests there, especially those of Standard Oil, owned by the Rockefeller family. Allen spent much time learning this new form of commercial diplomacy. As the world's navies were converting from coal-powered to oil-powered warships, marking the beginning of the petroleum age, he worked to ensure that the United States won its share of access to the resource that would shape the unfolding century.

Between trips to the Middle East, Allen found enough time to attend evening and early-morning classes at George Washington University Law School, from which he graduated in 1926. Nonetheless he sensed his career and life stalling. He was in his thirties, living on a civil servant's salary and a modest inheritance from "Grandfather Foster." His work had little impact. Once he found a packet of his reports lying unopened in a State Department closet.

Life with Clover was increasingly complicated. At one point Allen confronted her with an exorbitant bill from Cartier's, and she calmly explained that she had learned of his relationship with another woman and had bought herself an emerald necklace as "compensation." She then announced that she intended to buy a new piece of jewelry each time she discovered one of his affairs. This would have led the couple quickly to bankruptcy, and she did not carry out her threat.

A decade had passed since the exciting days of World War I, when Allen had spent mornings dispatching agents on clandestine missions across Europe, afternoons with his mistress of the moment, and long evenings debriefing spies over cognac at the Bellevue Palace Hotel in Bern. He longed to be a case officer again, but the United States had no intelligence service. His path was uncertain. Later he called this period "the slough of my Despond."

2

THE TAINT OF MY ENVIRONMENT

On a breezy day in May 1926, a crowd of Long Island swells gathered at the Oyster Bay Yacht Club to watch the season's first regatta. Around mid-morning, several noticed that one yacht, the *Snookabus*, was drifting dangerously. Another sailor pulled alongside. He found a body lying on the deck.

The victim, Royall Victor, had for a decade been one of the three senior partners at Sullivan & Cromwell. Just forty-eight years old, he had suffered a heart attack and died instantly.

This was the second heavy blow to the firm in less than a year. Another of its senior partners, Alfred Jaritzky, had recently died of stomach cancer. That left just one member of the triumvirate, Henry Pierce, but he was ailing and chose to retire rather than take over. One of his last acts was to urge the firm's co-founder and overseer, William Nelson Cromwell, to promote John Foster Dulles. Cromwell did so.

Foster became part of a four-man team running the firm, and a few months later, Cromwell made him the sole managing partner. He was thirty-eight years old and just fifteen years out of law school. Thus began his quarter century as one of the American elite's most ruthlessly effective and best-paid courtiers.

During these years, wealthy Americans eagerly spread their money—and their interests—around the world. The United States went from being a debtor nation to a creditor nation for the first time. New York replaced London as the world's financial capital. Clients clamored for Sullivan &

Cromwell's services. The list of those Foster represented reads like a guide to the upper reaches of American commerce, manufacturing, and finance.

In the 1920s, working for banks including Brown Brothers, Lazard Frères, Goldman Sachs, and First National Bank of Boston, Foster arranged seventeen loans to Latin American countries totaling nearly $200 million—equivalent to more than $2 billion in the early twenty-first century—and also three loans to China from J. P. Morgan. His special focus was Europe, where his clients lent more than a billion dollars during the 1920s, most of it to Germany. He had helped draft the complex terms of German reparation payments, designing a system under which Germany would borrow from foreign banks to pay off its war debts. This created a highly lucrative market in an abstruse field that he understood as well as any American. With his guidance, American banks began investing in banks in Germany, and also lending to German utility companies, private firms like Hansa Steamship Lines, the cities of Berlin, Munich, Hanover, Frankfurt, Breslau, and Nuremberg, and the state of Prussia.

The idea for these loans often came not from needy borrowers, but from Foster and his agents, who scoured Europe and especially Germany for places they could profitably place their money. "A Bavarian hamlet, discovered by American agents to be in need of about $125,000, was urged and finally persuaded to borrow $3 million in the American market," according to one study of this practice. American banks had discovered how much money they could make by lending abroad. Foster prospered by connecting them to borrowers.

In his 1911 letter to Janet reporting the glorious news that Sullivan & Cromwell had accepted him, Foster predicted that he would himself soon be hiring new lawyers for the firm, and that came true soon after he was named managing partner. Two of the first applicants he considered would go on to play important roles in American life. One was a graduate of Columbia Law School named William O. Douglas. Later, after Douglas became chairman of the Securities and Exchange Commission and then a Supreme Court justice, Foster would say that he turned Douglas down because he didn't seem sharp enough. Douglas told the story differently.

"I saw John Foster Dulles and decided against him because he was so pontifical," he wrote in a memoir. "He seemed to me like a high churchman out to exploit someone. In fact, I was so struck with Dulles's pomposity that when he helped me on with my coat as I was leaving the office, I turned and gave him a quarter tip."

Foster and Douglas were profoundly different kinds of Americans. Beneath their encounter lay opposing beliefs about how law should be practiced, how the United States should act in the world, and, in the end, how life should be lived. Foster was a tight-lipped patrician who had become rich by serving America's most powerful corporations and banking houses. Douglas was a passionate iconoclast who sympathized with underdogs and admired foreign cultures. One embraced religious and political certitudes, abhorred upheaval, and viewed the world from paneled suites in New York, Washington, and European capitals. The other rejected dogma, learned about the world by taking rugged trips through remote lands, and believed the United States should approach other countries "with humility" and let them solve their problems "in their own way."

"I'm not sure I want to go to heaven," Douglas mused later in life. "I'm afraid I might meet John Foster Dulles there."

Not long after Foster's odd encounter with Douglas, he interviewed another promising lawyer for a position at Sullivan & Cromwell. This one had nothing approaching Douglas's legal mind—it took him three tries to pass the bar exam—but compensated with another asset. He was Foster's brother.

Allen had pursued his law degree in the hope that it would open new horizons for him in the foreign service. After he earned it, however, he was offered only a posting in China at an annual salary of $8,000. He asked his older brother for advice, and Foster had an immediate suggestion: quit the foreign service and come to work for Sullivan & Cromwell. His salary would be considerably above what new lawyers normally made, and there would be other chances for enrichment. Allen accepted and joined the firm in October 1926. Ending a ten-year career at the State Department was, he wrote to a friend, "a tremendously hard decision." He understood that he was venturing into a moral and ethical twilight.

"I want to keep as good a reputation as I can," he wrote, "notwithstanding the taint of my environment."

Other lawyers at Sullivan & Cromwell expressed some resentment over the way Allen was brought into the firm, but his network of global contacts quickly paid off. Within the firm he became known as "the little minister."

Although he often worked in Europe, he also became the firm's key man for deals in Latin America. During his first year as an associate, with help from former colleagues in the State Department, he arranged for banks he represented to lend $13 million to Bolivia and $10 million to Colombia.

The first important new client Allen brought to the firm, a Social Register dandy named Arthur Bunker, had through family connections come into possession of a rich oil concession in Colombia. Royal Dutch Shell challenged his claim, but after Allen traveled to London in 1928 to present his client's case to Sir Henri Deterding, the legendary Shell chairman, Deterding backed off. Two years later, in 1930, Colombia held a presidential election that the muckraking Washington columnist Drew Pearson accused Allen of fixing to ensure the victory of a candidate pledged to protect Bunker's oil concession.

In recognition of these and other achievements, Allen was made a Sullivan & Cromwell partner in 1930. His first assignment was to spend a year in Paris, where the firm's silver-haired patriarch, William Nelson Cromwell, was enjoying semi-retirement. Allen left Clover behind with instructions to join him in three months, and during those months he lived at Cromwell's "swell suite" on Avenue Foch. Foster had by this time come to consider Cromwell an undisciplined and occasionally embarrassing eccentric, but Allen became, by his own account, "really fond" of the aging master. They developed something of the father-son relationship that Allen had lacked at home, where the stern Reverend Dulles favored his stern firstborn son.

While Allen was in Paris, Reverend Dulles died at the family home in Watertown, New York. Allen did not return for the funeral or memorial service, partly because he was occupied with a captivating woman named Gregoire. When not with her, he was sampling other pleasures, often with Cromwell. In one letter home he reported that they had taken two ladies to lunch at the Trianon Palace in Versailles, and afterward "gave the girls a good time." Even Clover's arrival with their three small children did not slow him down. Paris was a carnival of the senses, and Allen, as one biographer wrote, "lived it to the hilt: a playground of monarchs reigning and deposed, where Morgans and Vanderbilts, maharajahs from India and stars from Hollywood, old wealth and new, sought perpetual gaiety in reckless expenditure, escape from the spreading depression back in America. Far from feeling revulsion at the gaudy display, Allen reveled in the luxury that other people's money could buy."

Indulging his desires was not all that occupied Allen in Paris. This was also the time when he solidified his reputation as a world-class international lawyer. Money was flying across Europe for reparation payments, war debts, corporate mergers, and countless investments both legal and illegal. Tottering nations were fighting for survival. Whether advising central bankers who met quietly in Basel to shape the continent's future, pressing E. H. Harriman's bid to buy Poland's electric system—a bid that Prime Minister Jozef Pilsudski ultimately vetoed—or helping the J. Henry Schroder Bank expand from Germany to become a global financial power, Allen showed a flair for discreet deal making. He completed the transition from insightful but obscure diplomat to potent advocate for America's richest men, banks, and corporations.

"He never bothered to understand the technical aspects of financial maneuverings," one historian has written, "but under the influence of Foster and the firm, he grew sensitive to the elite's goal of transnational power to generate prosperity for the world and, of course, themselves."

After fourteen months in Paris, Allen returned to New York in March 1931—without Clover and their children, whom he had packed off to spend the spring and summer in Switzerland. Besides giving him time for his private pursuits, this interlude also allowed him to contemplate the scale of the economic collapse that had enveloped the United States and was spreading to Europe. Millions were out of work. Thousands of banks had failed. Between 1929 and 1932, corporate profits would fall by more than half. So would the value of American exports. Social upheaval threatened. For anyone deeply invested in the stability of global financial networks, as both Dulles brothers were, the Depression was a terrifying example of how crazy the world can become if it is not skillfully managed.

Despite the crisis, a remarkable amount of money still coursed through the circles surrounding the Dulles brothers. Some of Sullivan & Cromwell's biggest fees came from victims of the crash, notably $540,000 for negotiating on behalf of bondholders swindled by Ivar Kreuger, the Swedish financier and "match king" who committed suicide after his pyramid scheme collapsed in 1932. Foster's expertise in arcane matters of international debt restructuring was in more demand than ever. His banking clients continued to lend money abroad, mostly to refinance existing debts. Enough post-war reconstruction was still under way in Europe to bring profit, though at a reduced rate, to the engineering, mining, utility, machine tool, commodity, and transport companies he represented. No fewer than fifteen of these companies—including Grand Union, Babcock & Wilcox, American Bank Note, Western Power, North American Edison, International Nickel, and American Agricultural Chemical—brought Foster onto their boards of directors or trustees.

Neither brother lacked for money. Foster earned about $300,000 per year from Sullivan & Cromwell—the equivalent of nearly $5 million in the early twenty-first century—plus stock dividends and fees for his service on corporate boards. He was often described as the highest-paid lawyer in the United States. Allen took home about half as much, princely by the standards of the time, which allowed him to buy a Manhattan town house at 239 East Sixty-First Street and a retreat at Lloyd Neck, on the north shore of Long Island. Both homes were more than comfortable, though the town house was less impressive than Foster's, thirty blocks north at 72 East Ninety-First Street, and his home at Lloyd Neck was also smaller than Foster's in nearby Cold Spring Harbor. Allen also did well with timely investments in several companies his firm represented, among them International Nickel, Babcock & Wilcox, and United Fruit.

"Where he was an asset to the firm was in his ability to bring in business to Sullivan & Cromwell," one of Allen's partners later recalled. "He was a great customers' man. He loved the life in New York, and you began to see him everywhere, particularly where the tycoons, the company president, or their wives gather—opening nights at the Metropolitan Opera, charity balls, club dinners, squash sessions at the New York Athletic Club, tennis parties. He was a good tennis player and he knew when to lose. If he was playing with a tycoon's wife, he made certain they would win. But if the tycoon himself was in the opposite court, he'd keep the game ding-donging along until practically the final volley, when Allen would fumble and flub. That way the tycoon felt marvelous, having won a hard-fought game, and his wife didn't feel too bad either—after all, it wasn't her fault they'd lost—and both felt benevolent toward Allen. Such a good loser he was, too."

Foster brought something quite different to Sullivan & Cromwell. From his grandfather he had learned the delicate art of accumulating influence and wielding it to benefit his clients. He had a deep understanding of the global financial system, especially the bond market, and of the opportunities it presented for wealthy Americans. Although he was famously unable to remember the names of junior partners, he drew on a mind filled with legal minutiae. His appetite for work was legendary. So was his toughness in negotiation.

From a client's perspective, they made an ideal team: one brother was great fun and a gifted seducer, the other had uncanny skill in building fortunes.

The Third Avenue elevated train had a car informally reserved for men with chesterfield overcoats—a motorman steered others away—and when Allen stepped aboard on his way to Wall Street in the morning, he often ran into his brother, who boarded three stops earlier. On many Friday afternoons, both men took the 4:50 train from Pennsylvania Station to Long Island. Once there, they found different ways to amuse themselves. Foster had a yacht and sailed when weather allowed. When it did not, he spent most of his time at home, where he relaxed by reading a detective story in front of the fireplace while his wife knitted. Allen spent his Long Island weekends partying, often at his own home. Regular guests included Archie Roosevelt, a son of Theodore's and co-founder of an investment bank; Charles and Anne Morrow Lindbergh, one of America's dream couples; Rebecca West, who when asked years later if she had been one of Allen's mistresses replied, "Alas, no, but I wish I had been"; Hamilton Fish Armstrong, Allen's best friend from Princeton; and a parade of Manhattan neighbors ranging from John Gunther to Tallulah Bankhead. Allen's party skipped from weekend to weekend and year to year. With his cultivated charm, endless supply of stories, well-stocked wine cellar, predatory interest in women, wealth from uncertain sources, stylish blazers, and buttoned loafers, he could have stepped from the pages of *The Great Gatsby.*

"My father was very, very extroverted," his daughter Joan later recalled. "He loved to be on the go constantly. He would work hard and then he would want to go to a party, or to give a party. He wanted people around him, movement, action. My mother was an introvert and liked to have time to think about things, to read and to be alone. For an introvert, it often is painful to be around an extrovert who crowds himself and others in around you."

During his fifteen years at Sullivan & Cromwell between the wars, Allen made eleven extended foreign trips. Letters he wrote home to Clover were full of references to other women that could at best be read as insensitive, at worst as taunting. In one he wrote of a night out with "an attractive (not beautiful) Irish-French female whom I took to Scheherazade, where we stayed until the early hours." In another, the subject was "an English girl . . . rather good-looking. . . . Danced and drank champagne until quite late." Other women he reported meeting included "a charming widow," "a most pleasant companion," "a young English damsel," "a very delightful person," and "a sensible soul, also by no means ugly." After one Atlantic crossing he proudly wrote to Clover that "on the whole I have kept rather free from any entanglements, and in particular there have been no ladies on board with whom I have particularly consorted."

"I don't feel I deserve as good a wife as I have, as I am rather too fond of the company of other ladies," he confessed in another letter. His sister Eleanor later wrote that "there were at least a hundred women in love with Allen at one time or another—and some of them didn't even get to close quarters with him."

Clover responded by focusing her attention on her son and two daughters. She also took up the cause of penal reform, and often visited prisons. While walking the streets of poor New York neighborhoods, she would stop for long conversations with beggars and people in breadlines. In letters to friends, she suggested that the ease of upper-class life made her feel guilty and ashamed. Her husband, by contrast, was an unrepentant elitist who was known never to pick up a napkin when he dropped one at dinner, preferring to wait for a servant to do it.

Soon after returning home from Paris in 1931, Allen began an affair with a tall, blond Russian émigré who had turned up at the Cold Spring Harbor Tennis Club and whose husband was chronically ill. He made no effort to hide the relationship, raving freely not just to friends but to his wife and children about his wonderful new "tennis partner." Unapologetic adultery had become an established aspect of his character. It remained so all his life.

"Sex, it appears, was to Allen Dulles a form of physical therapy, something one did to keep himself fit for more important things," one biographer has surmised. "Clover's insistence on staying home with the children and her increasing preoccupation with prisoners' rights were treated by him as a kind of betrayal of her obligation to be his good and faithful companion. . . . If Clover would not travel when Allen asked, then he could not really be blamed if he diverted himself with other women, always of his own class and station."

Allen's near-pathological womanizing, and his evident lack of interest in building a strong relationship with his wife, contrasted sharply with Foster's endless devotion to Janet. Yet the two brothers were strikingly similar in their relationships with their children. Both were distant, uncomfortable fathers.

Foster's three children were raised by nannies and discouraged from intruding on their parents' world. The eldest, John Watson Foster Dulles, was moody and withdrawn, by one account "touchy, oversensitive, and highly emotional." When he lost a game of checkers or backgammon, he would burst into tears, a reaction that shocked his ever-stoic father. Their relationship was further strained when John dropped out of college because he could generate no enthusiasm for the legal career his father had planned for him. They never found a connection, emotional or otherwise. John became a mining engineer and spent much of his life in Latin America.

His younger brother, Avery, moved even further away, not geographically but spiritually. Strolling beside the Charles River one day while a student at Harvard, Avery was struck by what he called a revelation. Soon afterward he renounced his family's generations of Presbyterian tradition and converted to Roman Catholicism. Foster was apoplectic. Upon receiving the news, he telephoned Arthur Dean, his closest colleague at Sullivan & Cromwell.

"He called Dean," the journalist Marquis Childs later recalled, "and said, 'I want you to cancel all your appointments. The greatest crisis of my life has come up. I want you to read this letter I'm sending to Avery.' And the letter was: 'Never darken my door again. Never speak to me again. Never communicate with me again. You are no longer my son.' And then, according to Dean's story, from about four o'clock in the afternoon or 4:30 until 8:30 at night, he hashed this over with Dulles and persuaded him not to send the letter."

Avery entered the priesthood and went on to become a Jesuit scholar of conservative bent. He published two dozen books and hundreds of articles on theological topics and taught religion at Fordham University. He finally reached an awkward reconciliation with his father. Near the end of his life, Pope John Paul II made him a cardinal. As Cardinal

Dulles, one of his last public pronouncements was a statement criticizing the United States Conference of Catholic Bishops for being too "extreme" in seeking to expel accused pedophiles from the priesthood.

Foster's middle child, Lillias, offended her father's sense of order by announcing that she wished to attend college and, like her aunt Eleanor, make a career for herself. Foster believed education spoiled women, and disapproved. "He didn't want her to learn anything, except maybe the feminine charms, which he thought she lacked," Eleanor later wrote. Finally Lillias persuaded her father to allow her to attend Bennington College, which he mistakenly believed to be a finishing school. Later she became a Presbyterian minister, but even that did not bring her back into her father's good graces. He remained as cool to his daughter as he was to his sons.

"His work was very important to him, and he felt a real sense of obligation toward colleagues and subordinates," Eleanor wrote of her elder brother. "He couldn't neglect them for his children."

Allen's relationship with his three children was no happier. His son, Allen Macy Dulles, tried everything to win his father's attention, from learning chess to studying international politics, but to no avail. Acutely aware that Allen never found him "tough" enough, he enlisted in the Marine Corps. He was sent to Korea and, at the age of twenty-two, was almost killed when a shell fragment tore off part of his skull. Brain damage kept him in and out of sanatoriums and intensive care units for years.

Both of Allen's daughters, Joan and Clover Todd, known as Toddy, were taken out of school at an early age and educated at an informal academy on the estate of their Long Island neighbor Archie Roosevelt. There they read romantic poetry and played with a select group of other children—among them Roosevelt's nephew Kermit, who would later go to work for Allen and enter history as the CIA officer who directed the overthrow of Iran's government. Joan married a prominent Austrian, then divorced him and married another Austrian, a diplomat. She returned to the United States and lived an apparently fulfilling life.

Her older sister, Toddy, was less happy. She evidently inherited her mother's inclination to depression, and periodically suffered psychological "crises" that all but paralyzed her. Emotional imbalance disrupted both her home and school life. While in her early twenties she eloped with a college athlete her mother had hired to teach her brother sports. She married him, but the marriage soon failed. Later she married a Norwegian banker and moved with him to London. Her symptoms never abated, and she required periods of hospitalization throughout her life.

The Dulles brothers also had to deal with their independent-minded sister Eleanor, who, much to Foster's distress, had refused to settle into marital anonymity or submit to family codes. Soon after winning her doctorate in economics with a thesis on the causes of inflation in France, Eleanor visited Paris and, at a party in Montparnasse, met an older, divorced American named David Blondheim. They began dating, and when her parents came for a visit a few months later, she told them she was engaged. Reverend Dulles, already unwell, was taken aback by the news, since Blondheim came from an Orthodox Jewish family. Foster was also unhappy, and tried to dissuade his sister from going through with the marriage. Not wishing to cause further distress, she decided that she would quietly move in with her lover instead of marrying him. Blondheim also hid the affair from his parents, knowing they too would disapprove of the "mixed" match. Finally, after Reverend Dulles died in 1931, they married. No relative of the bride or groom attended the wedding.

The discomfort Eleanor's family felt at this cross-cultural marriage was mirrored by the disdain her husband suffered. David Blondheim's brother broke relations with him and told him he had been shut out of the Blondheim clan forever. He was already depressive, and this devastated him. Reports about the plight of Jews in Europe upset him further. When Eleanor told him in the spring of 1934 that she was pregnant, he responded not with joy but with pangs of guilt for having fathered a half-Christian child at a moment when Jewish survival was under threat. That autumn, shortly before the child was born, he committed suicide. Eleanor was crushed. At Foster's suggestion she dropped her married name as a way of insulating herself from memories of the tragedy.

Soon after President Franklin Roosevelt was inaugurated in 1933, he invited Allen and an older veteran of global diplomacy, Norman Davis, who had made a fortune in the Cuban sugar trade, to the White House for a chat. They sat on the rear veranda, overlooking the Washington Monument. Though a private attorney still in his thirties—and a Republican—Allen felt at home advising Roosevelt. His background and upbringing had prepared him to move comfortably in such elevated circles.

"It was almost informal," he wrote to Clover afterward, "and the President put on no airs."

At the end of their chat, Roosevelt asked the two men to travel to Europe as his emissaries. They would stop in London to heal a dispute with Britain over issues of disarmament and war reparations, then proceed to Paris for an economic conference. A few days later they departed, and in Europe they held a round of meetings with Prime Minister Ramsay MacDonald of Britain, Prime Minister Édouard Daladier of France, and other statesmen. The one they most wanted to meet, though, was the fiery National Socialist leader who had just come to power in Germany.

So it was that on Allen's fortieth birthday—April 7, 1933—he was riding a train to Berlin on his way to meet Adolf Hitler.

At four o'clock the next afternoon, the two emissaries were ushered into the Reichskanzlei, which sat just across Wilhelmstrasse from the American embassy where Allen had served as a junior diplomat thirteen years before. They were among the first foreign delegations the Führer received. Prime Minister Daladier had told Allen in Paris that Hitler had no clear foreign policy ideas, and their meeting confirmed it. Hitler spoke at length about the injustice of harsh reparations payments and insisted that he favored universal disarmament. He rambled through subjects ranging from the American Civil War to the perfidy of Poland. When Davis asked him about reports of "excesses" against dissidents, Hitler, well briefed on his guests' role in global finance, replied that he was simply imposing order "to protect the millions in foreign capital that are invested in Germany."

Gangs of Nazi thugs were beating Jews on German streets while Allen was there, but he came home without animus toward Hitler. When he returned to Berlin two years later, though, he found conditions worse and had what he called a "sinister impression." He was disturbed by stories he heard from Jewish clients, and worried about the implications of Sullivan & Cromwell's work fueling German financial and industrial power. Nazism became the first and only important subject on which the Dulles brothers seriously disagreed. Allen sensed what was coming and wished to spare Sullivan & Cromwell the stigma of collaboration. Foster could not bear to turn away.

Despite his lifelong devotion to France—which had awarded him the Legion of Honor for his work on the Versailles treaty—no country appealed to Foster more deeply than Germany. His father had studied theology at Göttingen and Leipzig, and awed him with stories of the country's rich intellectual tradition and role in the Reformation. He had made his first visit there when he was barely into his teens. At the Paris peace conference he argued unsuccessfully that Germany should not be forced to make crushing reparation payments to the victorious allies, and later he came to believe, probably correctly, that by insisting on those payments, the world helped push Germany toward aggression. In the period between the world wars, when Foster's legal practice became truly global, he devoted himself most assiduously to Germany. He had already developed an emotional attachment, based on his admiration for Germany's centuries of achievement and the rigor of its social order, and a political one, stemming from his belief that it was a rising nation and a bulwark against Bolshevism. Years of work for German clients gave his attachment an economic basis as well.

From his course with Henri Bergson after graduating from Princeton, Foster had picked up the concept of "dynamic" forces in eternal conflict with "static" ones. Bergson used this dichotomy as a way to understand religion and morality, but Foster applied it to global politics, which he interpreted as "the cyclical struggle between the dynamic and the static forces of the world." This was a way of placing nations into neat groups, which appealed to his ordered mind. During the 1930s he began describing France and Britain as "static" societies, interested only in defending what they had, and predicting that the future would be shaped by three newly creative and "dynamic" powers: Germany, Italy, and Japan.

"These dynamic peoples," he wrote in one article, "are determined to mold their states into a form which would permit them to take their destiny into their own hands and to attain that enlarged status which, under a liberal and peaceful form of government, had been denied them."

None of this would have mattered if Foster's closest engagement with Germany had not come while National Socialists were consolidating power.

Foster had helped design the Dawes Plan of 1924, which restructured Germany's reparation payments in ways that opened up huge new markets for American banks, and later that year he arranged for five of them to lend $100 million to German borrowers. In the seven years that followed, he and his partners brokered another $900 million in loans to Germany—the equivalent of more than $1 trillion in early-twenty-first-century dollars. This made him the preeminent salesman of German bonds in the United States, probably the world. He sharply rejected critics who argued that American banks should invest more inside the United States, and protested when the State Department sought to restrict loans to Germany that were unrelated to reparation payments or that supported cartels or monopolies.

Foster made much money building and advising cartels, which are based on agreements among competing firms to control supplies, fix prices, and close their supply and distribution networks to outsiders. Reformers in many countries railed against these cartels, but Foster defended them as guarantors of stability that ensured profits while protecting economies from unpredictable swings. Two that he shaped became global forces.

Among Foster's premier clients was the New Jersey–based International Nickel Company, for which he was not only counsel but also a director and member of the executive board. In the early 1930s he steered it, along with its Canadian affiliate, into a cartel with France's two major nickel producers. In 1934 he brought the biggest German nickel producer, I.G. Farben, into the cartel. This gave Nazi Germany access to the cartel's resources.

"Without Dulles," according to a study of Sullivan & Cromwell, "Germany would have lacked any negotiating strength with [International Nickel], which controlled the world's supply of nickel, a crucial ingredient in stainless steel and armor plate."

I.G. Farben was also one of the world's largest chemical companies—it would produce the Zyklon B gas used at Nazi death camps—and as Foster was bringing it into the nickel cartel, he also helped it establish a global chemical cartel. He was a board member and legal counsel for another chemical producer, the Solvay conglomerate, based in Belgium. During the 1930s he guided Solvay, I.G. Farben, the American firm Allied Chemical & Dye, and several other companies into a chemical cartel just as potent as the one he had organized for nickel producers.

In mid-1931 a consortium of American banks, eager to safeguard their investments in Germany, persuaded the German government to accept a loan of nearly $500 million to prevent default. Foster was their agent. His ties to the German government tightened after Hitler took power at the beginning of 1933 and appointed Foster's old friend Hjalmar Schacht as minister of economics.

Allen had introduced the two men a decade earlier, when he was a diplomat in Berlin and Foster passed through regularly on Sullivan & Cromwell business. They were immediately drawn to each other. Schacht spoke fluent English and understood the United States well. Like Dulles, he projected an air of brisk authority. He was tall, gaunt, and always erect, with close-cropped hair and high, tight collars. Both men had considered entering the clergy before turning their powerful minds toward more remunerative pursuits. Each admired the culture that had produced the other. Both believed that a resurgent Germany would stand against Bolshevism. Mobilizing American capital to finance its rise was their common interest.

Working with Schacht, Foster helped the National Socialist state find rich sources of financing in the United States for its public agencies, banks, and industries. The two men shaped complex restructurings of German loan obligations at several "debt conferences" in Berlin—conferences that were officially among bankers, but were in fact closely guided by the German and American governments—and came up with new formulas that made it easier for the Germans to borrow money from American banks. Sullivan & Cromwell floated the first American bonds issued by the giant German steelmaker and arms manufacturer Krupp A.G., extended I.G. Farben's global reach, and fought successfully to block Canada's effort to restrict the export of steel to German arms makers. According to one history, the firm "represented several provincial governments, some large industrial combines, a number of big American companies with interests in the Reich, and some rich individuals." By another account it "thrived on its cartels and collusion with the new Nazi regime." The columnist Drew Pearson gleefully listed the German clients of Sullivan & Cromwell who had contributed money to the Nazis, and described Foster as chief agent for "the banking circles that rescued Adolf Hitler from the financial depths and set up his Nazi party as a going concern."

Although the relationship between Foster and Schacht began well and thrived for years, it ended badly. Schacht contributed decisively to German rearmament and publicly urged Jews to "realize that their influence in Germany has disappeared for all time." Although he later broke with Hitler and left the government, he would be tried at Nuremberg for "crimes against peace." He was acquitted, but the chief American prosecutor, Robert Jackson, called him "the facade of starched respectability, who in the early days provided the window dressing, the bait for the hesitant." He baited no one more successfully than Foster.

During the mid-1930s, through a series of currency maneuvers, discounted buybacks, and other forms of financial warfare, Germany effectively defaulted on its debts to American investors. Foster represented the investors in unsuccessful appeals to Germany, many of them addressed to his old friend Schacht. Clients who had followed Sullivan & Cromwell's advice to buy German bonds lost fortunes. That advice, according to one study, "cost Americans a billion dollars because Schacht seduced Dulles into supporting Germany for far too long."

Foster never took responsibility for this fiasco, but Allen referred to it during an after-dinner speech at a Wall Street club. He admitted that Sullivan & Cromwell had "permitted debt to pile up too fast and too high and took bad moral risk," but insisted that it had given lenders "the finest legal protection," and that all should realize there was "no safeguard against economic conditions such as the last few years." With war spreading in Europe—and with Sullivan & Cromwell a powerful force not to be alienated—even investors who took huge losses saw no alternative to accepting them.

Foster had clear financial reasons to collaborate with the Nazi regime, and his ideological reason—Hitler was fiercely anti-Bolshevik—was equally compelling. In later years scholars would ask about his actions in the world. Did he do it out of a desire to protect economic privilege, or out of anti-Communist fervor? The best answer may be that to him there was no difference. In his mind, defending multinational business and fighting Bolshevism were the same thing.

Since 1933, all letters written from the German offices of Sullivan & Cromwell had ended, as required by German regulations, with the salutation *Heil Hitler!* That did not disturb Foster. He churned out magazine and newspaper articles asserting that the "dynamic" countries of the world—Germany, Italy, and Japan—"feel within themselves potentialities which are suppressed," and that Hitler's semi-secret rearmament project simply showed that "Germany, by unilateral action, has now taken back her freedom of action." Allen felt quite differently. After returning from Berlin in 1935, he told his brother that the time had come for the firm to close its Berlin office and the subsidiary in Frankfurt.

Foster was stunned by his brother's suggestion that Sullivan & Cromwell quit Germany. Many of his clients with interests there, including not just banks but corporations like Standard Oil and General Electric, wished Sullivan & Cromwell to remain active regardless of political conditions. He agreed. If the firm's Jewish clients in Germany were in difficulty, he suggested, its lawyers could avoid trouble by simply staying away from them.

For years Foster had done richly rewarding work at the Sullivan & Cromwell office in Berlin, a splendid suite at the Hotel Esplanade that was decorated with gold ornaments. A combination of sentiment and political blindness left him unable to step back and ask himself larger questions that might have shaken his view of the world.

This put Foster at odds not only with Allen but also with their sister Eleanor, who had traveled to Nazi Germany and was horrified by what she saw. She appealed to Foster to change his mind, but he never took her seriously and told her she was "working herself up" over nothing. He rejected President Roosevelt's denunciations of repression in Germany as demagoguery aimed at "drumming up mass emotionalism." Much of his political energy during the 1930s, the lawyer-diplomat John J. McCloy later recalled, was aimed at "rationalizing this Hitler movement."

On a summer day in 1935, Sullivan & Cromwell partners met in their Wall Street conference room to decide whether to cease operations in Nazi Germany. Foster opened the meeting with an impassioned speech warning that pulling out would cost the firm much money and "do great harm to our prestige." Allen replied that his recent trip had convinced him staying in Germany was impossible.

"You couldn't practice law there," Allen said. "People came to you asking you how to evade the law, not how to respect the law. When that happens, you can't be much of a lawyer."

The other partners agreed. "It would seem better to me if we didn't represent in any way any German clients," said Arthur Dean, perhaps the most respected of them. Finally it was left to Foster to ask, "Who is in favor of our closing down our operation in Germany?" All raised their hands.

"Then that is decided," he said. "The vote is unanimous."

By some accounts, Foster wept after pronouncing those words. Later he backdated the announcement by a year, to make it appear that the firm had closed its German offices in 1934 rather than 1935. He and Janet, however, continued to visit Germany as the Nazi regime tightened its grip on power, making trips in 1936, 1937, and 1939. Apparently nothing he saw disturbed

him. He supported the neutralist America First committee—Sullivan &
Cromwell drew up its articles of incorporation without charge—and
roused its members with speeches denouncing Churchill, Roosevelt, and
other "warmongers." Hitler impressed him as "one who from humble
beginnings, and despite the handicap of alien nationality, had attained the
unquestioned leadership of a great nation."

"Only hysteria entertains the idea that Germany, Italy, or Japan con-
templates war upon us," he assured businessmen at the Economic Club of
New York on March 22, 1939. This was a year after Hitler had incorpo-
rated Austria into the Reich, and barely a week after his troops seized
Czechoslovakia.

Not even the Nazi invasion of Poland later that year changed Foster's
mind. Two months afterward he gave a speech lamenting Britain's declaration of war against Germany and asserting that there was "neither in
the underlying causes of the war, nor in its long-range objectives, any
reason for the United States becoming a participant." This set off bitter
arguments between the brothers, often over dinner at Foster's retreat in
Cold Spring Harbor. Foster had published a plea for "alterations of the
international status quo" in order to head off "powerful forces emotion-
ally committed to exaggerated and drastic change." Allen understood this
as a call for accepting the rise of Nazism as a way to fight Bolshevism, and
he was appalled.

"How can you call yourself a Christian and ignore what is happening
in Germany?" he demanded of his brother. "It is terrible."

At least one other senior partner at Sullivan & Cromwell, Eustace Seligman, was equally disturbed. In October 1939, six weeks after the Nazi invasion of Poland, he took the extraordinary step of sending Foster a formal
memorandum disavowing what his old friend was saying about Nazism.

"I regret very much to find myself, for the first time in our long years
of association, in fundamental disagreement with you," Seligman wrote.
"Your position is that the Allies' moral position is in no respect morally
superior to Germany's, and in fact you go further by implication and
apparently take the view that Germany's moral position is superior to
the Allies'. . . . I can see nothing in it which furnishes any logical basis
for the position you have now come to. I think it is unfortunate from your
own point of view that you are taking this position publicly."

Allen had made his final visit to Nazi Germany in 1938. Upon returning to New York, chilled by Hitler's rise and perhaps eager to find a career more fulfilling than corporate law, he surprised his family and friends by announcing that he had decided to run for a seat in Congress from Manhattan's East Side. He jumped into the Republican primary and proved to be an eager if uninspiring candidate, speaking to neighborhood groups, giving radio interviews, and winning endorsements from both the *New York Times* and the *New York Herald Tribune*. In a rare show of family togetherness, his teenage daughters and eight-year-old son handed out leaflets on street corners and stuffed envelopes at campaign headquarters in the Belmont Plaza Hotel. On the stump Allen denounced "state socialism" and pledged to work for the "restoration of private enterprise," but did not demonize President Roosevelt in the fashion of more militant Republicans. On the night of the primary, he followed the returns from home, and before retiring he understood that he had lost. It was no great trauma, and in fact the race won him admiration in Republican circles. Some even mentioned him as a possible future candidate for governor.

Foster criticized the New Deal far more forcefully than his brother. Soon after Roosevelt proclaimed the first of his relief programs, Foster wrote a letter to the *New York Times* asserting that instead of launching new programs, Roosevelt should have taken the opposite approach by "radically" cutting government spending. Later he accused Roosevelt of "attempting to stir up class feeling." He was outraged by Roosevelt's desire to regulate the securities industry, and testified against the proposed Securities Act at a congressional hearing. After it passed, he told his clients it was unconstitutional and advised them, "Do not comply; resist the law with all your might, and soon everything will be right." He tried to persuade a Supreme Court justice, Harlan Fiske Stone, to resign and direct Sullivan & Cromwell's ultimately unsuccessful challenge to the law. Stone declined—and lamented in passing that the flow of talented lawyers to firms serving corporate power "has made the learned profession of an earlier day the obsequious servant of business, and tainted it with the morals and manners of the market-place in its most anti-social manifestations."

The Dulles brothers were paragons of the Wilsonian idea that came to be known as "liberal internationalism." They believed that trouble in the world came from misunderstandings among ruling elites, not from social or political injustices, and that commerce could reduce or eliminate this trouble. This was a refined version of the "open door" policy the United

States had embraced for decades—a policy that might better be called "kick in the door" because it was aimed at forcing other countries to accept trade arrangements favorable to American interests. At its core was the reassuring belief that whatever benefited American business would ultimately benefit everyone.

For Woodrow Wilson, the Dulles brothers, and nearly every powerful American business leader of their eras, the label "internationalist" was a badge of honor. They believed that business should be the vanguard of American expansion, and that state power should be used whenever necessary to promote and defend it. Their enemy, for much of the 1920s and '30s, was isolationism, the belief that the United States should pull back from foreign engagements. Isolationists saw internationalists as agents for bankers and others who profited by ensnaring Americans in the web of global finance—which is precisely what the Dulles brothers were.

Wilson's agonizing and ultimately unsuccessful campaign to win congressional approval for American entry into the League of Nations showed the Dulles brothers and others on Wall Street that internationalism had potent enemies. To resist those enemies, and to work toward a world that would welcome American corporate and political power, the brothers and a handful of their friends had decided to create an invitation-only club, based in New York, where the worldly elite could meet, talk, and plan. Above all they were moved by the conviction that as the United States grew to global power, its political leaders urgently needed guidance from bankers, businessmen, and international lawyers. To provide this guidance in a systematic way, they brought their new club into being in 1921. They called it the Council on Foreign Relations. Its motto was a single Latin word that spoke volumes: *ubique*, meaning "everywhere."

This was an era when American foreign policy was the province of a small elite, and the men who founded the council were all certified members. Its first president, Norman Davis, was an eminent diplomat who had been Wilson's assistant treasury secretary and undersecretary of state—and who, a decade later, would accompany Allen to Berlin to meet Hitler. Among its other founding members were Elihu Root, a corporate lawyer who had been Theodore Roosevelt's secretary of war; Newton Baker, who had been Wilson's secretary of war and then co-founded the Baker Hostetler law firm, which represented multinational corporations; and other former Wilson advisers including Isaiah Bowman and Archibald

Coolidge. Coolidge was the founding editor of the council's journal, *Foreign Affairs*, which made its debut in the summer of 1922 with articles by Foster and Root, among others. After Coolidge's death in 1928 the editorship passed to Allen's lifelong friend Hamilton Fish Armstrong. He held the job for nearly half a century, including a period in the 1940s when Allen served as the council's president.

"No nation can reach the position of a world power, as we have done, without becoming entangled in almost every quarter of the globe in one way or another," Foster wrote in what could be taken as a summary of the council's internationalist credo. "We are inextricably and inevitably tied to world affairs."

In the 1930s and 1940s members of the council, including Foster, produced more than six hundred classified policy memos for the State Department. So secret was this pipeline that even members of the council who were not directly involved did not know it existed. Nonetheless the council's intimacy with senior policy makers in Washington was evident, leading some to view it as a nerve center of America's hidden "permanent government." The journalist and historian Peter Grose may have been closer to the truth when he described it as "part research center, part influence on government, and throughout a club of cultivated gentlemen (women were admitted to membership only the year after Allen's death) who comfortably smoked cigars and pondered matters of state over their glasses of port. . . . Allen also found the Council to be a useful forum for flattering distinguished foreign guests. He would invite them to speak and, over dinner afterward, develop friendly relations that could be turned to business advantage."

Promoters of "internationalism" were eager above all to preserve stability. Like many of them, Foster saw authoritarian leaders like Hitler as valuable allies in the fight against Bolshevism. Regimes that maintained order and disciplined themselves economically, he believed, were always better than those that pandered to groups impatient for social change.

"It is a well ordered domestic economy which provides the greatest assurance of peace," Foster told the International Chamber of Commerce in Berlin in 1937. "The problem of international peace is but an extension of the problem of internal peace."

In the period between the two world wars, Sullivan & Cromwell became the largest law firm in the United States. Even calling it a law firm, as Peter Grose has written, was missing the point. He described it as "a strategic nexus of international finance, the operating core of a web of relationships that constituted power. . . . The firm did offer legal associates to draft contracts, preserve estates, and argue in courtrooms, but this was not the profession of law as practiced by Foster and Allen Dulles. Their Sullivan & Cromwell sought nothing less than to shape the affairs of all the world for the benefit and well-being of the select, their clients."

Success allowed the Dulles brothers to become rich, establish themselves as pillars of private power, and set out on courses that would shape history. Yet although they came to see the world through the same polished lens, their personalities remained opposite. A European banker who worked with both men wrote afterward that he was struck by the contrast.

"What a difference between them!" he marveled. "John Foster looked like a clergyman . . . vivid and somewhat nervous. Allen [was] quiet, relaxed, but at the same time hard-working. . . . Allen relied on his brains, and John Foster on his faith. . . . Allen was certainly more broadminded than his brother, and that is why his contacts with people were so much easier. I think Allen was loved by the men who worked with him, while John Foster was respected."

Eager to promote his ideas—and himself—Foster produced a stream of articles, not just for sophisticated journals like *Foreign Affairs*, the *New Republic*, and the *Atlantic Monthly* but also for mass-circulation magazines like *Life* and *Reader's Digest*. Business groups sought him out for speeches. He emerged as a foreign policy "wise man" and moved steadily toward public life. His interest in the Republican Party deepened through his relationship with Thomas Dewey, a promising lawyer he had sought to hire as a litigator for Sullivan & Cromwell. Dewey chose instead to run for district attorney. He was elected and won several headline-grabbing cases, including one against leaders of the organized crime syndicate known as Murder, Inc. In 1938 Dewey became the Republican nominee for governor of New York and, although he lost, his campaign made him a rising star in the party. Foster became his mentor in matters related to foreign affairs, thereby finding a new and powerful channel toward political influence.

Some of the men Foster met and worked with during these years imagined him as a future Supreme Court justice. His own ambition ran further.

He believed he had become one of the few Americans who truly understood what his country and the world needed. In unguarded moments he
dared to reflect on his prospects of rising to the presidency.

Allen was hardly less ambitious. He never considered himself a possible president, but for years imagined becoming secretary of state. He
thought he might be on his way when President Roosevelt considered
naming his friend Norman Davis to the post in 1933. Roosevelt, however,
was disturbed by the taint of scandal that had enveloped Davis as a result
of his business dealings in Cuba, and chose Senator Cordell Hull of Ten-
nessee instead.

One of the most striking aspects of the Dulles brothers' careers in the
period between the world wars was the ease with which they moved
between service to government and to private clients. Sometimes they
served both at once. In a later age, their conflicts of interest would have
been considered not just unethical but illegal. Yet no one asked them for
financial disclosures, and few eyebrows were raised when they found ways
to profit from their diplomatic assignments.

While "Uncle Bert" was a senior State Department official and later
secretary of state, Foster did not hesitate to ask him to do favors for Sullivan & Cromwell clients. Lansing gave Foster letters of introduction that
allowed him to reach elite circles during his first trips abroad on Sullivan &
Cromwell business, and dutifully showed up at dinners Foster arranged to
impress his clients. When he sent Foster to represent the United States in
Central America in 1917, he knew that Sullivan & Cromwell was pressing
President Chamorro of Nicaragua to accept a loan from one of its clients,
Seligman Bank, and was also legal counsel to the government of Panama.
While Foster worked for the War Trade Board, he helped direct loans
worth $400 million to railroads, cotton growers, food producers, and
manufacturers, including several that were his clients. His work helping
to design the Dawes Plan for German reparation payments and its succes-
sor, the Young Plan, opened rich new markets for banks that Sullivan &
Cromwell represented.

Allen also benefited from the clubby ethos that shaped political and
corporate cultures in this era. The columnist Drew Pearson wrote that he
often secured State Department approval for foreign loans through connections to former colleagues, arranged "over a few rounds of golf." In
1927, just five months after he began work at Sullivan & Cromwell, the

State Department named him legal counsel to the American delegation attending a naval disarmament conference in Geneva. For the next six years he divided his time between representing the United States at conferences like this one and working as a Sullivan & Cromwell lawyer. His legal clients included shipbuilders, steelmakers, and others with direct interest in the outcome of disarmament conferences. Pearson repeatedly accused him of conflict of interest for taking on diplomatic assignments while earning his living as an "operator for the bankers." Later, Allen admitted that there might have been some truth to the charge.

"Possibly I shouldn't have done it," he wrote to a friend. "You remember what happened to Lot's wife."

During the late 1930s, as war began spreading across Europe, Allen became involved in a secret organization known enigmatically as "the room." It was a private forum, based in an unmarked apartment on East Sixty-Second Street, where bankers, businessmen, and corporate lawyers—a total of about three dozen—met to exchange the most sensitive information they had gathered about events unfolding around the world. Nearly all had either backgrounds in intelligence or unusually deep contacts in foreign capitals. Among them were Winthrop Aldrich, chairman of the Chase Manhattan Bank; Vincent Astor, who became known as "the richest boy in the world" after his fabulously wealthy father went down with the *Titanic*; the investment banker Theodore Roosevelt Jr., a son of the former president; David Bruce, a son-in-law of the banker Andrew Mellon who went on to become the only American to serve as ambassador to Britain, France, and West Germany; the publisher and investment banker Marshall Field III; Sir William Wiseman, a broker at the Wall Street firm of Kuhn, Loeb & Co., who had served as liaison between the British and American intelligence services during World War I; and William Donovan, a war hero who had become a Wall Street lawyer and was honing his interest in intelligence. These patricians not only advised the Roosevelt administration on covert operations abroad, but willingly arranged corporate cover for agents undertaking them.

In 1940 Allen and Foster looked forward to the Republican National Convention in Philadelphia, which they hoped would nominate Thomas Dewey for the presidency. The delegates did not cooperate, choosing instead a lawyer from Indiana, Wendell Willkie. Allen was disappointed.

Foster, who loathed Willkie for his militant anti-Hitler views and sympathy with the New Deal, was disgusted.

After the final vote in favor of Willkie, Allen, who was a delegate from New York, was easing his way back through his crowded hotel lobby when another delegate approached, clapped him on the back, and said, "Let's go into the bar and talk." It was William Donovan, one of Allen's friends from "the room." Like others in the secret group, Donovan was concerned that the United States seemed about to enter a global conflict without a real intelligence service. He laid out his arguments and finished with a simple observation that would change Allen's life and the course of history.

"We'll be in it before the end of 1941, and when we are, there are certain preparations which should already have been made," Donovan said. "That's where you come in."

Not for nothing had Donovan become known as "Wild Bill." Ten years older than Allen, he was a wiry and pugnacious Irishman who had led a cavalry troop against Pancho Villa in 1916 and won the Medal of Honor for valor in France during World War I. After the war he had become a successful corporate lawyer and was the Republican candidate for governor of New York in 1932. He had a fascination with combat, and had made his way to the front lines during Italy's invasion of Ethiopia and the Spanish Civil War. Despite being a Republican, he had a good relationship with Roosevelt from the days when they were both active in New York politics.

During his barroom chat with Allen, Donovan revealed a secret. He had just returned from London, where he had been on a private mission for Roosevelt. A series of meetings with Prime Minister Winston Churchill had convinced him that the war would continue, and that ultimately the United States would fight.

"While in Britain he also made a study of the organization and techniques of British intelligence," Allen later wrote. "He was convinced that America's military planning and its whole national strategy would depend on intelligence as never before, and that the American intelligence setup would have to be completely revamped."

In 1940 there was little in the way of an "intelligence setup" in Washington. Networks established during World War I had been allowed to atrophy. At least eight government agencies, including the Federal Communications Commission and the departments of state, treasury, labor, and commerce, gathered foreign intelligence, but none knew what the others were doing. Much of what the White House learned about foreign countries came from private citizens like Donovan, who during the late 1930s spent part of his time as a self-appointed intelligence agent in Europe. In Washington, one of Donovan's aides later recalled, he "began to beat on Roosevelt about the importance of a central intelligence, a strategic intelligence function. He had made a life's study of the impact of intelligence on world events. He had collected enough for four or five volumes on the subject."

Donovan was assembling a team of clandestine officers to work for an agency that did not yet exist, to serve a president who had yet to be persuaded. Allen Dulles, who was one of America's few experienced spies, was an obvious recruit. He had never really left the intelligence business. Sullivan & Cromwell told clients that it had "unusual and diversified means of obtaining information," and much of it came from Allen. He was thrilled to realize that the era of privatized, hit-or-miss intelligence gathering was ending, and that Washington would soon return to the business of coordinated espionage and covert action.

Diplomacy had shown Allen the ways of the world. Corporate law had made him rich. Now Donovan was offering him a chance to return to the shadows in which he had worked so successfully during World War I. He would play just the kind of role he wanted in the world: decisive but secret.

"When do you want me to start?" he asked when Donovan finished making his pitch.

"As soon as the election's over," came the reply. "I'll call you."

3

DULL, DULLER, DULLES

Because the most famous spy in modern history, James Bond, is a fictional character, he did not accompany the chief of Britain's naval intelligence service into the Oval Office one day at the beginning of 1941. His creator, however, did. The two of them, Admiral John Godfrey and his aide, Lieutenant Commander Ian Fleming, carried an urgent message from Winston Churchill to Franklin Roosevelt: the United States must build a modern intelligence service.

Roosevelt needed little persuasion. He had sent the irrepressible "Wild Bill" Donovan on a three-month tour of battlefronts in the Balkans and North Africa, and Donovan returned with a report stressing the value of resistance, sabotage, and covert operations. Impressed, Roosevelt gave him an office in the basement of the White House and asked him to write a proposal outlining what an American intelligence agency might be and do. On June 11, 1941, not long after Roosevelt met with Churchill's secret envoys, Donovan presented it. A week later Roosevelt sent a directive to the Bureau of the Budget ordering it to create a new agency called the Coordinator of Information, assign it $100 million in funds already appropriated for "preparedness," and list Donovan as its founding director.

"Donovan was a born leader of men," Allen Dulles later wrote of the dynamo who became his wartime boss. "He had indefatigable energy and wide-ranging enthusiasm combined with great courage and resourcefulness.... He knew the world, having traveled widely. He understood people. He had a flair for the unusual and for the dangerous, tempered with judgment. In short, he had the qualities to be desired in an intelligence officer."

Three weeks after Roosevelt created the Coordinator of Information, an innocuous notice appeared in the *Federal Register* announcing it. The COI, it said, would "collect and analyze all information and data which may bear upon the national security," send it to the president and "such departments and officials as the president may determine," and carry out "such supplementary activities as may facilitate the securing of information important for national security, not now available to the Government."

With that, the United States established its first full-fledged intelligence agency by presidential decree.

When Japanese bombers attacked the American base at Pearl Harbor on December 7, 1941, Americans instantly ceased to debate whether their country should enter the war. Whatever sense of security they felt had been shattered. In Washington, shock over the attack quickly gave way to a realization that it had been the result of a profound intelligence failure. Congress and the executive branch rushed to give the COI whatever support it needed.

Part of what it needed was the skill and experience of Allen Dulles. A few weeks after the Japanese attack on Pearl Harbor, Donovan approached him through a mutual friend, David Bruce. It was the call for which Allen had been waiting. Bruce told him that Donovan needed a man for a job. He said nothing about the job, only that it required "absolute discretion, sobriety, devotion to duty, languages, and wide experience." Allen accepted instantly.

Like many stories about Allen during these years, this one has come into question. By some accounts he was already working for Donovan at the time of the Pearl Harbor attack. What is clear is that by early 1942, he had closed his Sullivan & Cromwell cases and taken over as chief of the COI station in New York. He leased a large suite of offices on the thirty-sixth floor of the International Building at Rockefeller Center and brought dozens, scores, and then hundreds of men and women to work there: lawyers, financiers, former diplomats, businessmen, and professors. Officially they were financial consultants. To friends they were allowed to say that they worked for a "research unit" related to the war effort, while stressing its "dull, statistical" nature.

"New York was the logical first place, and Dulles was the logical guy because of his contacts," one of Donovan's aides later recalled. "He started bringing people in right away."

Allen had two principal assignments. First was to lay the groundwork for an intelligence network that could penetrate Germany and the German-held regions of Europe, which meant finding and interviewing immigrants, Americans who had lived in those regions, and others who might have valuable memories or contacts. Second was an even wider-ranging effort to debrief everyone in New York, especially merchant seamen and newly arrived immigrants, who could give information—the more precise, the better—about European cities, ports, roads, rail lines, airports, factories, and military bases. Allen's agents also swarmed over docks, sailors' registry offices, and holding pens for "enemy aliens," offering money for objects that immigrants might have considered worthless but that could be valuable to infiltrators. They bought old suits, neckties, overcoats, and shoes that could help agents blend in, and also identity cards, ration books, and other documents for forgers to use as models.

All manner of European exiles and refugees poured into the Rockefeller Center office; one, Heinrich Brüning, had been chancellor of Germany until 1932. The office swelled to fill four floors. When that proved insufficient, Allen rented eight more offices around the city, including one at 42 Broadway, near the docks. He quickly became fascinated with the possibilities for "direct action" operations in Europe, and established a front called the Mohawk Trading Corporation, through which he assembled an arsenal of sniper rifles, silencers, poison pills, and other tools of the black arts.

Allen had chosen his suite at Rockefeller Center in part because it adjoined one where another secret operation was under way, run by the legendary Sir William Stephenson, later revealed to be the spymaster Churchill called "Intrepid" and supposedly a model for Commander Fleming's fictional agent 007. Churchill had sent Stephenson to New York in 1940 to gather intelligence and try to push the United States toward entering the war. He established himself in Suite 3603 of the International Building, where the sign on the door said "British Passport Control Office." Britain was known as setting the gold standard in intelligence work, and Allen found in Stephenson a role model, inspiration, and guru.

"He had much to teach me," Allen said later. "I picked his brains."

On June 13, 1942, with the United States engaged in global war, Roosevelt signed an order transforming the Coordinator of Information from an intelligence-gathering agency into one authorized to conduct covert and paramilitary operations. There was no change in leadership, but a new name: the Office of Strategic Services. The OSS was authorized to do everything its predecessor had done and one thing more: "Plan and operate such services as may be directed by the United States Joint Chiefs of Staff."

"With this, Donovan's blueprint for the coordination of strategic intelligence collection with secret operations was realized," Allen wrote later. "An intelligence agency had been created for the first time in the United States which brought together under one roof the work of intelligence collection and counterespionage, with the support of underground resistance activities, sabotage, and almost anything else in aid of our national effort that regular armed forces were not equipped to do."

The OSS opened secret training camps for agents in Maryland and Virginia, and quickly ballooned to a staff of more than six hundred, most based in New York or Washington. Allen hired many of them. He described them as "military men and civilian leaders, teachers, bankers, lawyers, businessmen, librarians, writers, publishers, ballplayers, missionaries, reformed safe-crackers, bartenders, tugboat operators. . . . A bartender was hired not because he knew how to mix drinks but because he spoke perfect Italian and was at home in the mountain passes of the Apennines; a missionary because he knew the tribes and native dialects of Burma; an expert in engraving because his agents would need the most expert documentation to pass through enemy lines."

That was a romanticized description of the men and women who joined the OSS. There were mud-on-the-shoes types, of course, but Allen and other recruiters for the OSS looked mostly to people like themselves, people they knew from prep school, college, the practice of corporate law or investment banking, clubs, vacation resorts, or the Council on Foreign Relations. The upper reaches of the OSS comprised what Drew Pearson called "one of the fanciest groups of dilettante diplomats, Wall Street bankers, and amateur detectives ever seen in Washington." Many from this group would go on to help shape the United States in the second half of the twentieth century: Richard Helms, William Colby, Arthur Schlesinger Jr., Walt Rostow, Stewart Alsop, C. Douglas Dillon, Arthur Goldberg, William Casey, Ralph Bunche, and a parade of unlikelier figures ranging from Sterling Hayden to Julia Child.

Interviewing sailors and refugees in New York produced a trove of intelligence, and Donovan was eager to use it. In July 1942, just weeks after the OSS was created, he sent President Roosevelt notice that he was ready to launch operations in Europe.

> Switzerland is now, as it was in the last war, the one most advantageous place for the obtaining of information concerning the European Axis powers. . . . We have finally worked out with the State Department the appointment of a representative of this organization to proceed to Bern as "Financial Attaché." . . . However, we badly need a man of a different type; some person of a quality who can mingle freely with intellectual and business circles in Switzerland in order to tap the constant and enormous flow of information that comes from Germany and Italy to these people. . . . As soon as we find the man we need and check him with the Department of State, I shall advise you.

Donovan had already spoken to Allen about the possibility of moving abroad, and had offered him a post as deputy to David Bruce, whom Donovan had named to run the OSS station in London. Being anyone's deputy was not Allen's wish. He told Donovan he would prefer a post where "my past experience would serve me in good stead." Donovan understood what he meant: Switzerland.

On September 17, 1942, the *New York Times* published a short item announcing that Allen had resigned as treasurer of the Manhattan Republican Party to concentrate on "war work for the Office of Strategic Services." Few people knew what the OSS was. At Upper East Side and Georgetown cocktail parties, wives joked that its initials stood for "Oh So Secret" or, because of its Ivy League tint, "Oh So Social." Allen's friends, though, had little trouble guessing what he was up to. He had taken up strange but revealing habits like asking people who they knew in Switzerland, and meeting for dinner with odd-looking men who spoke with thick accents.

As Allen was preparing to leave for Bern, he received an alarming piece of secret information. Allied forces were planning to invade North Africa on November 8, a move that would presumably set off sweeping German reactions, including the seizure of French ports and perhaps even an invasion of neutral Switzerland. Allen had to reach Bern before that happened. That meant leaving immediately and traveling through Nazi-controlled France, which would make him the first OSS agent to cross enemy lines. Allen was forty-nine years old and suffering from intensifying attacks of gout, but impatient to return to the secret world where he felt most alive.

Clover, who understood that her husband was off to clandestine war but knew no more, drove him to New York Municipal Airport on November 2. Trouble began almost immediately. Bad weather forced his plane to land in the Azores, and he had to sit for two excruciating days before being allowed to fly on to Lisbon. The trip to Barcelona was also full of delays. It was November 8 when he finally reached the French border, at Portbou. There he ran into a Swiss diplomatic courier.

"Have you heard the news?" the man shouted. "The Americans and British are landing in North Africa!"

Allen realized that Nazi officers and their Vichy collaborators were certain to be searching trains. He was carrying secret documents, a certified check for one million dollars, and what he later called "certain of the more esoteric devices of espionage." If discovered, the best he could hope for would be years in an internment camp. Later he wrote that he considered turning back, but it is difficult to believe that he considered it seriously.

While my train made its way through France that night, I decided that if there were evidence of German controls, I would try to slip away at one of the stops and disappear into the countryside in hopes of making contact with the French resistance. . . .

At Annemasse, the last stop in France where all passengers for Switzerland had to alight to have their passports examined, I found that a person in civilian dress, obviously a German, was supervising the work of the French border officials. I had been told in Washington that there would probably be a Gestapo agent at this frontier. I was the only one among the passengers who failed to pass muster. The Gestapo man carefully put down in his notebook the particulars of my passport, and a few minutes later a French gendarme explained to me that an order had been received from Vichy to detain all Americans and British presenting themselves at the frontier and to report all such cases to Marshal Pétain directly. I took the gendarme aside and made to him the most impassioned and, I believe, most eloquent speech I have ever made in French. Evoking the shades of Lafayette and Pershing, I impressed upon him the importance of letting me pass. . . . I began to case the area in the hope of carrying out my plan of slipping away on foot to avoid being trapped there. It wouldn't have been easy.

Finally around noon, when it was about time for the train to leave for Geneva, the gendarme came up to me, hurriedly motioned for me to get on the train, and whispered to me, *Allez passer. Vous voyez que notre collaboration n'est que symbolique.* (Go ahead. You see our cooperation is only symbolic.) The Gestapo man was nowhere to be seen. Later I learned that every day, promptly at noon, he went down the street to the nearest pub and had his drink of beer and his lunch. Nothing, including landings in Africa, could interfere with his fixed Germanic habits. . . .

Within a matter of minutes I had crossed the French border into Switzerland legally. I was one of the last Americans to do so until after the liberation of France. I was ready to go to work.

One of the first people Allen contacted after arriving in Bern, an Austrian lawyer who had done work for Sullivan & Cromwell, helped him find an apartment at Herrengasse 23, part of a row of fourteenth-century town houses set above terraced vineyards. Its balcony offered an idyllic Alpine vista over the Aare River toward the peaks of the Bernese Oberland, capped by the majestic Eiger massif. There was also something any spy would want in his home: a hidden rear entrance.

Years of experience had honed Allen's talent as an intelligence officer, and he had mastered the techniques of teasing valuable information out of disparate scraps. Nonetheless his assignment was daunting. First he was to create a web of spies that would allow the United States to learn what was happening behind enemy lines and, ultimately, inside Nazi Germany itself. After that, he would begin parachuting agents into occupied countries, supplying weapons to partisans, and directing guerrilla attacks on Nazi targets.

Allen brought several other officers to work with him at the OSS station in Bern. The real work of penetrating Nazi-controlled Europe, however, had to be done by native-born field agents. Many refugees in Bern could become such agents, or knew others who could. An alert Swiss journalist helped some of them find him.

I had been in Switzerland only a few weeks when one of its most respected and widely read newspapers, alerted to the unusual circumstances of my

entry, came out with an article describing me as "the personal representative of President Roosevelt" with a "special duty" assignment. This flattering designation, in all its vagueness, was widely circulated, and even if I
had wished to do something about it, there was little I could do. Of course,
it had the effect of bringing to my door purveyors of information, volunteers and adventurers of every sport, professional and amateur spies, good
and bad. Donovan's operating principle was not to have his senior representatives try to go deep underground, on the very reasonable premise that
it was futile and that it was better to let people know you were in the business of intelligence and tell them where they could find you.

Nazi agents, who also read the newspapers, quickly established a watch
post across the street from Herrengasse 23, and kept it staffed day and
night for as long as Allen lived there. Nonetheless he racked up a quick
series of successes. Among his first recruits were a girlfriend of Admiral
Wilhelm Canaris, chief of military intelligence for the Nazi regime, and a
French officer who later provided precise information about German positions in France. He also nurtured bands of partisans in Italy, Poland, Austria, Yugoslavia, Bulgaria, Greece, Hungary, Belgium, and Czechoslovakia,
and assembled eight separate intelligence networks in France, including
one that found a channel into the highest reaches of the Vichy regime.

Allen had permanently shaken off the persona of the gimlet-eyed lawyer, which never quite fit him. He abandoned Wall Street suits for a tweed-
ier, more inviting look, favoring flannels and a rumpled raincoat. One
foreign agent filed a report describing him as "a tall, burly, sporting type . . .
healthy looking, with good teeth and a fresh, simple, openhearted manner."
For the rest of his life he presented himself this way: casual, genial, inviting.

Also during those first weeks in Bern, Allen found a mistress. She
shared his life as a spy, entertained him after hours, and introduced him
to one of the century's most remarkable mystic thinkers.

Mary Bancroft was a dynamic woman of the world. She had grown up
on Beacon Hill in Boston under the wing of her devoted step-grandfather,
C. W. Barron, the publisher of the *Wall Street Journal*. A former debutante, she had collected two husbands and an impressive number of lovers,
learned fluent French and German, and accumulated a modest fortune. In
Geneva she wrote feature articles for American newspapers, worked on a
novel, and presided over an informal salon that attracted journalists and

politicians, but also spiritualists, vegetarians, and others engaged in esoteric quests. She was thirty-eight years old and had been living in Switzerland for eight years when Allen arrived at the end of 1942 to set up the
OSS station. He hired her to write political analysis, and the rest followed
hard upon.

"We can let the work cover the romance, and the romance cover the
work," he told her as they began their affair.

Every morning at 9:20, Allen called Mary from his base in Bern with a
list of the reports and translations he needed that day, along with suggestions of who she should meet. A couple of times a week she would take
the train from Geneva to meet him, spending a few hours discussing
German troop movements or prospects for Balkan uprisings and then
retiring for what she called "a bit of dalliance." By her own account she
developed "overwhelming admiration for his abilities" and fell "completely
in love" with him. After a time, however, she became frustrated by his
self-involvement. Their romance began to cool after he appeared unan-
nounced at her apartment one day when he knew her husband was traveling and her daughter was at school, and shouted, "Quick! I've got a very
tricky meeting coming up, I want to clear my head."

"We settled onto the living room couch," she recalled in her memoir,
Autobiography of a Spy. "In scarcely more time than it takes to tell the
story, he was on his way again, pausing in the doorway only long enough
to say, 'Thanks. That was just what I needed.'"

Despite the swings in their long affair, Allen and Mary remained close
colleagues at work. He valued her advice and respected her command of
the spy trade. She also had an unusual circle of friends, among them the
pioneering psychoanalyst Carl Gustav Jung.

Although Mary was a vivacious extrovert, she suffered from painful
sneezing fits that she believed were the result of repressed emotional turmoil. She submitted herself to Jung's analysis, was cured, and became one
of his fervent advocates. Jung had reflected deeply about the cultural roots
of Nazism, and Mary often mentioned his views in reports she prepared
for Allen. The two men, spymaster and spiritual seeker, met at the beginning of 1943 and struck up what Allen called a "still-experimental marriage between espionage and psychology." Jung wrote a series of reports,
including psychological profiles of Hitler and other Nazi leaders, that
Allen said were of "real help to me in gauging the political situation."

Some reached the Allied commander, General Dwight Eisenhower, who sent Jung a letter of commendation after the war ended.

Allen's wartime record at the OSS station in Switzerland was, as is normal in the spy business, a mixture of success and failure. Some of the intelligence he reported proved false after being compared with enemy radio intercepts. After he had been in Bern for six months, one of Donovan's aides sent him a withering cable asserting that "all news from Bern these days is being discounted 100% by the War Department." A year later, in the spring of 1944, he made two wildly wrong predictions, first that the Nazi regime was "near collapse" and then that Allied troops would have an easy time landing in France on D-Day. Yet he also ran hundreds of agents across Europe, penetrated governments, and scored espionage triumphs.

Two began when strangers knocked on his door. The first was an anti-Nazi Austrian who led him to documents locating the factory where Nazis were building the V-1 and V-2 rockets they planned to rain down on London. Allen's information, confirmed by other sources, led to Allied bombing of the factory, in the Baltic town of Peenemünde. This delayed the launching of the London blitz by several months.

Allen's second walk-in was even more impressive. Fritz Kolbe, who contacted him through an intermediary and then came to the back door of Herrengasse 23 during a blackout, was a diplomat serving at the German foreign ministry in Berlin. Kolbe said he had access to all of the ministry's incoming and outgoing cable traffic and, motivated by hatred for the Nazi regime, wanted to hand whatever he could to the Americans. He passed Allen documents by the hundreds. Among them were minutes of Hitler's private meetings, damage assessments of Allied bombing campaigns, and clues that led to the discovery of a Nazi agent inside the British embassy in Turkey.

When Allen looked back over his OSS service in later years, he especially enjoyed recalling his role in two of the war's most spectacular clandestine operations.

The first was the attempted assassination of Hitler. Through one of his senior agents, an anti-Nazi German who lived in Switzerland, Allen learned of the conspirators' plot and the approximate date they would strike. As the date approached, they sent an emissary to meet him in Bern and propose a deal. If they could kill Hitler, they suggested, perhaps the Allies would alter their policy of demanding unconditional surrender from Germany and allow the country to come under a new regime without occupation. After consulting Washington, Allen replied with what he later called "an unconditional no." The plotters proceeded without him. On July 12, 1944, he sent a cable to Donovan alerting him to the "possibility that a dramatic event may take place up north." Eight days later the plotters struck, but the bomb they placed managed only to injure Hitler.

In the months after that failed attempt, it became clear that Germany would ultimately lose the war. Allen focused more intently than ever on a challenge he considered urgent: shaping post-war Europe in a way that would minimize Soviet power. His most audacious idea was to find Nazi commanders who recognized the futility of their cause and wished Germany to be ruled by Americans, not Russians, when the war ended. Once the Nazis were pushed out of France, the major active theater was Italy. Allen resolved to approach Nazi commanders there to see if they would ignore their fight-to-the-death orders and agree to a quick surrender.

At the end of 1944 and during the first months of 1945, Allen conceived and orchestrated Operation Sunrise, a multilayered plan that ultimately led to the Nazi surrender in Italy. One of his partners was General Karl Wolff, commander of SS forces there. A German court would later find Wolff complicit in the murder of 300,000 Jews, including the liquidation of the Warsaw ghetto, but by the end of the war he had fallen out with Hitler and was ready to deal with the Americans. Allen balanced Wolff's needs against those of various Italian exile and partisan groups, which sent him a stream of emissaries seeking American support for various plots. The emissaries ranged from a future prime minister, Ferruccio Parri, to a daughter of the renowned conductor Arturo Toscanini, Countess Wally Toscanini Castelbarco, whom Allen promptly seduced. His climactic secret meeting with Nazi commanders was held at a lakeside villa outside the Swiss town of Ascona, a couple of miles from the Italian border. It produced a dramatic accord that led to the sudden end of war in Italy and also in Austria, over which Nazi commanders in Italy had authority. On May 3, 1945, *Stars and Stripes* reported the news jubilantly:

The German armies in Italy and in part of Austria have surrendered—completely and unconditionally. . . . This means that vital cities like Salzburg and Innsbruck are ours without a fight. It means that Allied forces take over Austrian territory within ten miles of Berchtesgaden, where

Hitler built what he thought was a personal fortress so deep in the fast-
ness of the Alps that it would take months or years to approach it. . . . But
above all else, the surrender in Italy means that the valorous fighters of
the 5th and 8th Armies, who have fought their way up the entire length
of the relentless Apennines, need not begin the heartbreaking task of
conquering the mountains that lead to the Brenner Pass and into Austria. It means, too, the fliers of the Mediterranean Allied Air Forces need
not go plunging into the flak alleys around Brenner Pass or other narrow
passages among the Alps.

As the war wound down, Allen invited his wife to join him in Bern.
Soon after she arrived, he introduced her to his mistress, Mary Bancroft.
Clover had met several of Allen's female companions and formed a
remarkably strong bond with Mary. "I can see how much you and Allen
care for one another, and I approve," Clover told Mary soon after they
met. They often lunched together, and took to referring to Allen and Foster as "the sharks" because they seemed to need constant motion in order
to survive. Mary also introduced Clover to Carl Gustav Jung, whose help
she sought in dealing with her troubled marriage; by Mary's account it
was shaped by enraged arguments "which Allen invariably won by the
simple device of clamping an iron curtain between them." Contact with
Jung left a deep impression on both women. After the war Mary helped
edit a Jungian journal in California. Clover promoted Jung's work in New
York, and her younger daughter, Joan, became a Jungian analyst.

Allen was present at the red schoolhouse in Reims on May 7, 1945,
when General Alfred Jodl signed the instrument of surrender that ended
World War II in Europe. A few weeks later he set out for Washington to
discuss his future with Donovan—and to bask in the glory of Operation
Sunrise. Churchill congratulated him personally when he stopped in
London, and his opposite numbers in the British Secret Intelligence Service treated him like a hero. In Washington he was welcomed just as
warmly. Donovan encouraged him to tell the story of Operation Sunrise
publicly, and in September he published a breathless account of it in the
Saturday Evening Post. In this article and in a longer version he published
in 1966 as a book called *The Secret Surrender*, he portrayed the operation
as a brilliant success that spared the Allies a longer war in Italy. Some historians later saw in it an early warning sign of the Cold War. The OSS had

refused to let the Soviets in on the negotiations, leaving them feeling deceived and suspicious about America's plans for post-war Europe.

"What had been gained by two months of dickering with the Nazis?" the historian Gar Alperovitz asked in a review of Allen's book. "A mere six days. The fighting in Italy halted on May 2; the total collapse of the Reich was recorded on the evening of May 7–8. What had been lost? It is impossible to know precisely, but insofar as the possibility of peace depended on trust and mutual confidence, that possibility had been damaged. *The Secret Surrender* reminds us that the Cold War cannot be understood simply as an American response to a Soviet challenge, but rather as the insidious interaction of mutual suspicions, blame for which must be shared by all."

With the war over, the OSS had little reason to maintain a station in Bern. Nevertheless, there was still plenty of intelligence work to do, and Allen decided that he should become director of OSS operations in Europe. Donovan, however, considered Allen "an artist of intelligence" but a terrible administrator, and would not give him the job. Instead he became chief of the new OSS station in Berlin. He arrived in the bombed-out city on June 20, 1945, exactly eleven months after the abortive bomb attack against Hitler that he had encouraged. His first two projects were oddly contradictory: gathering evidence to be used at the Nuremberg war crimes trials and integrating the legendary Nazi spymaster Reinhard Gehlen and his far-flung espionage network into the OSS. Then, after he had been station chief for just three months, his assignment was cut short.

On September 20, 1945, the new American president, Harry Truman, signed an order abolishing the OSS. He feared that the secret powers it had accumulated during the war might, in peacetime, expand to threaten American democracy. To avoid this, he transferred the OSS research unit to the State Department and its espionage and counterespionage units to the War Department. Ten days after he issued his order, the OSS was no more.

The dissolution of the OSS cut Allen loose from his moorings. He had spent the war years in an adrenaline-charged secret world where any misstep could mean death or worse. Now he faced a new and in some ways more terrifying prospect: normal life at home.

The Dulles brothers were separated for most of World War II and followed strikingly different paths. Allen disappeared into the obscure world of espionage and covert action. Foster passed through a remarkable phase in which he spoke more fervently than ever for Christian principles and against selfish nationalism.

By the time Foster marked his fiftieth birthday in 1938, he was more influential than any other private lawyer in the United States. Nonetheless he was restive, and began to reflect on the future course of his life. He had his share of private disappointments; the vote to pull Sullivan & Cromwell out of Nazi Germany had shaken him, and he recognized his failure to build strong relationships with his children. The world seemed to be racing toward catastrophe. He began spending more time writing, speaking, and deepening his involvement in religious groups.

Foster's re-encounter with the earnest Presbyterianism of his youth began when he traveled to Oxford in the summer of 1937 to participate in a gathering of Christian leaders called the World Conference on Church, Community, and State. Religious thinkers including Reinhold Niebuhr, Paul Tillich, and T. S. Eliot joined in far-ranging discussions about how Christians could help shape a more peaceful world. After returning home, Foster persuaded the Federal Council of Churches to create a platform from which he could speak out on political and moral issues. It emerged as the Commission to Study the Bases of a Just and Durable Peace, and from 1940 to 1946 it was Foster's platform, his megaphone, and the center of his intensifying public activism.

During this period of his life, Foster moved closer than ever to the ideals of global cooperation. He never became a full-fledged "one-worlder," but he hammered relentlessly on the theme that self-defeating nationalism had caused devastating global conflicts that could be resolved only by new global organizations. Much of what he said and wrote seems startling in light of his post-war metamorphosis.

The society of nation-states, Foster asserted, had become a "society of anarchy," proving that "the sovereignty system is no longer consonant either with peace or justice." Americans in particular failed to see the urgent need for cooperation with other nations, and foolishly believed they could ensure their future security through "dependence on our strength alone." Peace could be guaranteed only by "a kind of supranational guild" that would balance the interests of all nations. It would emerge in stages, beginning with "economic and financial union, letting the political union work out of them if and when this becomes a natural development." People and nations should "avoid concentrating upon the admitted evils elsewhere, slurring over the admitted evils at home and thereby becoming, in my judgment, hypocritical and un-Christian."

Religious imagery began pervading what Foster said and wrote. He urged statesmen to cultivate "Christ-like qualities" and "not to identify national self-interest with righteousness." When news of the Bataan death march and other Japanese atrocities appeared in the press and a friend of his called them unforgivable, he replied, "Jesus Christ tells us that nothing is unforgivable." In 1943 he published a remarkable treatise called *Six Pillars of Peace* in which he ridiculed the "devil theory" of global politics and rejected the image of the world as made up of a "nation-hero" surrounded by "nation-villains." He scorned demagogues who "seek national unity by fomenting fear of other people," promote "a feeling that their nation is in danger," or "extol patriotism as the noblest emotion."

Foster's book, which also urged arms control, decolonization, and a new world organization, was widely discussed in the press, endorsed by the Rockefeller Foundation, and printed in a special edition for Protestant clergymen. Yet when he secured a meeting at the White House to present a copy to Franklin Roosevelt, he found the president preoccupied with winning the war and uninterested in discussing Christian imperatives. He hoped for a warmer reception in London, and through the American ambassador arranged a meeting with Foreign Secretary Anthony Eden and his undersecretary, Sir Alexander Cadogan. They too were unimpressed.

"Lunched with A. in his flat," Cadogan wrote in his diary. "J. F. Dulles there . . . J. F. D. the wooliest type of useless pontificating American. . . . Heaven help us!"

As the 1944 presidential election approached, Foster returned to the side of his younger friend Thomas Dewey, who had been elected governor of New York and was making a second run for the presidency. He tutored Dewey on foreign affairs and wrote speeches for him. This time Dewey won the Republican nomination but was defeated decisively in the general election, as Roosevelt won his fourth term. Foster emerged from Dewey's losing campaign as one of the Republican Party's two senior foreign policy spokesmen, along with Senator Arthur Vandenberg of Michigan, the ranking Republican on the Senate Foreign Relations Committee.

"To look at him you might think he had just finished contact with a green persimmon," began a magazine profile of Foster that appeared during the 1944 campaign. "To listen to him on the subject of his business (he is top senior partner in the Wall Street firm of Sullivan & Cromwell), you would only begin to guess that he can distill the poetry of action as well as a big income out of such things as reshuffling the corporate structure of the International Nickel Company."

The war had not yet ended when Roosevelt summoned world leaders to San Francisco for the historic effort to create what became the United Nations. He had been persuaded that the American delegation should be bipartisan, and the Republicans proposed Foster as a "legal adviser." Roosevelt was displeased.

"He will play it his way," Roosevelt told Secretary of State Edward Stettinius. "He will leak things. He will be a disruptive force. I don't like Foster Dulles. I won't have him there."

The Republicans insisted, and finally Roosevelt agreed to accept their choice. He died soon afterward, leaving Harry Truman to oversee the San Francisco talks.

From April 25 to June 26, 1945, delegates from fifty countries met at the San Francisco Opera House to design the new world body. During these nine weeks Foster was intensely in his element, pressing his views in public debates and private meetings. He and the other American delegates worked to shape the embryonic United Nations in ways that would serve American interests—ensuring, for example, that clauses on trusteeship and decolonization were worded so as not to threaten American control over Hawaii, Alaska, and Puerto Rico.

Reports in the American press depicted Foster as the wizard who managed the San Francisco conference from behind the scenes. They were the result of his practice of briefing reporters privately at the end of each day's proceedings, usually placing himself at the center of events. This greatly irritated the delegation's chairman, Secretary of State Stettinius, and its official spokesman, Adlai Stevenson, neither of whom had yet grasped the value of self-serving leaks.

Foster had become the only major figure in American public life who claimed both religious and political identities. While serving as the Republican Party's foreign affairs spokesman, he also ran the Just and Durable Peace commission for the Federal Council of Churches. He was simultaneously chairman of the Carnegie Endowment for International

Peace and an elder of the Park Avenue Presbyterian Church, a trustee of both the Rockefeller Foundation and Union Theological Seminary.

Despite his broadening interests in politics and religion, Foster continued to devote most of his time and energy to his law practice. Demand for his expertise in German debt refinancing had evaporated in the firestorm of global conflict, and to compensate for lost clients he had acquired a set of new ones: non-Americans with large interests in the United States, including the governments of China and the Netherlands and the national banks of Belgium and Poland. He also remained an active board member of half a dozen corporations whose legal affairs he had overseen for years. The rebirth of the intense religiosity of his youth and his emergence as a major figure in the Republican Party coincided with an ever-broadening law practice specializing in global finance and quiet Washington lobbying.

One of the most productive relationships Foster developed in the 1940s was with the ambitious journalistic entrepreneur Henry Luce, who had become the country's most powerful opinion maker. Luce's views reached one million subscribers to *Time*, four million subscribers to *Life*, eighteen million listeners who heard *The March of Time* each week on the radio, countless more who watched *The March of Time* newsreels, and an elite business audience that subscribed to *Fortune*—by one estimate "at least a third and perhaps considerably more of the total literate adult population in the country." No other media baron had anything approaching his reach or influence. His most famous article, "The American Century," which appeared in the February 17, 1941, issue of *Life*, was a stirring call for "the most powerful and vital nation in the world" to embrace world leadership.

"We are the inheritors of all the great principles of Western Civilization," Luce wrote. "It now becomes our time to be the powerhouse."

Foster had much in common with Luce. Both were internationalist, pro-business Republicans shaped by Calvinist principles and the missionary tradition; Luce's parents were missionaries, and he was born in China. Both believed Providence had ordained for the United States a unique role in the world. Both abhorred all forms of socialism, and saw in Moscow a godless tyranny dedicated to destroying the West. Fighting Communism was the challenge they believed history had assigned to their generation.

"The two Presbyterians, Luce and Dulles, would cause suspense and even terror in ensuing years because of their determination to reshape the world as closely as possible after the pattern of American transcendence," one of Luce's biographers has written. "Both had the good fortune of discovering that their religion and their politics were complementary. . . . Both Presbyterians were men of great mental vigor who sunk to narrowest parochialism in the area where the molten materials of their religion, patriotism, and politics fused into one cold and flinty mass. Such ferociously aggressive men were uncomfortable with ideological competition. . . . When either Luce or Dulles started talking about 'America's priceless spiritual heritage' or 'the hopes of all who love freedom,' lesser nations had reason to become uneasy."

Luce did as much as anyone to transmit the Cold War consensus to Americans. Somewhat unexpectedly, he found a partner in Foster, who was undergoing a remarkable transformation. In the space of less than a year, between late 1945 and the middle of 1946, Foster moved from preaching tolerance and forgiveness to promoting the "devil theory" he had formerly scorned. In a series of articles for *Life*, he painted a steadily more frightening picture of the Soviet threat. His first major volley was a two-part series, published in June 1946, entitled "Thoughts on Soviet Conduct and What to Do About It." In it he set the urgent tone that defined how he, the Luce press, the Republican and Democratic parties, and most Americans would view the world for a generation.

Soviet leaders, Foster wrote, had launched a worldwide campaign that aimed to subjugate the West; to "eliminate what are, to us, the essentials of a free society"; and to impose on conquered peoples a system "repugnant to our ideals of humanity and fair play." Already, he asserted, the Soviets had built a shadowy network of allies in non-Communist countries who pretended to be patriots but in reality "take much guidance from Moscow." This made Soviet Communism the unseen force directing nationalist movements in Asia, Africa, and Latin America.

"Never in history have a few men in a single country achieved such world-wide influence," he concluded.

Foster's view of the Soviet Union as the center of a global conspiracy did not place him on the outer fringes of public opinion. At times he used a more melodramatic vocabulary than President Truman, Senator Vandenberg, Secretary of State George Marshall, and foreign policy mandarins like George Kennan and Averell Harriman, but all shared the same essential view that Soviet Communism was, in Kennan's words, "a great political force intent on our destruction."

In 1947, responding to Soviet pressure on Greece and Turkey, Truman decided that the United States should make a new commitment to intervene anywhere in the world to stop what it deemed to be the spread of Communism. When he told Vandenberg he planned to make this sweeping commitment, Vandenberg replied, "Mr. President, the only way you are ever going to get this is to make a speech and scare the hell out of the country." Truman took his advice. In a speech to a joint session of Congress on March 12, 1947, he unveiled the far-reaching global project that became known as the Truman Doctrine.

"Totalitarian regimes imposed on free peoples, by direct or indirect aggression, undermine the foundations of international peace and hence the security of the United States," the president asserted. "At the present moment in world history, nearly every nation must choose between alternative ways of life. The choice is too often not a free one. One way of life is based upon the will of the majority, and is distinguished by free institutions. . . . The second way of life is based upon the will of a minority forcibly imposed upon the majority. It relies upon terror and oppression, a controlled press and radio, fixed elections, and the suppression of personal freedoms. I believe that it must be the policy of the United States to support free peoples who are resisting attempted subjugation by armed minorities or by outside pressures."

Congress accepted Truman's worldview and appropriated the $400 million he requested for military aid to countries where Communist influence was seen to be growing. Some historians pinpoint this as the moment when the Cold War began in earnest, as the United States proclaimed that it considered the entire world a battleground between the superpowers. World events helped drive this view, but it also reflected impulses and attitudes deeply woven into the national psyche. They include, as the diplomatic historian Townsend Hoopes has written, "American commitment to individual liberty, American will-to-win, American resistance to half-measures, [and] American frustration with the psychological strain, the danger, the complexity, and the persisting inconclusiveness of a challenge that had to be met, yet could not be eliminated."

In 1948 Foster traveled to Amsterdam for a religious assembly sponsored by the World Council of Churches. His speech was fiery, complete with vivid descriptions of the "diabolical outrages" perpetrated by Communist leaders, who he said "do not believe in such concepts as eternal justice," embraced an ideology based on "evil, ignorance, and despair," and were "conspiring to overwhelm mankind with awful disaster." What made this speech remarkable was what followed: a spirited reply to Foster's "grotesque distortions" from a prominent Czech-born theologian, Josef Hromadka, who had spent nearly a decade teaching theology at Princeton. Hromadka urged that the atheism of Communist leaders be understood as a reaction to the misuse of religion by the czars, "rather a tool and weapon of an anti-bourgeois and anti-feudal political propaganda than a distinctive faith." It was unfair, he added, to compare Soviet Communism with "democratic institutions and processes originated, grown and perfected under an utterly different historical sky." Instead it should be seen as a "historical necessity in a country consisting of multiple ethnic, in part culturally backward elements, and in a nation which for many reasons had not been privileged to enjoy political liberties and popular education."

The official report of the Amsterdam assembly included long quotes from this speech and only a couple of brief lines from Foster's. He saw this as reflecting a dangerous weakening of Christian resolve in the face of peril, and the drift of Protestant theology toward "left wing and socialist tendencies."

Foster's newfound militancy was the final stage of a political voyage that stretched over a quarter century. He had always hated Bolshevism, but in the 1920s he recognized the Soviet Union as disorganized, economically prostrate, and no threat to the West. In 1924 he described America's refusal to recognize its government as an "absurdity." For much of the 1930s he focused his attention on defending Nazi Germany as a bulwark against Bolshevism as an ideology, but once the United States entered the war in 1941 and became a military ally of the Soviets, American criticism of the Soviet system was muffled. During the war years, Foster saw the Soviet Union as a conventional big power, protective of its own interests and rationally weighing its relations with other countries. As late as the San Francisco Conference of June 1945, at which the United Nations was founded, he publicly urged Western leaders to "proceed on the assumption that Russia will come to practice genuine cooperation."

For much of his life, Foster had believed that the root of conflict and global instability was the failure of nations to cooperate. After the war he abandoned this view. In his new theology, threats to peace came not from the recklessness of nations, but the recklessness of one nation: the Soviet Union.

What led Foster to this turnaround? His own explanation was twofold. First, he said he had never before thought deeply enough about the nature of Communism to develop "a clear understanding of the fundamentals." He began obsessively reading and rereading *Problems of Leninism*, a collection of Stalin's essays and speeches. By one account he "owned six or more pencil-marked copies, and kept one in each of his work places." To him it was a revelation: a chilling blueprint for world conquest, to be achieved by weakening rival powers and seizing control of emerging nationalist movements.

> The October Revolution has shaken imperialism not only in the centers of its domination, not only in the "metropolises." It has also struck at the rear of imperialism, its periphery. . . . Having sown the seeds of revolution both in the centers of imperialism and in its rear, having weakened the might of imperialism in the "metropolises," and having shaken its domination in the colonies, the October Revolution has thereby put in jeopardy the very existence of world capitalism as a whole.

At least as important as Foster's immersion in *Problems of Leninism* was what he called the "very great transformation" in Soviet behavior. Within two years of the war's end, the Soviets had sought to intimidate Iran and Turkey, had supported Communist fighters in the Greek civil war, and had imposed pro-Moscow regimes in Poland, Romania, and Bulgaria. Foster saw this as evidence that Stalin was pursuing precisely the aggressive strategy he had publicly proclaimed.

In speeches and articles, Foster began warning that Soviet leaders were bent on "eradicating the non-Soviet type of society," and that if the United States did not strike back, an "alien faith will isolate us and press in on us to a point where we shall be faced with surrender or with new war." He painted the Soviet Union as pursuing not simply age-old Russian strategic goals, but power over the whole world; it posed to the West not just the sort of threat that assertive powers have always posed to one another, but "a challenge to established civilization—the kind of thing which occurs only once in centuries."

"In the tenth century after Christ the so-called Christian world was challenged by an alien faith," he wrote. "The tide of Islam flowed from Arabia and swept over much of Christendom. . . . Now another ten centuries have rolled by and the accumulated civilization of these centuries is faced with another challenge. This time the challenge is Soviet Communism."

This was not only harsher rhetoric than Foster had ever used against Communism, but also far surpassed any criticism he had ever made of Nazism. The threat posed by Communism seemed to him infinitely greater. He had come to recognize Nazism as an ideology that led to great crimes, but during the 1930s he accepted it because he considered its identity essentially Western, Christian, and capitalist. Communism was none of those. In it Foster saw something he never saw in Nazism: an ultimate evil with which no compromise could ever be possible.

"The outlook for world peace seems to be getting dull, duller, Dulles," lamented Frank Kingdon, a Methodist minister and columnist for the *New York Post*.

Occasionally a voice emerged to offer a less apocalyptic view of Soviet intentions. The columnist Walter Lippmann urged Americans to "stop beating our heads against stone walls under the illusion that we have been appointed policeman to the human race," and warned that Washington's fixation on the Cold War "is misconceived, and must result in a misuse of American power." These warnings, however, were overwhelmed by a fast-developing national consensus that the world had been divided between godly forces and others that were evil. John Foster Dulles gave voice to that belief.

"We are the only great nation whose people have not been drained, physically and spiritually," he declared in one speech. "It devolves upon us to give leadership in restoring principle as a guide to conduct. If we do not do that, the world will not be worth living in. Indeed, it will probably be a world in which human beings cannot live."

This stridency drew Foster apart from the era's most eminent Protestant theologian, Reinhold Niebuhr. The two had served together on the Just and Durable Peace commission and shared a passionate interest in the application of ethics to global politics. Niebuhr, however, never sought a political role. Instead he remained reflective, and was uncomfortable with Foster's emerging good-versus-evil view of the world. It contradicted his own belief in moral ambiguity, the danger of self-righteousness, the imperfection of human institutions, and what he called "the similarity between our sin and the guilt of others." Foster believed the principal threat to the United States came from Moscow; Niebuhr saw it in the egotism of Americans and their leaders.

"If we should perish," Niebuhr warned, "the ruthlessness of the foe would be only the secondary cause of the disaster. The primary cause would be that the strength of a great nation was directed by eyes too blind to see all the hazards of the struggle, and the blindness would be induced not by some accident of nature or history, but by hatred and vainglory."

Such introspection is rarely popular in any country, and in any case Niebuhr emerged only slowly as a public intellectual. Foster, meanwhile, continued making news as the Republican member of American diplomatic missions. Several times he clashed dramatically with Andrei Vishinsky, the fire-breathing Soviet deputy foreign minister, who had been chief prosecutor at Stalin's grotesque Great Purge trials. He would later write that Vishinsky's arrogant intransigence was for him "a streak of lightning that suddenly illuminated a dark and stormy scene. We saw as never before the magnitude of the task of saving Europe for Western civilization."

Vishinsky combined a confrontational style with an absolute insistence on squeezing every bit of advantage for his side, which he believed embodied the future of humanity. During one summit he was so relentlessly demanding that American delegates retreated to regroup. One of them wondered aloud what Vishinsky might have become if he had been born and raised in the United States.

"Why, there's no doubt about it," General Walter Bedell Smith answered. "He would have been senior partner at Sullivan & Cromwell."

4

THAT FELLA FROM WALL STREET

What does a wartime spymaster do when the fighting ends and his government has no more use for him? John Foster Dulles saw his brother facing this dilemma after the guns fell silent in Europe. He had an answer: come back to Sullivan & Cromwell. The only strong argument he could make was that legal work would offer rich returns. Foster stressed it in letters to his brother.

"An awful lot of things are opening up," he wrote. "We'll clean up!"

Allen was less than thrilled at the prospect, but with the Office of Strategic Services shutting down he had no better option. At the end of 1945 he resigned from government service for the second time. He returned to law practice under his brother's supervision, and with some difficulty began feigning interest in bonds, debentures, and indemnities. "Much of the sparkle and charm went out of Allen's personality as I had known it," Mary Bancroft later wrote. "It was rather like the way an exuberant young person behaves when his parents suddenly show up."

Allen spent hours writing nostalgia-filled letters to former OSS comrades. "Most of my time is spent reliving those exciting days," he admitted in one of them.

Several of Allen's closest ex-comrades became his favorite companions. Kermit Roosevelt, who was part of Allen's smart set on Long Island, spent hours with him, officially to collect stories for a history of the OSS but often just to reminisce. Tracy Barnes, another Long Islander whom Allen had sent on a daring operation to photograph the secret diaries of Mussolini's daughter, stopped by almost as often. Two others with whom Allen often shared drinks, cigars, and memories were young agents who had worked for him during his truncated assignment as OSS station chief in Berlin. Frank Wisner, once his partner in the operation to recruit the "Gehlen Group" of former Nazi spies, had also returned to work at a Wall Street law firm, and they spent weekends on Long Island grousing about Washington's lack of interest in covert operations. Richard Helms, who had gone from selling advertisements for the *Indianapolis Times* to running Allen's counterintelligence operation in Berlin, was also eager to return to the front lines.

These restless warriors, with a handful of others, would soon shatter the world.

In the years immediately after the war, world events unfolded in ways that convinced President Truman and many other American leaders of the need for a secret intelligence service. The nation was gripped by a fear that Soviet Communism was winning victories around the world while the United States was standing still or losing. Soviet takeovers in Eastern Europe, coupled with the emergence of nationalist movements in Asia, Africa, and Latin America, seemed to many in Washington a centrally organized campaign aimed at conquering the world. In this climate, Allen and his fellow OSS veterans found officials in Washington increasingly receptive to their idea that the United States not only needed a peacetime intelligence agency—something it had never had—but that this agency should have powers greater than any such agency had ever exercised in a democratic country.

Western secret services had always kept the collection of intelligence strictly separate from the analysis and possible action that might follow from it, since concentrating those functions in a single agency was thought likely to lead to intelligence reports tainted by pressure from covert operatives. This principle had been allowed to lapse during wartime, and the OSS men became accustomed to doing every part of the job: collecting intelligence, analyzing it, and acting on it. President Truman had created a loose body called the Central Intelligence Group to advise him on intelligence matters, but he gave it no authority to carry out covert operations. Allen wished this to change.

"The collection of secret intelligence is closely related to the conduct of secret operations," he argued in one confidential report. "The two activities support each other and can be disassociated only to the detriment of both."

Allen's ability to press his case improved sharply after the 1946 congressional elections, in which Republicans took control of both houses for the first time in sixteen years. The new chairman of the Senate Foreign Relations Committee, Arthur Vandenberg, named one of Allen's old OSS comrades, Lawrence Houston, to his staff. Houston had directed many covert operations and shared Allen's love of them. Together they drafted a bill that would create a National Security Council to advise the president on foreign policy, and a Central Intelligence Agency authorized to collect information and to act on it. "Wild Bill" Donovan, the widely admired former OSS director, lobbied for the bill in Congress but found some members reluctant. Several wanted the State Department, not a secret new agency, to oversee covert operations, but their case was weakened when Secretary of State Marshall announced that he did not want his department to be involved in such operations. The bill made its way through Congress in a matter of weeks. On July 26, 1947, Truman signed it into law.

"There were strong objections to having a single agency with the authority both to collect secret intelligence and to process and evaluate it for the President," according to one history. "The objections were overruled, and CIA became a unique organization among Western intelligence services, which uniformly keep their secret operations separate from their overall intelligence activities."

The new National Security Act contained a tantalizing clause worded to allow endlessly elastic interpretation. It authorized the CIA to perform not only duties spelled out by law, but also "such other functions and duties related to intelligence affecting the national security as the National Security Council may from time to time direct." This gave it the legal right to take any action, anywhere in the world, as long as the president approved.

"The fear generated by competition with a nation like the USSR, which had elevated control of every aspect of society to a science, encouraged the belief in the United States that it desperately needed military might and counterespionage by agencies that could outdo the Soviet spymasters," the historian Robert Dallek has written. "Dean Acheson [who would succeed Marshall as secretary of state] had the 'gravest forebodings' about the CIA, and 'warned the President that neither he nor the National Security Council nor anyone else would be in a position to know what it was doing or to control it.' But to resist the agency's creation seemed close to treason."

Donovan, who had all the experience necessary to head the new CIA, could not aspire to the job because of his poor relationship with Truman; he was an archetype of the slick Wall Street lawyer Truman detested, and he also epitomized a belief in secrecy and covert action that Truman did not share. Allen, who might also have been a candidate, was disqualified as a Republican associated with his brother's partisanship—although Truman did offer to make him ambassador to France, a prospect he declined in part because Foster feared that having a brother working for a Democratic president would weaken his Republican credentials. Instead Truman chose Admiral Roscoe Hillenkoetter, a quiet, steady officer who had been naval attaché in Moscow, as the first CIA director.

Although OSS veterans failed to place one of their own at the top of the CIA, they had won most of what they wanted. The intelligence service they considered essential to their country's security—and to their own personal fulfillment—had been established. It had been given more power than any of its counterparts in the Western world. The only remaining obstacle was President Truman, who showed no inclination to use the CIA as Allen and his friends wished it to be used.

"It was not intended to be a 'Cloak and Dagger Outfit'!" Truman wrote in frustration years later. "It was intended merely as a center for keeping the President informed on what was going on in the world."

If that was Truman's vision, it faded almost immediately. Just six months after the CIA was established, it had a rude shock when Communists in Czechoslovakia staged a "constitutional coup" that brought them to power. That event focused urgent attention on the upcoming elections in Italy, where the Communist Party was surging. The CIA sent its men into action, spending $10 million on operations that included supporting pro-American parties like the Christian Democrats, recruiting Catholic priests and bishops to denounce the Communist threat, and flooding Italy with letters, pamphlets, and books warning of Communism's danger. Allen took a quiet leave of absence from Sullivan & Cromwell to help direct this campaign. It may not have been quiet enough, since ten days before the Italian election, the *Boston Globe* ran a story about his involvement headlined "Dulles Masterminds New 'Cold War' Plan Under Secret Agents." The result, however, was a grand success: the Christian Democrats won a resounding victory at the polls.

The CIA's early covert operations were in Europe, where the subversive threat was thought to be most urgent. Its first two major ones—intervention in the 1948 Italian election and the hiring of Corsican gangsters to break a Communist-led dockworkers' strike in the French port of Marseille—were successful. Around the same time, however, an explosion of violence closer to home shook the assumption that Europe would be the main battleground of the unfolding covert war.

On April 9, 1948, while Secretary of State Marshall was attending the Ninth Inter-American Conference in Bogotá, Colombia, one of Colombia's most popular politicians was assassinated, setting off riots in which thousands died. Historians have unanimously understood this episode, known as the *Bogotazo*, as part of an intensifying civil war that shook Colombia for decades. In Washington, though, it was seen as a Moscow-inspired effort to challenge the United States by destabilizing Latin America. Outraged politicians and editorial writers demanded to know why there had been no warning. In the fearful climate of that era, few in Washington could imagine that the *Bogotazo* stemmed entirely from conflicts within Colombia. They assumed it was part of a plot hatched in the Kremlin.

Soon after these early Cold War skirmishes, the Allied commander in Europe, General Lucius Clay, sent Washington a chilling warning that a Soviet attack could come "with dramatic suddenness." This threw American leaders into what a later Senate report called "near-hysteria." The year-old National Security Council reacted by issuing a secret directive called NSC 10/2, approved by President Truman, that gave the CIA more explicit power than it had ever had. It was dated June 18, 1948—four months after Communists took power in Czechoslovakia and two months after the Italian election and the *Bogotazo*. These events, it concluded, showed that the Soviet Union had launched a "vicious" campaign against the United States. In response, the NSC empowered the CIA to engage in "propaganda, economic warfare, preventive direct action including sabotage, anti-sabotage, demolition and evacuation measures, [and] subversion against hostile states, including assistance to underground resistance movements, guerrillas and refugee liberation groups." These operations were to be "so planned and executed that any US government responsibility for them is not evident to unauthorized persons, and that if uncovered the US government can plausibly disclaim any responsibility for them."

As the CIA evolved in the way Allen wished, Foster also began sensing

THAT FELLA FROM WALL STREET

events moving in his direction. He believed he could direct American diplomacy better than Secretary of State Marshall or anyone else working for "that shirt salesman from Kansas City," as he called Truman. In 1948 he saw a chance to prove it. The one politician to whom he was truly close, Governor Thomas Dewey of New York, who had lost the Republican presidential nomination in 1940 and won it in 1944, only to lose the election to Roosevelt, was making a third run that seemed likely to succeed. It was widely assumed that after his victory, he would name Foster secretary of state.

Foster had been part of American delegations to half a dozen international conferences in the three years since the war ended. Through the reporting of the Luce press and the other journalists he cultivated, like his Princeton classmate Arthur Krock of the *New York Times* and the syndicated columnist Roscoe Drummond, he had the image of a principled hard-liner who forced the weak-kneed Truman administration to show backbone and resist Soviet demands. At home he found his adversaries not just among Democrats, but also in the group of Republicans who wished the United States to play a less intrusive role in the world. Their leader, Senator Robert Taft of Ohio, who ran against Dewey for the Republican presidential nomination in 1948, rejected the idea that destiny was calling Americans to overspread the globe.

"It is based on the theory that we know more about what is good for the world than the world itself," Taft said in one speech. "It assumes that we are always right and that anyone who disagrees with us is wrong. . . . Other people simply do not like to be dominated, and we would be in the same position of suppressing rebellions by force in which the British found themselves during the 19th century."

The contest for the Republican presidential nomination in 1948 was not just between Dewey and Taft, but between the "internationalist" and "isolationist" wings of the party. Foster was Dewey's foreign policy adviser during the campaign, and through Dewey, he pressed his internationalist views. In a series of memos for the candidate, he argued that the United States faced imminent threat and was called to forward defense around the world. "The enemies of human freedom are ever present and constantly looking for what seem to be soft spots," he wrote. He also published an article in *Life* pledging that Republicans would move the United States "from a purely defensive policy to a psychological offensive, a liberation policy which will try and give hope and a resistance mood within the Soviet empire."

As the election approached, Foster began making plans for after the victory. In one memo he sketched out ideas for the transition, including a suggestion that "the President-elect" make a quick trip to Europe to solidify alliances there. The press treated him reverently. "He has a sense of history, and he is good at the vanishing art of simple speech and definition," James Reston wrote of Foster in a *Saturday Evening Post* profile. Reston's only fear was that Foster "might be tempted to use the power of office to launch something of a crusade."

Election night found Foster in Paris, attending a diplomatic conference with Secretary Marshall. His days there were heady, with foreign statesmen pressing to see him and all but ignoring Marshall, whom they considered a lame duck. On the morning of November 3, however, the world awoke to news that voters had re-elected Truman in one of the great upsets in American political history.

"You see before you the former future secretary of state," Foster ruefully told an American correspondent.

Foreign Minister Carlos Romulo of the Philippines had unwisely arranged a "victory banquet" for that evening, with Foster as the guest of honor. Foster gamely went through with it, but the shock of Dewey's loss was, as he admitted in a letter to Allen, "quite a bombshell." For the next four years Truman, the man he had ridiculed—and who had returned the favor by scorning him as "that fella from Wall Street"—would direct American foreign policy. Someone else, not he, would whisper in the president's ear. Dewey was clearly finished in presidential politics. At the age of sixty, Foster had reason to wonder whether his time was running out as well.

Allen rode the same political roller coaster in 1948. He was a close, day-to-day adviser to Dewey—unlike his brother, who disdained electoral politics. During the campaign he also wrote a private proposal urging that the CIA, which had been given broad powers but made only limited use of them because Truman mistrusted it, be unleashed and sent to launch operations "including covert psychological warfare, clandestine political activity, sabotage, and guerrilla activity." Allen planned to present this proposal to Dewey after the election, in the hope that Dewey would endorse it and then name him to head a more aggressive CIA.

Like all Dewey supporters, Allen was prepared to celebrate on election night. Instead he wound up paying a somber call on the defeated candidate, whom he found in a room at the Roosevelt Hotel, standing quietly in his bathrobe. Rather than becoming leader of the Free World, Dewey would be returning to Albany.

Although both brothers faithfully tended to the interests of their Sullivan & Cromwell clients during the post-war years, their hearts were not in their work. Allen thought constantly about what he could do to push the United States back into the business of covert action. Foster served as the token Republican on diplomatic delegations and testified in Washington in favor of the security alliance that became the North Atlantic Treaty Organization. Both were uncharacteristically adrift.

The first break came to Foster, most unexpectedly, on a summer day in 1949.

He was vacationing with Janet at Duck Island in Lake Ontario, a former rumrunners' haunt that he had bought eight years earlier and where he maintained a spartan retreat without electricity or telephone. If there was urgent news, a nearby lighthouse keeper who had a radio would motor over. That day he brought a puzzling message: call Governor Dewey immediately. Dutifully Foster sailed back to the mainland.

Dewey had an offer few could resist. Senator Robert F. Wagner had just resigned due to poor health, and Dewey wished to appoint Foster to replace him. The rough-and-tumble of electoral politics, where compromise is a way of life and few succeed without the common touch, was hardly Foster's natural habitat. Nonetheless the offer was a magnificent gift. Foster realized that it would propel him back to the center of national debate just when he feared his future was dimming. On July 8, 1949, he resigned from Sullivan & Cromwell, where he had worked for thirty-eight years. Later that day he took the oath of office as a United States senator.

Foster was an outsider in the ritualized environment of the Senate. He was aloof by nature, and in any case had little to offer as the body's lowest-ranking member. Rather than respect the tradition that new senators should bide their time before making their maiden speeches, he waited just four days before unburdening himself of a long discourse depicting the Soviets as warmongers and the United States as "a living instrument for righteousness and peace." In the following weeks he made several more speeches in the Senate, and although he had no real authority, he was exhilarated by his new position in Washington and the deference that came with it.

"They even cut your hair free of charge," he marveled.

Three months after Foster took his seat in the Senate, Communists under Mao Zedong won the civil war in China. Foster had known Chiang Kai-shek, leader of the defeated Nationalists, for more than a decade, and was also close to the equally autocratic President Syngman Rhee of South Korea. Both were not simply anti-Communist but Christian, which made Foster especially zealous in their defense. He had once described the two men as "modern-day equivalents of the founders of the Church." They helped shape his view of East Asia, which was based on the presumption that all upheaval there was fomented by Moscow.

One formidable obstacle stood between Foster and a career in the Senate. His appointment was temporary, until a special election could be held for the balance of Wagner's term. Dewey had chosen Foster with the hope that his sober image would make him a strong candidate, but as the campaign unfolded, he proved to be stiff, uncomfortable in crowds, and out of touch with the lives of ordinary people. His opponent, Herbert Lehman, a folksy Democrat and former governor who championed causes like public housing and unemployment insurance, brought these shortcomings into high relief. Lehman ran as a friend of labor and the poor. Foster, playing to his own strength, campaigned in an open car bedecked with a banner reading "Enemy of the Reds."

"Six-footer John Foster Dulles looks like a serious, mild-mannered professor, but don't let his looks fool you," his campaign brochure urged. "He's serious all right, but the way he's handled the Reds has proved he's far from mild. He's downright serious about keeping the world from going Communist. From the front row, he's watched the Red menace creep over one-third of the face of the globe, and he's learned some bitter truths. The Reds know he knows those truths. That's why Andrei Vishinsky screamed, 'That man should be put in chains.' Can you think of a better tribute or a greater reason for keeping him in the Senate? The Commies dislike Foster Dulles for the same reason you will like him. He knows that their greatest threat to us is internal penetration by fellow-travelers. That's why he fights Socialism and every sign of this political cancer in this country. . . . No wonder the Russians don't want him in Washington!"

The special election was set for November 8, 1949, and as it approached, the campaign turned ugly. Foster charged that Lehman was "pushing us down the road to socialism" and toward "a very serious loss of personal liberties," which explained why "the Communists are in his corner." The Democrats replied that Foster's work for the Schroder Bank and other German-based firms made him "a lawyer for those who built up the Nazi Party." They also charged that his speeches during the 1930s had "justified German, Japanese, and Italian land grabs" and that his legal work for the Bank of Spain suggested sympathy for Francisco Franco's fascist regime. There was enough truth in this to throw Foster off balance. During a campaign swing upstate, he told a crowd: "If you could see the kind of people in New York City making up this bloc that is voting for my opponent, I know you would be out, every last one of you, on election day." Lehman denounced this as anti-Semitic and "a diabolical and deliberate insult to the people of New York." In the end Foster was defeated by a decisive 200,000 votes.

"I'm glad that duck lost," Truman said after hearing the news.

Political campaigns—and shared, though still diffuse, ambition—kept the Dulles brothers close during the late 1940s and early 1950s. The difference between them was that while Allen was happy to remain obscure, Foster sought ways to stay in the news. He returned to Sullivan & Cromwell after his brief stint in the Senate but was also an American delegate to early sessions of the United Nations General Assembly, considered the possibility of seeking the presidency of Princeton or Columbia University, and even inquired indirectly about the prospect of a job in the Truman administration.

"What, that bastard?" Truman replied when the idea was put to him. "Not on your life."

Several months of persuasion, led by Senator Vandenberg, finally led Truman to soften his view. In May 1950 he agreed to name Foster "adviser to the Secretary of State." To everyone's surprise, since Foster had been mainly associated with policy toward Europe, his first major assignment was to negotiate a final peace treaty with Japan. He guided talks that produced the treaty and, in the first months of 1952, lobbied Republicans in the Senate to ensure its ratification. Truman was impressed and offered to make him ambassador to Japan. He turned down the job because he saw "no point in being at the end of the transmission line if the power house itself was not functioning."

That Foster would speak so dismissively of Truman reflected new political realities. Truman's term was ending. Cold War fears had intensified as the Soviets tested a nuclear weapon, Communists consolidated their rule in China, and a Communist army invaded South Korea. Foster had re-established himself as a successful diplomat and polemicist. His old dream seemed once again within reach.

Allen's prospects were also brightening. He and his coterie of former OSS men never relented in their quiet but insistent efforts to transform the CIA from an intelligence collection agency into a globally aggressive force. In 1950 two developments, one secret and one front-page news, strengthened their case.

First was Truman's acceptance of a chilling policy decree called NSC-68, which the National Security Council produced and which guided American foreign policy for the next decade and beyond. Its central premise was that the Soviet Union "is inescapably militant because it possesses and is possessed by a world-wide revolutionary movement, because it is the inheritor of Russian imperialism, and because it is a totalitarian dictatorship." Truman adopted it without open debate and never referred to it in public. It remained secret for decades.

> The Soviet Union, unlike previous aspirants to hegemony, is animated by a new fanatic faith, antithetical to our own, and seeks to impose its absolute authority over the rest of the world. Conflict has, therefore, become endemic and is waged, on the part of the Soviet Union, by violent or non-violent methods in accordance with the dictates of expediency. With the development of increasingly terrifying weapons of mass destruction, every individual faces the ever-present possibility of annihilation should the conflict enter the phase of total war. . . .
>
> Any substantial further extension of the area under the domination of the Kremlin would raise the possibility that no coalition adequate to confront the Kremlin with greater strength could be assembled. It is in this context that this Republic and its citizens in the ascendancy of their strength stand in their deepest peril. . . . The issues that face us are momentous, involving the fulfillment or destruction not only of this Republic

but of civilization itself. They are issues which will not await our delib-
erations. With conscience and resolution, this Government and the
people it represents must now take new and fateful decisions.

Less than two months after Truman turned NSC-68 into official U.S.
policy, Communist soldiers from North Korea invaded South Korea.
Documents released decades later make clear that this invasion was not
part of a grand Soviet plot and was not even Stalin's idea, but at the time
no one knew that. NSC-68 had portrayed the Soviets as bent on conquering the world, and the invasion of South Korea seemed to prove it. Truman immediately asked Congress for $10 billion to buy new weaponry,
and more to expand the size of the United States Army.

"Somehow or other, the North Korean attack came soon to appear to a
great many people in Washington as merely the first move in some 'grand
design,' as the phrase went, on the part of the Soviet leaders to extend their
power to other parts of the world by the use of force," George Kennan, a
former ambassador to the Soviet Union, wrote years later. "The unexpect-
edness of this attack—the fact that we had no forewarning of it—only
stimulated the already existent preference of the military planners for
drawing their conclusions only from the assessed capabilities of the adversary, dismissing his intentions, which could be safely assumed to be hostile. All this tended to heighten the militarization of thinking about the
Cold War in general, and to press us into attitudes where any discriminate
estimate of Soviet intentions was unwelcome and unacceptable."

The fact that there had been no warning of the North Korean attack
disturbed Truman, and he resolved to dismiss Admiral Hillenkoetter
and name a new director of central intelligence. On August 18, 1950, he
announced his choice: General Walter Bedell Smith, who had been Dwight
Eisenhower's chief of staff during World War II and then served as ambassador to the Soviet Union.

"I know nothing about this business," General Smith admitted after
his appointment was announced. That was precisely why Truman chose
him. The president mistrusted spies and covert operatives, and wanted
their agency to be run by someone who shared his mistrust.

Allen was one of the few Americans with long experience in the clandestine world, so it was all but inevitable that he would find his way to the
CIA. In the autumn of 1950, soon after taking over as director, "Beetle"

Smith—who had known Allen for thirty years, dating back to the days in Paris when they patronized Le Sphinx together—hired him on a six-week consultant's contract. When the six weeks expired, Smith offered him a post he had just created: deputy director for operations. It was not the agency's number-two job—that went to William Harding Jackson, a Wall Street lawyer and investment banker who had been an intelligence officer during the war—but it gave Allen control over all covert operations carried out by the United States abroad. He resigned from Sullivan & Cromwell, quit his post as president of the Council on Foreign Relations, and told Clover they would be moving to Washington. On January 2, 1951, he formally began his career at the CIA.

He had already won a concession from his boss. His title would not be "deputy director for operations," but "deputy director for plans," which he found more suitably obscure. The Soviets were not deceived. They had closely followed Allen's career, and when he joined the CIA, the Soviet journalist Ilya Ehrenburg took note.

"Even if the spy Allen Dulles should arrive in Heaven through someone's absentmindedness," Ehrenburg wrote in *Pravda*, "he would begin to blow up the clouds, mine the stars, and slaughter the angels."

From the beginning, Allen's relationship with Smith was troubled. Style was part of the reason. Allen had emerged from a life of comfort and privilege, wore worsted jackets, smoked a pipe, told witty stories, and relied heavily on his legendary charm. Smith was a gruff, no-nonsense soldier who had worked his way up through the ranks without a West Point education and never got on well with "silver-spoon" types. More important were their divergent views of intelligence work. Allen was a compulsive activist who rarely saw a plot he didn't like or a foreign crisis in which he did not want the United States to intervene; Smith was less partial to covert action. Allen believed the CIA should simultaneously engage in intelligence gathering, analysis, and covert action; Smith feared mixing these functions. By one account Smith "did not trust Allen's capacity for judgment or self-restraint in the exercise of powers that, by their secret nature, had to operate beyond the normal discipline of accountability." Nonetheless he allowed Allen to launch a series of operations whose ambition and variety foreshadowed the work he would do over the next decade.

"Once one gets a taste for it," Allen admitted to a friend, "it's hard to drop."

Not long after Allen came to Washington, the post of DDCI—deputy director of central intelligence—became vacant when William Harding Jackson returned to Wall Street after less than a year. This was the job Allen had wanted from the beginning, and on August 23, 1951, Smith gave it to him. This brought him to the heart of a hidden global network that was full of potential, but still unformed and unfocused.

As Allen was moving up, Congress approved the CIA's request for $100 million to be used for arming paramilitary exile groups "or for other purposes." He persuaded General Smith that much of this money should be spent on the most ambitious CIA project yet, an effort to foment guerrilla uprisings behind the Iron Curtain. Over the next few years, he sent waves of agents into Eastern Europe and Asia, nearly all of them exiles, with missions ranging from collecting earth samples to launching armed attacks. Nearly every man he sent into action was quickly discovered, and many were executed—hundreds in Europe, thousands in Asia. These losses did not disturb him.

"At least we're getting experience for the next war," he reasoned.

Not until more than a decade had passed did one reason for this epic failure become clear. The senior British intelligence officer assigned as liaison to the CIA, Kim Philby, was a double agent working for the Soviets. Philby spent years in Washington and knew the top CIA men as well as any outsider. Later he wrote that he had found General Smith to have "a precision-tooled brain," but was less impressed with Allen.

"He had a habit of talking around a problem, not coming to grips with it," Philby wrote after defecting to Moscow in 1963. "I find recurring, with inexorable insistence, the adjective 'lazy.' Of course, AD was an active man, in the sense that he would talk shop late into the night, jump into aeroplanes, rush around sophisticated capitals and exotic landscapes. But did he ever apply his mind hard to a problem that did not engage his personal interest and inclination; or was he a line-of-least-resistance man. . . . Personally, I liked him a lot. He was nice to have around: good, comfortable, predictable, pipe-sucking, whiskey-drinking company."

All the men Allen recruited, and who became his comrades for much of the next decade, shared his eagerness to launch a global war against Communism. Taking his old job as deputy director for plans was Frank Wisner, who had been set afire with anti-Communist passion when the Romanian royal family, with whom he was close, was brutally pushed from power by Soviet-backed forces. Tracy Barnes, who had parachuted behind enemy lines in France during the war and then become one of Allen's favorite agents in Bern, quit his law practice and became one of Wisner's deputies. Richard Bissell, also an OSS veteran, became Allen's special assistant. Kermit Roosevelt took over the Middle East division. James Jesus Angleton, who had helped direct the CIA campaign to influence the 1948 election in Italy, became the agency's liaison to the nascent Israeli secret service and then its counterintelligence chief. Harry Rositzke, who had worked for the OSS in Germany while posing as a wine merchant, became chief of the Soviet Division and was sent to Munich to oversee anti-Soviet guerrilla operations.

"All were gregarious, intrigued by possibilities, liked to do things, had three bright ideas a day, shared the optimism of stock market plungers, and were convinced that every problem had its handle and that the CIA could find a way to reach it," the intelligence historian Thomas Powers has written. "They also tended to be white Anglo-Saxon patricians from old families with old money, at least at the beginning, and they somehow inherited traditional British attitudes toward the colored races of the world—not the pukka sahib arrogance of the Indian Raj, but the mixed fascination and condescension of men like T. E. Lawrence, who were enthusiastic partisans of the alien cultures into which they dipped for a time and rarely doubted their ability to help, until it was too late."

These were the "best men" who formed the core of the early CIA. Most came from privileged backgrounds that isolated them from ordinary life and had gone on to the right schools: Wisner graduated from the University of Virginia, Barnes and Bissell from Groton and Yale, Roosevelt from Groton and Harvard, Angleton from Yale and Harvard Law. Rositzke had a doctorate in German philology from Harvard. During the war they had traded genteel lives for death-defying adventures. Upon returning home, they found the quiet routines of peace unfulfilling. They yearned to fight again, and either found or helped create an enemy so terrifying that fighting became essential. On the outcome of this shadowy war, they convinced themselves, hung the fate of the United States, civilization, and humanity itself.

"They were pining to get back," one of Allen's friends later recalled. "They were boy scouts who were bored in their law jobs. They were like fighter pilots in England after the Battle of Britain. They couldn't adjust. They were . . . great romantics who saw themselves as saviors of the world."

In his effort to "get back" during the early 1950s, Allen sought to decide the fate of three nations.

His first operation, in the Philippines, was remarkably successful. It also led him into a long and fateful relationship with Edward Lansdale, a former advertising executive who became one of the most admired CIA operatives of his age. Lansdale conceived a strategy, based in part on manipulating superstitions, religious beliefs, and rumors, by which he believed the army of the Philippines could defeat a Communist-led insurgency. He had also discovered a rising Catholic politician, Ramon Magsaysay, and was grooming him for national leadership.

"Lansdale operated with very little money," according to one account. "His mode of operation was to gain the confidence of the Filipinos and to persuade them to take the necessary actions to promote Magsaysay, and to do this to help their own country and not to help the United States. However, on one of his trips to Washington, Allen Dulles offered Lansdale five million dollars to finance the CIA operations in the Philippines. Lansdale was uneasy about this amount of money and asked if he was supposed to buy votes with it. . . . He did finally accept one million dollars, which was delivered to him in cash by another CIA operator in the Philippines."

Lansdale's counterinsurgency campaign was brilliantly designed and brought near-total victory. He also helped make Magsaysay a global symbol of anti-Communist nationalism, guiding him first onto the cover of *Time* and then to the presidency of the Philippines. Allen was thrilled. His appetite whetted, he twice offered to overthrow a foreign government.

The first country where Allen wished to foment a revolution was Guatemala. Its nationalist government was cracking down on United Fruit, the country's largest landowner and a longtime Sullivan & Cromwell client. Communists were active in the labor and agrarian movements. American newspapers ran articles with headlines like "Red Front Tightens Grip on Guatemala" and "United Fruit Becomes Victim of Guatemala's Awakening."

In mid-1952 the Nicaraguan dictator, Anastasio Somoza, visited Washington and told his hosts that if they gave him weapons, he would "clean up Guatemala for you in no time." Allen liked the idea. With General Smith's approval—and by some accounts with indirect encouragement from the White House—he assembled a small team of CIA operatives that conceived a plot aimed at setting off a coup in Guatemala.

On the afternoon of October 8, CIA officers presented this plot, called Operation Fortune, to their counterparts at the State Department. Frank Wisner said that the CIA was seeking approval "to provide certain hardware to a group planning violence against a certain government." Another officer asserted that the operation was necessary because "a large American company must be protected." State Department officials at the meeting, according to one account, "hit the ceiling." One of them, David Bruce, Allen's old OSS comrade, told him that the State Department "disapproves of the entire deal."

The next morning Smith gave his men the bad news. J. C. King, chief of the Western Hemisphere division, recorded the meeting in a memorandum.

> The Director explained to [initials not declassified] that all plans for the operation were canceled. [Initials not declassified] then pointed out the responsibilities we have toward the people who are already in the field and who have committed themselves, and the dangers to the entire Caribbean of the decision reached yesterday. The Director replied that he was fully aware of the dangers inherent in such a decision, but that this Agency is merely an executive agency to carry out the policies of the Department of State and the Department of Defense, and if they instruct us not to engage in a certain operation, we shall not engage in that operation. [Initials not declassified] then commented that the Department of State might very well change its position in the near future. . . . To this the Director agreed.

While making his unsuccessful effort to push the United States into action in Guatemala, Allen promoted another intervention on the other side of the world. His second target was Iran, which like Guatemala had produced a nationalist government he considered unfriendly to Western power. Winston Churchill was outraged at Iran's nationalization of its oil industry, long dominated by Britain, and wished to promote a coup, but could not do so without American help. Senior CIA officers wanted to join the plot. That would require approval from Secretary of State Acheson, however, and they knew he would not give it.

"I didn't feel like raising the matter with him," Kermit Roosevelt later wrote. "Neither did Allen Dulles. . . . We saw no point in getting the outgoing administration involved in something we thought they might be less enthusiastic about than the Republicans."

Allen's attempts to send the CIA into action against the governments of Iran and Guatemala were aborted, but he did not forget them. Two seeds were left to germinate.

By the end of Harry Truman's term, the CIA had established its role as not simply a collector of intelligence but also an advocate of covert operations. It had shown its willingness to go beyond what it had done before, even to the extreme of overthrowing governments. Allen and his friends could not do all they wished because Truman would not allow it, but they were ready. All they lacked was a friend in the Oval Office.

Allen and Foster looked forward to the 1952 election with different degrees of interest. "Beetle" Smith had made clear that he would leave the CIA once a new president took office, and as the agency's number-two man, Allen was positioned to become director no matter who won. Foster, however, was an unabashed Republican. His dream could come true only if a Republican won the presidency.

The likely nominee, General Dwight Eisenhower, was a career military officer who had rarely come into contact with the New York elite or the world of global finance in which Foster had spent his life. Foster was eager to establish a personal connection. He arranged to be invited to give a speech in Paris, where Eisenhower was serving as supreme Allied commander. They had two long conversations, and Foster left the general with the manuscript of an article called "A Policy of Boldness" that he had just written for *Life*. It charged Democrats with following a cowardly policy seeking only "containment" of Communism. Republicans, Foster vowed, would take the offensive. They would secure "liberation" of "captive nations" and crush Communist "stooges" around the world.

"There is a moral or natural law not made by man which . . . has been trampled on by the Soviet rulers," he wrote. "For that violation they can and should be made to pay."

Given Eisenhower's age and breadth of international experience, Foster could not hope to establish the sort of father-son relationship he had enjoyed with Dewey. Nonetheless he wrote some of Eisenhower's campaign speeches and was the main force in drafting the Republican Party's foreign policy platform, which condemned the "containment" policy as "negative, futile and immoral" because it consigned "countless human beings to despotism and Godless terrorism."

"We charge that the leaders of the administration in power lost the peace so dearly earned by World War II," the platform asserted. "Communist Russia [has] a military and propaganda initiative which, if unstayed, will destroy us."

Eisenhower scattered lines like this through his campaign speeches, though unlike Foster he often added that he wished to achieve his goals peacefully. He pledged that "liberating the captive peoples" would be one of his priorities in office, and vowed not to rest "until the enslaved nations of the world have in the fullness of freedom the right to choose their own path." His running mate, Senator Richard Nixon of California, scorned the Democrats for treating the confrontation with Communism as a "nicey-nice little powder-puff duel." Foster's own speeches and writings hammered on the same theme: the Democrats had left a "heritage of appeasement" and followed policies "which at best might keep us in the same place until we drop exhausted." When a television interviewer asked him whether the United States was stronger "as against Russia" than it had been a year earlier, his reply was gloomy.

"Probably not," he replied. "The tide is still running against us. Everywhere I look around the world, the question is what maybe we're going to lose next, you know, and we seem to be on the defensive and they're on the offensive. You can look around the whole circle of the world and you find one spot after another after another after another where the question is, are we going to lose this bit of the free world?"

In retrospect this seems exaggerated. During Truman's term, as the historian Stephen Ambrose has written, the United States "forced the Russians out of Iran in 1946, came to the aid of the Greek government in 1947, met the Red Army's challenge at Berlin and inaugurated the Marshall Plan in 1948, joined the North Atlantic Treaty Organization in 1949, and hurled back the Communist invaders of South Korea in 1950, all under the umbrella of the Truman Doctrine, which had proclaimed

American resistance to any advance by Communism anywhere." Nonetheless the confusing rush of world events provoked emotions that pushed many Americans to the brink of panic. "We were all hysterical at the time," Harry Rositzke wrote decades later.

> Even now, as the emotions of the time can be recollected with relative tranquility, it is hard to define the precise quality of the public mood in which we began our work. Words like *hysteria* and *paranoia* come to mind, and if the main element in the first is "emotional excitability" and in the second "systematized delusions of persecution," both are relevant. . . . The Cold War prism saw the main threat to America in the halls of the Kremlin. The bogey was Stalin, a despot and a devil, a devious plotter with a Blueprint for World Domination. . . . The world was divided into two parts: "Communist" and "free." All countries were either good or bad. Those who did not take sides were bad. . . . The Cold War became a holy war against the infidels, a defense of free God-fearing men against the atheistic Communist system.
>
> There was no serious dissent from this view for a decade. The White House, the secretaries of state, both parties in Congress, the press, and the reading public all viewed the Communist Threat through the same prism. It was the last great consensus in America on our foreign purposes. . . .
>
> As it turned out, the image was an illusion. The specter of a powerful Russia was remote from the reality of a country weakened by war, with a shattered economy, an overtaxed civilian and military bureaucracy, and large areas of civil unrest. The illusory image was at least partly due to a failure of intelligence. . . . Had there been even the rudiments of an American intelligence effort in the Soviet Union during the war, or had we concentrated on intelligence operations against Russia and Eastern Europe in the postwar lull, the course of the Cold War might have been different. It was our almost total ignorance of what was going on in the "denied area" behind the Iron Curtain that helped create the false image of a super-powerful Soviet Union.

In the election of November 4, 1952, Eisenhower won a landslide victory over Governor Adlai Stevenson of Illinois. Foster was the likely secretary of state but not a sure thing. His clipped, sanctimonious manner had irritated many in Washington. Others objected to his Manichean

worldview. Some European statesmen thought him lacking in grace, subtlety, and wisdom. The British foreign secretary, Anthony Eden, went so
far as to write Eisenhower asking him to choose someone else. For a time
Eisenhower seemed to be leaning toward John J. McCloy, who had run the
World Bank and then became high commissioner for Germany. He also
considered Paul Hoffman, the administrator of the Marshall Plan—which
covertly funneled 5 percent of its budget to the CIA—and Walter Judd, a
militantly anti-Communist congressman from Nebraska. Judd turned
aside an overture and recommended Foster.

"Well, he is being considered," Eisenhower replied. "But he's got a lot
of opposition."

The most surprising move to block Foster came from his old comrade
Henry Luce, who passed Eisenhower a letter recommending Thomas
Dewey instead. Dewey had no background in foreign affairs, which has
led historians to suspect Luce of a hidden motive. "Although it was believed
a foregone conclusion that John Foster Dulles would become Eisenhower's secretary of state, and Luce greatly admired Dulles's moral outlook on
foreign policy, perhaps he still had a lingering hope to edge out his fellow
Presbyterian," one has written. "It might [have been] a Luce maneuver to
toss the State appointment up in the air in the hope that it might light
on him."

Foster had known more than a dozen secretaries of state personally
and had worked for eight. This was a pedigree for the job that no American
has ever matched. It helped give his nomination an air of inevitability.
After a few weeks of deliberation, Eisenhower chose him.

At his confirmation hearing before the Senate Foreign Relations Committee, the secretary-designate graphically laid out his view of the world.
Soviet Communism, he asserted, was "not only the gravest threat ever
faced by the United States, but the gravest threat that has ever faced what
we call Western civilization, or indeed any civilization which was dominated by a spiritual faith."

> We shall never have a secure peace or a happy world so long as Soviet
> Communism dominates one-third of all of the peoples that there are, and
> is in the process of trying, at least, to extend its rule to many others....
> Therefore, a policy which only aims at containing Russia where it now is,
> is in itself an unsound policy; but it is a policy which is bound to fail,

because a purely defensive policy never wins against an aggressive policy. If our only policy is to stay where we are, we will be driven back. It is
only by keeping alive the hope of liberation, by taking advantage of that
wherever opportunity arises, that we will end this terrible peril which
dominates the world.

Foster was widely respected in Washington, and the Senate confirmed
his nomination by voice vote, the equivalent of consensus. Some were
dubious. The polemicist I. F. Stone covered Foster's confirmation hearing
and reported afterward that the secretary-designate had "worked himself
into a positive crescendo of righteousness" by repeatedly declaring his
"obsessive hatred for socialism." This, Stone warned, would intensify global
tensions and push moderates in other countries away from the United
States.

"Smooth is an inadequate word for Dulles," Stone wrote. "His prevari-
cations are so highly polished as to be aesthetically pleasurable. . . . Dulles
is a man of wily and subtle mind. It is difficult to believe that behind his
unctuous manner he does not take a cynical amusement in his own monstrous pomposities. He gives the impression of a man who lives constantly
behind a mask. . . . It is fortunate for this country, Western Europe and
China that he was not at the helm of foreign policy before the war. It is
unfortunate that he should be now."

Allen's path to the top was also indirect. His boss, "Beetle" Smith,
whom Eisenhower nominated to be undersecretary of state, did not want
his deputy to succeed him. By one account Smith "made no secret of his
concern over Allen's enthusiasm for extravagant covert actions and, mir-
roring Eisenhower's hesitancy about Foster, he worried what Allen would
do with the expanding resources of the CIA without a cool hand to guide
him." Another of Allen's former bosses, "Wild Bill" Donovan, warned
Eisenhower that Allen did not have the ordered mind required to administer a large organization. Donovan, however, was waging a quiet campaign for the director's job himself, so Eisenhower may not have taken his
warning to heart.

Weeks dragged on. There was speculation that the CIA job might go
to General Alfred Wedemeyer, who had been commander of American
forces in China and then became a hero to American politicians who
sought to overturn Mao Zedong's victory there. At one point Allen told

his friend Nelson Rockefeller that if he was not named to direct the CIA, he might seek to become president of the Ford Foundation, which was already a cover for much covert action. The *Washington Post* published an editorial asserting that some CIA operations seemed "incompatible with democracy," but it did not mention the fact that the agency's deputy director was hoping for a promotion. Inauguration Day came and went without an announcement. Finally, at the end of January, Eisenhower gave Allen the job. He would be the third director of the Central Intelligence Agency, and the first civilian to hold the post. On February 26, 1953, the Senate confirmed his appointment without opposition.

During his OSS days, Allen's cryptonym had been simply a number, 110. This time he chose a more mysterious one: Ascham. It was the name given to an elite warrior class in ancient Egypt, and is said to mean "those who stand at the left hand of the king."

As the Dulles brothers reached pinnacles of power, their sister Eleanor found her career stalled. She had spent six years helping to administer the new Social Security system, and then, because of her familiarity with Germany, was recruited to join the State Department's "Germany Committee" during World War II. When the war ended, she worked for a time at the Commerce Department and then returned to State. Her assignments brought her to the front line of the Cold War and gave her the chance to work with many prominent Europeans, including the future West German chancellors Konrad Adenauer, Willy Brandt, and Helmut Schmidt. Because she was a woman, though, she faced discrimination at every stage. Her boss at the Commerce Department frankly told her she had "the best brain in this building," but that he would not promote her because "I don't believe in women getting too high up."

Attitudes like these still outraged Eleanor when, in the 1970s, she reviewed her career in a memoir. "Women in the State Department are a problem—to themselves and to the men in the department," she wrote. "Not until men, who hold nine-tenths of the power, are willing to train women the way they do the young men on their staffs will there be a serious chance for women."

Whatever personal pleasure Eleanor took from Eisenhower's victory stemmed from what it meant not for her, but for her brothers. Neither was young by the time he reached the pinnacle of power; Foster was sixty-five years old, Allen sixty. Long experience had hardened their view of the world. As the most intense phase of the Cold War began, it became the official view of the United States.

Foster was shaped above all by a lifetime working for international banks and businesses, whose interests he had come to identify with those of the United States. His mastery of complex legal and financial codes reflected a rigorously organized mind, but he was not a deep thinker. The few new ideas he developed were modest in scale, dealing with matters like tariffs and exchange mechanisms. His ideology was the defense of the two principles that he believed best served global commerce: free enterprise and American-centered internationalism. He was driven to find and confront enemies, quick to make moral judgments, and not given to subtlety or doubt.

Allen's ideology was in all essentials identical to his brother's. Both saw the world at war in ways that ordinary people could not comprehend, and both were eager to fight. Allen, however, was less moved by religious and ethical imperatives, more laconic and closer to cynicism. He felt a compulsive need to act, to strike and then strike again. Nations were to him like women: a succession of challenges to be mastered. He could not abide the idea of allowing history to take its course. Instead he wished to shape it.

Dwight Eisenhower took office on January 20, 1953. "Forces of good and evil are massed and armed and opposed as rarely before in history," he declared in his inaugural address. "Freedom is pitted against slavery, lightness against the dark."

Never before had siblings directed the overt and covert sides of American foreign policy. It was an arrangement fraught with danger. The Dulles brothers had shared such common backgrounds, and spent so much time together over so many years, that their minds had come to function as one. They knew, or believed they knew, the same deep truths about the world. Their intimacy rendered discussion and debate unnecessary. There would be no reason for State Department and CIA officers to meet and thrash out the possible advantages and disadvantages of a proposed operation. With a glance, a nod, and a few words, without consulting anyone other than the president, the brothers could mobilize the full power of the United States anywhere in the world.

"It has always surprised me that more of a fuss was not made over the constellation of power resulting from Foster at State and Allen at the CIA," Mary Bancroft wrote years later. "Undoubtedly the only reason that there was not more criticism of this particular combination was that Eisenhower was in the White House. The American people had placed their faith in Daddy—and Daddy could do no wrong."

PART II

SIX MONSTERS

Dawn had not yet broken over Manhattan when the door to 60 Morningside Drive swung open. Two men emerged, slipped into a waiting Cadillac limousine, and sped away. They drove through the darkness to Mitchel Air Force Base on Long Island. A guard waved them in. They made their way toward a runway where a Constellation airliner was waiting. The driver, a Secret Service agent, pulled to a stop, jumped out, and opened the rear door. President-elect Dwight Eisenhower stepped into the morning light.

On that Saturday, November 29, 1952, Eisenhower was setting out to redeem his most electrifying campaign promise: "I shall go to Korea." This homespun pledge helped propel him to the presidency. News of Communist victories in Korea was sending shock waves through the United States. Eisenhower had vanquished Nazi armies in Europe. Voters hoped that if he went to Korea, America could win there too.

A fragile cease-fire had taken hold in Korea. Eisenhower arrived carrying the first piece of official advice he received from John Foster Dulles, his secretary-of-state-to-be. Dulles urged him to renounce the cease-fire, send armies across the demilitarized zone, and not rest "until we have shown, before all of Asia, our clear superiority by giving the Chinese one hell of a licking." After three days of meetings with diplomats and field commanders, Eisenhower decided to do the opposite: accept the cease-fire and agree to end the war in a stalemate. A new offensive, he concluded, would cost many lives and risk a wider war with no certain outcome.

General Douglas MacArthur, the revered former American commander in Korea, was outraged. So were many Republicans in Congress. Some grumbled that if President Truman had accepted such a truce, he would have been impeached. Eisenhower's popularity and unique military credentials, however, made it impossible for anyone to challenge him.

The carnage of World War II had given Eisenhower a visceral understanding of war's costs. He was determined not to send American troops back to fight on foreign soil. The risk of retaliation was too great and the price of war too high. Nor could Eisenhower realistically hope to overthrow any of the world's ten Communist governments, which ruled the Soviet Union, China, and eight countries in Eastern Europe. Yet despite these limitations, he was determined to strike back against what seemed to be Communism's global advance. He wanted to fight, but in a different way.

Many historians have observed that, as Stephen Ambrose put it, "Eisenhower and Dulles continued the policy of containment. There was no basic difference between their foreign policy and that of Truman and Acheson." Eisenhower, though, combined the mind-set of a warrior with a sober understanding of the devastation that full-scale warfare brings. That led him to covert action. With the Dulles brothers as his right and left arms, he led the United States into a secret global conflict that raged throughout his presidency.

In the secrecy-shrouded 1950s and for long afterward, the scope of this unseen war remained obscure. Truths about it have emerged slowly, episodically, in isolated pieces over the course of decades. Woven back together in their original sequence, they tell an illuminating tale.

Truman used the CIA to carry out covert operations, but drew the line at plotting against foreign leaders. That line evaporated when he left office. Eisenhower wished to wage a new kind of war. Secretary of State John Foster Dulles plotted it. His brother, Director of Central Intelligence Allen Dulles, waged it.

"The White House and this administration have an intense interest in every aspect of covert action," Allen told his men soon after taking office.

Since Eisenhower never admitted ordering plots against foreign leaders, it is impossible to be certain why he favored them. Revelations since his death, however, make two things clear.

First, historians now know that covert operations were far more important during World War II than outsiders understood at the time. Spectacularly effective ones, including the breaking of German codes, remained secret for decades. As the Allied commander, Eisenhower was of course privy to all of them. Understanding the role they played in winning the war must have left him with a deep appreciation for what covert action can achieve.

Eisenhower would also have seen covert action as humanitarian. It was a way to fight high-stakes battles at low cost. Never foreseeing the long-term effects these operations might have, he imagined them as almost bloodless.

"He was a great admirer of covert operations," one veteran CIA officer recalled decades later. "He's the reason we got caught up in so many of them. He had experienced war and saw that covert operations were the alternative. And of course in those days, you had this notion of plausible deniability. You could really believe no one would ever know what you had done. If somebody said, 'Mr. President, I don't understand why you authorized that operation against Arbenz,' he would look you in the face and say, 'I don't know what you're talking about.' That's the way things were done in those days."

During the late 1940s and early 1950s, many Americans projected the worst images of their World War II enemies, including the Nazi campaign of mass murder, onto Soviet Communism. Americans were told, and came to believe, that Soviet leaders were actively plotting to overrun the world; that they would use any means to ensure victory; that their victory would mean the end of civilization and meaningful life; and that there-fore they must be resisted by every means, no matter how distasteful.

John Foster Dulles and Allen Dulles personified this worldview. They crystallized the Cold War paradigm. Everything in their background pre-pared them for this role. The forces that shaped them are quintessential strains in the American character.

First was missionary Christianity. "I see the destiny of America embod-ied in the first Puritan who landed on those shores, just as the human race was represented by the first man," Alexis de Tocqueville wrote at the beginning of the nineteenth century. This destiny reached apotheosis in the Dulles brothers. They were raised in a parsonage and taught from childhood that the world is an eternal battleground between righteousness and evil. Their father was a master of apologetics, the discipline of explain-ing and defending religious belief. They assimilated what the sociolo-gist Max Weber described as two fundamental Calvinist tenets: that

Christians are "weapons in the hands of God and executors of His providential will" and that "God's glory demanded that the reprobate be compelled to submit to the law of the Church."

The second force that shaped the brothers was American history. They could only have been awed by its upward arc. Their grandfather John Watson Foster had helped tame the frontier and campaigned for Abraham Lincoln; they spread American power to every corner of the globe. In their belief that the United States knew what was best for the world, as in their missionary Christianity, they reflected dominant strains in the society that produced them.

As adults, Foster and Allen were shaped by a third force: decades of work defending the interests of America's biggest multinational corporations. Although not plutocrats themselves, they spent their lives serving plutocrats. They were among the visionaries who developed the idea of corporate globalism—what they and other founders of the Council on Foreign Relations called "liberal internationalism." Their life's work was turning American money and power into global money and power. They deeply believed, or made themselves believe, that what benefited them and their clients would benefit everyone.

Both brothers were moved by compulsive activism, a conviction that they were instruments of destiny, and a reflexive sense of loyalty to the business elite that had made them rich.

Foster and Allen shared much in the years before they assumed high office, but their paths diverged in one important way. Foster spent his entire life devoted to a single cause: promoting American economic and political power in the world. He became famous and lived comfortably in the global elite.

Allen also earned a handsome living by brokering international deals for his Sullivan & Cromwell clients, and had no more sympathy than Foster for those who challenged the ruling world order. Yet unlike his older brother, he found Wall Street unfulfilling. He began lusting for adventure as a young man and never stopped. At the CIA he hired restless souls like himself: sons of privilege who graduated from elite schools, went to work for law firms or investment banks, left their jobs to do clandestine work for the Office of Strategic Services during World War II, rebelled against the boredom of routine when the war ended, and during the 1950s found—or made—a covert war to fight. By temperament, training, and inclination, Allen was ideally suited to enforce Foster's threats.

These two brothers were triumphs of cultural and political evolution. In the United States, pioneers had subdued wildness, redemptive religion had become ingrained in national culture, and concentrated economic power had produced great fortunes. Foster and Allen, more than any other Americans of their age, were heirs to this legacy.

Because Eisenhower made clear—despite his campaign rhetoric—that he would not approve "rollback" campaigns aimed at overthrowing established Communist regimes, Foster and Allen had to find other enemies. For years they had been warning about stooges in poor countries who served Moscow while posing as patriots, nationalists, or anti-colonialists. These would be their targets.

In his famous Independence Day speech to the House of Representatives on July 4, 1821, Secretary of State John Quincy Adams proclaimed that the United States "goes not abroad in search of monsters to destroy." The Dulles brothers, however, did. Six impassioned visionaries in Asia, Africa, and Latin America became the monsters they went abroad to destroy. Their campaigns against these six were momentous battles in the global war the United States waged secretly during the 1950s.

This war comprises a hidden chapter of American history. It shaped the world—and still does.

5

A WHIRLING DERVISH WITH
A COLLEGE EDUCATION

Invitations to the Council on Foreign Relations for the evening of November 21, 1949, said the event would be "a small private dinner." It was also the geopolitical version of a debutante's coming-out party. Singly and in small groups, nearly one hundred powerful men strode out of the darkness and into the elegant salon on East Sixty-Eighth Street in Manhattan. Their host, Allen Dulles, who was balding and wore rimless glasses, greeted each of them: Nelson Rockefeller, chairman of Chase Manhattan Bank and a former assistant secretary of state; Henry Luce, crusading publisher of *Time* and *Life*; even the legendary "Wild Bill" Donovan, America's most famous spymaster. All had come to meet Allen's new protégé, Mohammad Reza Shah Pahlavi of Iran.

The young shah—he had just turned thirty—was living through a turbulent year. A few months earlier he had been wounded in an assassination attempt. He attributed his survival to divine intervention, and took it as a sign that he was fated to rule Iran. As he recovered, he cast about for a way to show the grandeur of his vision. Allen found him one.

After years of law practice that bored him, Allen had finally acquired a client with global ambition that matched his own. It was a radically conceived new company, Overseas Consultants Inc., formed by eleven large American engineering firms, that aimed to do nothing less than change the world by making poor countries—and themselves—rich. The visionaries who ran OCI were looking for a country to transform. They settled on Iran, which the United States viewed as a strategic prize. Iran desperately needed development and, since it was receiving more than $50 million in oil royalties every year and had access to loans from the United States, would be able to pay for it.

The elaborate OCI proposal to Iran, five volumes long, envisioned huge-scale projects including hydroelectric plants, rebuilt cities, and new industries imported from abroad. Mohammad Reza Shah, who had grown up mainly in Europe and knew little of his homeland, was captivated but uncertain. The directors of OCI needed a special envoy to close the deal. They hired Allen, who was a famous charmer as well as the former head of the State Department's Bureau of Near Eastern Affairs.

In the autumn of 1949, Allen flew to Tehran to meet the shah. He must have been persuasive. Soon after he returned home, it was announced that Iran had agreed to pay OCI a staggering $650 million—more than half a trillion in the early twenty-first century—to complete a massive seven-year enterprise. This would be the largest overseas development project in modern history. It was the greatest triumph of Allen's legal career. For Sullivan & Cromwell it opened a world of possibilities.

"OCI provided the King of Kings with a blueprint for economic revolution," *Time* reported, "and US and Western European businessmen with a guide to a vast new area of relatively untapped markets."

A month later, Allen stood before his brethren at the Council on Foreign Relations and introduced his new friend. When the applause subsided, His Imperial Majesty spoke. He introduced himself as a committed democrat who embraced "progressive ideas" and wished for no more power than the king of Sweden. As for Iran's future, it would be shaped by "the seven-year development plan which, as you no doubt know, has been drawn up with the aid of American engineering consultants."

"My government and people are eager to welcome American capital, to give it all possible safeguards," the shah told his audience. "Nationalization of industry is not planned." During the question period he added, "Iran's resources are still virgin and are yet to be developed."

This was what these lords of corporate globalism wished to hear. On that night, the American foreign policy elite accepted Mohammad Reza Shah as its Iranian partner. Allen had sealed a highly promising relationship.

Since he had recently been in Iran, however, Allen knew that the shah had not forthrightly described what was happening there. Far from embodying what he called "democratic values common to our two countries," the shah had become the chief enemy of Iran's democratic movement. Just weeks before he flew to New York, a throng of protesters, angered by his attempt to pack parliament by stealing an election, had marched to his palace, camped on the lawn, and vowed not to leave until he agreed to call a new vote. Not wishing to come to the United States with election-rigging charges swirling around him, he agreed. That cooled the confrontation momentarily, but no one imagined it was over.

During his visit to Iran, Allen had not only sealed his friendship with the shah but seen the frightening alternative. The democratic movement seemed a volatile mob stirred by demagogues. Among these demagogues, one was the unchallenged leader. It was he who led protesters onto the shah's palace lawn, he who denounced royal privilege, he who directed every campaign against foreign influence in Iran.

This was Allen's first close-up view of Mohammad Mossadegh.

Mossadegh's upbringing was eerily similar to that of the Dulles brothers. He was born in 1882, not long before they were. He enjoyed a privileged childhood, was tutored by eminent relatives, attended a fine university, and pursued graduate studies in Europe. From an early age he was fascinated by the world and his country's place in it. That drew him to public life.

Besides coming from the same generation, Mossadegh and the Dulles brothers shared essential beliefs. They embraced the principles of capitalist democracy, detested Marxism, and felt driven to defend their respective countries against what they considered mortal threats. The worlds from which they emerged, however, made them enemies.

Mossadegh grew up watching outsiders loot his prostrate country. Through corrupt deals, predatory foreign companies acquired the right to establish Iran's banks, print its currency, and run its post office, telegraph service, railroads, and ferry lines. One Western firm bought the caviar industry, another the tobacco industry. At the beginning of the twentieth century oil was discovered in Iran, but British officials bribed a puppet monarch, Mozaffar al-Din Shah, into signing it away. The ocean of petroleum that lay beneath Iran's soil became the property of the Anglo-Iranian Oil Company, owned principally by the British government. Mossadegh came of age in an era when Iran was found to have a spectacularly rich resource, but before Iranians could make use of it, foreigners had snatched it from them.

Educated Iranians of Mossadegh's generation absorbed a tragic sense of life. They had two options: continue their humiliating submission to foreign power or launch a rebellion that was certain to fail. Mossadegh chose rebellion. He came from a national and religious tradition that celebrates martyrdom, and he was comfortable with it. Bargaining over the details of Iran's oil contract with Britain did not interest him. He demanded full Iranian control of Iranian resources and was undaunted by the prospect of defeat.

"We were, perhaps, slow in realizing that he was essentially a rich, reactionary, feudal-minded Persian inspired by a fanatical hate of the British and a desire to expel them and their works from the country regardless of the cost," Secretary of State Dean Acheson wrote in his memoir.

Mossadegh emerged from an ancient culture enveloped in fatalism, poetry, and a belief that most problems will never be solved because injustice rules the lives of men. A very different culture shaped the Dulles brothers. They grew up as their country soared toward prosperity and global power. Like many Americans of their generation, they were boundlessly optimistic and self-confident. They believed that their country was uniquely blessed, that God wished it to project influence around the world, and that good people would welcome this influence because it was righteous, benevolent, and civilizing.

The Dulles brothers were negotiators and deal makers; Mossadegh was utopian. American history taught them that the future would certainly be better than the past; Iranian history taught him that this was nonsense. They believed that poor countries could progress only by welcoming outsiders; he hated what foreign power had done to Iran.

Mossadegh had been a law student at the University of Neuchâtel in Switzerland when, in the summer of 1919, Britain announced that it had imposed a one-sided "agreement" on the dissolute Iranian monarchy under which it would take control of Iran's army, treasury, and transport system. This sent him into paroxysms of outrage. "He talked and corresponded with other prominent Iranians in Europe, published leaflets, and wrote to the League of Nations protesting against the agreement," one biographer has written. "He even traveled to Bern for the sole purpose of having a rubber stamp made for the Comité de Résistance de Nations, in whose name the anti-agreement statements were issued."

Here is grist for a tantalizing historical fantasy. The young Mossadegh was in Bern pursuing his anticolonial passion in the autumn of 1919. Allen Dulles, even younger, was also there, closing down his World War I espionage operation and preparing to leave for the Paris peace conference.

Neither could have been aware of the other. There is no way to know whether they ever crossed paths—say, Mossadegh paying for his rubber stamp while Allen walked past the shop window—but the spirit of coincidence would wish it so.

Mossadegh never stopped agonizing over his country's forced submission to foreign power. After World War II he emerged as leader of the nationalists in parliament. He was most famous for denouncing British ownership of his country's oil industry, but in 1950 he found another audacious foreign project to oppose: the seven-year development plan Allen had negotiated for Overseas Consultants Inc. He and other nationalists denounced it as a sellout to foreign potentates.

Even some in the United States had doubts about the OCI project. Dean Acheson, who was secretary of state when it was announced, called it "a grandiose plan beyond the capacity of the Iranian government." Yet the company, encouraged by Sullivan & Cromwell, pressed ahead.

Mossadegh's loose political alliance, the National Front, led the opposition to the OCI contract. During debates over the contract in parliament, one National Front deputy warned that its cost would "break the back of future generations." Another argued that "Iran should not blindly follow the advice of a foreign power" and should entrust its development "not to American advisers, but to trained Iranian experts who are qualified by experience." These speeches struck a patriotic chord, and in December 1950 parliament, by refusing to appropriate funds for the project, effectively killed it. This liquidated with a single stroke the giant endeavor from which Allen and OCI had hoped to earn great profits—and which would have been an ideal base for projecting American influence throughout Iran and the Middle East.

Not content with striking this heavy blow against the position of foreign capital in Iran, Mossadegh soon dealt another. Parliament chose him as prime minister on April 28, 1951. Before accepting, he asked for a vote in favor of nationalizing the country's oil industry. It was unanimous.

This dramatic step boded ill for another of Allen's most important clients, the J. Henry Schroder Banking Corporation, which served as financial agent for the Anglo-Iranian Oil Company and on whose board he sat. It also jolted Foster, who was then seeking business in Iran for another Sullivan & Cromwell client, the Chase Manhattan Bank. Beyond that, it was a frontal attack on the structure of the petroleum industry, with which the firm had been deeply involved for decades and which had become a foundation of the global economy.

Mossadegh's opposition to Western privilege made him the sort of leader the Dulles brothers instinctively mistrusted. Their mistrust turned to enmity when he helped kill the OCI contract. It sharpened further when he nationalized his country's oil industry. He embodied one of their nightmares: a populist rabble-rouser who stirs the masses by rejecting the way the world is run.

This made Mossadegh the first monster the Dulles brothers set out to destroy. Deposing him was among their highest priorities for 1953. They had developed a deep grudge against him during their years at Sullivan & Cromwell. Upon assuming power, they acted on it.

As Foster and Allen settled into their new jobs, Washington society saw the sharp personality differences that had separated them since childhood. Foster remained somber and withdrawn. He rarely ventured out at night, preferring to sit at home working on a speech, reading a detective novel, or playing backgammon with Janet. His one regular public appearance in Washington was at National Presbyterian Church every Sunday morning, where he sat in the pew that "Grandfather Foster" had used half a century before. He was an awkward dinner guest, often inelegantly dressed in off-green suits, with distracting habits like stirring his drink with his index finger and stretching his legs to reveal stretches of pale skin. During one dinner, the wife of an undersecretary of the navy noticed him picking melted wax from a candle, squeezing it into a ball, and chewing it.

"Now, Mr. Dulles, I scold my children for doing that," she told him. "It's bad manners and it messes up the tablecloth."

Foster quickly apologized for his "terrible habit" and later acknowledged the lady's gift of a box of candles to soothe any hurt feelings. Social graces were not his strength at work either. His confidence in his own judgment was so strong that he felt little need to consult State Department professionals, and he often treated them brusquely. During meetings he doodled incessantly on yellow legal pads, taking breaks to sharpen his pencil with a pocket knife. When lost in thought he made what the columnist Stewart Alsop called "small clicking noises with his tongue." The extended silences between his sentences were legendary.

"His speech was slow," the future British prime minister Harold Macmillan wrote after one meeting, "but it easily kept pace with his thoughts."

Allen was just the opposite: buoyant, outgoing, a sparkling presence on the diplomatic party scene. No one knew what he was up to, but everyone suspected enough of the truth to give him an air of mystery. His pipe provided a smoky halo that enhanced the mystique. Attacks of gout sometimes forced him to use crutches, but this had an endearing advantage: he was the only member of President Eisenhower's inner circle who was allowed to wear slippers in the Oval Office.

Their old friend Henry Luce put each of the brothers on the cover of *Time* during their first year in office. Allen was pictured with his ubiquitous pipe, smoke curling up toward a black-cloaked figure carrying a dagger, above the title "In an Ancient Game, New Techniques and a New Team." Foster followed a couple of months later. Wrinkled and sullen, staring out from beneath a black homburg in front of a globe encircled with red, white, and blue banners, he looked worthy of what *Time* described as his mission: "To Unite Principle and the Facts of Life."

Luce's friendship was only one of many assets that helped Foster and Allen project their views into the American press. Foster built a dense network of media contacts, and once Allen became director of central intelligence he went even further. Allen established discreet contact with owners, publishers, and editors of influential daily newspapers, magazines, and broadcast networks. Among his regular collaborators were William Paley of CBS, Arthur Hays Sulzberger of the *New York Times*, Alfred Friendly of the *Washington Post*, and James Copley of Copley News Service. Through them, and through journalists who were veterans of the Office of War Information, the U.S. government's official propaganda arm during World War II, he regularly planted stories about foreign countries and their leaders. By one account he could "pick up the phone and edit a breaking story, make sure an irritating foreign correspondent was yanked from the field, or hire the services of men such as *Time*'s Berlin bureau chief and *Newsweek*'s man in Tokyo." The columnist Allen Drury called him "a man of notoriously thin skin who is not above trying to get the jobs of newspapermen who criticize his agency."

Years later it became clear that Allen's efforts to influence the American press were not casual or episodic, but part of a multifaceted project called Operation Mockingbird. Through it he funneled information, some of it classified, to journalists disposed to promote the CIA world-view, among them James Reston of the *New York Times*, Benjamin Bradlee of *Newsweek*, and the influential columnists Joseph and Stewart Alsop. Operatives also planted stories in smaller news outlets and then arranged for them to be amplified through networks controlled by friendly media barons. Frank Wisner, who helped oversee Mockingbird, called it the CIA's "mighty Wurlitzer."

Home life remained as complicated for Allen as it was simple for his older brother. The pace of his romantic adventures slowed, though he continued his on-and-off affair with Mary Bancroft—who became so friendly with Clover that at one point they considered collaborating on an illustrated book about Jungian dream theory. He also reconnected with Countess Wally Toscanini Castelbarco, whom he had met when she was a courier for the Italian resistance, and after a period of coolness Clover accepted her, too.

While Allen cultivated an enigmatic, diaphanous image, Foster's fire-and-brimstone Cold War sermons made him a major national figure. In his first speech as secretary of state, delivered on January 27, 1953, on national television, he dramatically unveiled a map of the world that showed a vast region, "from Kamchatka, near Alaska . . . right on to Germany in the center of Europe . . . which the Russian Communists completely dominate." He warned that the population of this region, totaling eight hundred million people, was "being forged into a vast weapon of fighting power backed by industrial production and modern weapons that include atomic bombs."

"We have enemies who are plotting our destruction," he concluded. "Any American who isn't awake to that fact is like a soldier who's asleep at his post."

Whether this was a sober estimate of Soviet power or a wild exaggeration, it both reflected and intensified the sense of fear that many Americans felt. Foster sought to make nuclear combat seem a real, imminent possibility. He conveyed a terrifying worldview. Most Americans came to share it.

Enveloped in a world entirely disconnected from Cold War pathologies, and even further distant from the imperatives of global business, Mohammad

Mossadegh never realized that he had potent enemies in the United States. He was puzzled that Truman had not rallied to his cause, and when Eisenhower was elected, he dared to hope for a change. The first response seemed encouraging. In January 1953 Mossadegh sent Eisenhower a message asking the new president to help Iranians regain their "natural and elementary rights," and Eisenhower promised to "study those views with care and with sympathetic concern."

Even before Eisenhower took office, however, members of his incoming administration had begun discussions with agents of Britain's Secret Intelligence Service about a plot against Mossadegh. Their interlocutor was Christopher Montague Woodhouse, a former chief of the British intelligence station in Tehran, who made a secret trip to Washington soon after the election. At the State Department and again at the CIA, he argued that Mossadegh should be overthrown not as punishment for seizing Britain's oil company, but because he had become too weak to resist a possible Soviet-backed coup.

"When we knew what the prejudices were, we played all the more on those prejudices," Woodhouse later wrote of his dealings with American officials. "A powerful ally was Frank Wisner, who was then director of [CIA] operations. Allen Dulles was also receptive. . . . He proved to be shrewd and practical, and he greatly helped in convincing the CIA that between us we could carry out an effective operation."

Eisenhower assumed the presidency without any of the anti-Mossadegh fervor that gripped the Dulles brothers. According to one of his biographers, Jean Edward Smith, he "initially took little interest" in the idea of fomenting revolution in Iran, but Foster pressed it, and "over drinks in the evening Ike was brought around to accept a coup, providing America's hand would not be visible."

Once Foster had persuaded the president to authorize Mossadegh's overthrow, Allen began to plan it.

"On February 18, 1953, the newly installed chief of the British Secret Intelligence Service arrived in Washington," the intelligence historian Tim Weiner has written. "Sir John Sinclair, a soft-spoken Scotsman known to the public as 'C' and to his friends as 'Sinbad,' met with Allen Dulles and proposed Kim Roosevelt as field commander for a coup. The British gave their plan the prosaic title of Operation Boot. Roosevelt had a grander name: Operation Ajax, after the mythical hero of the Trojan War (a strange choice, as legend has it that Ajax went mad, slew a flock of sheep thinking they were warriors, and killed himself in shame after coming to his senses)."

A series of vivid dispatches from Loy Henderson, the American ambassador in Tehran, fueled Foster's enthusiasm for Operation Ajax—which may have been named for the household cleanser, not the tormented Greek. Henderson reported "the fact that the Iron Curtain is about to envelop Iran," asserted that Mossadegh's nationalism pleased "only those sympathetic to the Soviet Union and to international communism," and urged policies that would "starve Mossadegh out of power." These reports reinforced what Foster already believed and stiffened his determination to proceed.

Mossadegh had given both Dulles brothers many reasons to wish him gone. Once in office, each found a new one.

Foster had identified an emerging enemy of freedom in the world: neutralism. He defined it as the "immoral and shortsighted" belief that countries could hold themselves apart from the Cold War confrontation. This put him at odds with emerging statesmen like Prime Minister Jawaharlal Nehru of India, who wanted his country "to avoid entanglement in power politics and not to join any group of powers as against any other group," and the new Egyptian strongman Gamal Abdel Nasser, who reasoned that there was no reason for Egypt to oppose the Soviets because "we've never had trouble with them."

Mossadegh shared their view. He did not use the term "neutralism" to describe his foreign policy, but came up with one that meant the same thing: "negative equilibrium." Foster realized that if Mossadegh thrived, leaders of other countries might follow him toward neutralism. If he were to fall, neutralism would seem less tempting.

Allen was eager to strike against Mossadegh for the same reasons as his brother, plus one of his own: he wanted action. His first two years at the CIA had been frustrating because Truman would not authorize the kind of world-shaking operations he longed to run. Now he had a president eager to wage clandestine war, and full command of what would later be called "the invisible government."

"They might be more or less invisible in terms of the ongoing public debate about foreign policy, but that simply made them all the more powerful," David Halberstam wrote of Allen and the men around him. "They were the real players in a real world, as opposed to the world that newspapers wrote about and Congress debated."

> The temptation to do things covertly grew; it was easier, less messy. In this netherworld of power and secrecy it was particularly comforting to the more established figures of Washington to have a man like Allen Dulles as head of the CIA. His job so readily lent itself to the abuse of power, but he was a comforting figure. . . . He was affable as his brother, Foster, was not. Even more importantly, he lacked Foster's dogmatism and righteousness and rigid certainties. . . . A man that accessible, that open and gregarious, could hardly be a part of a world of invisible men with false identities who worked in the darkness. Rather, he seemed a thoughtful, fair-minded, humane public servant who seemed to offer reassurance that whatever things his men were doing, they were the kind of things that everyone at the party would approve of. He was not only the head of the closed society, he was its ambassador to the open one.

The Dulles brothers' antipathy to Mossadegh might not, by itself, have been enough to propel the United States to the extreme of overthrowing him. That became possible only when several other factors converged.

First was the imperative of scoring a public "win," somewhere or other, in the global struggle against Communism. The Eisenhower administration came to office pledging to lead the United States out of what Vice President Richard Nixon had called "Dean Acheson's college of cowardly communist containment." Pressure to act became more acute after the shock of Eisenhower's decision to accept a truce in Korea, which some saw as a sign of weakness. His refusal to pardon the convicted atomic spies Julius and Ethel Rosenberg, who were executed on June 19, 1953, toughened his image, but it was not enough. He needed a quick success. With the Soviet Union, China, and Eastern Europe ruled out as unrealistic targets, another had to be found.

Iran had an open society, meaning that covert action would be relatively easy. It shared a long border with the Soviet Union. It had rich oil reserves and, as the historian James Bill has written, "the United States clearly had an interest in gaining entry to the Iranian oil business." And although Mossadegh was far from a Communist, Foster and Allen saw him as weak and unstable, an Iranian Kerensky who would be unable to resist if the Communists struck against him.

"If disorders flare up in Iran as a result of nationalization, the Russians may intervene, grab the oil, even unleash World War III," *Life* warned. "To call Mossadegh a fanatic may be correct, but it explains almost nothing. Mossadegh is a far more complex character than the most baffling men the West has yet had to deal with, including misty yogis like Nehru and notably unmisty commissars like Josef Stalin. . . . Mohammad Mossadegh, with his faints, his tears and wild-eyed dreams, is a whirling dervish with a college education and a first-rate mind."

Striking against Mossadegh was also tempting because of the political risk of not doing so. Senator Joseph McCarthy and other anti-Communist zealots in Congress were denouncing diplomats they blamed for the "loss" of China. If Iran were somehow to be "lost," Eisenhower and the Dulles brothers would be accused of having failed to act. They could avoid this danger by seizing control of events there.

The final factor in this equation was pressure from Britain. Losing access to Iranian oil, a foundation of British economic and military power, was difficult for British leaders even to contemplate. They had been forced to surrender India; Kenya was afire with anticolonial passion; and now the Iranians had nationalized their oil industry. One British diplomat warned plaintively that if this momentum was not stopped, "we will be driven back to our island, where we shall starve."

To avoid this fate, British leaders had launched a campaign of escalating pressure on Iran in 1951 and 1952. It not only failed but provoked Mossadegh to close the British embassy in Tehran, expelling all diplomats including secret agents. Prime Minister Winston Churchill's last hope was to reach across the Atlantic for help. He invited President Truman to "gallop together" with him against Mossadegh. Truman refused, for two reasons. First, he did not believe the CIA should overthrow governments, and second, he was an anticolonialist who had no sympathy for what he called the "block headed British."

Secretary of State Acheson conveyed this message clearly. "Only on the invitation of the Iranian government, or Soviet military intervention, or a Communist coup d'état in Tehran, or to evacuate British nationals in danger of attack, could we support the use of force," he declared. Later he wrote that a "distinct cleavage" separated American and British attitudes toward oil nationalization and Mossadegh.

That cleavage disappeared when Eisenhower replaced Truman in the White House. His secretary of state and director of central intelligence were impatient to "gallop together" into the world of covert action. A fateful alignment of forces led them to choose Mossadegh as their first target:

- They arrived in high office mistrusting him.
- They wanted to win a strategic victory somewhere.
- Iran was a tempting target.
- The British were urgently interested and eager to help.

Behind all of this lay the overwhelming reality of the Cold War. Eisenhower came into office believing that Iran "stands today at the same place China did only a very few years ago," and that the United States had to find "some scheme or plan that will permit that oil to keep flowing to the westward." The Dulles brothers won his support for a coup by framing their antipathy to fit Cold War fears. Even Ambassador George McGhee, who had been Truman's liaison to Mossadegh and considered him "a patriotic Iranian nationalist with no reason to be attracted to socialism," understood the imperative.

"If it weren't for the Cold War," McGhee mused as the coup was being planned, "there's no reason why we shouldn't let the British and the Iranians fight it out."

On some days, Foster spoke personally or by telephone with Eisenhower as many as ten times. At dusk he often visited the White House for a chat over drinks. No one else was present at these meetings, and no notes were taken. Nor were any taken during the weekend lunches Foster and Allen often shared at their sister's home in suburban McLean, Virginia, or during their many private conversations. Allen often dropped by Foster's house after work, and by one account they "spoke on the telephone to each other daily, often many times, in quick, shorthand conversations that bypassed layers of bureaucracy." Making far-reaching decisions secretly fit well with the new administration's commitment to covert action.

"The line between intelligence and policy wore thin from the start," according to the biographer Peter Grose. "Allen was ever imaginative in devising intelligence operations that by their very nature determined the shape of national policy."

In Washington the CIA was seen as a bastion of relative liberalism. Allen believed—not surprisingly for a spymaster—that he had a deep and subtle understanding of the world. In speeches and interviews, he avoided the heated rhetoric that was his brother's trademark. He recommended against the execution of Julius and Ethel Rosenberg, arguing that it would stir anti-American sentiment abroad. His analysts often seemed sharper and more imaginative than their counterparts at the State Department.

"Many of the liberals who were forced out of other departments found a sanctuary, an enclave, in the CIA," Robert F. Kennedy recalled later. "So some of the best people in Washington, and around the country, began to collect there."

Allen even tried to hire George Kennan, one of the era's most thoughtful American diplomats, after Foster pushed him out of the State Department. Kennan, recently returned from a truncated term as ambassador to the Soviet Union, was the author of the "containment" doctrine Foster professed to abhor. He had been quoted as calling Foster "a dangerous man" seized by "emotional anticommunism." The State Department could not accommodate them both. Foster's rise implied Kennan's fall. Rather than dismiss him outright, Foster suggested that he might be happier at the CIA. Allen was ready to hire him, but Kennan demurred.

"I felt that if I could not be where I had grown up and belonged, i.e., in the State Department, I would rather not be anywhere," Kennan wrote afterward.

By 1953 the CIA had become a truly global organization, six times larger than when it was founded in 1947. Allen commanded fifteen thousand employees in fifty countries, with an annual budget in the hundreds of millions of dollars, no accounting necessary. He had remarkably little to show for it. All three of his main operations in Eastern Europe, aimed at stirring anti-Communist resistance in Poland, Ukraine, and Albania, collapsed in defeat. His analysts did not foresee Stalin's death or its first major consequence, the emergence of Nikita Khrushchev as the new Soviet leader. He sought to use Burma and Thailand as staging grounds for guerrilla warfare against "Red China," but his secret armies won no victories.

The operation in Burma was an early example of how closely the two brothers collaborated—and of how often their projects produced unintended consequences. Eager to destabilize the Communist regime in China, they created a guerrilla force of Chinese Nationalists in northern Burma, drawn from remnants of Chiang Kai-shek's defeated army. Directed by Allen's men, these fighters staged a series of raids into southern China. Foster's role was to provide diplomatic cover, which he did by denying repeatedly that the United States was connected to the insurgency. He even kept the operation secret from his diplomats in the region. By the end of 1953, however, it became clear that the CIA was the outside force dropping arms to the insurgents and seeking to provoke war on a volatile border. This led to a burst of patriotic outrage in Burma, a decision by Prime Minister U Nu to stop accepting American aid, and a sharp improvement in Burma's relations with "Red China." Burma soon fell into a long cycle of military coups, repression, and ethnic war.

While the secret war in Burma was under way, Foster and Allen proposed an even more ambitious operation to President Eisenhower and the National Security Council. They asked that the CIA be authorized to do something it had never done before: overthrow a foreign leader. Their target would be Mossadegh. Less than two months after taking office, the brothers were bringing American foreign policy into a new age.

Truman had periodically convened the National Security Council—a shifting group of cabinet secretaries, military commanders, and senior intelligence officers—but under Eisenhower it assumed a central role as the official rubber stamp for foreign and security policy. It met once a week. Eisenhower presided, but Foster and Allen dominated most meetings. Allen, who was the council's "security adviser," would open with a twenty-minute review of world events. Foster would follow, usually echoing his brother's views and recommendations. There was little debate. Eisenhower used the council to endorse decisions that he, Foster, and Allen had already made.

On March 4, 1953, the National Security Council met to consider overthrowing Mossadegh.

Allen gave a summary of intelligence from Iran, which he said pointed to "a Soviet takeover." Foster took the threat further, predicting that after the takeover, "other areas of the Middle East, with some 60 percent of the world's oil reserves, will fall under Communist control." All agreed that this threat required urgent action. Only one participant was conflicted:

Eisenhower. He still hoped Iran and Britain could reach some accord that would make intervention unnecessary. At one point he exploded in frustration, demanding to know why it was so difficult "to get some of the people in these downtrodden countries to like us instead of hating us." Moments later he added, "If I had five hundred million dollars of money to spend in secret, I would get a hundred million of it to Iran right now." He was quickly assured that the Mutual Security Administration could assemble "as much as the situation required," but he did not pursue his impulse. Nor, in the end, did he discourage the idea of a plot. All knew this meant he had approved it. He made his approval clear again at the next week's NSC meeting, silently assenting to Foster's recommendation that the United States become "senior partners with the British" in a plot against Mossadegh.

"Moscow's involvement in Iran was negligible," the historian Richard Immerman later concluded, "but [Foster] Dulles could not distinguish between indigenous nationalism and imported communism."

Operation Ajax occupied more of Foster's interest than his time. In his frequent travels and many speeches, he made occasional disapproving remarks about Iran but never directly threatened Mossadegh. When the State Department's cooperation in the plot was required, he gave it through his deputy Walter Bedell Smith. His role was to approve, to encourage, and to keep the president discreetly informed.

"Eisenhower participated in none of the meetings that set up Ajax; he received only oral reports on the plan; and he did not discuss it with his cabinet or the NSC," Stephen Ambrose wrote in his biography of Eisenhower. "Establishing a pattern he would hold to throughout his presidency, he kept his distance and left no documents behind that could implicate the President in any proposed coup. But in the privacy of the Oval Office, over cocktails, he was kept informed by Foster Dulles, and he maintained a tight control over the activities of the CIA."

On April 4, exactly one month after Eisenhower gave Operation Ajax his tacit approval, Allen signed an order approving the expenditure of $1 million to be used "in any way that would bring about the fall of Mossadegh." Never before had an official of the United States government approved such an order. The chain of command was elegantly direct: from the president to the secretary of state, and from the secretary of state to his brother, the director of central intelligence.

Declassified records show that on this same day, April 4, Allen set in motion another of his extraordinary projects: MKULTRA, a mind-control experiment that aimed to test the value of drugs in black operations. He received a proposal from one of his trusted operatives, Richard Helms, recommending that the CIA "develop a capability in the covert use of biological and chemical materials" that could be used in "discrediting individuals, eliciting information, and implanting suggestions and other forms of mental control." Soon afterward he approved MKULTRA with a budget of $300,000. It included experiments in which LSD was administered to CIA and other government employees, doctors, prisoners, mental patients, and prostitutes and their clients. One prisoner who participated, the future New England gang leader James "Whitey" Bulger, later wrote that the experiments were "nightmarish" and "would plunge me into the depths of insanity." Another participant, an army researcher who was unwittingly given LSD, was reported to have leaped through a window to his death. A Senate investigating committee later found aspects of this project "clearly illegal."

Allen never recoiled from the use of coercive violence. He established secret prisons in Germany, Japan, and the Panama Canal Zone, where suspected double agents were subjected to what would later be called "enhanced interrogation." At the same time he intensified CIA commando operations behind the Iron Curtain. His men trained bands of mercenaries and exiles, armed them, packed them into planes at clandestine airfields in Greece, Germany, Britain, and Japan, and air-dropped them into Eastern Europe, the Soviet Union, and China.

One of the farthest-reaching projects Allen directed during this period was the creation of underground armies in Europe that would be ready to rebel and spread terror in case of Soviet invasion or the election of leftist governments. The CIA created these clandestine networks—collectively known as "Gladio," after the name the force was given in Italy—in fifteen countries, sometimes with help from the British secret service MI-6. William Colby, a CIA officer who helped run the project, later wrote that to be sure fighters were properly armed, "specialized equipment had to be secured from CIA and secretly cached." In 2000, a report to the Italian parliament concluded that some of the killings and bombings that threw Italy into turmoil during previous decades had been perpetrated by "men linked to the structures of United States intelligence." Not until 2005 did the first serious studies of Gladio appear. In one of them, the Swiss scholar Daniele Ganser reported that in eight of the fifteen countries where the CIA shaped "stay-behind" armies—Italy, Turkey, Germany, France, Spain, Portugal, Belgium, and Sweden—"links to terrorism have been either confirmed or claimed."

> In order to guarantee a solid anti-Communist ideology of its recruits, the CIA and MI-6 generally relied on men of the conservative political Right. At times, former Nazis and right-wing terrorists were also recruited . . .
>
> It is greatly upsetting to discover that Western Europe and the United States collaborated in establishing secret armed networks which in the majority of countries are suspected of having had links to acts of terrorism. In the United States, such nations have been called rogue states and are the objects of hostility and sanction. Can it be that the United States itself, potentially in alliance with Great Britain and other NATO members, should be on the list of states sponsoring terrorism, along with Saudi Arabia, Pakistan, and Iran?

Rumors about these operations began to circulate in Washington and caused some alarm. In the spring of 1953 a subcommittee of the House Appropriations Committee summoned Allen, Frank Wisner—who as deputy director for plans was in charge of covert operations—and four other senior CIA officers for two days of secret testimony. No hearing like this had ever been held in the United States, and there were extended negotiations over who should attend, including whether a stenographer was necessary. Wisner spoke first and was remarkably candid. He told the subcommittee that the CIA "engages in covert psychological, political, and economic warfare" and directs "a very substantial program of covert and 'unconventional' military activities, including guerrilla warfare, counter-guerrilla operations, sabotage and counter-sabotage, and the development of escape and evasion networks in enemy or potentially hostile territory." Allen gave the subcommittee a list of CIA operations—it has never been fully declassified—and when the subcommittee asked for more, he provided it.

Allen appeared regularly before congressional committees, often in closed session and accompanied by as many as seven of his deputies. He presented the CIA budget to the House Appropriations Committee and shared top-secret assessments of Soviet nuclear capability with the Joint Committee on Atomic Energy. He assured a House Armed Services subcommittee that he withheld "no secrets" from Congress. In fact, he was never fully forthcoming. When one committee sent investigators abroad to assess the work of CIA stations, he sent a cable telling his men that the investigators were "completely unwitting" of what the agency was doing "and should remain unwitting."

As Allen pursued his covert projects, Eisenhower proclaimed an important shift in American defense posture that became known as the "New Look." One of his constant themes was that military and economic strength must go hand in hand and that, as he declared at one cabinet meeting, "We cannot defend the nation in a way which will exhaust our economy." Immediately after taking office he began a series of sharp cuts in the defense budget, achieved mainly by reducing the number of troops under arms. Rather than relying on conventional forces, the "New Look" envisioned a rapid buildup of nuclear weapons, which Eisenhower believed would provide the same security at less cost. In 1954 he announced a $7.4 billion tax cut. Secretary of the Treasury George Humphrey followed with an announcement that defense spending would be cut by $2 billion.

Eisenhower's "New Look" policy had three components: a smaller army, nuclear deterrence, and covert action. The first two were public. Few knew about the third.

One Friday night in the spring of 1953, a celebrity-studded crowd gathered at Radio City Music Hall in New York City for an event that had nothing, but also everything, to do with America's newly fortified determination to shape world events. It was the premiere of the year's most poetic film, Shane, starring Alan Ladd as a brooding, noble gunman in the old West. His character personified the way the Dulles brothers perceived America's role in the world.

Shane unfolds in a frontier valley where thugs are threatening peaceable people. One good man with a gun appears. Nobody has invited him, but decent folk understand that he has come to free them. He kills the thugs, and with that violent act brings peace to the valley. His service complete, he rides away. All are grateful.

Crowds thronged to Radio City during the film's four-week run, and it turned out to be an Oscar-winning triumph. The *New York Times* called it "a disturbing revelation of the savagery that prevailed in the hearts of the old gun-fighters, who were simply legal killers under the frontier code." It was that and more. The hero acts precisely as many Americans believe their country acts in the world. He is an enforcer of morality and a scourge of oppressors; he comes from far away but knows instinctively what must be done; he brings peace by slaying wrongdoers; he risks his life to help others; and for all this he wishes no reward other than the quiet satisfaction of having done what was right. *Shane* reinforced a cultural consensus that steadied America's self-image during the disorienting early years of the Cold War. Whether Foster or Allen saw it is unrecorded, but they imagined themselves like its hero: a morally centered warrior who assumes burdens—even the moral burden of murder—in order to ensure the ultimate triumph of justice.

Another film classic of the early 1950s became Eisenhower's favorite: *High Noon*, starring Gary Cooper as a peaceable lawman who is forced to confront criminals alone because no one else can or will. Eisenhower watched it three times. He cannot have avoided seeing himself and the United States in the sheriff's role: reluctant to fight, but moved to do so because otherwise good people will suffer.

"In their recognition of the inevitability of armed conflict, these films present the politics of containment," the critic Stanley Corkin has written. "The need to quarantine the misdirected and potential threats to civil society resounds throughout these films. . . . While *High Noon* and *Shane* offer some notion of the ideal state and function of the aggregate, they also assert the desirability of the extraordinary individual's riding to the rescue."

Soon after *Shane* opened in New York, Foster set off on his first trip to the Middle East as secretary of state. He spent three weeks traveling, with stops in Syria, Lebanon, Jordan, Egypt, Saudi Arabia, Israel, Libya, and Turkey, along with Pakistan and India. The absence of Iran from this list drew much comment. In Pakistan a reporter asked Foster if he was seeking to undermine Mossadegh. He replied that the United States had "no disposition to meddle in the affairs of others."

Foster returned to Washington on May 24, and four days later Eisenhower received another message from Mossadegh. Iran's economy was collapsing as a result of British sanctions. Mossadegh was not only unaware that Eisenhower had ordered his overthrow, but still believed what nearly every Iranian believed about the United States: that it was a friend of democracy and an opponent of colonial exploitation. Not realizing how fully the climate in Washington had changed, he appealed for Eisenhower's help.

"Although it was hoped that during Your Excellency's administration, attention of a more sympathetic character would be devoted to the Iranian situation, unfortunately no change seems thus far to have taken place in the position of the American government," Mossadegh wrote. "As a result of actions taken by the former Company and the British Government, the Iranian nation is now facing great economic and political difficulties. There can be serious consequences, from an international viewpoint as well, if this situation is permitted to continue."

This last sentence, which suggested that Mossadegh might consider steering Iran closer to the Soviet Union, set off new alarm in Washington and resolved any lingering doubts about Operation Ajax. On June 25, Foster summoned the principals to his office for a final go-ahead. He and half a dozen senior diplomats represented the State Department; Allen and Kermit "Kim" Roosevelt, a grandson of Theodore Roosevelt, who had been chosen as field commander, came from the CIA. Roosevelt began by reporting that "the Soviet threat is indeed genuine, dangerous, and imminent." Then he handed Foster a twenty-two-page summary of the action plan, which British and American agents had written during a series of brainstorming sessions in Cyprus.

"So this is how we get rid of that madman Mossadegh," Foster said as he leafed through the document.

All understood that the plot would not have advanced this far without the president's approval. This meant that, as Roosevelt later wrote, "anything but assent would be ill-received." Roosevelt recalled Henry Byroade, the assistant secretary of state for Near East affairs, "accepting the fact that discussion would be useless" and "drumming his fingers on a knee, his black brows forming an uncompromising line that matched his equally straight, uncompromising mouth. . . . In fact, I was morally certain that almost half of those present, if they felt free or had the courage to speak, would have opposed the undertaking."

Roosevelt outlined the plan, which envisioned a series of operations aimed at weakening Mossadegh, throwing Tehran into chaos, and encouraging pro-shah military officers to stage a coup. Then Ambassador Henderson, whom Foster had summoned from his post in Tehran, summed up the case for it. "Mr. Secretary, I don't like this kind of business at all," he concluded. "But we are confronted by a desperate, a dangerous situation, and a madman who would ally himself with the Russians. We may have no choice but to proceed with this undertaking. May God grant us success."

This was what Foster wished to hear and knew he would hear. "That's that, then," he said. "Let's get going."

Roosevelt was one of the last to file out. As he was leaving, he saw Foster pick up the white telephone that connected him to the Oval Office. The secretary of state, he guessed, was calling the president to report that he had set Operation Ajax in motion.

A few days later Eisenhower sent a tart answer to Mossadegh's letter, which had been sitting on his desk for a month. "It would not be fair to the American taxpayers for the United States Government to extend any considerable amount of economic aid to Iran so long as Iran could have access to funds derived from the sale of its oil," he wrote. "I note the concern reflected in your letter at the present dangerous situation in Iran and sincerely hope that before it is too late, the Government in Iran will take such steps as are in its power to prevent the further deterioration of that situation."

As the United States was setting out to depose a non-Communist government in Iran, it faced a sudden opportunity to strike inside the Soviet bloc. On June 16, 1953, several thousand construction workers in East Berlin walked off their jobs rather than accept new government work rules. Their protest spread. Crowds besieged government buildings. As word spread through the city, people raced to the scene. One was the chief of the State Department's Berlin Desk, Eleanor Lansing Dulles.

Eleanor had been given this post, which she said "came close to being the dream job," just before Foster became secretary of state, but no fraternal influence was involved. In fact, soon after his appointment was announced, he told her that he would not give her any position in the State Department—though he would not fire her if she was on the job by Inauguration Day. Soon afterward James Riddleberger, head of the Office of German Affairs, asked Eleanor to create an unofficial "Berlin Desk" to coordinate "all the work on the political, military, cultural, and economic aspects of Berlin." She accepted and began commuting to Berlin. After her first trip, she returned to a rude shock: her brother wanted to fire her. They had drifted apart, and he did not appreciate her habit of lecturing him. During the presidential campaign she had privately reprimanded him for refusing to distance himself from Senator McCarthy, and more than once she offered him unsolicited advice on economic policy.

"Jimmy Riddleberger went to see Foster and said he couldn't fire me because I was in the department first, it wouldn't be fair," Eleanor later recalled. "And Foster told him he just couldn't have me around, it didn't look right, or something. And Riddleberger said, 'Look, give her a chance. Give her a year and if she doesn't get into trouble, it will probably be all right.' And Foster agreed. And after a hard year, it all blew over. But I never understood why he did what he did."

On the morning of June 16, Eleanor was discussing food stockpiles with city officials in West Berlin when a man burst in and shouted, "There is trouble!" Racing to East Berlin, she found surging crowds charged by bold denunciations of Walter Ulbricht's Soviet-backed regime and chanting of "Get Ulbricht Out!" and "We Want Freedom!" One group of protesters begged for help, pleading, "Why don't the Americans give us guns?" Soviet tanks were approaching. If the Eisenhower administration had been looking for a chance to jump into an anti-Communist uprising, here was one.

"By midnight on June 16, the basic decision for restraint had been made," Eleanor later wrote. "The risk of nuclear war and the Soviet firmness in holding on to restive areas made clear that any action to help those in revolt would bring imminent danger of World War III. . . . If the revolting workers had been given arms, in their wild bid for freedom, a bloody confrontation would have resulted."

Soviet officials were most unhappy at having had to face this uprising. A radio report from East Berlin fixed blame: "The fascist putsch was staged on the direct instruction, and under the guidance, of Allen Dulles." There was at least some truth to this.

"Some of the provocateurs captured by the Communist authorities were too well equipped with blueprints for sabotage to have managed the business alone," the intelligence historian Andrew Tully has written.

"Rioters had in their pockets plans for blowing up railroad bridges and railway terminals, and detailed floor plans of governmental buildings. They had forged food stamps and fake bank drafts to be used to spread confusion in the food-rationing system and to disrupt East German bank credits. It seemed indisputable that they were getting their espionage pay checks from the CIA's top German spy . . . Reinhard Gehlen."

The imperative of liberating "captive nations" was a staple of Washington rhetoric, but neither Allen, Foster, nor President Eisenhower ever took it literally. They understood that providing military aid to protesters in Eastern Europe could draw the superpowers toward nuclear confrontation. Deposing a government under Moscow's direct control was not a realistic goal. Foster and Allen looked for other places to win victories.

Operation Ajax had already been set in motion, but by law the National Security Council had to give final approval. At its July 1 meeting, Foster asserted that Iran "woefully lacks any prospect of effective political leadership," and then pronounced his verdict.

"The United States must concentrate on changing the situation there," he said.

Acting on this recommendation, the council gave its approval. Preparations proceeded methodically—with one glaring exception. Neither Foster nor Allen ever convened subordinates or anyone else to discuss whether overthrowing Mossadegh was a good idea. They never considered alternatives. Instead they acted on an unspoken consensus: Mossadegh was in rebellion against the West; his rebellion exposed Iran to Soviet influence; therefore he must be deposed.

Foster avoided debate at the State Department through the simple expedient of not informing either of its Iran specialists that a plot was under way. Allen had to do a bit more. The CIA station chief in Tehran, Roger Goiran, was penciled in as a key player in Operation Ajax, but wrote himself out of the script by firing off an angry cable warning that deposing Mossadegh would serve only the interests of "Anglo-French colonialism." This might have been a warning bell, but Allen treated it as an annoyance. He pulled Goiran out of Tehran and replaced him with a station chief who knew less and would act as ordered.

No American who might have spoken against the coup could do so because none knew that a coup was being planned. One prominent public figure, however, became a fervent Mossadegh supporter: Supreme Court

Justice William O. Douglas. This was the moment when Douglas emerged most clearly as the anti-Dulles.

In 1949 Allen had traveled to Iran for meetings with the shah and his courtiers aimed at securing the ill-fated OCI contract. Douglas also visited Iran that year, to travel on horseback through tribal homelands. He was one of the few Americans of his generation to become thoroughly absorbed with Iran. In interviews, articles, and a book called *Strange Lands and Friendly People*, he championed Mossadegh as "a great popular hero" who was "passionately Persian and anti-Soviet in his leanings," embraced "democratic ideals," and "offers an alternative to Communist leadership." This was exactly opposite to the Dulles view. Foster and Allen saw Mossadegh through an ideological prism, as an enemy of global capitalism and therefore a threat to the West. Douglas saw him as Iran's liberator and did not much care whether he served American interests.

"If you and I were in Persia," he wrote in the *New Republic* in April 1952, "we'd be for Mossadegh 100 percent."

By this time the political climate in Washington had become not just fiercely anti-Communist, but increasingly influenced by the crusading Senator McCarthy. For several years he captivated the nation by charging that Communists had launched "a conspiracy so immense and an infamy so black as to dwarf any previous venture in the history of man." Among the agencies he singled out as having been infiltrated by Communists were the State Department and the CIA.

Foster never forgot the trauma of Woodrow Wilson's collapse after his failure to win Senate approval for American entry into the League of Nations. From it he drew the lesson that makers of American foreign policy must work closely with Congress and avoid alienating any of its prominent members. This made him eager, in his own words, "to find a basis for cooperation with McCarthy." Since McCarthy considered the State Department a nest of dissolute leftists, that meant firing people.

During his first weeks in office, Foster dismissed twenty-three diplomats as security risks, apparently after being told that they might be homosexual. In another gesture to McCarthy, he turned East Asia policy over to a group of militant anti-Communists known as the "China Lobby," who were convinced that traitors or fellow travelers inside the State Department had helped the Communists defeat their hero Chiang Kai-shek in the Chinese civil war four years earlier. They singled out John

Carter Vincent, whom Foster fired in 1953 for "failure to meet the standard" expected of American diplomats, and John Paton Davies, whom Foster dismissed the next year after concluding that he had "demonstrated a lack of judgment, discretion, and reliability." McCarthy was a leading promoter of the loose but powerful "China Lobby." So was Henry Luce, who used *Time* and *Life* to promote the view that China had been "lost" in part because of perfidy in the State Department; he featured Chiang on no fewer than ten *Time* covers. Foster appointed a "China Lobby" favorite, a Virginia banker named Walter Robinson, as assistant secretary of state for Far Eastern affairs. Eisenhower picked another, Admiral Arthur Radford, as chairman of the Joint Chiefs of Staff.

In a gesture to McCarthy, Foster hired one of the senator's protégés, a former FBI agent named Scott McLeod, to enforce "positive loyalty" in the State Department by rooting out subversives and other undesirables. Together they imposed a rigorous program of security clearances, loyalty oaths, investigations, and cross-examinations that ended the careers of many diplomats. Morale suffered. Applications to join the foreign service dropped.

McCarthy's pressure on Foster was steady. For Allen it crashed down suddenly, on July 9, 1953.

Roy Cohn, McCarthy's chief investigator, called the CIA that morning and demanded that a veteran CIA officer and old friend of Allen's, William Bundy, present himself immediately for questioning. Cohn had discovered that Bundy had contributed $400 to the Alger Hiss defense fund, and considered this incriminating enough to require explanation. Allen immediately recognized Cohn's summons as the beginning of an attack on his institution and power. It was also an assault on his social class. Bundy was one of his "old boys," with a trajectory that ran through Groton, Yale, Harvard Law School, marriage to Dean Acheson's daughter, clandestine work during World War II, and legal practice at the elite Washington firm of Covington and Burling. Allen quickly sent Bundy on "personal leave" and announced that he was out of town, a maneuver McCarthy denounced as a "most blatant attempt" to defy the will of Congress. A couple of days later, Allen drove to Capitol Hill for a meeting with McCarthy and other Republicans on his investigating committee.

"Joe, you're not going to have Bundy as a witness," Allen said.

The senators were startled, but Allen held fast and departed cheerfully.

Later that day he called Vice President Nixon and asked him to use his influence to calm McCarthy. Nixon did so. Never again did any of McCarthy's investigators seek to question a CIA officer. Some quietly cheered Allen's successful defiance, though Walter Lippmann warned that it would strengthen "the argument that the CIA is something apart."

Allen had reason to believe that his agency was indeed a thing apart. With the approval of the president and secretary of state, he was about to give "Kim" Roosevelt an assignment never before given to an American intelligence officer: overthrow a government.

Robust but bespectacled and professorial, Roosevelt was a thirty-seven-year-old Harvard graduate who had joined the Office of Strategic Services during World War II, returned to civilian life for a while, and then was recruited by Allen, his Long Island neighbor, as chief of the CIA's Middle East division. He had written a few articles about the region for the *Saturday Evening Post* and a book about the role of oil there, but had none of the deep cultural knowledge or language skills that distinguished many British agents and diplomats. Yet he showed some of his famous grandfather's adventurous spirit. It is a marvelous twist of history: President Theodore Roosevelt helped usher the United States into the "regime change" era, and half a century later his grandson followed him into the business of deposing governments.

Roosevelt crossed into Iran from Iraq on July 19, 1953, carrying a passport that identified him as James Lochridge. He made his way to Tehran and, working with a handful of American and Iranian agents, quickly set to work. The team bribed journalists and newspaper editors to publish anti-Mossadegh diatribes, paid mullahs to denounce Mossadegh in their sermons, built a network of dissident military commanders, and, after much difficulty, won the fearful shah's cooperation.

While Roosevelt marshaled his forces in Tehran, Foster and Allen coordinated overt and covert pressures on Mossadegh. Foster tightened diplomatic screws and issued grave warnings. On July 28 he told reporters in Washington that "the growing activities of the illegal communist party in Iran, and toleration of those activities, has caused our government great concern." Allen and his team in Tehran, meanwhile, launched the operation of which Foster professed to be ignorant.

It took Roosevelt just a couple of weeks to throw Tehran into chaos. On the night of August 15, he sprung his trap. He sent the elite Imperial

Guard, sworn to obey only the shah, to Mossadegh's house with orders to arrest him. The operation went disastrously wrong. Mossadegh had learned of the plot, and the Imperial Guard, which was to have captured him, was itself captured by loyal soldiers. Upon hearing this news on the radio at six o'clock the next morning, the shah panicked, grabbed a couple of suitcases, and fled to Rome.

This first attempted CIA coup was worse than a failure. Not only did Mossadegh survive, but the shah, America's best Iranian friend, had scurried into exile.

Roosevelt might have quit and returned home in defeat. He still, however, had a key advantage. Mossadegh was a trusting soul, unwise to the ways of the covert world, and never imagined that a CIA officer was in Iran directing the rebellion; he presumed that the shah had been behind it, and that with the shah gone the danger was past. He relaxed security restrictions and released prisoners. Taking advantage of this misjudgment, Roosevelt decided to stay in Tehran and try again. He paid street gangs to terrorize the city, marshaled dissident military units, and, at midday on August 19, helped guide a mob toward Mossadegh's house. Three hundred people were killed in the climactic battle. By dawn the Mossadegh government was no more. The shah returned, reclaimed the Peacock Throne, ruled with increasing repression for a quarter century, and then was overthrown in a revolution that brought fanatically anti-Western clerics to power.

Eisenhower wrote in his diary that Mossadegh's fall had been "a serious defeat" for the Soviets. By one account he "genuinely believed that Russia was poised to enter Iran in 1953, and that only the CIA had prevented a Communist victory." Having directed battles in which thousands were killed, he also marveled that the operation had been carried out with the loss of just a few hundred lives, none of them American. Foster understood what a potent new tool he now had at hand. Allen had shown that he could crush foreign leaders secretly, cheaply, and almost bloodlessly. All wanted to do it again.

6

THE MOST FORTHRIGHT PRO-COMMUNIST

For most of his life, Allen retreated whenever he could to his house on the north shore of Long Island. On the outside it looked much like others nearby. Inside it was dazzlingly distinct. Bright-colored fabrics from Guatemala hung on several walls. A Guatemalan rug lay in front of the fireplace. Delicate Guatemalan figurines decorated the mantelpiece.

Allen had visited Central America during his years at Sullivan & Cromwell, mainly to do legal business for the United Fruit Company. He took Clover, and she fell under the spell of Guatemala's rich culture. The souvenirs they brought back to Long Island made Guatemala a more vivid physical presence in Allen's life than any other foreign country.

In the early 1950s, Allen and his brother began to focus on Guatemala as something more than a banana land and a producer of bright-colored handicrafts. In their Cold War cosmology, it became the place where Moscow's global conspiracy reached closest to American shores, led by a Kremlin puppet masquerading as a nationalist. Drawn to Guatemala by their work for United Fruit, they became arbiters of its fate.

"Some paradox of our nature," the essayist Lionel Trilling has observed, "leads us, when once we have made our fellow men the objects of our enlightened interest, to go on to make them the objects of our pity, then of our wisdom, ultimately of our coercion."

The concept "Guatemala" was an invention of Spanish conquerors, diffuse and aspirational. Quite different was the concept "United Fruit." This company was everything Guatemala wished to be: powerful, independent, skilled at marshaling resources, wise to the ways of the world, and rich enough to provide steady income for all its people. In some countries, governments control and regulate corporations. The opposite was true in Guatemala. United Fruit was the power, Guatemala a subsidiary.

"If the finance minister were to overdraw his account or the archbishop wanted six nuns transported from Germany," *Fortune* reported, "if the president's wife wished her gallstones removed, or the minister's wife liked fresh celery from New Orleans, or the president wanted three blooded cows served by a blooded bull; if anyone wants almost anything, then United Fruit's 'contact man' is the one who can quickly get it."

Sporadic use of violence, sometimes backed by the threat of American military intervention, helped keep this Boston-based company profitable for nearly half a century. For most of its existence it was a prized Sullivan & Cromwell client. Both Foster and Allen did legal work for United Fruit, and both reportedly held substantial blocks of United Fruit stock. Sullivan & Cromwell also represented the two affiliated companies through which United Fruit secured its power over Guatemala: American & Foreign Power Company, which owned Empresa Eléctrica de Guatemala, producer of most of Guatemala's electricity, and International Railways of Central America, which owned its rail network. The J. Henry Schroder Banking Corporation, another longtime Sullivan & Cromwell client, served as financial agent for all three companies.

The one-sided agreements that Sullivan & Cromwell conceived to promote United Fruit's interests in Latin America were legendary. One of them, signed in 1936 with General Jorge Ubico, the dictator of Guatemala, gave the company rule for ninety-nine years over tracts that comprised one-seventh of the country's arable land, as well as control of its only port. These contracts were engineered by the lawyer who had more experience than any other American in the exquisite art of squeezing concessions out of weak countries.

"John Foster Dulles, back in the early days when his law firm of Sullivan & Cromwell represented United Fruit, was reputed to be the author of the actual concessions which the firm negotiated on our behalf," a former United Fruit vice president, Thomas McCann, wrote in his history of the company. "I was told this by Sam G. Baggett, longtime United Fruit general counsel and the man who should have known."

United Fruit's long rule in Guatemala began to crumble in 1944, when reformist officers deposed General Ubico. They called an election, and a democratic regime came to power. It adopted a labor code that set minimum wages and limited the workweek to forty-eight hours.

For decades United Fruit had run its plantations as private fiefs. Now a government was asserting its right to penetrate that domain. A United Fruit executive told the *New York Times* that if this was tolerated, it would certainly lead to "legal and pseudo-legal assaults on foreign enterprises in many places."

President Truman sympathized with United Fruit's plight and authorized initial planning for a CIA coup. Secretary of State Acheson, however, was strongly opposed—by one account he believed "no development in Latin America merited risking the international standing of the United States"—and managed to kill the operation. The banana company could only bide its time until events moved in its direction. They finally did, as Thomas McCann recalled.

"Guatemala's government was the region's weakest, most corrupt, and most pliable," he wrote. "Then something went wrong: a man named Jacobo Arbenz became President."

Arbenz was the son of a Swiss immigrant whose suicide left him without money to pay for college. He entered the military academy, became a brilliant cadet and officer, and in 1944 helped organize the revolution that brought democracy to his country. He served for six years as defense minister, then won the second free election in Guatemalan history.

On March 15, 1951, full of patriotic fervor and just thirty-seven years old, Arbenz stood before a cheering crowd as the presidential sash was draped across his chest. In his inaugural address he committed himself to "three fundamental objectives: to convert our country from a dependent nation with a semi-colonial economy to an economically independent country; to convert Guatemala from a backward country with a predominantly feudal economy into a modern capitalist state; and to make this transformation in a way that will raise the standard of living of the great mass of our people. . . . Foreign capital will always be welcome as long as it adjusts to local conditions, remains always subordinate to Guatemalan laws, cooperates with the economic development of the country, and strictly abstains from intervening in the nation's social and political life."

Short of proclaiming himself a Bolshevik, Arbenz could have said little that would so effectively provoke the wrath of Americans committed to defending transnational capitalism.

After barely a year in office, Arbenz did something that confirmed Washington's worst fears: he won passage of the first serious land reform law in Central American history. It required large landowners to sell the uncultivated part of their holdings to the government, for distribution to peasant families. United Fruit owned more than half a million acres of the country's richest land and left 85 percent uncultivated. It took this law as a declaration of war. So did the Dulles brothers, who enjoyed steady income from United Fruit legal fees and stock dividends. They could not strike back against Arbenz, but looked forward to a time when that might change.

The land reform law need not have sealed Arbenz's fate. It was not even sealed when, five months after it was adopted, American voters elected Dwight Eisenhower to the presidency. But once Eisenhower chose Foster and Allen Dulles to design and carry out his foreign policy, the die was cast. Arbenz became the second monster they went abroad to destroy.

During their first eight months in office, the Dulles brothers were pre-occupied with overthrowing Mossadegh. Once they accomplished this, with barely a pause, they set out against the other world leader who had struck heavy blows against Sullivan & Cromwell clients: Arbenz. These were the two heads of government they arrived in office determined to depose. There is no record of them responding to news of Mossadegh's overthrow with the expression, "One down, one to go," but that was the essence of their reaction.

"On Friday, September 4, 1953, I reported at the White House," Kermit Roosevelt wrote at the end of his account of Operation Ajax. "[My report] was, I thought, very well received. One of my audience seemed almost alarmingly enthusiastic. John Foster Dulles was leaning back in his chair. Despite his posture, he was anything but sleepy. His eyes were gleaming; he seemed to be purring like a giant cat. Clearly, he was not only enjoying what he was hearing, but my instinct told me that he was planning as well. . . . Within weeks I was offered command of a Guatemala operation already in the making."

Roosevelt declined the offer. That did nothing to slow the Guatemala plot, but something else happened around the same time that might have. The chief justice of the United States, Fred M. Vinson, died of a heart attack, and Eisenhower offered Foster his job "because of my belief that he was one of the few men who could fill the post with distinction." Rarely has an American been given such an extraordinary choice: continue as secretary of state or become chief justice.

"He eliminated himself instantly and unequivocally," Eisenhower wrote in his memoir. "He said, in effect, 'I have been interested since boyhood in the diplomatic and foreign affairs of our nation. I'm highly complimented by the implication that I might be suited to the position of chief justice, but I assure you that my interests lie with the duties of my present post. As long as you are happy with my performance here, I have no interest in any other.'"

Foster's decision to remain as secretary of state opened the way for the appointment of Earl Warren as chief justice. If he had decided otherwise and left the State Department, Allen would undoubtedly have continued to press the anti-Arbenz project. Whether another secretary of state would have shared his passion for it is an intriguing question for which there can be no answer.

As Allen plotted, Foster relentlessly warned Americans about the threats they faced from a hostile world. He denounced the Soviet Union, "Red China," and creeping neutralism. In Europe he rejected every proposal for demilitarization or neutral zones, and worked instead to rearm Germany and strengthen NATO.

Forged in the bazaar of the Paris peace negotiations nearly half a century earlier, where statesmen bartered the fate of nations, and shaped by decades of business diplomacy, Foster accepted the traditional definition of the world that mattered: Europe, the United States, and a couple of East Asian powers. The nationalist passion sweeping through Asia, Africa, and Latin America was foreign to his experience. He considered it threatening but never sought to understand it on its own terms, apart from the Cold War context.

At the end of 1953, Foster accompanied Eisenhower to Bermuda for a summit with Prime Minister Joseph Laniel of France and a strikingly feeble Winston Churchill. The atmosphere was tense. Stalin had been dead for eight months, and the interim Soviet leader, Georgi Malenkov, was sending out peace feelers. Churchill and Laniel proposed another summit to which Malenkov would be invited. Foster was adamantly opposed and blocked the idea.

"This fellow preaches like a Methodist minister," Churchill complained privately. "His bloody text is always the same: that nothing but evil can come out of a meeting with Malenkov. Dulles is a terrible handicap. Ten years ago I could have dealt with him. Even as it is I have not been defeated by this bastard. I have been humiliated by my own decay."

From Bermuda, Foster traveled to Europe to press his no-negotiations case, but his visit only deepened the transatlantic divide. He set off a storm of protest in France by warning that if its National Assembly did not ratify a treaty creating a new military alliance with a supranational army, called the European Defense Community, the United States would begin "an agonizing reappraisal" of its commitment to Western Europe. This threat rang immediately false—there was no real prospect of Washington abandoning Europe—but many in France were outraged. In a last-ditch effort to save the treaty, Allen gave one of his salaried informants, a member of the French cabinet, half a million dollars to bribe members of the assembly. It proved insufficient. Fearing that Foster's militancy might drag Europe back toward war, the assembly rejected the treaty, and the European Defense Community was stillborn.

"Employed to inspire the allies to draw together in the face of the Soviet threat, rhetorical diplomacy actually endangered the unity of the Western alliance," the State Department historian Chris Tudda concluded years later. "In their zeal to cast European interests as part of their larger scheme to confront the Soviet threat and increase the security of the Free World, Eisenhower and [Foster] Dulles instead weakened European confidence in their ability to provide that security. The European public and press resisted Washington's efforts to 'educate' them, and reacted angrily whenever the United States tried to coax Europe to follow its lead."

Less than a month after Foster came up with the concept of "agonizing reappraisal," he unveiled a second trademark phrase: "massive retaliation." This, he warned in a speech to his old friends at the Council on Foreign Relations, was what the United States was ready to rain down on Moscow in response to a provocation anywhere in the world. It too sounded like an empty threat, since no one believed the United States would launch nuclear war over a border skirmish somewhere. It was also an imprecise transcription of Foster's words, since his actual threat was "massive retaliatory power." The same thing happened to the third phrase with which he is permanently associated: the "rollback" of Communism. He preferred to call his encouragement of anti-Communist revolt a "liberation policy." In any case it too was rhetorical, as his failure to support rebelling workers in East Berlin had shown. All three of the concepts that Americans associated most directly with Foster—rollback, the agonizing reappraisal, and massive retaliation—were devoid of serious meaning. During his years in power, the United States never actively sought the "liberation" of nations under Communist rule, never considered a "reappraisal" of support for Western Europe, and was never prepared to use nuclear weapons in response to a local proxy war.

Foster recognized the gap between his rhetoric and the reality of American foreign policy. It did not trouble him, because he believed that portraying the Soviets as unrelentingly evil was a way of sharpening people's fear and thereby promoting readiness and national unity. Eisenhower agreed. In public, both men insisted that they were open to the possibility of accords with the Soviet Union, but in fact they believed any substantial agreement was impossible. Foster told the National Security Council that disarmament negotiations were an "operation in public relations." Eisenhower encouraged the secretary of state to come up with proposals that would have "some real appeal, both to our own people and the people of the world," but they agreed that these should not be truly new departures—only old proposals in "different packages" tied together with "different colored ribbons."

"The perception that the USSR was using negotiations to rally public opinion against American intransigence, and to pressure the United States to engage in unsafeguarded nuclear disarmament, led American policy makers to discount Soviet proposals as mere propaganda," one historian has written. "US officials believed that if they accepted a Soviet proposal, they would add respectability to the Soviet leadership and enhance Moscow's prestige. In their view, consenting to a Soviet initiative was tantamount to receiving a propaganda defeat before world opinion. . . . The objective became out-maneuvering the opponent in the battle for public opinion; positions were put forward more to win public acclaim than to pave the way for compromise at the bargaining table."

During their early years in office, Foster and Allen perceived imminent Communist threats to four far-flung "outposts of freedom": Iran,

Guatemala, Korea, and Indochina. Both, however, had been conditioned by education and experience to consider Europe the center of the world. That led them to vivid fears, not only because Europe seemed vulnerable to a possible Soviet attack, but because many Europeans wished for conciliation rather than confrontation. Staggered by the carnage of World War II, they resisted Washington's rhetoric of fear and enmity, and often elected leaders who sought to calm tensions on their continent rather than sharpen its division.

For years Foster had promoted the idea of European unity. After Churchill declared in 1946 that an "Iron Curtain" had descended across the continent, Foster adjusted his vision to mean Western European unity—if not political, then at least military. By the time he took office in 1953, this imperative seemed to him more urgent than ever, both because of the Soviet threat and because President Eisenhower's dogged devotion to balanced budgets made it impossible for the United States to blanket the continent with troops. His sense of urgency fueled his campaign for the European Defense Community, which failed after France and Britain refused to participate. Neither country's leaders shared Foster's view— especially after Stalin's death—that the Soviet Union was implacably hostile and therefore negotiations were pointless.

With both of America's main European allies dubious about Foster's approach to Communism, he was thrilled to find a soul mate in Chancellor Konrad Adenauer of West Germany. No statesman was ever as close to Foster as Adenauer. This closeness extended to Allen, who with Adenauer's blessing built strong ties between the CIA and the West German secret services, and to their sister Eleanor, who was one of the most prominent Americans in Germany during the 1950s. She was the first member of the family Adenauer met, over lunch at the beginning of 1953.

"Adenauer wanted to know all he could about John Foster Dulles," Eleanor wrote in her memoir. "I told him that Foster had a new, but close, relationship with our President. I said that he had also been in Germany a number of times. . . . That lunch was my first encounter with this truly great man, who was to be a friend to me and my brothers."

Soon afterward, Foster arrived in Bonn and met Adenauer for the first time. Their compatibility began with personality. Both were cool and formal, rarely entertained, confided in no one, and followed moral codes shaped by traditional Christianity. Ideology drew them closer. Adenauer believed that West Germany should tie itself irrevocably to the United States and do whatever necessary to maintain their alliance—a policy that became known as *Westbindung*. He was the only European leader, and one of the few in the world, who shared Foster's anti-Communist militancy and denounced the Soviet Union in terms Foster could approve, as when he described it as wielding the "cataclysmic powers of ungodly totalitarianism." So close was their relationship that in advance of the West German election in late 1953, Foster warned publicly that the defeat of Adenauer's Christian Democratic Union would be "disastrous" for the West. Opposition leaders protested, but Adenauer was handily re-elected. Foster visited him more often than any other world leader, a total of thirteen times during his six years in office.

Adenauer's friendliness allowed Allen to proceed with one of his most ambitious early projects, the digging of a tunnel from West Berlin to a point in the East from which the CIA could tap Soviet-bloc communication systems. Allen had admitted to the National Security Council that his agency's understanding of the Soviet Union was crippled by "shortcomings of a serious nature." The first spy he sent to Moscow was seduced by his housekeeper, who turned out to be an agent of the Soviet KGB, photographed in bed with her, blackmailed, and summarily fired when the truth emerged. The second was quickly discovered and expelled. Then, at the end of 1953, one of Allen's men in Berlin, assigned to photograph letters purloined from the East Berlin post office, came across plans for a new underground switching station near the East-West border. Allen shared this discovery with his British counterpart, Sir John Sinclair, and they agreed to dig together.

While this operation was under way, Allen launched another promising covert project. At a dinner party he heard a University of Chicago professor rave about new developments in high-altitude photography. He called the professor to his office, gave him a series of tests, and became a believer. A team that he assembled, led by James Killian, the president of the Massachusetts Institute of Technology, and including Edwin Land, the inventor of Polaroid photography, shaped what became a large-scale operation to spy on Communist countries by taking photographs from aircraft flying far above their territories. It would produce valuable intelligence, but would also lead to one of the great foreign policy debacles of the Eisenhower era.

During the year that stretched from mid-1953 to mid-1954, Allen was occupied most intently with the plot against Arbenz. Tensions in Guatemala rose steadily. The Arbenz government expropriated nearly four hundred thousand acres of fallow land owned by United Fruit and offered to pay in compensation what United Fruit had declared the land to be worth for tax purposes: $1,185,115.70. In reply, the State Department—not the company—scornfully demanded more than ten times that.

"This law has affected United Fruit Company land . . . that has been fallow and unproductive for many years and has provided no benefit to the company or its stockholders," the Guatemalan government insisted. "This permanent lack of production has harmed our people and our national economy. . . . The Government of Guatemala maintains friendly relations with all countries, naturally including the United States, and notes with concern that the monopoly interests of a company that has caused so much harm to Guatemala are harming the cordial relations between the Government of Guatemala and the Government of the United States, and threaten to harm them further. . . . The Government of Guatemala declares that it rejects the claim of the Government of the United States."

Foster and Allen were not accustomed to being addressed this way by leaders of small countries. Nor were others in the Eisenhower administration, several of whom also had ties to United Fruit.

John Moors Cabot, the assistant secretary of state for inter-American affairs, came from a family that held United Fruit stock, and his brother, Thomas, had been the company's president. Another member of their family, Henry Cabot Lodge, the American ambassador to the United Nations, had defended the company so vigorously during his years as a U.S. senator from Massachusetts that he became known as "the senator from United Fruit." Robert Cutler, the president's national security adviser, was a former member of United Fruit's board of directors. Undersecretary of State Walter Bedell Smith spoke of his wish to join the United Fruit board of directors, and did so after leaving the State Department at the end of 1954. Ann Whitman, Eisenhower's private secretary, was married to United Fruit's publicity director, Ed Whitman, who had produced a film called *Why the Kremlin Hates Bananas*. No American company has ever been so well connected to the White House.

In the middle of the twentieth century the United States was the world's behemoth, richer and more powerful than any other country. Its army was 140 times the size of Guatemala's, its territory ninety times larger, its population fifty times greater. American companies were the decisive factor in Guatemalan life, while Guatemala had no influence in Washington. The United States was tied through a web of alliances to many of the world's mightiest powers. Guatemala was surrounded by a constellation of hostile tyrants: Anastasio Somoza in Nicaragua, Rafael Trujillo in the Dominican Republic, Fulgencio Batista in Cuba, François "Papa Doc" Duvalier in Haiti, and Marcos Pérez Jiménez in Venezuela. Despite this imbalance, the Dulles brothers considered Arbenz a grave threat to the United States.

Many in Washington were guided by a conviction that spread through the corridors of American power after the 1948 "constitutional coup" in Czechoslovakia: any government that allowed Communists even the slightest influence would sooner or later fall to Moscow's power. Four Communists held seats in Guatemala's fifty-six-member Congress. Two others were close advisers to Arbenz.

"In Czechoslovakia, the government appointed a Communist interior minister, and then one day there was a reshuffle and suddenly the Communists were in power," one CIA veteran recalled years later. "The lesson we drew was that you can't let any Communist into power in any position, because somehow that would be used to take over the government. And if a country didn't follow that rule, it became our enemy."

At the end of 1953 the CIA produced its first proposal for the operation it called PB/Success, "a general, over-all plan of combined overt and covert operations of major proportions" in Guatemala. It began with a list of Arbenz's transgressions. He had turned Guatemala into "the leading base of operations for Moscow-influenced Communism in Central America," installed a "Communist dominated bureaucracy," and pursued "an aggressively hardening anti-US policy targeted directly against American interests."

"CIA has placed top operational priority on an effort to reduce and possibly eliminate Communist power in Guatemala," the paper concluded. "Appropriate authorization has been received to permit close and prompt cooperation with the Departments of Defense, State, and other Government agencies in order to support the CIA task."

This authorization could only have come from Eisenhower. Soon after receiving it, Allen told his men that this operation was "the most vitally important one in the agency."

"Allen Dulles became the executive agent for Project PB/Success [and] kept in close touch with the planning through personal assistants," the intelligence historian John Prados has written. "The key conversations took place in Allen Dulles's own office. . . . [He] rounded off the CIA budget to a cool $3 million when he went to the White House to ask for the money."

Arbenz, unaware of these proceedings, continued to speak defiantly. Early in 1954 he declared that "it is entirely up to Guatemala to decide what kind of democracy she should have," and demanded that outside powers treat Latin American countries as more than "objects of monopolistic investments and sources of raw materials." *Time* called this "the most forthright pro-Communist declaration the President has ever uttered."

As planning for PB/Success continued, Allen launched another operation in Central America that was smaller in scale though arguably more damning. He and Foster had developed a strong dislike for the region's other outspoken democrat, President José Figueres of Costa Rica. Figueres was elected to the presidency in 1953 after defeating a Communist-supported uprising, which should have made him a hero in Washington, especially since he had been educated in the United States, married an American woman, and deeply absorbed New Deal principles. Once in office, however, he promoted land reform and abolished the Costa Rican army. Worst of all, he ceaselessly denounced Central American and Caribbean dictators who were allies of the United States, encouraged plots against them, and sheltered many plotters, including Communists. Costa Rican landowners who dreamed of overthrowing Figueres approached Allen. He was sympathetic. In mid-1954 Senator Mike Mansfield of Montana publicly accused the CIA of tapping Figueres's telephone, an offense that he said could have "tremendous impact" on the region. This did not stop Allen from encouraging the anti-Figueres plotters, but they failed for two reasons. First, Allen was preoccupied with deposing Arbenz in nearby Guatemala; second, since there was no army in Costa Rica, he had no instrument through which to carry out a coup. Nonetheless, this episode reflected something disheartening about the policies Foster and Allen pursued in America's "backyard." They embraced the region's dictators while working to undermine its few democracies.

"Our main enemy," Figueres recalled after peacefully leaving office in 1958, "was Mr. John Foster Dulles in his defending corrupt dictatorships."

One of the oddest aspects of the Dulles brothers' approach to Latin America was that as they assaulted the leaders of Guatemala and Costa Rica, they happily accepted a president of Bolivia who was in some ways more radical than either one. The Bolivian leader, Victor Paz Estenssoro, came to power in 1952 after a violent rebellion supported by armed workers and powerful Marxist factions—rather than through an election, as Arbenz and Figueres had. In his first May Day speech, Paz accused the United States of trying to sabotage Bolivia's economy by manipulating the world market for tin, the country's main export, and pledged to respond by building closer ties to Communist countries. Soon afterward he nationalized his country's strategic tin and tungsten resources. Yet the official position of the United States, as pronounced by Assistant Secretary of State John Moors Cabot, was that the Paz government "is sincere in desiring social progress," while Arbenz was "openly playing the Communist game." A State Department spokesman justified American aid to Bolivia with the odd explanation that the Paz government was "Marxist rather than Communist." As he spoke, the Eisenhower administration was tightening its noose around Guatemala.

Scholars who have pondered this paradox offer various explanations. "Bolivia was far from the United States and from the Panama Canal, and there was no chance to train an army of emigres to invade the country or establish another government," one has written. "Guatemala was nearby; it had a seacoast; there was an available alternative regime; and local satraps in Nicaragua or Honduras could be suborned or persuaded to provide help for an invasion. . . . The Bolivian leaders . . . eliminated all Communists from government offices. . . . The Guatemalan leaders showed no such flexibility, no comparable understanding of the obligations of neighborliness, no recognition of the fact that, to avoid destruction, they must evict Communists from their administration."

The United States had not deposed a Central American leader in decades, and Arbenz may have believed it was out of practice or no longer in that business. If so, he miscalculated. Like Mossadegh, he failed to grasp the intensity of the Cold War fears that had come to envelop Washington.

He saw his reform program as no more radical than the New Deal—without realizing that many in the new Republican elite, including Foster, considered the New Deal to have been an abomination.

Foster and Allen were driven to attack Arbenz for much the same reasons they had attacked Mossadegh. The world that had shaped them was based on the premise that powerful countries, especially the United States, had the right to set the terms of their commerce with countries whose resources and markets they coveted. Mossadegh and Arbenz rejected this premise. Their crackdowns on corporate power led Foster and Allen to presume that they were serving Soviet ends. Two reasons for striking at them—defending corporate power and resisting Communism—blended into one.

Declassified transcripts refer to only one moment when a State Department diplomat, left unnamed, questioned this consensus. This foreign service officer suggested that Arbenz might be only a homegrown nationalist unconnected to the Kremlin. Before he could say more, Undersecretary Walter Bedell Smith, who was always loyal to Eisenhower, cut him off.

"You don't know what you're talking about," Smith told the offender. "Forget those stupid ideas and let's get on with our work."

Thousands of new officers joined the CIA during the 1950s, but because the agency was still highly clandestine, Allen never considered conventional hiring techniques. Instead he stuck with the agency's traditional recruiters: college professors, deans, and presidents. This ensured that some of America's "best men" would be discreetly brought into covert service. It also fostered an inbreeding that helped seal the agency into a cocoon of groupthink and overconfidence.

Agents who joined while Allen was director felt the thrill of setting off on a grand crusade. One recalled it half a century later:

> The CIA recruiter asked my college president if there were any students who might be interested in the CIA as a career. The president selected several political science majors and me, an English major. I'm sure he chose me because he knew I was a devious son of a bitch. Before becoming president of the student body in my junior year, I had been involved in all kinds of hell-raising, which continued to some extent even after I became student body president. There was no other reason. I hadn't read

a newspaper in years, being immersed totally in such writers as Chaucer, Milton, Shakespeare, and Yeats. I had no idea what the CIA was. I was, though, an Air Force ROTC cadet, which meant I had a three-year obligation to serve in the Air Force after graduation. The recruiter was impressive, and I was inclined to pursue it further, but the three-year commitment stood in the way. When the recruiter told me he'd get me out of my three-year ROTC commitment half-way through, I saluted and told him I was ready. Everything worked out the way he promised.

It was a patriotic feel-good function for people in academia to steer people to the CIA. The Ivy League schools were notorious in that respect. Nearly every college had a contact that helped "spot" likely recruits for the CIA. Right from the outset after recruitment you felt a little special, perhaps because you were constantly being told you were special and doing special things for your country. . . .

Everyone revered [Allen]. He was seen as the father of the entire organization. He was God. One of the first things we were told was that the CIA was not a military organization and that you were not expected to say "sir" or salute. The only person for whom you had to rise to your feet when he entered the room was Allen Dulles. He was called "Mr. Director" and "Sir."

He was known for spending a lot of time with the station chiefs, one by one, when they returned to headquarters for some reason, discussing what was happening in their countries. His experience in Switzerland was about that kind of thing: slow, quiet, personal contact. He was great at that. He always insisted on a personal relationship with his station chiefs. Whether he was up to running a big international organization, which the agency became during his term—I don't think so. At least it would not seem so, given how badly botched the Bay of Pigs operation was.

He had another endearing trait: whenever he had to be briefed on an operational case, he insisted that the case officer directly in charge of the operation be present, no matter how low his rank. Dulles wanted access to the operational detail, and he feared higher level officers doing the briefing would sift it out either deliberately or out of ignorance. Lower level officers naturally very much appreciated this attitude. He was a very quiet, soft-spoken guy, not a voluble person or a table-thumper. He was very much an Eastern Establishment gentleman. Even though he was not a terribly riveting person, everyone hung on his every word. He was totally at ease, as if he didn't feel any need to explain himself or impress you.

Like other recruits, this young man was sent for training to a sprawling camp that may have been the world's largest and most elaborate school for spies. Located on a nine-thousand-acre military reservation officially called Camp Peary, near Williamsburg, Virginia, it was known in the agency simply, and even affectionately, as "the farm." During World War II it had been used as a training base for Navy Seabees, then as a secret jail for prisoners of war. For a few years afterward it was a forestry preserve. The CIA took it over in 1951, and within a couple of years Allen had transformed it into a center for advanced study of the black arts. Here agents-to-be learned how to wear disguises, pick locks, enter secured buildings, plant listening devices, use invisible ink, and surreptitiously open and reseal letters and packages. Then they graduated to techniques of illegal border crossings, which they practiced at full-scale mock-ups of crossings between countries in Western and Eastern Europe, complete with armed "guards" and snarling watchdogs. They learned how to recruit informants and supervise their work. Most were taught paramilitary skills ranging from parachute jumping to the use of explosives and small arms. On trips to nearby Richmond, they practiced urban techniques like passing messages and eluding surveillance. Some were subjected to extreme pressures like sleep deprivation and mock executions.

Many graduates of "the farm" went on to join the Office of Policy Coordination, which according to one of its longtime officers, Joseph Burkholder Smith, "was a cover title that disguised the fact that the real missions of the office were covert psychological warfare, covert political action, and covert military action." In his memoir, *Portrait of a Cold Warrior*, Smith recalls what a briefing officer told him and other new recruits when they were hired.

"You've just joined the Cold War arm of the US government," the officer said. "We're not in the intelligence business in this department. We're an executive action arm of the White House. . . . Some people call us the 'dirty tricks' department, but that's too superficial a thing to say. What we are doing is carrying out the covert foreign policy of the United States government. Obviously we can't let the Soviets or Chinese or anyone else know this is the case, but everything we do is authorized by the President's own National Security Council, and organizationally speaking, our chain of command is through the NSC directly to the President."

As Allen's power reached a peak, he faced his first criticism from

Congress. In a speech to what one reporter called a "hushed and attentive" Senate, Mike Mansfield delivered the sharpest public critique of the CIA that had ever been heard in Washington. Since the agency was "freed from practically every ordinary form of Congressional check," Mansfield said, no one could be sure whether it was "staying within the limits established by law" or exceeding them to become "an instrument of policy." The chairman of the House Appropriations Committee, Representative John Taber, who according to one historian had an "aggressive and suspicious nature," forced the CIA to answer a long series of questions and summoned Allen for extended testimony. Taber concluded that the CIA was inefficient and wasteful, and he imposed a temporary hiring freeze. Mansfield went further, proposing a bill to create a "watchdog commission" that would oversee the CIA, for which he found twenty-seven cosponsors. Allen resisted fiercely. With the help of friends in the Senate—including Leverett Saltonstall of Massachusetts, home to United Fruit—he managed to derail the bill.

In quick succession during that spring of 1954, the United States tested a massively powerful hydrogen bomb at Bikini Atoll in the Pacific; Vietnamese Communists led by Ho Chi Minh won decisive battles in their war against France; a "loyalty board" in Washington questioned the country's most famous nuclear scientist, J. Robert Oppenheimer, about charges that he was a Soviet agent; and televised hearings exposed millions of Americans to Senator McCarthy's charges that Communists had infiltrated the United States Army. Allen was able to persuade Congress that this was no moment to rein in the CIA.

"Never before or since has the CIA had more support from the State Department, or, because Secretary Dulles was so powerful, more freedom to infiltrate U.S. embassies, consulates, and the U.S. Information Service offices in foreign countries," the biographer Leonard Mosley has written. "It had complete freedom to undertake projects of enormous tactical or strategic significance with little or no oversight of its expenditure or the nature of its activities. In 1954 the CIA had four hundred of its agents operating out of London alone, controlled not only by the local station chief but by a resident director, or senior representative, reporting directly to Allen Dulles. . . . The [National Security] Act of 1947 had set up the National Security Council to oversee operations in which the Agency's many arms were now engaged, but in the two years since Allen had been operating as director of the CIA, the Council had no real control over the activities that he ordered and approved—manifold activities, which were protected from interference by Foster's brotherly wing."

Despite his political successes, Allen faced private difficulties. His marriage remained unhappy. Clover began spending extended periods traveling. Allen's legendary libido slowed; he had an affair with a woman who worked for him, and perhaps others, but he was not prowling with anything near the enthusiasm he had once shown. Attacks of gout sometimes forced him to take to bed. Drugs he took for his condition had painful side effects. Nonetheless his enthusiasm for work never flagged. Once a reporter asked him what the CIA was.

"The State Department for unfriendly countries," he replied.

Most of the officers Allen chose to run his Guatemala operation reflected the insularity of the early CIA. They came from elite backgrounds and were connected to each other through webs that ran through elite boarding schools, colleges, and law schools, the OSS, Wall Street law firms and investment banks, the Council on Foreign Relations, and cocktail parties on the north shore of Long Island at which, by one account, they drank "phenomenal" quantities of alcohol. Allen liberated these men from what might otherwise have been humdrum lives and brought them into an incomparably exciting world. They joined the CIA not to observe, reflect, analyze, and ponder, but to plot, act, fight, confront, strike, and subvert. Most spoke no Spanish and had never set foot in Guatemala.

The field commander of PB/Success would be Albert Haney, a former Chicago businessman who headed the CIA station in Seoul and had directed paramilitary forays into North Korea. The handsome and well-spoken Tracy Barnes, whose pedigree ran through the Ivy League, the Office of Strategic Services, and the Wall Street law firm of Carter Ledyard & Milburn, would direct the crucial psychological-warfare aspect of the plot. His chief propagandists would be David Atlee Phillips, assigned to create a fake "Voice of Liberation" radio station that would broadcast disinformation into Guatemala, and the future Watergate burglar E. Howard Hunt, who produced anti-Arbenz cartoons, posters, pamphlets, and newspaper articles for use in Guatemala and the rest of Latin America. Above them the chain of command ran through J. C. King, chief of the Western Hemisphere division; deputy director for plans Frank Wisner; Richard Bissell, Allen's special assistant; and at the top of the pyramid Allen himself.

With his covert team in place, Allen had to confront one last personnel problem. The CIA station chief in Guatemala, Birch O'Neill, had proven reluctant to plant tendentious propaganda in the local press, did not believe that Arbenz's land reform law was communistic, and seemed, as John Prados has written, "too cautious for a swashbuckling covert action." Allen liked to believe that each of his station chiefs knew more about the country where he served than any other American. This one, however, did not see Guatemala as he did. Following the pattern he set when his man in Tehran opposed the coup against Mossadegh, he removed O'Neill and replaced him with an officer who was less experienced but more obedient.

As Allen was ensuring that his man on the scene would obey orders, Foster did the same. The American ambassador to Guatemala, Rudolf Schoenfeld, was intensely anti-Arbenz but also a professional diplomat with thirty years in the foreign service. Foster concluded he would be hesitant to help overthrow a government to which he was accredited, and replaced him with John Peurifoy, who in his brief tenure at the State Department had earned a reputation as one of the most outspokenly undiplomatic of American diplomats.

Foster then removed two other Latin American specialists who he feared might doubt the conspiracy. First to go was John Moors Cabot, the assistant secretary of state for inter-American affairs, who was a United Fruit stockholder and staunch anti-Communist but considered the Guatemalan situation "very ticklish" because "there was a good deal of sentiment in Latin America that the government of Guatemala was leftist, yes, but not Communist." Then Foster replaced the American ambassador in Honduras, John Draper Erwin, who knew the country intimately, with Whiting Willauer, a veteran of clandestine air operations over China.

Having assembled his diplomatic team, Foster set out to obtain some kind of international sanction for what he and Allen planned to do—without explicitly revealing what that was. The Organization of American States, which was headquartered in Washington and largely submissive to the U.S. government, had planned a summit in Caracas, Venezuela, and he decided to attend. At the climactic session, he gave a dramatic speech warning that Latin America was under attack "by the apparatus of international Communism, acting under orders from Moscow."

"There is ample room for national differences and for tolerance between the political institutions of the different American States," he said. "But there is no place here for political interests which serve alien masters."

The chief Guatemalan delegate, Guillermo Toriello, replied that "conspirators and the foreign monopolies that support them" were attacking his government because it was seeking "to put an end to feudalism, colonialism, and the unjust exploitation of its poorest citizens." The *New York Times* reported that applause following his speech lasted twice as long as that given to Foster. One delegate told *Time* that Toriello "said many of the things some of the rest of us would like to say if we dared."

In the end, the power of the United States, which Foster applied in a series of private meetings, proved overwhelming, and on March 28 the OAS approved his resolution. It declared that "the domination or control of the political institutions of any American state by the international Communist movement . . . would call for appropriate action in accordance with existing treaties."

The Caracas resolution was a masterpiece of diplomatic legerdemain. Toriello later marveled at its ingenuity.

"Asking other American republics to take joint action against Guatemala in any way would appear to be what it really was: interference in the internal affairs of a member nation in clear violation of the basic principles of the inter-American system," he wrote. "Happily for the State Department, Mr. Dulles's talent, so successfully proven in various diplomatic triumphs in Europe and Asia, managed to square the circle with a clever solution: in order not to be accused of intervening, let us say that there has been a foreign intervention in an American nation and that we are coming to its aid. Let us call the hateful nationalist-democratic movement in Guatemala 'communist intervention' and, claiming that we are moved by the great democratic tradition of the United States and the need to save 'Christian civilization,' liberate that country from this foreign aggression."

PB/Success would have proceeded regardless of what the OAS decided, but the Caracas resolution gave the plot a fig leaf of legality. The *Washington Post* hailed the resolution as "a striking victory for freedom," and the *New York Times* called it "a triumph for Secretary Dulles, for the United States, and for common sense in the Western hemisphere." President Eisenhower said at a press conference that it was "designed to protect, and not to impair, the inalienable right of each American state freely to choose its own form of government and economic system."

As the date for launching PB/Success drew near, Allen visited its base of operations, set up in a complex of unused hangars at an air force base in Opa Locka, Florida. It was bustling with activity. CIA-contracted pilots were preparing to fly bombing raids over Guatemala. David Atlee Phillips was writing scripts for radio messages aimed at convincing Guatemalans that a full-scale rebellion was under way. Other agents were building a legend around Carlos Castillo Armas, the cashiered Guatemalan colonel the CIA had chosen to command its phantom "liberation army." This was one of the largest bases the CIA had ever built. Allen was thrilled.

"Continue the good work and give 'em hell!" he told his men.

Allen understood that Arbenz remained popular in Guatemala, and feared that people might rise up to defend him when the attack began. To prevent that, he sought to capture their minds. A decade earlier, during his collaboration with Carl Gustav Jung in Switzerland, he had speculated on the possibilities of a "marriage between espionage and psychology." In Guatemala he consummated it.

The essence of PB/Success was not military or political but psychological. Allen knew that his ragtag "liberation army" would hardly be able to win a battle, much less a war. His plan was to destabilize Guatemala so fully that military commanders would conclude they had no choice other than to overthrow Arbenz. This required him to dig deep into his tactical arsenal.

American hearts and minds had already been won. Thanks largely to a brilliantly executed propaganda campaign paid for by United Fruit and directed by the legendary opinion-maker Edward Bernays, press coverage of Arbenz in the United States was overwhelmingly negative. When a *New York Times* reporter in Guatemala, Sydney Gruson, began filing stories about the benefits of land reform, Allen quietly protested, and the *Times*'s publisher, Arthur Hays Sulzberger, obligingly had Gruson recalled. Even when Guatemala erupted in violence, no newspaper suggested that the United States might be involved. The phrase "Central Intelligence Agency" had rarely appeared in print and would have been unfamiliar to most Americans.

Although Allen and his friends at United Fruit had managed to turn Arbenz into a demon for most Americans, they had a harder time persuading Guatemalans. Techniques the CIA had used before seemed unpromising. False or misleading articles in the press would be of limited value since most Guatemalans were illiterate. Fake radio broadcasts would reach only those who owned radios—about one of every fifty. Bombs dropped on military targets would frighten only those who lived nearby. Allen looked for another way to mobilize the emotions of Guatemala's poor masses. He found it in their spiritual soul.

Religious belief is deeply woven into the human psyche, and powerful figures have long sought to turn it to their benefit. Rarely in American history have they done so as successfully as during the 1950s.

The rise of John Foster Dulles, an elder of the Presbyterian Church who often denounced Communism as an "alien faith," was hardly the only reflection of this surge in public religiosity. Church attendance rates rose steadily. President Eisenhower, who came from a family of Mennonites and Jehovah's Witnesses, accepted baptism as a Presbyterian soon after taking office and, in a nationally televised speech endorsing the American Legion's "Back to God" campaign, asserted that "without God, there could be no American form of government nor an American way of life." His cabinet voted to open each meeting with a prayer. A new Revised Standard Version of the Bible appeared in 1953 and sold an astonishing twenty-six million copies within a year. It was closely followed on the best-seller list by *The Power of Positive Thinking* by Norman Vincent Peale, who proudly proclaimed that "no one has more contempt for communism than I have" and advised "companionship with Jesus Christ" as the best defense against it. Another evangelist, Billy Graham, who preached on national radio every Sunday and wrote a column that was syndicated in 125 newspapers, declared that Communism was "inspired, directed, and motivated by the devil himself, who has declared war on Almighty God." The actor and singer Pat Boone announced that he would refuse to kiss his leading ladies on-screen for religious reasons. Congress passed a bill adding the phrase "under God" to the Pledge of Allegiance, and then another making "In God We Trust" the nation's official motto.

Since early childhood, the Dulles brothers had been steeped in the power of religious faith. As adults they saw how deeply it permeated life and politics. Since no institution in Guatemala had as direct a tie to as many ordinary people as the Roman Catholic Church, Allen decided to try tapping its power.

The CIA had no direct channel to Archbishop Mariano Rossell y Arellano of Guatemala, but its indirect channel was ideal. The most prominent Catholic prelate in the United States, Francis Cardinal Spellman of New York, was not only outspokenly anti-Communist, but also a crafty global power broker with deep contacts throughout Latin America. Among his friends were three dictators—Batista, Trujillo, and Somoza—who detested Arbenz. Spellman had a special interest in Guatemala, not only because Archbishop Rossell y Arellano shared his political views—he admired Francisco Franco and considered land reform "completely communistic"—but also because of Guatemalan history. In the 1870s Guatemala had been the first Latin American country to embrace the principles of anticlericalism: lay education, civil marriage, limits on the number of foreign-born priests, and a ban on political activity by the clergy. The Church had an old score to settle there.

"An official of the Central Intelligence Agency approached Spellman in 1954 with a relatively simple request," one of his biographers has written. "The agent wanted him to arrange a 'clandestine contact' between one of the CIA men in Guatemala and Archbishop Mariano Rossell y Arellano. . . . Thus, as during the Italian elections, the Church and the U.S. government joined forces. Spellman decided to help the Dulles brothers overthrow the Arbenz government. . . . He acted swiftly. After Spellman's meeting with the CIA agent, a pastoral letter was read on April 9, 1954, in all Guatemalan churches."

The pastoral letter was a masterpiece of propaganda, steeped in the vocabulary of faith, fear, and patriotism.

> At this moment, we once again raise our voice to alert Catholics that the worst atheistic doctrine of all time—anti-Christian Communism—is continuing its brazen advance in our country, masquerading as a movement of social reform for the needy classes. . . .
>
> The honorable Guatemalan nation must oppose those who are suffocating our freedom, people without a nation, the scum of the earth, who have repaid Guatemala's generous hospitality by preaching class hatred with the goal of completing the pillage and destruction of our country. These words from your Pastor are to bring Catholics into a just and dignified national campaign against Communism. The people of Guatemala must rise up like a single man against this enemy of God and the nation. . . .

Who can uproot it from our land? The grace of God can do anything—if you Catholics, wherever you are, by every means given to us as
free beings, in a hemisphere not yet subjected to the Soviet dictatorship,
and with the sacred freedom given to us by the Son of God, fight this
gospel that threatens our religion and Guatemala. Remember that
Communism is atheism and atheism is anti-patriotic. . . . Every Catholic
should fight Communism for the simple reason that he is Catholic.
Christian life is at the heart of our campaign and our crusade.

This broadside, which was reprinted the following morning in Guatemalan newspapers, had a profound impact. Ordinary people who had
until then admired Arbenz heard for the first time that he was in fact their
enemy. Most important, the warning came from their pastors, who many
considered veritable messengers of God. It had a deep, transformational
effect on Guatemala's collective psyche. Overjoyed by this success, CIA
operatives in Opa Locka directed their Guatemala team to use religious-
based propaganda "on a continuous and rapidly increasing scale."

"Underscore fear that commies will interfere with religious instruction in schools," they advised. "Awaken popular revulsion against
communism . . . by describing graphically how the local church would be
turned into a meeting hall for the 'Fighting Godless,' how their children
would have to spend their time with the 'Red Pioneers,' how the pictures
of Lenin, Stalin, and Malenkov would replace the pictures of the Saints in
every home, and the like."

Arbenz had drifted leftward during his presidential term—his wife
speculated years later that by the time of the coup he "considered himself a
communist"—but no one in Guatemala doubted that he would step down
after the 1956 election. All of the leading candidates to succeed him were
more conservative than he was, and Guatemala's constitution required the
army to depose any president who sought to violate the ban on re-election.
Foster, Allen, and their boss in the White House, however, were in no
mood to wait patiently for a couple of years while events took their course
in Guatemala.

Any doubts about Arbenz that may have remained in Washington were
resolved with the news in mid-May that his government had received a shipment of arms from Czechoslovakia. The United States had stopped supplying weapons to the Guatemalan army and intervened to prevent half a dozen

other countries from doing so, giving Arbenz a plausible excuse for looking elsewhere. In Washington, though, the shipment was taken as proof of a Guatemala-Moscow connection. Foster pronounced it "a development of gravity," and at his advice, President Eisenhower sent fifty tons of weapons to the pro-American dictators in Nicaragua and Honduras, which according to the *New York Times* now faced threats of "Guatemalan aggression."

On the morning of June 16, 1954, Foster, Allen, and Eisenhower's other top national security aides met with the president for breakfast in the family quarters of the White House. Allen reported that all was ready in Guatemala.

"Are you sure this is going to succeed?" Eisenhower asked. Allen said it would.

"I want all of you to be damn good and sure you succeed," the president told them. "I'm prepared to take any steps that are necessary to see that it succeeds. When you commit the flag, you commit it to win."

Two days later, Castillo Armas led a band of 150 "rebels" from Honduras into Guatemala. They advanced six miles, then stopped. Over the next two weeks, they fought only a few skirmishes with government troops. Their main assignment was to sit and wait while the Dulles brothers worked their magic.

Mendacious radio broadcasts crackled across Guatemala's airwaves, pretending to be from insurgent commanders reporting battlefield victories and defections from the army. CIA pilots, flying from clandestine bases in Honduras and Nicaragua, bombed high-profile targets including the principal military base in Guatemala City. Arbenz asked the United Nations to send fact finders, but Ambassador Lodge maneuvered to prevent that from happening.

Few American journalists suspected the truth. One who did was James Reston of the *New York Times*. In a later era he might have produced a sweeping story exposing the true nature of the "liberation army." Genteel journalistic standards of the age, coupled with a widely shared sense that all Americans faced a mortal threat from Communism and were obliged to support their government's struggle against it, made that all but unthinkable. Instead Reston crafted a column that some may have read as nothing more than idle speculation, but that Washington insiders could decode. It was headlined "With the Dulles Brothers in Darkest Guatemala."

"John Foster Dulles, the Secretary of State, seldom intervenes in the

internal affairs of other countries, but his brother Allen is more enterprising," Reston wrote. "If somebody wants to start a revolution in, say, Guatemala, it is no good talking to Foster Dulles. But Allen Dulles, head of
the Central Intelligence Agency, is a more active man. He has been watching the Guatemalan situation for a long time."

Reston's hunch about CIA plotting in Guatemala was correct. He had
no way of knowing, however, that soon after his column appeared, the plot
came so close to collapsing that Allen had to make an emergency rescue
run to the White House.

Bombing raids by CIA planes were having their desired effect in Guatemala. They symbolized Washington's determination to depose Arbenz,
and because of their supposed effect on him and his supporters, they
became popularly known as *sulfatos*—laxatives. Then, within a matter of
hours on June 21–22, the *sulfato* force was decimated. One plane was dis-
abled by ground fire, another crash-landed, and two more were forced
down in Mexico after bombing a border town. Only a couple remained—
not enough to maintain the operation's momentum.

"Air power could be decisive," Allen's men on the scene told him in an
urgent cable on June 23.

Within hours, Allen was in the Oval Office. He explained the situation
and asked Eisenhower to authorize immediate deployment of several air
force planes to Nicaragua, where the dictator, Anastasio Somoza, would
release them for use in PB/Success. When he was finished, Henry Holland, the State Department's legal adviser, presented the contrary case,
arguing that further bombing would violate international law and promote anti-Americanism. Eisenhower decided in Allen's favor, and the
planes were deployed. Later he told one of his close military comrades,
General Andrew Goodpaster, that it was an easy choice.

"If you at any time take the route of violence or support of violence,"
he said, "then you commit yourself to carry it through, and it's too late to
have second thoughts."

Reinforced by the new planes, Allen's campaign against Arbenz intensified. Guatemala's senior military commanders, taking broad hints from
Ambassador Peurifoy, realized that the United States was behind the
assault and would not relent until Arbenz was gone. On June 27 the commanders gave Arbenz what one called a "final ultimatum." A few hours
later he appeared on Guatemalan radio to announce that he had made a

"sad and cruel judgment," and would surrender to "the obscured forces which today oppress the backward and colonial world."

Arbenz then walked from the Presidential Palace to the nearby Mexican embassy, where he was granted asylum. After a brief interregnum, Colonel Castillo Armas, the CIA's chosen "liberator," was installed as his successor. His first acts included dissolving Congress, suspending the constitution, disenfranchising three-quarters of the population by banning illiterates from voting, and decreeing repeal of the land reform law that had enraged United Fruit. Ten years of democratic government, the first that Guatemalans had ever known, were over.

"Heartiest congratulations upon outcome," Wisner wired in a cable to his men. "A great victory has been won."

Soon afterward, as he had done following the triumph in Iran ten months earlier, Eisenhower invited the victorious warriors to visit him and explain how they had carried out their coup. The group was ushered into a small theater in the East Wing. There they found not just Eisenhower waiting, but also Foster, the Joint Chiefs of Staff, and about two dozen other high-ranking officials including Vice President Nixon and Attorney General Herbert Brownell. All were riveted by their presentations. When they finished, Eisenhower shook everyone's hand, saving his last handshake for Allen.

"Thanks, Allen, and thanks to all of you," he said. "You've averted a Communist beachhead in our hemisphere."

Some were dubious. "Commie argument that 'invaders' and 'Yankee imperialists' [are] anxious to wipe out agrarian reform appears to be most dangerous not only for Guat consumption, but for effect wherever in world agrarian reform questions vitally important, including Latin America, Asia, Africa, even certain European countries," the Opa Locka command post reported to Allen. "Recommend therefore you suggest State Dept. immediate countermeasures."

Allen brought this message to Foster, and they agreed that the best "countermeasure" would be a disingenuous speech by Foster. He delivered it over national radio and television on June 30, the day after the last pro-Arbenz forces in Guatemala capitulated.

Tonight I should like to talk with you about Guatemala. It is the scene of dramatic events. They expose the evil purpose of the Kremlin. . . .

Guatemala is a small country. But its power, standing alone, is not a measure of the threat. The master plan of international communism is to gain a solid political base in this hemisphere, a base that can be used to extend Communist penetration to the other peoples of the other American Governments. . . .

We regret that there have been disputes between the Guatemalan Government and the United Fruit Company. . . . But this issue is relatively unimportant. . . . Led by Colonel Castillo Armas, patriots arose in Guatemala to challenge the Communist leadership—and to change it. Thus the situation is being cured by the Guatemalans themselves. . . .

The events of recent months and days add a new and glorious chapter to the already great tradition of the American States. . . . Communism is still a menace everywhere. But the people of the United States and of the other American Republics can feel tonight that at least one grave danger has been averted.

A few months later, from exile in Mexico, the Guatemalan diplomat Guillermo Toriello published his own account. "The break of day on June 29th, 1954, brought with it the triumph of foreign aggression against Guatemalan democracy," he wrote. "A combination of the State Department, the Central Intelligence Agency, and the Banana Empire had finally managed to crush this small nation, indefensible and inoffensive, one hundred times smaller than its adversary, and drown in blood a flowering democracy dedicated to the dignity and economic liberation of its people. The next day, John Foster Dulles announced the 'glorious victory' and proclaimed his delight at the crime's consummation."

Allen brought the CIA into its golden age by showing that he could topple governments with minimum cost and almost complete discretion. Foster understood the power this implied. The world had become their battlefield. The brothers came to power determined to depose the leaders of two countries on opposite sides of the world. Both were now gone. Flushed with success, they moved on to their third target.

7

A MATCHLESS INTERPLAY OF
RUTHLESSNESS AND GUILE

Spymasters are usually discreet, but Allen Dulles had overthrown two governments in the space of ten months and did not feel compelled to deny it. In the summer of 1954 he invited a pair of reporters from the *Saturday Evening Post* into his confidence. Through them, he gave the world an account of his first year on the job. It emerged as a three-part series called "The Mysterious Doings of the CIA."

"The *Post* presents its own exclusive report on America's 'silent service'— the super-secret Central Intelligence Agency," read the legend on the opening page, below a large photo of Allen. "Here, revealed for the first time, are its methods, how it gets its operatives and money, and its accomplishments—in Guatemala, Iran, and behind the Iron Curtain."

These articles reported that CIA operatives in Eastern Europe were fomenting strikes, mining rail lines, and blowing up bridges. More surprisingly, they made clear that the CIA had been behind the overthrows of Arbenz and Mossadegh. The reporters, presumably reflecting Allen's views, wrote that Arbenz had been deposed because he was a "communist puppet" engaged in "unbridled subversion of the Guatemalan people," and that had he remained in office, "we might have faced the necessity of sending Marines to reinforce the Panama Canal and save Latin America."

"Another CIA triumph was the successful overthrow, in 1953, of old, dictatorial Premier Mohammad Mossadegh and the return to power of this country's friend, Shah Mohammad Reza Pahlavi," they wrote. "A helping hand in the rescue of one country such as Guatemala or Iran from communism is worth the CIA's annual budget many times over. Whether the squeamish like it or not, the United States must know what goes on in those dark places of the world where our overthrow is being plotted by communists."

As Allen basked in this publicity, *Time* chose Foster as "Man of the Year" and put him on the cover of its first issue of 1955. He was a good choice. Few were fighting Communism more vigorously, and nothing less than the survival of humanity seemed to hinge on the outcome of that fight. The *Time* profile was flattering and self-congratulatory, as much about America's destined role in the world as about an individual. It called Foster "a practical missionary of Christian politics" who had given Americans "a feeling of firm confidence in the U.S. economy and in dynamic capitalism as an economic way of life."

The article devoted a page to challenges that lay ahead for Foster. Staring out from the center of that page was a thin, bearded figure with Asian features, hands crossed over his knees and wearing a field jacket. His face was not yet well known in the United States. Below his portrait was a simple caption: "Indo-China's Ho." He was about to become the third monster Foster and Allen went abroad to destroy.

In 1953, overthrowing Mossadegh had been the Dulles brothers' obsession. The next year it was Arbenz. Now they focused on Ho Chi Minh, the Communist leader of Vietnam's anticolonial movement. They singled him out not simply because of who he was, but where he was. Europe had settled into its Cold War pattern, and although Foster and Allen still considered it the center of the world, they believed the front line had moved to East Asia. They mistakenly saw China as a pawn of the Soviet Union, and Ho, also mistakenly, as a puppet of both. Crushing him, they decided, would be the most potent next blow they could strike against "international Communism."

In the decades that had passed since Ho's failed appeal to Woodrow Wilson at the end of World War I, he had become Vietnam's nationalist hero. By many accounts he admired the United States. He had been spellbound by the Statue of Liberty and East River bridges in New York. During World War II he collaborated closely with the OSS in the fight against the Japanese occupiers of his country.

Ho was a leader of anti-Japanese guerrillas, and in 1945 the OSS

dropped a team into his jungle base with instructions to locate and support a "Mr. Hoo." Team members trained Ho's men in the use of American weaponry, which they received in air drops, and gave copies of U.S.
Army field manuals to Ho and other English-speaking guerrilla leaders.
Reports filed by team members suggest that they were mightily impressed
with Ho. When the fighting ended with Japan's surrender in August, the
team commander, Major Allison Thomas of the U.S. Army, had a farewell
dinner with him and asked him if he was a Communist.

"Yes," Ho replied. "But we can still be friends, can't we?"

A month later, Ho declared Vietnam independent. He became its first
leader, and in his Independence Day speech he quoted American scripture by declaring, "All men are created equal; they are endowed by their
creator with certain unalienable rights; among these are life, liberty, and
the pursuit of happiness." In November he wrote to the new secretary of
state, James Byrnes, asking if he could send to the United States "a delegation of about fifty Vietnam youths with a view to establish friendly cultural relations with American youth on the one hand, and carrying on
further studies in engineering, agriculture, as well as other lines of spe-
cialization, on the other." Receiving no reply, he sent a letter to President
Truman asking him to keep faith "with the idealistic loftiness and gener-
osity expressed by your delegates to the United Nations assembly, Messrs.
Byrnes, Stettinius, and J.F. Dulles."

> The French colonialists, who betrayed in wartime both the Allies and the
> Vietnamese, have come back, and are waging on us a murderous and
> pitiless war in order to re-establish their domination. . . . This aggression
> is contrary to all principles of international law and the pledge made by
> the Allies during World War II. It is a challenge to the noble attitude
> shown before, during, and after the war by the United States government
> and people. . . .
>
> [Western powers] ought to keep their words. They ought to interfere
> to stop this unjust war, and to show that they mean to carry out in peace-
> time the principles for which they fought in wartime. . . . What we ask
> has been graciously granted to the Philippines. Like the Philippines, our
> goal is full independence and full cooperation with the United States.
> We will do our best to make this independence and cooperation profit-
> able to the whole world.

Truman did not reply, and Ho's letter was kept secret for a quarter century. Meanwhile, American diplomats in Vietnam reported in dispatches that Ho was "the outstanding representative of the native peoples" and a "wily opportunist" known for "straddling the fence." Justice William O. Douglas wrote after traveling through Indochina that this "tubercular Communist" was one of the most "amazingly successful" revolutionaries of his era.

"He was hunted by every French policeman but never found," Douglas reported. "He was a phantom, a ghost, who seemed to move at will, casting a shadow on the French regime. Peasants spoke of him in whispers. The hopes of thousands of miserable people went with him wherever he moved."

The Dulles brothers' campaign against Ho began in Geneva, where countries concerned with Indochina met in the spring of 1954. Foster at first said he would not attend the conference because a Chinese delegation would also be there. French leaders persuaded him that if he did not, their government would fall and France might move toward an open break with the United States. When Foster announced at a Washington press conference that he would indeed travel to Geneva, he vowed to make no concessions either to the Chinese or to Ho, whom he presumed to be their puppet.

Q: What would you regard as a reasonable satisfactory settlement of the Indochina situation?

DULLES: The removal by the Chinese Communists of their apparent desire to extend the political system of Communism to Southeast Asia.

Q: That means the complete withdrawal of Communists from Indochina?

DULLES: That is what I would regard as a satisfactory solution.

Q: Is there any compromise that might be offered if that is not entirely satisfactory to the Communists?

DULLES: I had not thought of any.

Foster arrived in Geneva with a single goal: to prevent any compromise with Ho. Every other delegation, except for the one representing Vietnam's old emperor, Bao Dai, favored compromise. Rather than accept the consensus, Foster resolved to lead the United States on a course of its own. In time this would lead it to war in Vietnam.

For years Foster had worked assiduously to isolate the Communist government of China. He considered the Nationalists on Taiwan to be China's legitimate rulers, and he resolutely defended their right to the Chinese seat at the United Nations. Since he did not recognize the Communist regime, he refused to negotiate with it. He also used the State Department's control over passports to ban all travel to China for American citizens, including journalists.

The Geneva conference of 1954 gave Foster his first chance to reassess this absolutist policy. China's delegation to the conference would be headed by Zhou Enlai, the formidable prime minister and foreign minister. Zhou would be across the table from him during negotiating sessions, and available for a chat anytime. This stirred interest in Washington. A reporter asked Foster if he could imagine meeting the Chinese leader when they crossed paths in Geneva.

"Not unless our automobiles collide," he replied.

That was a remarkably droll answer from a man not known for wit. Behind it lay the three assumptions Foster carried with him to Geneva. This makes them the assumptions that drew the United States into Vietnam:

- World Communism is a monolithic movement directed from the Kremlin.
- Having been checked in Europe, this movement now seeks to conquer Asia.
- Its most active agent there is Ho, which makes him America's new enemy.

Many in Washington had shared these assumptions for years. "Question whether Ho as much nationalist as Commie irrelevant," Dean Acheson had written in one cable. "All Stalinists in colonial areas are nationalists."

President Harry Truman had agreed. "To lose those countries to the rulers of the Kremlin would be more than a blow to our military security and our economic life," he once warned. "It would be a terrible defeat for the ideals of freedom—with grave spiritual consequences for men everywhere who share our faith in freedom." In 1950, eager to win French support for the American-led war in Korea, Truman put aside his anticolonial impulse and agreed to begin subsidizing France's war in Vietnam. He sent $100 million. By 1952 this aid had tripled to $300 million. Two years later it was nearly $1 billion.

One mid-level figure in the State Department, Paul Kattenburg, who was the desk officer for Vietnam during much of Foster's tenure, suggested to a colleague that instead of continuing to spend money fighting Ho, the United States should offer him $500 million in reconstruction aid. This, he reasoned, would allow Ho to draw away from China and the Soviet Union, while also keeping the United States out of war. This unorthodox view was heresy, and Kattenburg did not push it. Later he wrote a poignant account of the mind-set he faced.

> Few if any policy practitioners in Washington or among American representatives in Asia would dare to say in 1950, for example, when Ho Chi Minh was beginning to defeat the French: "Ho is certainly a Communist, but he has great appeal; he is regarded as a champion of nationalism and of anti-colonialism; he is forging an unbreakable bond with his people; he will win his revolutionary struggle regardless of the odds, for we can see, hear, and sense that the masses of the people support him and not the French or their puppets." Stilling or silencing voices such as these, and hearing instead only those who said, "Ho is a Communist, therefore he cannot really represent the aspirations of his people, and moreover they regard him as a tool of Russia or China," led American leaders—and people as well—into an anti-Communist climate of deafness and blindness.... It is one of the most dangerous, in fact potentially suicidal, things a great nation can do in world affairs: to cut off its eyes and ears, to castrate its analytic capacity, to shut itself off from the truth because of blind prejudice and a misguided dispensation of good and evil.

Foster first hoped to keep Ho from power by continuing to support the French army in its war against his movement, the Viet Minh. The United States paid most of the cost of this war, more than $2 billion between 1950 and 1954. It was not enough to turn the tide.

Late in 1953, Viet Minh attackers surrounded the strategic French outpost at Dien Bien Phu, in Vietnam's mountainous northwest. All understood that a decisive battle was at hand. If France faced defeat, might the United States send troops to relieve the besieged garrison? When this question was raised at a National Security Council meeting on January 8, 1954, according to the official transcript, President Eisenhower reacted "with vehemence."

Princeton University Library

The Dulles brothers grew up in one of America's most extraordinary families. Here Allen Dulles is standing at left while John Foster Dulles stands at right, with his father and mother beside him. The boys' grandfather John Watson Foster, seated at center, was secretary of state in the 1890s. Their uncle Robert Lansing, standing with his dog, held the same post during World War I. Their talented sister Eleanor sits at left foreground.

SULLIVAN & CROMWELL
JUNE 25, 1934

Princeton University Library

John Foster Dulles became managing partner of the Wall Street law firm Sullivan & Cromwell, a unique repository of global power. He is seated at center right. The firm's audacious co-founder, William Nelson Cromwell, is at center left.

Allen Dulles was a successful spymaster based in Switzerland during both world wars.

John Foster Dulles denounced the "containment" policy that Secretary of State Dean Acheson followed after World War II. He urged policies to promote the "liberation" of Communist countries.

In 1953 John Foster Dulles (left) became secretary of state, and Allen Dulles became director of the Central Intelligence Agency. It was the only time in history that siblings controlled the overt and covert sides of American foreign policy.

As secretary of state, Dulles worked intimately with President Dwight Eisenhower. Both supported covert action and "regime change" operations.

Prime Minister Mohammad Mossadegh of Iran (left) was the first "monster" the Dulles brothers set out to destroy. His most prominent American supporter was Supreme Court justice William O. Douglas.

After deposing Mossadegh, the Dulles brothers set out against President Jacobo Arbenz of Guatemala. He was strip-searched as he departed to exile after being deposed in 1954.

European diplomats reluctantly concluded in the mid-1950s that there was no way the Communist leader Ho Chi Minh could be kept from power in Vietnam. The Dulles brothers refused to agree. They embarked on a campaign against him that led to a long and costly war.

President Sukarno of Indonesia admired American icons from the Founding Fathers to Marilyn Monroe. His neutralist policies, however, led the Dulles brothers to launch a clandestine war against him.

Prime Minister Patrice Lumumba of the Congo was the next Dulles target. He was captured and executed after less than a year in office.

The last Dulles nemesis, the Cuban revolutionary leader Fidel Castro, met Vice President Richard Nixon when he visited New York soon after seizing power.

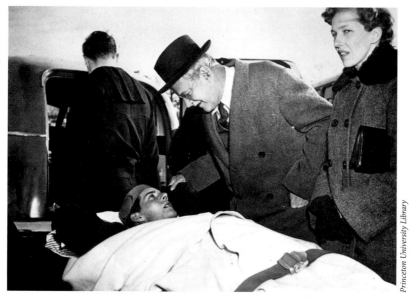

Allen Dulles was an enthusiastic adulterer and had a difficult relationship with his wife, Clover. Their son, Allen, was severely wounded in Korea.

John Foster Dulles was stern, self-righteous, and devoted to his wife, Janet. She accompanied him on many foreign trips, as on this visit to Ceylon (now Sri Lanka).

Princeton University Library

SECRETARY DULLES FLIES AGAIN

DESTINATION IMMORTALITY

WORLD'S PEOPLE

WORLD PEACE

THE TIMES-PICAYUNE, NEW ORLEANS. MAY 26, 1959

John Foster Dulles did not live to see his reputation decline. When he died in 1959, the nation was grief-stricken.

CUBAN CRITICISM

ALLEN DULLES

CIA RESIGNATION

JFK

GIB CROCKETT
WASHINGTON STAR

"I'VE HAD ENOUGH OF THE CLOAK AND DAGGER BUSINESS!"

Fate was less kind to Allen Dulles. The first covert operation he recommended to President John F. Kennedy was an attempt to overthrow Fidel Castro by landing an exile army at the Bay of Pigs in southern Cuba. It failed disastrously. Kennedy fired him soon afterward.

Diego Rivera's vivid mural *Glorious Victory* depicts the American-sponsored coup in Guatemala. The Dulles brothers are at the center, Foster being thanked by his Guatemalan lackey while Allen stands beside him, his satchel full of cash. Eisenhower's face decorates a bomb. Allen was delighted with the way *Glorious Victory* portrayed him and proudly handed out small-format copies.

"[There's] just no sense in even talking about United States forces replacing the French in Indochina," he said. "If we did so, the Vietnamese could be expected to transfer their hatred of the French to us. I cannot tell you . . . how bitterly opposed I am to such a course of action. This war in Indochina would absorb our troops by divisions."

Foster had not specifically recommended the dispatch of ground troops, though by some accounts he seemed to favor it. Once the president pronounced himself so forcefully, however, the option of sending American soldiers to war in Vietnam had to be discarded. Foster looked for others.

"Nothing could hold Dulles back," David Halberstam wrote. "There was an absolute belief in our cause, our innocence and worthiness, also a belief that it was better politically to be in than to be out. It was mostly Dulles's initiative."

Pressure for a new policy was intense because Viet Minh fighters were closing in on Dien Bien Phu, which according to *Time* had been transformed "from a scratch on the map to one of the most important places in the world." *Time* called Ho "a matchless interplay of ruthlessness and guile," and warned that defeating him "will take power, humanity, and steely nerve."

On April 5 a cable arrived in Washington conveying France's request for "immediate armed intervention of US carrier aircraft" for bombing raids on Viet Minh positions around Dien Bien Phu. Eisenhower "actively contemplated taking the United States directly into the war," the historian Fredrik Logevall has written, and sent Foster to Capitol Hill for hurried meetings with congressional leaders. They told him they would oppose any intervention in Vietnam unless other countries joined.

"I sat listening to him talking about sending American boys off to fight in a war like that," Senator Richard Russell told the *New York Times* afterward, "and suddenly I found myself on my feet shouting, 'We're not going to do that!'"

Foster's only hope was to enlist Britain, which had substantial forces of its own and could also mobilize those of Australia and New Zealand. Together with the United States and two subservient allies it could enlist, Thailand and the Philippines, this would make a modestly credible coalition. Eisenhower appealed to Prime Minister Churchill in a letter, reminding him that the West had allowed Hitler's rise "by not acting in unity and in time." He was asking Britain to join the United States in launching a new war.

Churchill, who believed Ho's power was irresistible, demurred. Foster then flew to London to make a personal appeal to Foreign Secretary Anthony Eden. He told Eden he was "greatly disturbed" by Britain's refusal to fight alongside the United States, and warned that it could prove "disastrous" for relations between their countries. This too fell on deaf ears.

"The loss of the fortress must be faced," Churchill reluctantly advised his American friends.

Nineteen fifty-four was a congressional election year in the United States, and domestic politics was one reason some around Eisenhower felt compelled to reject Churchill's advice and plunge into Vietnam. Foster had spent years denouncing the Democrats for what he called "appeasement of Communism." He realized that if he were to accept a settlement in Vietnam that gave even limited power to Ho, he would be overwhelmed by charges of hypocrisy. Vice President Nixon predicted that Democrats would call any settlement "a sellout." Eisenhower's press secretary, James Hagerty, warned that it would "give the Democrats a chance to say that we sat idly by and let Indochina be sold down the river to the Communists without raising a finger or turning a hair."

Eisenhower wished to crush Ho—to keep him from power at all costs, and preferably destroy his popularity at the same time—without using military force. No one in Washington could imagine how this might be done. The only alternative to intervention, however, was to face the reality that Ho was overwhelmingly powerful in Vietnam and could not be defeated. Britain recognized this, and France was about to. The United States could not.

"In certain areas at least, we cannot afford to let Moscow gain another bit of territory," Eisenhower told one National Security Council meeting. "Dien Bien Phu may be just such a critical point."

A few dissenters raised doubts. Senator Edwin Johnson of Colorado declared himself "against sending American GI's into the mud and muck of Indochina on a blood-letting spree to perpetuate colonialism and white man's exploitation in Asia." From London, Foreign Secretary Eden warned that only "intervention on a Korean scale, if that, would have any effect on Indochina." One of Eisenhower's advisers, C. D. Jackson, wrote in a private memorandum that dreams of stopping Ho were fantasies produced by "wishful thinking, rosy intelligence, oversimplified geopolitical decisions . . . and unwillingness to retreat from previously taken policy decisions."

These calls for caution went unheeded. A powerful Republican, Senator William Knowland of California, warned that any compromise with Ho would be a "Far Eastern Munich." Eisenhower agreed. He was determined to confront Ho. So were his secretary of state and director of central intelligence. The question was not whether they would fight, but how.

Foster and Allen decided to try the same brotherly combination that had succeeded in Iran and Guatemala. One would orchestrate political and diplomatic pressure on Ho while the other launched a covert war. They gave themselves authority in a directive they wrote and the National Security Council approved: "The Director of Central Intelligence, in collaboration with other appropriate departments and agencies, should develop plans, as suggested by the Secretary of State, for certain contingencies in Indochina."

Foster launched his part of the campaign with a speech to the Overseas Press Club in New York on March 29, 1954. His central challenge was to explain to Americans why they must resist Ho. The answer was what he called the "domino theory."

> If the Communist forces won uncontested control over Indochina or any substantial part thereof, they would surely resume the same pattern of aggression against the other free people in the area. . . . The entire Western Pacific area, including the so-called "offshore island chain," would be strategically endangered. . . . The imposition on Southeast Asia of the political system of Communist Russia and its Chinese ally, by whatever means, would be a grave threat to the free community. The United States feels that possibility should not be passively accepted, but should be met by united action. This might involve serious risks. But the risks are far less than those that will face us a few years from now if we dare not be resolute today.

The "united action" Foster wanted was a military alliance committed to denying Ho control over any territory. No other country, however, wished to join that effort. That forced a choice on the United States. It decided to fight alone.

None of the three Americans who pushed their country into the Vietnam quagmire at this decisive moment—Eisenhower and the Dulles
brothers—underestimated the challenge Ho posed. Nonetheless they
believed they could defeat him. Much of their confidence stemmed from
their conviction, strengthened by their successes in Iran and Guatemala,
that covert operations could turn the tide of foreign battles. Foster would
play his part in the drama, but it was Allen and his clandestine operatives
on whom the outcome would mainly depend.

As soon as Eisenhower approved this project, Allen set out to bring
down his third monster. Eisenhower cheered him on. So did Foster. Neither wished to know details.

Although Ho was a dominant figure on the geopolitical radar that guided
Foster and Allen during the mid-1950s, they operated in complex worlds
far beyond Vietnam. There was no place on earth where they did not seek
to win influence or guide the course of events. Vietnam may have been
their most urgent project during this tense phase of the Cold War, but it
was hardly their only one.

Allen devoted much effort to building a global network of informants.
Often he recruited them personally, during secret trips abroad. In select
company he claimed to have cabinet-level sources in every Western and
neutral government.

He even had an agent in the Soviet military intelligence service, Pyotr
Popov, who offered himself to the CIA in 1953 by slipping an American
diplomat a note that said, "I am a Soviet officer. I wish to meet with an
American officer with the object of offering certain services." Over the
next six years, Popov betrayed valuable secrets including details of Soviet
military capacities, names of Soviet spies in Europe, and information
about Soviet plans to plant long-term agents in the United States. The CIA
asked the FBI to follow one of these agents, who was living in New York.
She realized what was happening and notified her superiors in Moscow.
They quickly determined that Popov, who had been her control officer,
was a traitor. He was arrested in 1959 and executed the following year.

Much of what Allen was able to discover about life behind the Iron
Curtain came from the espionage network General Reinhard Gehlen created to serve the Nazi regime and then, after the war, turned over to the

CIA. Allen paid him a reported $6 million annually for his services, much to the displeasure of some of his British counterparts, who harbored wartime grudges against Gehlen. His other close German partner was Otto John, the chief of West Germany's domestic security service. Allen was jolted when, just a few days after John visited CIA headquarters in mid-1954, he defected to East Germany, saying he could not bear Konrad Adenauer's commitment to remilitarization and his appointment of ex-Nazis to government posts. A roundup of Western agents operating in the East soon followed.

In Japan, Allen turned the ruling Liberal Democratic Party into a client. He backed a rising politician, Nobusuke Kishi, who later became prime minister; doled out cash to other party leaders; and worked to subvert the rival Socialist Party. This operation continued for more than a decade and helped keep Japan allied with the United States for the duration of the Cold War.

"We ran Japan during the occupation, and we ran it in a different way in these years after the occupation," the officer who directed this operation later recalled. "General MacArthur had his ways. We had ours."

Beyond running "penetration" projects like these, Allen pursued his interest in propaganda and mass psychology. Convinced that the United States could improve its standing in the world by showcasing the vibrancy of its culture, he spent millions of dollars subsidizing tours by American jazz bands, traveling exhibitions of abstract art, and magazines in countries from Britain to Brazil. He funneled money to supposedly independent groups like the Congress for Cultural Freedom and the National Student Association, and to cultural figures—sometimes without their knowledge—including Dwight Macdonald, Ted Hughes, Derek Walcott, James Michener, and Mary McCarthy. Through Radio Free Europe and Radio Liberty, on which he spent about $30 million annually, he beamed pro-Western propaganda into the Soviet Union and Eastern Europe. The CIA secretly financed the publication of hundreds of books, and regularly placed articles in *Foreign Affairs*, the *Times Literary Supplement*, and other publications read by intellectuals. In Europe, where this "hearts-and-minds" campaign was most intense, CIA operatives were swimming in cash as a result of a secret arrangement that allowed them access to Marshall Plan funds. They distributed millions of dollars through fake philanthropies and real ones like the Ford, Carnegie, and Rockefeller Foundations.

"These covertly sponsored activities sounded many of the themes that permeated American official and unofficial propaganda," one CIA officer based in Europe wrote years later. "Politics was reduced to a simple black-and-white formula of East or West, slavery or freedom. Liberalism was attacked as an ally of communism, with ex-Communists playing a leading role as the only men who really knew what communism was all about. 'Neutralism' was a dirty word, since no one could be detached from the great battle for men's minds. Intellectuals, writers, and artists raised the angel-devil issue to a sophisticated level of international polemics."

Law prohibited the CIA from operating within the United States, but Allen interpreted it loosely. He sought to shape coverage of world events in the American press through calls to editors and publishers. After Europeans began citing the absence of African American actors in Hollywood films as evidence of racism in the United States, he assigned an officer to visit producers and urge them to hire more. Perhaps his most imaginative media operation was taking control of the animated film version of George Orwell's anti-totalitarian classic *Animal Farm*. The book's ending, in which animals realize that both ruling groups in the barnyard are equally corrupt, is a trenchant rejection of the binary worldview. Allen realized that this message implicitly contradicted much of what the United States was saying about the Cold War. By investing in the film and influencing its content through a team of operatives that included E. Howard Hunt, a veteran of PB/Success, he arranged for the film version to end quite differently. Only the pigs are corrupt, and ultimately patriotic rebels overthrow them. Orwell's widow was disgusted, but the film reached a wide audience. The United States Information Agency distributed it around the world.

Although Allen was skilled at recruiting high-level informants and found the subtleties of "psy-war" intriguing, he was never happier than when immersed in covert operations. By one account he "had a child's enjoyment of the adventures of his officers." His deputy director for plans, Frank Wisner, shared his zeal. Together they spent as much money as they wished on endlessly ambitious operations in dozens of countries.

"Dulles was enthralled with covert operations," according to one history of the CIA. "He was called 'the Great White Case Officer' because he was so fascinated with the details of these operations. Another reason why he favored covert warfare was that it sustained Congress's and the

President's support for the new intelligence agency. . . . An operation like Guatemala dazzled the politicians who controlled the CIA purse strings."

Eisenhower may have been dazzled, but he was not blinded. During his first years in office he commissioned several outside reviews of executive agencies. In 1954 it was the CIA's turn. He asked General James Doolittle, who had won fame for leading air raids on Tokyo during World War II and who then became a Shell Oil executive, to review the agency's operations. Doolittle's conclusions were terrifying.

"It is now clear that we are facing an implacable enemy whose avowed objective is world domination by whatever means and at whatever cost," Doolittle wrote. "There are no rules in such a game. Hitherto acceptable norms of human conduct do not apply. If the United States is to survive, long-standing concepts of 'fair play' must be reconsidered. We must develop effective espionage and counter-espionage services and must learn to subvert, sabotage, and destroy our enemies by more clever, more sophisticated, and more effective weapons than those used against us. It may become necessary that the American people be made acquainted with, understand and support this fundamentally repugnant philosophy."

Although Doolittle's language bordered on the apocalyptic, the CIA reforms he proposed in his report, such as better hiring procedures and increased use of polygraphs, were bland. His real recommendation was so sensitive that he decided to deliver it orally: fire Allen Dulles.

Doolittle made his case to Eisenhower at a meeting in the Oval Office on October 19, 1954. He said he admired Allen's "unique knowledge" of the covert world but warned that he was guided by "emotionalism . . . far worse than it appeared on the surface." As for the CIA, Doolittle reported that it had "ballooned out into a vast and sprawling organization." No one controlled it, he said, because of the "family relationship" between its director and the secretary of state.

"It leads to protection of one by the other, or influence of one by the other," he warned. Before he could continue, Eisenhower stopped him. The CIA, he told Doolittle, was "one of the most peculiar types of operation any government can have, and it probably takes a strange kind of genius to run it."

"I am not going to be able to change Allen," he said. "I'd rather have Allen as my chief intelligence officer, with his limitations, than anyone I know."

Allen was a poor administrator. Many around him also noted a lack of intellectual engagement. He often turned aside probing discussion by telling a story, or musing about his favorite baseball team, the Washington Senators. His mind was undisciplined. By one account he "seemed almost scatterbrained." A senior British agent who worked with him for years recalled being "seldom able to penetrate beyond his laugh, or to conduct any serious professional conversation with him for more than a few sentences."

Eisenhower had given his private endorsement of Allen's leadership to Doolittle just two weeks after accepting the resignation of one of his oldest friends and collaborators, Walter Bedell Smith. The two retired generals had worked closely during World War II. "Beetle" became director of central intelligence under Truman, and Eisenhower made him undersecretary of state. His departure marked a loss for Eisenhower but a decisive leap in power for Foster and Allen. Foster no longer had a second in command with direct access to the Oval Office. Allen's predecessor was no longer looking over his shoulder. With "Beetle" gone, no one was left to challenge their commanding role in shaping and carrying out American foreign policy.

Early in 1955 Allen scored a quietly celebrated triumph when the phone-tapping tunnel his men had spent months digging in Berlin "went live." Construction had required a maze of cover stories and diversions, and the work of cutting into underground cables without provoking service interruptions was delicate. The taps produced a stream of information, though nothing truly startling or explosive. One day, after the operation had been running for a year, Soviet agents suddenly charged into the tunnel from the East German side. CIA officers fled wildly. A few days later the chief of the Soviet KGB station in East Berlin invited reporters to see the CIA's handiwork. This allowed Allen to take open credit. In Washington he was celebrated for an audacious success. Years later it was discovered that a British agent who helped supervise the digging project, George Blake, was actually a KGB "mole" and that the Soviets had monitored it from the beginning.

Allen's other great success of this period was also less spectacular than it first appeared. In 1956 he thrilled Eisenhower and the National Security Council by producing a copy of the top-secret speech in which the new Soviet leader, Nikita Khrushchev, denounced Stalin's brutality. He took ostentatious pride in this accomplishment and described it as "one of the major coups of my tour of duty." Years later it became clear that the Israeli secret service, acting through a Jewish operative in the government of Poland, had actually obtained the speech and that Allen had received it only after the Israelis decided to send him a copy.

Part of the reason Allen was able to cultivate an image of success was that he managed to keep his failures quiet. The most glaring of them was his inability to foment upheaval inside the Soviet Union, but there were others. One was his effort to seize control of the oil-rich Buraimi Oasis on the Persian Gulf. The oasis was controlled by Oman and Abu Dhabi, whose leaders were aligned with Britain, and Allen wished to bring it under the rule of Saudi Arabia, where both King Saud and his brother, Prince Faisal, were on the CIA payroll. Allen sent Kermit Roosevelt to run a covert operation that involved infiltrating Saudi soldiers into the oasis, offering Saudi citizenship to its inhabitants, and tempting its ruling sheikh with an air-conditioned Cadillac and $90 million in gold. The sheikh, however, proved loyal to his British patrons. Ultimately the dispute was submitted to an international tribunal in Geneva. Allen sought to bribe its members, but they resisted. In the end, Saudi troops were forced to withdraw. This conflict made worldwide headlines, but it was portrayed as an inter-Arab dispute rather than a skirmish between the power that had long dominated the Middle East and the one that sought to replace it. The true story did not emerge until decades later.

Allen had long experience in the Middle East and paid it special attention. In 1952 he sent $12 million in cash to one of the emerging rulers of post-royalist Egypt, General Muhammad Naguib, but the money was discovered in a search of Naguib's house, and one of his rivals, Gamal Abdel Nasser, used the resulting scandal to push him out of power. Later Allen sent another bribe—also $12 million—to the mother of King Hussein of Jordan, in the hope that she would guide her son into the American orbit. Hussein was not tempted, perhaps because the British were already subsidizing him.

More successful was Allen's cultivation of Saudi leaders, to whom he passed tens of millions of dollars. This solidified a partnership that gave Americans access to a seemingly unlimited supply of oil. It also bolstered a deeply radical regime devoted to promoting forms of anti-Americanism that would ultimately prove more devastating to the United States than anything emanating from Moscow.

Allen worked from an unmarked building at 2430 E Street, in the Foggy Bottom section of Washington. One day as he was arriving for work, he overheard a guide telling a group of tourists, "This is where the spies work." He concluded that it was foolish to pretend otherwise, and ordered a sign put up in front that said CENTRAL INTELLIGENCE AGENCY.

This building was across the street from the State Department, a proximity that was more than casual. Foster and Allen had discovered that by working together, they could shake the world. They cooperated ever more closely. This created a nexus of power unmatched in American history.

"The process of delegation was carried a step beyond Eisenhower's delegation of powers to John Foster Dulles," Senator Eugene McCarthy wrote in his memoir. "Dulles's own delegation included his giving, in some cases, powers that he did not have to the Central Intelligence Agency, directed then by Allen Dulles, brother of the Secretary of State. The CIA became a major force in executing and formulating foreign policy. There were two particular advantages in such delegation. First, the CIA was more free of congressional intervention and supervision than was the State Department, and second, it was free to use methods that would not otherwise have been allowed."

Confidence in the power they wielded led Foster and Allen to believe they could begin defeating Ho in the spring of 1954. France was losing its will to fight him. Britain could generate none. At the Geneva conference, the United States began assuming the role its allies refused to play.

Negotiators from Cambodia, Laos, and the two enemy factions in Vietnam—one led by Ho, the other anti-Communist—gathered around a horseshoe-shaped table at the old League of Nations headquarters with the foreign ministers of France, Britain, the United States, the Soviet Union, and China. The timing could not have been better for Ho. On May 7, soon after delegates began their work in Geneva, his Viet Minh forces overran the French garrison at Dien Bien Phu. The Western powers were split on how to respond. Britain and France reluctantly agreed that Ho had won the right to at least a portion of power. Foster found this abhorrent and could not accept it.

The Geneva conference was, among other things, a diplomatic debut for the five-year-old People's Republic of China, the first time its diplomats had appeared on the world stage. Zhou Enlai arrived with an entourage of two hundred. He installed himself in a twenty-room château where Rousseau had once lived. At his first grand reception, Scotch whisky and Italian vermouth were served along with caviar and frogs' legs.

No American attended this reception, because Foster had instructed his delegation to have no contact with the Chinese. During plenary sessions he refused to acknowledge Zhou's presence and, according to one British diplomat, projected "almost pathological rage and gloom" with his "mouth drawn down at the corners and his eyes on the ceiling, sucking on his teeth." By another account he "conducted himself with the pinched distaste of a puritan in a house of ill repute."

This determination to reject corporal reality for diplomatic reasons led Foster to the oddest and perhaps most wounding contortion of his public career.

"At the first meeting," the American diplomat U. Alexis Johnson recalled years later, "when we went out into the reception hall for a break in the meeting, Zhou Enlai was there. . . . And when Dulles came in, Zhou Enlai moved towards him, obviously to shake his hand. A number of photographers were around, and Dulles quite brusquely turned his back. . . . This deeply wounded Zhou, and over the years, even up to now, Zhou recounts this incident to visitors, and it very deeply, I think, affected his attitude. I'm not saying political factors would have changed, but this was a loss of face, of course, and a deep wound as far as Zhou Enlai was concerned, and this had some effect. I knew this. I saw it and I could see it reflected throughout the rest of the conference."

Nearly everyone in Washington still believed that China and the Soviet Union were marching in lockstep, rather than careening toward a bitter split. The dismissal of the State Department's senior East Asia experts, and their replacement by "China Lobby" partisans, left no one to explain subtleties or argue for a diplomatic overture. Any suggestion that Foster meet with Zhou, or even shake his hand, would have disappeared into a fog of unexamined assumptions.

"Unfortunately, there are governments or rulers that do not respect the elemental decencies of international conduct so that they can properly be brought into the organized family of nations," Foster said in explaining his behavior at Geneva. "That is illustrated by the regime which now rules the Chinese mainland."

Soon after the Geneva talks began, Foster sensed that his nightmare scenario was unfolding. It took him just a week to realize that he had no hope of keeping Ho from power. As soon as he did, he flew home. It is the only time in American history that a secretary of state has abandoned a big-power conference before it ended.

"Dull, unimaginative, uncomprehending," Churchill said of Foster when he learned of his abrupt departure from Geneva. "So clumsy I hope he will disappear."

Three months of talks at Geneva, interrupted by the fall of the French government, finally produced an accord. Vietnam would be partitioned at its waist, along the seventeenth parallel. Ho would rule from Hanoi in the north, while France and her allies would shape a pro-Western regime in the south, headquartered in Saigon. Partition would last for two years, during which outside powers would refrain from sending troops or weapons to support any faction. In July 1956 an election would be held "under the supervision of an international commission." The country would be reunited under whoever won.

France's ambassador in Washington and future foreign minister Maurice Couve de Murville candidly described this as "an agreement to leave it to the Communists because nobody could prevent it." The Paris newspaper *Le Figaro* said France was "in mourning," but welcomed the accord because it meant "French blood will no longer flow in a hopeless battle." Foster considered it calamitous. The United States refused to sign the Geneva accord. Foster issued a statement saying that the United States would respect it as long as doing so did not weaken American security and would "refrain from the threat or use of force" to disturb it.

Had Foster accepted the Geneva accord and persuaded Eisenhower to do so, the United States could have avoided involvement in Vietnam. Instead he resisted it, did not consider the United States bound by its provisions, and ultimately acted to subvert it. He believed the United States had a duty, in Indochina as elsewhere, to "fill the vacuum of power" left by retreating colonial powers—and to maintain "not merely the ability to act in an emergency, but day in, day out presence."

Once it became clear that Vietnam would be partitioned, Foster and Allen realized that the temporary new state to be created in the south would be their platform. They would have to find someone to lead it. Their ideal candidate would be a figure inspirational enough to displace Ho as

the country's national hero and then defeat him, either politically or mili-
tarily. This was the first of many impossible tasks the United States set out
to achieve in Vietnam.

Ngo Dinh Diem, a portly Catholic mandarin, had been a minor official in Vietnam and was interior minister for three months in 1933. He
had not held a job in the more than two decades since then, living instead
in seminaries, including one in Lakewood, New Jersey, that was overseen
by the redoubtable Cardinal Spellman. His Christianity made him an
unlikely leader of his homeland—Vietnam is 90 percent Buddhist—but
Americans appreciated it. Spellman introduced him to opinion makers
like Henry Luce, and Catholic politicians like Senators Mike Mansfield
and John F. Kennedy. When the time came for American leaders to choose
a savior for South Vietnam, they knew no one else.

Some who had worked with Diem doubted that anyone would be able
to turn him into a statesman. General Paul Ely, the French chief of staff,
considered him "extremely pig-headed." Emperor Bao Dai, who had ruled
the country with French support before retiring to Cannes, called him
"a psychopath who wishes to martyrize himself even at the price of
thousands of lives," but offered to name him prime minister because he
believed—correctly, as it turned out—that Diem would be able to lure the
United States into the role France was abandoning.

"I had said to Foster Dulles when we were at a meeting, 'I don't think
Diem is the man for that,'" Pierre Mendes-France, the French prime minister, recalled years later. "Number one, he is a man from the north. He is
not a man from this country. He's coming from the north, so the people in
this South Vietnam country don't feel he belongs, you understand? Number two, he's Catholic. . . . Here is something which, again, doesn't belong
in that country. Number three, he's connected with very reactionary military circles, and I don't think he is able to make any democratic reforms.
You cannot count on him for agrarian reform, for example, because he has
too many landlords in his entourage. . . . Number four, he's a man having
too much confidence in the police, in some kind of government which is
always treading toward a Fascist conception."

Mendes-France was designing the Geneva accord that Foster considered a craven surrender, so his words had little effect. Foster and Allen
decided Diem was the best candidate available. With their blessing, Bao
Dai offered him the leadership of South Vietnam. He accepted and, on

June 25, 1954, flew from Paris to Saigon to take over a country that did not yet exist.

Allen chose one of his favorite operatives, Edward Lansdale, to coach Diem toward popularity and ultimately to victory over Ho. In the Philippines during the early 1950s, Lansdale had raised an obscure politician, Ramon Magsaysay, to national leadership and helped him crush a guerrilla insurgency, using tactics ranging from folklore-based propaganda to election rigging to napalm bombing. Now Lansdale would be sent to Saigon, with the rank of an air force colonel and cover as an assistant air attaché, to work the same magic with Diem.

"I want you to do what you did in the Philippines," Foster told Lansdale at a send-off meeting.

The day Diem arrived to assume leadership of his new country, he met the man Allen had sent to guide him toward victory.

Lansdale strode into Gia Long Palace, formerly the French governor's residence, and found Diem walking down a corridor in one of his trademark white suits. He introduced himself, and the two men withdrew for the first of what would be countless private talks. This was the beginning of a long and intense partnership between two men and two governments.

Just hours after this fateful meeting, in faraway Guatemala, President Jacobo Arbenz resigned. On a single weekend—June 26–27, 1954—the second Dulles target fell and covert action against the third began.

Diem was installed as prime minister ten days later. In the months that followed, Lansdale saved him twice, once from a coup by his army chief of staff and then from an uprising by powerful gangs and religious sects. Using the blank check Allen had given him, Lansdale paid $12 million to rebel leaders who agreed to call off their plots, and hired mercenaries to crush the sect that would not be bribed.

The violence of this crackdown, along with Diem's corruption and refusal to broaden his government beyond his own narrow clique, set off a wave of angry speeches and editorials in the United States. Eisenhower felt compelled to send a special envoy to Vietnam, and when the envoy, General J. Lawton Collins, returned, he recommended that Diem be replaced. Allen, however, had received a cable from Lansdale arguing that despite his flaws, Diem "represented a better chance of success" than any possible replacement. Allen passed this verdict to Foster, who in turn brought it to Eisenhower. All accepted it. There was no more talk of replacing Diem.

This was the moment at which United States involvement in Vietnam became a Dulles project. Foster and Allen decided to throw in their lot with Diem. They persuaded Eisenhower. That set a fateful course.

Long-secret documents from mid-1954 make clear that both sides realized they were heading toward a clash. In August the National Security Council, where Foster and Allen held decisive influence, adopted a directive entitled "U.S. Policies Toward Post-Geneva Vietnam," which declared that France must be made to "disassociate" itself entirely from Vietnam so the United States could fight Ho in its own way.

Ho also saw war coming.

"Up to now we have concentrated our efforts on wiping out the forces of the French imperialist aggressor," he told his comrades at a clandestine meeting. "But now the French are having talks with us, while the American imperialists are becoming our main and direct enemy. So our spearhead must be directed at the latter. Until peace is restored, we shall keep fighting the French. But the focus of our attention, and that of the world's people, should be on the United States."

At the Saigon Military Mission, as Lansdale's covert cell was known, agents were busy carrying out Allen's multi-pronged strategy. They sent teams trained at Clark Air Base in the Philippines to carry out operations in the north, ranging from sabotaging bus depots and train lines to attacking government outposts. After several months it became clear that these operations were having little effect; by one account, every Vietnamese agent they sent northward defected to Ho's army. Lansdale also launched a series of rumor campaigns, most aimed at playing on traditional Vietnamese superstitions. In the second half of 1954 alone, he helped publish more than 150 different books, pamphlets, and leaflets and distributed fifty million copies of them. This effort also produced no palpable results.

Allen pressed Lansdale to come up with a more imaginative and audacious "psy-war" project. Ideally it would be one that would both wound Ho and persuade Americans that fighting him was vital to their freedom and security. This was the genesis of what the historian Bernard Fall called "an extremely intensive, well-conducted and, in terms of its objective, very successful American psychological warfare operation." Like the pastoral letter that Allen had used to turn Guatemalans against Arbenz, this one aimed to mobilize religious sentiment for political purposes.

Lansdale seized on a provision of the Geneva accord that allowed anyone in North or South Vietnam to move freely to the other part of the
country. More than one million Catholics lived in the north. Communists had not treated Catholics well in Indochina, and CIA officers
launched a large-scale propaganda campaign aimed at frightening them
into abandoning their homes and fleeing to the south. They bribed sooth-
sayers to predict doom in the north, persuaded priests to tell their parish-
ioners that "the Virgin Mary has fled to the south," and distributed leaflets
suggesting that Ho's regime was plotting anti-Catholic pogroms, had
invited Chinese troops into the country who were raping Vietnamese
women, and expected an American nuclear attack. Tens of thousands,
then hundreds of thousands, responded to this campaign. Carrying their
belongings on their backs, they flooded into the harbor town of Haiphong,
where U.S. Navy warships were waiting to carry them south. This is said
to have been the largest-scale naval evacuation in history.

Lansdale, steeped in the principles of advertising and "psy-war," concluded that the story of Operation Passage to Freedom would resonate
more deeply if he could find a single figure to personify it. Americans
associated the anti-Communist crusade with dour scolds like Foster, Senator McCarthy, and Cardinal Spellman. Lansdale wished to give it a
brighter face.

The face he chose belonged to a young man named Tom Dooley, a
handsome young Notre Dame graduate who had become a doctor, enlisted
in the navy, and thrown himself into the noble mission of rescuing Christians from Ho. Within months of his arrival, Lansdale began steering
journalists to him. They pounced on the human aspect of his story, and he
quickly became a popular hero in the United States.

Americans admired Dooley because he reflected them as they believed
themselves to be. He was an idealist, like Shane, who wished only to help
others. In his best-selling book, *Deliver Us from Evil*, Dooley described Ho
as "a Moscow puppet" who had launched his revolution "by disembowel-
ing more than 1,000 native women in Hanoi." Fortunately for the Vietnamese, "our love and help were available, just because we were in the
uniforms of the U.S. Navy." Dooley provided a narrative calculated to
move the American soul: Christians in a foreign land were being brutal-
ized by Communists; these Communists also wished to harm Americans;
therefore, the United States must act.

"The American press reported on the million-person migration as if it were a spontaneous rejection of communism and the manifestation of a natural yearning of people for freedom," according to one study. "The media portrayed the typical refugee as a devout Catholic who wished to practice his or her religion freely. Newsreels depicted U.S. naval vessels crammed with humble and hungry huddled masses being transported to freedom by kindhearted and white-uniformed sailors of the U.S. Navy. Photographs showed the small, stooped, frightened, and bedraggled Vietnamese peasants finding safety in the arms of their big, clean, strong American protectors. . . . What the American public was not told, however, is that much of what they were seeing and hearing was the result of a CIA-instigated propaganda campaign designed to frighten Catholics in North Vietnam and to elicit sympathy for them in the United States."

The Tom Dooley story was a masterstroke for Allen, Lansdale, and the CIA. It might have been tarnished when Dooley was forced out of the navy for homosexuality, but the facts were hushed up. A poll in the late 1950s found him to be one of the ten most admired people in the United States. For a time after his death in 1961, the Catholic Church considered canonizing him.

"As a key agent in the first disinformation campaign of the Vietnam War," one scholar wrote of Dooley, "he performed the crucial propaganda function of making the American people knowledgeable of and willing to fight Communism in Southeast Asia."

While Allen and his agents in Saigon escalated their covert war against Ho, Foster attacked on the diplomatic front. Eager to show that the United States still had friends in the world after the debacle at Geneva, he flew off for meetings in Europe but pointedly left France off his itinerary. This produced much unhappiness in Paris, where people had been stunned by the loss of their colony in Indochina and were sensitive to insult. One French newspaper lamented that Foster had shown "a remarkable lack of psychology."

Foster's next step was to pull pro-American governments into a new regional alliance, the Southeast Asia Treaty Organization, or SEATO, modeled on the robust NATO alliance in Europe. He imagined it as a symbol of resolve in the face of Communism and a font of support for the new state the United States was creating in South Vietnam. Despite his efforts, SEATO never became a major political or military force. Its member states—Britain, France, Australia, New Zealand, Thailand, the Philippines, Pakistan, and the United States—committed themselves only to "consult" in case of emergency, not to come to each other's defense in time of war or establish a joint military command.

SEATO may have done more harm than good. Foster, often with quiet help from Allen, used all the pressure he could muster to pull regional leaders in. The most popular among them, however, were neutralists who wanted fewer, not more, military alliances in the world. Among those who were deeply unhappy with the emergence of SEATO were Sukarno of Indonesia, U Nu of Burma, and Prince Sihanouk of Cambodia. Sihanouk later wrote about his decision not to join.

> U.S. Secretary of State John Foster Dulles and his brother, CIA Director Allen Dulles, each visited me and attempted to persuade me to place Cambodia under the protection of SEATO. I kindly declined the offer, preferring to adopt a neutral stance in the conflict between our neighbors and the U.S. I considered SEATO an aggressive military alliance directed against neighbors whose ideology I did not share but with whom Cambodia had no quarrel. I had made all this quite clear to John Foster, an acidy, arrogant man, but his brother soon turned up with a briefcase full of documents "proving" that Cambodia was about to fall victim to "communist aggression" and that the only way to save the country, the monarchy, and myself was to accept the protection of SEATO. The "proofs" did not coincide with my own information, and I replied to Allen Dulles as I had replied to John Foster: Cambodia wanted no part of SEATO. We would look after ourselves as neutrals and Buddhists. There was nothing for the secret service chief to do but pack up his dubious documents and leave.

At least as damaging to United States security over the long run was Foster's determination to bring Pakistan into the alliance, despite the fact that it is not in Southeast Asia. He dealt mainly with Pakistani generals, to whom he promised $250 million in aid so they could quadruple the size of their army, and let them know that he considered them, not the elected civilian government, as America's preferred partner in Pakistan. This appalled Prime Minister Jawaharlal Nehru in neighboring India, who believed SEATO was "more likely to promote mistrust and suspicion than security." Nehru presciently warned that Pakistani membership would weaken that country's nascent democracy, push it toward militarism, and subject it to endless pressures from Washington. "When military aid comes in, the whole country becomes a base," he told the Indian parliament. "It is not a question of an odd base here or there. It is the whole country which can be utilized for purposes laid down by other peoples and countries."

The *New York Times* reported that "nothing in the realm of foreign affairs has so exercised India since she became free as the proposed extension of United States military aid to Pakistan," and that SEATO had led to a "sharp deterioration in relations between India and the United States." This was fine with Foster, who detested Nehru. He encouraged Pakistani generals to exercise authority in ways that deformed their country's political system and ultimately led the United States to much grief. Even at the time it seemed hard to understand, and Walter Lippmann asked him about it in an interview.

"Look, Walter," Dulles told him, "I've got to get some real fighting men into the south of Asia. The only Asians who can really fight are the Pakistanis. That's why we need them in the alliance. We could never get along without the Gurkhas."

"But Foster," Lippmann replied, "the Gurkhas aren't Pakistanis."

"Well, they may not be Pakistanis, but they're Moslems."

"No, I'm afraid they're not Moslems, either. They're Hindus."

"No matter!" Foster replied, and launched into a half-hour lecture about the dangers of Communism in Asia.

Foster was at the founding SEATO meeting in Manila when, on September 3, 1954, artillery batteries on the Chinese mainland unleashed a barrage of fire at the small islands of Quemoy and Matsu, which lay close to the mainland but were controlled by the Nationalist regime in Taiwan. The administration's leading hawk, Admiral Radford, saw this as a chance to wage the war for which he and others in the "China Lobby" were eager. Supported by two of the other three Joint Chiefs of Staff—the dissenter was General Matthew Ridgway of the army—he urged Eisenhower to bomb China in retaliation. Foster was sympathetic and brought up the possibility of using nuclear weapons, which he claimed could "utterly

destroy military targets without endangering unrelated civilian centers."
He abandoned this proposal after CIA analysts estimated that a nuclear
attack on China would kill twelve to fourteen million civilians. Eisenhower was relieved.

"We're not talking now about a limited, brush-fire war," the president
told the National Security Council. "We're talking about going to the
threshold of World War III."

In this mini-crisis, Foster behaved much as he had during the debate
several months earlier over Dien Bien Phu. His instinct was to respond to
global challenges by using, or at least threatening to use, military force.
Eisenhower was more cautious, preferring to navigate what he called the
"narrow and dangerous waters between appeasement and global war."

Foster did manage, however, to persuade Eisenhower that he should
not give "Red China" an apology for covert air flights over Chinese
territory—even though it might have produced the release of two captured CIA fliers.

Late in 1954 the Chinese government announced that the two, John
Downey and Richard Fecteau, whose plane had been shot down while on
a mission to pick up a CIA courier inside China, had been tried, convicted
of espionage, and sentenced to long prison terms. Both men had pleaded
guilty. Prime Minister Zhou Enlai suggested that he was open to negotiating their release, and even invited the men's relatives to visit them. Foster
forbade these visits and denounced the Chinese for their "reprehensible"
imprisonment of two Americans on "trumped up charges." He might
have used this case as a way to begin a dialogue with China. As he had
shown by snubbing Zhou at Geneva a few months earlier, however, he was
disposed in the opposite direction.

In 1957 Zhou made another overture, offering to free the two airmen
if Foster would allow a delegation of American journalists to visit China,
but Foster scorned this as "blackmail." There the case lay for more than a
decade, until Chinese-American hostility finally began to fade. In the
warmer climate that surrounded President Nixon's visits to Beijing in
the early 1970s, the United States finally made the admission for which
China had been waiting: the two men were intelligence officers. Fecteau
was released in 1971. Downey came home two years later.

"One must look to Secretary of State John Foster Dulles to understand fully the complex and disappointing course of the prisoner affair," one study concluded years later.

> The Secretary's extraordinary animosity toward the Chinese Communists and communism in general, combined with his tendency toward over-simplification and exaggeration, precluded him from cooperating with the Chinese. A moralist to the end, Dulles consistently saw the Downey-Fecteau case as a fight between good and evil, between right and wrong, and thus compromise was never a realistic possibility. Further, Dulles's strong allegiance to the conservative "China Lobby" and McCarthyites in Washington gave his moral revulsion to the Chinese a degree of political legitimacy. While these characteristics may have been common among American officials during the 1950s, as Secretary of State (and one with the unflinching trust of the president), Dulles's personality had extraordinary influence on American policy and action. Thus it was the unlucky, but not coincidental, fate of John Downey and Richard Fecteau to be imprisoned for two decades after flying covertly over China at the height of the Cold War, with a stubborn, anticommunist, anti-Chinese figure serving as the American Secretary of State.

Since few leaders in other countries considered the world to be as irreconcilably divided as Foster believed it to be, he was often isolated. His relations with Britain were especially poor. He considered Foreign Secretary Eden soft, weak, and unwilling to confront the Soviet menace— hardly better than the French, whose decision to abandon Indochina he found unforgivable. According to one of Foster's close aides, he had "absolutely no regard" for Eden's positions on world affairs and believed "you could simply not count on the British." Eden, who fruitlessly pleaded with Foster to soften his attitude toward China, returned this low esteem. He considered Foster a narrow-minded ideologue and deplored his vivid denunciations of Communism. According to a memoir by one of Eden's advisers, the British foreign secretary saw Foster as "always ready to go on the rampage."

Churchill agreed. After one of their meetings he remarked, "Foster Dulles is the only case I know of a bull who carries his own china shop around with him."

Although Foster and Allen continued to share an almost identical worldview, their private lives remained as different as ever. Allen loved being the center of attention at dinners and parties where he could impress men and flirt with women. Sometimes he did more than flirt. One of the women with whom he is reported to have conducted an affair during the mid-1950s was Clare Boothe Luce, the wife of his old friend Henry Luce—who was then seeing Allen's longtime partner Mary Bancroft. Another of his conquests, according to several accounts, was Queen Frederika of Greece, formerly a German princess. Luce may have been sharing a private joke when he put Frederika on the cover of *Time* with the caption, "My Power Is the Love of the People."

One foreign correspondent who covered the Middle East during this period met Allen at a reception in Cairo, where he was trying to arrange the overthrow of President Gamal Abdel Nasser. "We were talking animatedly about Arab-Israeli problems," the correspondent wrote afterward, "when a long-legged Swedish blonde passed by, showed all her teeth in a large smile, and said, 'Why, Allen Dulles!' He was off in her direction like a shot."

Foster had a different way of relaxing. Every few months he and Janet would decamp to their rough-hewn cabin on Duck Island in Lake Ontario. During these stays he dropped out of contact with Washington, refused all visitors, and devoted himself to sailing, fishing, hiking, and whatever else might take his mind off work and bring back boyhood memories. In 1955 he turned sixty-seven but seemed remarkably vigorous.

"When you figure that he had thromboid phlebitis, very bad eyes, malaria, a slipped disc, diverticulitis, quite serious hay fever if he didn't watch it, and finally cancer, which is quite a complement of physical ills, it's amazing how he refused to let them limit his activities or cloud his brain," his sister Eleanor later marveled. "He got about as much out of his body and mind as he could possibly have done."

Foster's sojourns on Duck Island and his ceaseless foreign travels were in part a way to escape from his administrative responsibilities, in which he had no interest. He wanted to run the world, not the State Department. To those around him he projected what one contemporary called "the heavy opaqueness of a large bear—massive in physique, in energy, in capacity for work, in self-certitude." His closeness to Eisenhower made him powerful, but he remained the reserved, distant figure he had always been. Once he asked an aide to make a list of interesting guests who might enliven the formal dinners he hosted for visiting dignitaries. When he saw Marlene Dietrich's name on the list, he was taken aback.

"Perhaps the department has gone too far," he said.

Resplendent in embroidered robes that billowed in the tropical wind, wrapped in saffron pajamas like those worn by Buddhist monks, and even, in a few cases, wearing business suits and bowler hats, leaders of twenty-nine Asian and African nations gathered at the provincial Indonesian city of Bandung for one of the twentieth century's most remarkable summits, the Asian-African Conference. If there was a historical moment when the modern Third World or "non-aligned movement" was born, this was it. Never before had leaders of so many former colonies— their countries had 1.6 billion inhabitants, more than half of humanity— gathered to set a common course. Most shared the neutralist passion of their host, President Sukarno of Indonesia, who welcomed them on April 18, 1955, with a speech calling on big powers to give up their interventionist mind-set and adopt the "live and let live principle."

"How terrifically dynamic is our time!" Sukarno cried. "We can mobilize all the spiritual, all the moral, all the political strength of Africa and Asia on the side of peace. Yes, we! We, the people of Asia and Africa!"

Foster considered neutralism a Kremlin project and the Bandung conference "a communist road show," as *Time* called it. In a speech broadcast on national radio and television, he warned Americans not to be fooled by what might come out of "a so-called Afro-Asian conference." He saw the conference not as a chance for leaders of emerging nations to meet and clamor for change, but as part of a Soviet effort to seduce and conquer the Third World. In private his aides scorned it as "the Dark-Town Strutters' Ball."

As Foster feared, the ringing doctrine of neutralism stirred delegates at Bandung. They cheered Nehru when he said, "I do not believe in the communist or the anti-communist approach." Nasser insisted that "the game of power politics in which small nations can be used as tools must be stopped." Most intriguingly, Prime Minister Zhou Enlai of China, in his second appearance at a major conference in as many years, made several thoughtful speeches insisting that Chinese leaders "do not want to have a war with the United States," and wanted to "discuss the question of relaxing tension in the Far East." Zhou met with diplomats from many countries, listened to their concerns about China, assuaged many of them, and seemed, as Foreign Minister Carlos Romulo of the Philippines put it, "affable of manner, moderate of speech." A correspondent for the *Economist* reported that Zhou "played his cards there with superb skill."

"He behaved very humbly and put the six hundred million people of China on the same level, say, as Ceylon or Laos," the correspondent wrote. "Bandung has been compared to the Magna Carta and the Gettysburg Address, and it had the same timeless quality of certainty about it. For the Chinese Communists it was a master stroke to place themselves at the center of such a gathering."

African and Asian leaders met at Bandung as the civil rights movement in the United States was beginning to grow. In 1953 the National Book Award for fiction was awarded to *Invisible Man*, Ralph Ellison's searing best seller about growing up black in America. A year later the Supreme Court ruled school segregation unconstitutional, and then ordered integration to proceed "with all deliberate speed." The murder in Mississippi of a black teenager, Emmett Till, set off a wave of outrage in the summer and fall of 1955. It had barely subsided when an Alabama woman, Rosa Parks, refused to move to the rear of a segregated bus, as required by law, setting off a boycott of buses in Montgomery that lasted for more than a year. A deeply ingrained paradigm of American life was being thrown into question.

Civil rights leaders in the United States would soon begin tying their campaign to a larger, transnational movement that was emerging in post-colonial countries. This was an enormous leap of consciousness. It may be traced in part to Bandung and its influence on American civil rights advocates.

Organizers of the Asian-African Conference invited the United States to send observers. Congressman Adam Clayton Powell Jr. of Harlem urged Foster to assemble "not an all-white Department of State team but a team composed of Negroes and whites, Jews and Gentiles, Protestants and Catholics" so the world would see "that America is a democracy of the people." Foster replied that he had no intention of recognizing the conference or sending anyone to represent the United States.

"The Department of State deliberately and calculatedly imperiled the future of the United States for perhaps the rest of our lives," Powell wrote in his memoir. "When I realized that our government's stupidity would not allow them to send an observer to this, one of the most significant conferences of our times, I then informed the administration that I was going to Bandung anyway, and I was going to pay my own way. Immediately all hell broke loose."

On the day the conference opened, twin front-page headlines in the *Observer*, Indonesia's only English-language newspaper, read "United States Refuses to Send Message to Asian-African Conference" and "Best Wishes for Asian-African Conference from Union of Soviet Socialist Republics." Powell wrote that "not a single journalist at Bandung could understand why our government had been so blind," and concluded, "We missed the boat in Bandung." After returning he sent Eisenhower a series of recommendations, including that he tour countries emerging from colonialism and consider calling a Third World summit of his own. Eisenhower rejected all except one: that he recruit more blacks into the diplomatic corps so American embassies would not present all-white faces.

After his return, Powell dropped by CIA headquarters to see Allen.

"Allen Dulles was a wonderful, dedicated man, usually in a tweed suit and always smoking a pipe," he wrote. "I was seated beside him, with the top espionage leaders of our country around the rest of the table. The soundproof room was guarded. I began to tell Allen Dulles about the final communiqué issued by the Asian-African powers. He became excited and asked, 'Where did you get this?' I said, 'They were printed in English and stacked on the desk at the Information Center for anyone who wanted one.' He pounded on the table. . . . He, the head of the Central Intelligence Agency, hadn't been informed of its release."

The other influential black American who was sufficiently intrigued by the promise of Bandung to travel there was the impassioned novelist and social critic Richard Wright, who like Powell saw links between the structures of American power at home and those it enforced abroad. Wright traveled to Bandung and interviewed scores of delegates.

"There was something extra-political, extra-social, almost extra-human about it; it smacked of tidal waves, of natural forces," he wrote afterward. "Over and beyond the waiting throngs that crowded the streets at Bandung, the conference had a most profound influence upon the color-conscious millions in all the countries of the earth."

Malcolm X did not attend the conference, but it strongly impressed him.

He told his followers it was "the first unity meeting in centuries of black people—and once you study what happened at the Bandung conference, and the results of the Bandung conference, it actually serves as a model for the same procedure you and I can use to get our problems solved."

Foster's diplomacy in the post-Bandung period was aimed not at softening the clash between superpowers, as neutralists wished to do, but sharpening it. One of his tactics was constructing anti-Soviet alliances, or what some in the press called "pactomania." Having created SEATO in 1954, he went on in 1955 to create CENTO, the Central Treaty Organization, whose founding members were Britain, Turkey, Iraq, Iran, and Pakistan. It began falling apart just three years later, when Iraq withdrew, and never had a substantial impact on regional events.

Although Foster willingly negotiated with smaller countries, many of which had little choice but to accept his terms, he continued to oppose direct talks with the Soviet enemy. In 1955, however, Eisenhower overruled him and agreed to meet the Soviet Union's post-Stalin leaders. The summit, which opened in Geneva on July 18, 1955, was staged in a tense climate. Eight months earlier Foster had won approval for one of his most cherished projects, the integration of West Germany into NATO, and in May 1955 the Soviets had responded by creating a military alliance of their own, the Warsaw Pact. Eisenhower made news at the summit by proposing a plan he called "Open Skies," under which the United States and Soviet Union would be allowed to photograph each other's territory from high-altitude planes, but nothing came of it. Foster had decreed before the talks began that no Americans should be photographed smiling or shaking hands with Russians. Eisenhower obeyed with some difficulty; the columnist Stewart Alsop later recalled that "his whole instinct was to smile and be friendly" but instead "he'd kind of draw back, remembering what Foster had said." This summit proved to be only a momentary Cold War icebreaker.

Two meetings of powerful leaders, held thousands of miles apart, reflected profoundly different views of the world. Leaders who gathered at Geneva presented the traditional Cold War narrative: two warring blocs led by Moscow and Washington. Those who convened at Bandung offered a counter-narrative. They saw a world divided not between Communists and anti-Communists, but between nations emerging from colonialism and established powers determined to continue influencing them. The summit at Geneva helped maintain a delicate peace between superpowers.

From the Asian-African Conference emerged a kaleidoscope of nationalist passions that would shape the next half century.

A year after the Dulles brothers set out to destroy Ho Chi Minh, he remained not only alive but strong, popular, and certain to win the nationwide election mandated by the Geneva accord. Eisenhower admitted at a press conference that Ho would take "possibly eighty percent" of the vote. This might have been the moment for a pause, even for soul-searching. For Foster and Allen it was not. Determined to block or topple Ho, they forged ahead.

In the spring of 1955, Foster traveled to Paris for talks with French leaders. His goal was to persuade the French that they must wash their hands of Vietnam and turn responsibility for its security over to the United States. Prime Minister Edgar Faure, who abhorred Diem but saw that the United States was determined to rise or fall with him, reluctantly agreed. Foster did not wish to formalize this accord into a treaty, but came home with a "kind of gentleman's agreement" that gave the United States freedom to wage war in Vietnam on its own terms.

"Suppression of alternatives, both on the general and particular level, led to a circularity in and reinforcement of existing policies," the Pentagon Papers concluded years later. "There is little indication that U.S. policymakers, their thoughts dominated by the objective of containing the monolithic communist bloc, faced up to the costs of winning the Indochina war, even while direct U.S. intervention was being considered."

Eisenhower played twenty-seven holes of golf at a Colorado resort on September 23, 1955, and then dined on hamburger and onions. Before dawn the next morning, he suffered what doctors called a moderate coronary thrombosis. The heart attack kept him away from Washington for six weeks. His senior aides made great efforts to maintain a public sense of stability. Foster traveled as planned to a summit of foreign ministers in Paris while his boss was hospitalized. He set off a tempest, however, with an interview he gave to *Life* in which he said that his diplomacy was aimed at bringing the United States "to the verge of war." His words struck many as terrifying. Newspapers around the world denounced him—one in London called him an "edgy gambler"—and James Reston of the *New York Times* wrote that he had become a "supreme expert" in the art of diplomatic blundering.

"He doesn't just stumble into booby traps," Reston observed. "He digs them to size, studies them carefully, and then jumps."

Half a world away at the Saigon Military Mission, Edward Lansdale was launching the next stage of his covert war. He and Diem agreed, with approval from Foster and Allen, that the national vote in July 1956, mandated by the Geneva accord, should not be held. "We will not be tied down by the treaty that was signed against the wishes of the Vietnamese people," Diem declared in announcing this decision.

Allen feared it would be difficult to persuade Americans to support a leader who had consolidated power by canceling an election. For their benefit, and also to remove the last obstacle to American influence in Vietnam, he encouraged Diem to stage a referendum in which voters would be asked if they wished to be ruled by him or Emperor Bao Dai. It was held on October 23, 1955. Lansdale arranged for ballots favoring Diem to be printed in red, considered lucky in Vietnam, while the Bao Dai ballot was green, the traditional color of misfortune. Campaigning for Bao Dai, who remained in France, was forbidden. Cartoons and other material, much of it designed by Lansdale's men, showed the emperor in pornographic poses with French women and defamed him as a "dung beetle who sold his country for personal glory." Local officials were ordered to bring peasants to the polls and tell them to vote for Diem.

As ballots were being cast, Lansdale advised Diem to announce that he had won 60 to 70 percent of the vote. This turned out to be one of the few times he could not bend Diem to his will. Diem insisted that his vote total be announced as 98 percent—and then decided on 98.2. In Saigon, where there were 450,000 registered voters, he claimed more than 600,000 votes.

Americans, wishing to believe they had found the "miracle man" who would woo the Vietnamese away from Ho, put aside their doubts and hailed Diem. "The people of Viet-Nam have spoken, and we, of course, recognize their decision," Foster said in a statement. His ambassador in Saigon, Frederick Reinhardt, pronounced the referendum a "resounding success." The *New York Times* called it "a sound democratic procedure [and] a public tribute to a strong-willed leader."

Three days after the vote, Diem proclaimed a rump Republic of Vietnam in his half of the country, with himself as president. Then he banned political parties and proclaimed a constitution that gave him the power to rule by decree for five years. This formalized his rejection of the all-Vietnam election that was to unify the country in 1956.

Ho would almost certainly have won the 1956 election, but no one can know what he would have done afterward. He might have established a regime that was Communist and repressive, but not fully subservient to Moscow and not anti-American—like the one he did in fact establish twenty years later. In a great failure of imagination, the political class in Washington never entertained this possibility.

"No systematic or serious examination of Vietnam's importance to the United States was ever undertaken," Leslie Gelb, the editor of the Pentagon Papers, wrote a quarter century later. "It was ritualistic anti-Communism and exaggerated power politics that got us into Vietnam. These were articles of faith and were not, therefore, ever seriously debated."

Yet at the same time that Foster and Allen were escalating their campaign against Ho, they not only accepted but embraced another Communist with whom the Vietnamese leader had much in common.

Josip Broz Tito, the leader of the patched-together country called Yugoslavia, committed himself to Communism in 1920, the same year Ho did. During World War II he, like Ho, led a resistance army that pinned down large numbers of occupying troops. Like Ho, he received support from the Office of Strategic Services despite his Communist convictions because he was bleeding the Axis. After the war, both leaders forged powerful Marxist movements, thereby making themselves enemies of the United States. Yet a few years after taking power, Tito broke with Moscow.

"No matter how much each of us loves the land of socialism, the USSR, he can in no case love his own country less," he wrote in a letter to Stalin.

For the first time, Foster considered the possibility that a Communist leader might also be a genuine nationalist, and not necessarily Moscow's lackey. At the end of 1955 he traveled to Yugoslavia to meet Tito. They sat on a terrace at Tito's villa on the Adriatic island of Brioni. During their talk, according to one account, Foster "became convinced once and for all of the Yugoslav commitment to independence." Upon his return he persuaded Eisenhower that although Tito was a Communist, he was not an enemy of the United States. The next year's American budget included $90 million in food aid to Tito's regime. It was an all but unimaginable gift, given Foster's implacable convictions. He showed something new: an ability to distinguish among various sorts of Communists.

Why was Foster able to see Tito this way, but not Ho? The best explanation stems from the Eurocentrism that was ingrained in his identity and that of almost every other American foreign policy specialist of his age. He, his brother, and Eisenhower had studied European history, were steeped in European politics, and understood the subtle interplays that for centuries had bound and separated European states. About East Asia, by contrast, they knew little. Blinded by their anger at "losing" China and robbed of expertise by the dismissal of the State Department's "China Hands," they never gave Ho the chance they gave Tito. Instead they drew closer to Diem, their anti-Ho.

"We have been exploring ways and means to permit our aid to Viet-Nam to be more effective and to make a greater contribution to the welfare and stability of the government of Viet-Nam," Eisenhower wrote to Diem in a letter dated October 23, the same day as the stage-managed referendum. "I am, accordingly, instructing the American Ambassador to Viet-Nam to examine with you in your capacity as Chief of Government, how an intelligent program of American aid given directly to your government can serve to assist Viet-Nam in its present hour of trial."

Three days later, in accordance with this offer, Secretary of Defense Charles Wilson directed the Joint Chiefs of Staff to prepare a "long-range program for the organization and training of a minimum number of free Vietnam forces necessary for internal security." Some historians point to the decisions of this week—Eisenhower's letter and Wilson's directive—as the beginning of a commitment to South Vietnam that would, over the next two decades, cost the United States more than $100 billion and the lives of more than fifty-eight thousand soldiers.

"None of [Foster] Dulles's actions was to bring forth a darker harvest than his refusal to allow the United States to support or even countenance a diplomatic settlement of the French colonial war in Indochina," Townsend Hoopes wrote two decades later. "Although he demonstrated tactical flexibility beneath a strident rhetoric, Dulles steadfastly refused to acknowledge the existence of any reasonable or legitimate claims on the Communist side."

During four years as a highly active secretary of state, Foster had become accustomed to being feted by world leaders. Allen normally traveled more discreetly, but in mid-1956, moved in part by the realization that he would certainly lose his job if Eisenhower was not re-elected that fall, he decided to take a grand tour. At the end of August, aboard the best-appointed plane the air force owned, the director of central intelligence set out to circle the globe in fifty-seven days.

At every stop Allen met with his station chiefs and case officers. He could not bring himself to keep a low profile, though. Dignitaries assembled to greet him wherever he landed. Heads of state and prime ministers hosted formal dinners for him. Reinhard Gehlen, the former Nazi spymaster who had become one of his closest collaborators, welcomed him in Bonn. Not one but two of his intimate friends, Clare Boothe Luce and Queen Frederika, met him in Athens. Turkey, Iran, Saudi Arabia, and Pakistan were next, followed by India, where Prime Minister Nehru complained to him about his brother's schematic approach to the world. In Thailand there were three days of feasting, complete with dancing girls. Vietnam was more work-oriented, including a formal meeting with President Diem and several sessions with Edward Lansdale. From there Allen flew to Manila, Hong Kong, Taipei, Tokyo, and Seoul. Everywhere he was hailed as a grand figure.

"I never saw him in later years," wrote Ray Cline, a CIA officer who accompanied him, "without our reminiscing about this famous trip, unique in the annals of the CIA, until tears of laughter came to our eyes."

Eisenhower's re-election campaign was going well when Allen returned to Washington, but whatever hopes he and Foster had for a tranquil autumn were wiped away with the sudden explosion of two world crises. Both were unexpected, and both exposed Foster and Allen to unaccustomed waves of criticism.

The crisis in Egypt began brewing soon after the Dulles brothers took office. They were suspicious of Colonel Gamal Abdel Nasser, the fiery nationalist who came to power after helping to topple the Egyptian monarchy in 1952, but for a time believed they could work with him. To their disappointment, he proved unwilling to accept the Cold War paradigm. When Foster warned him about the Soviet threat during their first meeting in mid-1953, he replied with the tart observation that the Soviets "have never occupied our country, but the British have been here for seventy years." Allen sent Kermit Roosevelt to help Nasser set up his security service and gave Roosevelt $3 million to spend in any way that might "harness Arab nationalism" to American purposes. A delegation of U.S. military commanders and CIA officers came to Cairo to offer Nasser a security partnership and $20 million in military aid. Foster suggested that if Nasser became an ally, the United States might even agree to finance Egypt's "dream project," the Aswan High Dam, which would open arid regions near the Nile to productive farming.

It was unrealistic to hope that any of this would shake Nasser from his neutralist principles. His cause, Arab nationalism, defined itself as resistance to power blocs. So virulently did he reject the idea of aligning Egypt with the United States that his ambassador in Washington, Ahmed Hussein, felt compelled to remind him that Foster and Allen knew how to destroy defiant leaders.

"Remember Guatemala," Ambassador Hussein warned him.

"To hell with Guatemala!" Nasser replied.

Foster was no less determined. He did not even reply to Nasser's detailed request for American weaponry and called Nasser's implicit threat to turn to the Soviets "immoral blackmail." In any case, he told aides, the threat was "surely a bluff—the Soviets just don't have that kind of surplus to sell or give away."

Seeking to intensify pressure on Nasser, Foster began retreating from his offer to finance the Aswan dam. "Washington began to treat Nasser's need for the dam as it had treated his need for arms, leaving his messages unanswered and its own promises unhonored," *New York Times* correspondent Kennett Love wrote afterward. Foster struck the final blow during a meeting with Ambassador Hussein on July 19, 1956.

"Please don't say you are going to withdraw the offer," the Egyptian ambassador pleaded. Patting his jacket pocket, he added, "We have the Russian offer to finance the dam right here."

"Well then," Foster replied curtly, "as you already have the money, you have no need of our support. The offer is withdrawn."

Nasser was outraged—"Americans, may you choke on your fury!"— and six days later, he lashed out against the West by nationalizing the Suez Canal, which was controlled by Britain and France. The British, desperate to hold their last major possession in the Middle East, decided to invade Egypt in the hope of deposing him. France, which was also bitter at Nasser for his support of rebels in French-controlled Algeria, agreed to join. So did Israel, which saw a chance to weaken a hostile Arab power and seize the Sinai peninsula. Planning for the invasion was kept so secret that not even the CIA learned of it.

As this crisis was about to explode, another one in Europe riveted the world's attention. A student-led protest rally in Budapest on October 23, 1956, gathered mass support and quickly snowballed into a revolt against Hungary's pro-Soviet regime. Military units rebelled, the border to Austria was opened, and Prime Minister Imre Nagy announced that Hungary would quit the Warsaw Pact and become "neutral" in the East-West conflict. The Soviets responded by ordering tanks to Budapest and crushing the uprising after several days of intense street fighting. Thousands were killed, a new pro-Moscow regime was installed, and Nagy was executed.

Foster had repeatedly called for the "liberation" of Eastern Europe. Allen had gone further, sending agents to encourage rebellion in every country behind the Iron Curtain. Yet when an uprising broke out in East Germany in 1953, the United States refused to aid the rebels. Three years later in Hungary, the story was much the same.

Street fighting was still raging in Budapest when, on October 29, the British, French, and Israelis launched their invasion of Egypt. Anticolonial outrage erupted across the Middle East and beyond. Eisenhower was furious, partly because he wished to see an end to European power in the Middle East in order to open the region to American influence. He began what turned out to be a successful effort to force the British, French, and Israelis to withdraw from Egypt. He also realized that the invasion had made Nasser a hero of epic proportions, and reluctantly told Foster and Allen that deposing him was no longer a realistic possibility.

"The President said that an action of this kind could not be taken when there is as much hostility as at present," according to notes of the meeting. "For a thing like this to be done without inflaming the Arab world, a time free from heated stress holding the world's attention, as at present, would have to be chosen."

This rush of events threw Foster and Allen off balance. They were publicly criticized for not having foreseen the invasion of Egypt, and also for having whipped up anti-Soviet feeling in Hungary and then done nothing when Hungarians rebelled against Soviet power. Before the year was out, they faced another new challenge when a project they had overseen produced results they did not expect.

Allen had worked for several years to build a capacity for high-altitude surveillance photography. He persuaded Eisenhower that this project should be run by the CIA rather than the Defense Department because the CIA, not hobbled by contract requirements, could move faster. The plane he developed with Lockheed Aircraft Corporation, the U-2, was able to take detailed photographs from seventy thousand feet, beyond the range of most antiaircraft weapons. On May 31, 1956, Eisenhower authorized the first U-2 flights over the Soviet Union. They began two weeks later, and photo analysts soon began producing reports on what they saw. Among their first findings was that the Soviets could not possibly be producing as many warplanes as the CIA had estimated. James Killian brought this finding to Eisenhower. He appreciated it but refused to agree with Killian that the overstated estimate reflected the "administrative inadequacies of Allen Dulles."

Eisenhower had appointed two thoughtful diplomats—Robert Lovett, a former secretary of defense, and David Bruce, who had been an OSS officer, ambassador to France, and undersecretary of state—to a body he had recently created, the President's Board of Consultants on Foreign Intelligence Activities, and in 1956 he asked the board to prepare a report on the CIA. The report, delivered several months later, warned about "the increased mingling in the internal affairs of other nations of bright, highly graded young men who must be doing something all the time to justify their reason for being." Bruce, Lovett, and others on the board made a series of suggestions to limit Allen's power, including moving his office to the White House and appointing a deputy to administer the CIA. Eisenhower rejected them all.

During Allen's first four years as director of central intelligence, Eisenhower repeatedly defended him and yielded to his judgment. He accepted Allen's advice that the United States continue to support Diem in South Vietnam even though his own personal envoy urged the opposite; he rejected General Doolittle's suggestion that he fire Allen; and he turned aside Killian's criticism of Allen's administrative ability. Following this pattern, he ignored his intelligence board when it recommended that he curb Allen's authority.

The nation that turned out to vote on November 6, 1956, was prosperous and largely united at home, despite rumblings from what would become the civil rights movement. What it feared lay abroad. In the weeks before the election, Soviet tanks had rolled into Budapest and three nations had invaded Egypt. This did not seem a good moment to change presidents. Eisenhower was overwhelmingly re-elected, preserving not only his own job but those of his secretary of state and director of central intelligence.

In his second inaugural address on January 20, 1957, Eisenhower described the world as he and most Americans saw it.

"The divisive force is International Communism and the power that it controls," he declared. "The designs of that power, dark in purpose, are clear in practice. It strives to seal forever the fate of those it has enslaved. It strives to break the ties that unite the free. And it strives to capture—to exploit for its own greater power—all forces of change in the world, especially the needs of the hungry and the hopes of the oppressed."

Once he had established the scope of this threat, Eisenhower vowed that the United States would resist no matter where it emerged. This was the essence of the "containment" doctrine that shaped American foreign policy for a generation.

"We recognize and accept our own deep involvement in the destiny of men everywhere," Eisenhower said. "And so the prayer of our people carries far beyond our own frontiers, to the wide world of our duty and our destiny."

Vietnam was the place "far beyond our own frontiers" where Eisenhower, along with Foster and Allen, saw the greatest danger. Yet their effort to undermine Ho was failing. Elaborately planned American operations had brought down two foreign leaders, but Ho proved more resilient.

This left Foster and Allen in search of a new target. During their first four years in office, they moved almost seamlessly from Mossadegh to Arbenz to Ho. With the presidential election behind them, they set out to choose their next victim.

8

THE SELF-INTOXICATED PRESIDENT

Rarely has a head of state anticipated a visit to the United States as eagerly as President Sukarno of Indonesia. American history fascinated him. As a boy he spent long evenings in imaginary conversations with Washington, Jefferson, and Lincoln. In his speech opening the Bandung Conference on April 18, 1955, he summoned Asian and African leaders to "the battle against colonialism," and then asked them, "Do you know that today is a famous anniversary in that battle? On April 18, 1775, Paul Revere rode at midnight through the New England countryside warning of the approach of British troops and the opening of the American War of Independence, the first successful anti-colonial war in history."

Sukarno spent much of his time crisscrossing Indonesia on trips that often lasted weeks, leaving little time for foreign travel. In 1956, however, after he had been in power for seven years and become one of the world's most magnetic leaders, he expressed interest in visiting the United States. John Foster Dulles was dubious. He detested Sukarno, not only for his neutralist politics but also for his personal style, which was unabashedly hedonistic and featured a parade of wives and girlfriends. Nonetheless, this towering figure was a strategic prize. Foster overcame his doubts and recommended that Eisenhower invite him.

"As the leader and personification of his people's struggle for independence, President Sukarno occupies a position of unique power and influence in Indonesia, the largest and most populous nation of Southeast Asia," he wrote in a memo to the president. "His lifetime efforts to separate

Indonesia from Dutch political and economic influence have biased his attitude toward many aspects of Western economic and political development. . . . I believe that we may broaden his outlook and increase his understanding by a visit to the United States."

Foster and Vice President Nixon were at National Airport to greet Sukarno when he arrived on May 16, 1956. The Indonesian leader was elegant as always in an impeccably tailored tunic, black felt cap, sunglasses, and inlaid baton. When he saw the animated crowd—twenty-five thousand people turned out to greet him—he broke away from his bodyguards and plunged in, shaking hands, kissing, and even squatting to introduce himself to a small boy wearing a cowboy outfit. Finally he returned to protocol, and rode with the secretary of state and the vice president to the White House. Eisenhower was waiting at the portico.

Their meeting was pleasant, though the two leaders did not resolve their differences. Sukarno objected to American support for the Dutch claim to western New Guinea, which Indonesia also claimed. Eisenhower, following Foster's advice, made no concessions and did not offer Sukarno any new aid. The two leaders lapsed into small talk. Eisenhower revealed that his favorite actor was Randolph Scott—not surprising, since many of Scott's films, like *Frontier Marshal* and *The Stranger Wore a Gun*, placed him in the role Eisenhower imagined as his own: a morally centered lawman who reluctantly uses violence to pacify dangerous places.

That evening, at a state dinner, Sukarno spoke warmly of the United States. "I am a brown man, an Indonesian, an Asiatic," he said. "Yet you accept me as a friend. Is that not real democracy?"

Sukarno charmed Americans. He told them he was "in love with your country" and had come "to appreciate you." Reporters swarmed around him. Their stories appeared under headlines like "Sukarno Captivates Washington" and "Indonesian President Wows Capital; Stops Tour to Kiss Ladies, Pat Babies." The *New York Times* hailed him as him "a sensitive Asian nationalist" with "an open-spirited, democratic nature much like that of the average American." Anticipation was high when he arrived on Capitol Hill to address a joint session of Congress. He did not disappoint and was interrupted repeatedly by applause—even when he asserted that nationalism, not Communism, was the most powerful political force in the world.

"Understand that, and you have the key to much of post-war history," he said. "Fail to understand it, and no amount of thinking, no torrent of words, and no Niagara of dollars will produce anything but bitterness and disillusionment."

Sukarno finished his speech with the wish that God would "give us, America and Indonesia, the best friendship which has ever existed between nations." The next day, accompanied by his twelve-year-old son, Gunter, he set off on a two-week tour of the United States. He was given a ticker-tape parade in New York, and then began a pilgrimage to honor the imagined companions of his youth. He visited Mount Vernon, Monticello, Independence Hall, and sites associated with Lincoln in Springfield, Illinois. To these he added Niagara Falls, the Grand Canyon, and Disneyland, where he was escorted by Walt Disney himself and photographed driving a "Dumbo" bumper car with his son. The high point was Hollywood, a dream destination for a self-described sybarite. One starlet he wanted to meet, Ava Gardner, was in Europe and could not accommodate him, but his other favorite, Marilyn Monroe, flew in from Canada, where she was filming *Bus Stop*, to attend a party in his honor at the Beverly Hills Hotel and sing for him.

On serious matters Sukarno took pains to avoid offense. He was mystified by Americans' fear of Communism, for example, but said so only indirectly. "I find only one fault with Americans," he observed. "They're too full of fear. Afraid of B.O. Afraid of bad breath. They're haunted by the fear they'll never get rid of dandruff. This state of mind I cannot understand."

Sukarno later wrote that he "tried to explain our nation's political color to John Foster Dulles," but concluded that "nonalignment can easily be misunderstood by America. America likes you only if you're on the side she selects. If you don't go along with her totally, you're automatically considered to have entered the Soviet bloc. Mr. Dulles' retort was, 'America's policy is global. You must be on one side or the other. Neutralism is immoral.'"

As a young man Sukarno had stirred crowds with passionate denunciations of colonizers who ruled what was then the Dutch East Indies. He had served terms in prison and "internal exile" in Borneo, emerged as leader of the anticolonial movement, and then, after the Dutch finally withdrew in 1949, became Indonesia's first president. Having dedicated his life to pulling his country away from an overlord, he was hardly ready to align it with a new one—even his beloved United States.

This drew Sukarno to neutralism. He called it *mendayung antara dua karang*—rowing between two reefs. By embracing it, he explicitly rejected Cold War dogma. That made him loathsome in the eyes of Cold War commanders like Foster and Allen.

Indonesia is vast—thousands of islands scattered across an expanse nearly as wide as the United States—and unimaginably diverse. Its central challenge has been to find a unifying identity. This requires synthesis above all: among regions, traditions, peoples, ideologies, languages, belief systems, and cultures. Sukarno rose to power largely because he was a master synthesizer. To transmit his vision of Indonesian identity he used spellbinding oratory, blending traditional and modern rhetorical styles and often evoking call-and-response frenzies. He was the revolutionary who imagined an emerging nation and came to incarnate it.

The success of Sukarno's trip to the United States led many in Washington to presume they had won him over. They were mightily displeased when, just a few months later, he traveled to China and made speeches praising its economic progress, then proceeded to the Soviet Union and hailed Lenin. The crowning blow came when Soviet leaders announced a $100 million loan to Indonesia.

For Sukarno, praising China and the Soviet Union after praising the United States was a way of "rowing between two reefs." In Washington it was taken as betrayal. Americans spoke bitterly of a treacherous guest, a knife in the back. *Time* reported that Sukarno had found "much common ground" with Communist leaders and warned that the $100 million loan "will place Soviet 'technicians' in strategic points in the sprawling republic, which already has a well-organized Communist Party."

Sukarno felt insulted and replied in kind. "To me, both the Declaration of Independence and the Communist Manifesto contain underlying truths, but the West doesn't permit a middle road," he complained. "The West keeps threatening, 'Do you want to be dominated by the Communists?' We answer, 'No, but neither do we want to be dominated by you.' At least Russia and China didn't call us names when we smiled sweetly at America."

Foster and Allen considered Sukarno's trip through the Iron Curtain a humiliating setback. In the months that followed, they watched with interest as two other developments reshaped Indonesia. First was a speech in which Sukarno declared that he was fed up with partisan bickering and wanted to "bury political parties." Second was a ripple of rebellion from within the military, showing itself in two attempted coups and secessionist rumblings on the islands of Sumatra and Sulawesi. The speech led Foster and Allen to conclude that Sukarno was preparing a leap toward Communism. Upheaval in the army suggested they might be able to stop him.

No known document records the beginning of the American campaign against Sukarno. None is likely to exist, because the idea almost certainly emerged during one of the countless unrecorded conversations Foster and Allen shared during their years in power. The moment when this idea moved into the realm of action can, however, be fixed: November 1956.

One day that month, Frank Wisner, the CIA's deputy director for plans, summoned the newly appointed chief of the agency's Far East division, Al Ulmer, and gave him a far-reaching assignment. Ulmer understood that Wisner was speaking for Allen, and implicitly for the secretary of state and president.

"I think it's time we held Sukarno's feet to the fire," Wisner said.

With that, Foster and Allen launched one of the largest-scale covert operations of the decade. Using the resources of the State Department, the CIA, and the United States Army, Navy, Air Force, and Marines, they armed and trained a rebel army numbering more than ten thousand fighters; requisitioned transport vessels, cruisers, submarines, and a fleet of fifteen B-26 warplanes fitted with .50-caliber machine guns; directed a sustained bombing campaign; and even produced what may have been the first CIA-made pornographic movie.

Less than a year after Americans thronged to welcome Sukarno, he became the fourth monster Foster and Allen went abroad to destroy.

"During the late 1950s, the Eisenhower administration provoked and strongly abetted a major rebellion and civil war in Indonesia that tore the country apart," begins one of the few accounts of this operation, published forty years later. "Both the available documentary evidence and the consensus among State Department and CIA members interviewed indicate that among the top leaders of the Eisenhower administration, John Foster Dulles was the most aggressive and consistent in forwarding this policy."

The campaign against Sukarno, which became known as "Archipelago," remained secret for longer than most others Foster and Allen waged. By the mid-1950s, their involvement in overthrowing Mossadegh and Arbenz was an open secret in Washington, clear to anyone who could read the *Saturday Evening Post*. Press reports about their campaign against Ho

Chi Minh appeared periodically as the Vietnam War escalated. Archipel-ago, however, went almost entirely unreported, and remained virtually unknown for decades afterward.

If the hidden story of the Dulles brothers is the covert war they waged against six enemies, their anti-Sukarno operation is its most hidden episode.

A night of ecstasy lay ahead for Sukarno during a visit he paid to Cairo. Being a man of generous spirit, he decided to invite his host, the fiery Egyptian leader Colonel Gamal Abdel Nasser, to share the delights. He may have guessed that the CIA was tapping his telephone, but this did not inhibit him.

"I have three gorgeous Pan American stewardesses here with me and they'd like to have a party," the president of Indonesia told the president of Egypt.

Nasser curtly declined and hung up. That showed the two heads of state to be of different temperaments. Politically, however, they were remarkably similar. Both had been anticolonial firebrands, rose to power in the years after World War II, emerged as global leaders at the Bandung Conference of 1955, and considered the Cold War a costly distraction from the world's true challenges. They were titans of neutralism, twin nightmares for Foster and Allen.

The Americans were stunned when, in 1956, Egypt began receiving weapons from the Soviet Union—not just small arms, but hundreds of tanks and MiG jet fighters. Then, in what may have been an even greater shock, the Soviets agreed to give Egypt a low-interest loan of $1.1 billion to begin construction of the Aswan High Dam.

This was a spectacular triumph for the Soviets. It brought their power to the Arab world for the first time. Most remarkably, this happened not as the result of a coup or subversion of a weak political system, but at the open invitation of a popular leader. Foster's strategy had produced the very result he had hoped to avoid.

New friendship between Egypt and the Soviet Union was partly the result of miscalculation in Washington, but it also represented the first major success for a changed Soviet approach to the Third World. Marxist dogma taught that revolution would explode in countries where masses of industrial workers were oppressed by factory owners. This excluded Africa and most of the colonial world, and during the Stalin era the Soviet Union had sent no aid to developing countries. In 1956, sensing the energy of emerging postcolonial governments, Nikita Khrushchev changed course. He announced that countries "not part of the world socialist system . . . now need not beg their former oppressors for modern equipment. They can obtain such equipment in the socialist countries." Then he set off on a series of trips to neutral countries, including Burma, Indonesia, and Afghanistan—countries Foster believed Eisenhower should not visit because their loyalty was uncertain. Suddenly the United States had an active competitor for influence in countries emerging from colonialism.

This might have led Foster to soften his us-or-them tone when dealing with Third World countries. Instead he did the opposite, becoming angry at any regime he saw as flirting with both Cold War adversaries. That alienated some nationalist leaders and gave the Soviets new opportunities in Africa and Asia.

While Khrushchev cultivated an image as friend of the Third World, he also took a series of conciliatory steps in Europe. He withdrew Soviet troops from Austria and Finland, and made peace with Tito's neutralist regime in Yugoslavia, which Stalin had stigmatized. The world began seeing a different Moscow.

"Countries with differing social systems can do more than exist side by side," Khrushchev declared. "It is necessary to proceed further, to improve relations, strengthen confidence between countries, and cooperate."

Foster and Allen saw this as a clever gambit to win propaganda points, without a shred of sincerity. They circulated intelligence estimates warning that Khrushchev's softer line was "a strategy to defeat the West without war" and "an even more serious threat to the Free World than . . . Stalin's aggressive post-war policies." Eisenhower agreed, and lamented "the seductive quality of Soviet promises and pronouncements."

"Far from seeing the policy of 'peaceful coexistence' as a cause for optimism, Eisenhower and his advisors viewed it as a greater threat to the free world than Stalinism," the historian Kenneth Osgood has written. "To American policy makers, peaceful coexistence represented a menacing political warfare strategy of the most treacherous kind. It raised doubts about the entire Cold War enterprise, and it bred 'false hopes' that a negotiated settlement might be possible."

Changing attitudes in the Kremlin did, however, give Allen two new intelligence opportunities.

The first came when Khrushchev announced that he would loosen Stalin-era restrictions on tourism in the Soviet Union. Rather than train CIA officers to pose as tourists, Allen chose to rely on private citizens who decided on their own to visit the Soviet Union. His men interviewed many, determined which ones were willing to cooperate, reviewed their itineraries, and gave them individual assignments. Some were asked to buy specific products, or note details like the color of smoke emerging from an industrial plant. A few, mostly Russian-speaking scholars, were brought to Washington, given several days or weeks of CIA training, and assigned to photograph sensitive installations like submarine bases and missile launchpads.

"These tourists provided an extraordinary amount of information on high-value targets," one CIA officer later wrote. "The KGB was perfectly aware of the CIA program. They simply chose to turn a half-blind eye on eager tourists who did not go too far."

Khrushchev also began a program of military aid to neutral countries. This allowed Allen, who had worked intently to obtain information about Soviet weaponry, to begin obtaining the weaponry itself. He authorized CIA officers to pay rewards up to hundreds of thousands of dollars for specific items. They bought everything from machine guns to manuals for surface-to-air missiles. Specialists pored over this trove, and used what they learned to reshape American weapons systems and tactical doctrine.

Egypt was one of the first countries to reap political benefit from the Soviet Union's new interest in the Third World. Emboldened by Moscow, Nasser intensified his calls for revolution in Saudi Arabia, Iraq, and Jordan—all ruled by pro-Western monarchs. Then he announced a plan to break down borders between Arab countries and create a giant pan-Arab state. In Washington it was presumed that this new state would be pro-Soviet. "Nasser might have become a tool for the Russians," Foster told Eisenhower. During a visit to Cairo, Allen erupted in frustration when a case officer briefed him on Nasser's growing power.

"If that colonel of yours pushes us too far," he vowed, "we'll break him in half!"

This bravado faded after the British-led invasion of Egypt in late 1956. Eisenhower and the Dulles brothers saw the invasion as an intolerable attempt to reassert European power in the Middle East. Besides, they had been working on an anti-Nasser plot of their own, and once Nasser emerged from the Suez crisis as a hero, all prospect of mobilizing Egyptians against him evaporated. Yet despite this setback, the Americans were still eager to strike. Eisenhower told the National Security Council that he wanted to take "measures, even drastic ones."

Those measures became a plan known as "Omega." It began as a plot to destroy Nasser, but Nasser's great popularity, sealed by his triumph at Suez, forced Foster and Allen to adjust it. They reduced Omega to a smaller-scale operation aimed at harassing Nasser and limiting the spread of his influence in other Arab countries. This was a long-unrecognized effect of the Suez crisis: it helped lead Foster and Allen to give up their covert campaign to depose Nasser.

"Given the conception of Omega," the historian Ray Takeyh has written, "Suez must be reduced to its proper dimension: a sideshow that disrupted Eisenhower's policy of covertly undermining Nasser and his radical allies."

Omega envisioned a campaign of escalating coercion, but had no fixed goal. At various points, it aimed at forcing Nasser to cut his ties with the Soviet Union, recognize Israel, stop subsidizing nationalists in other Arab countries, and order "a public reorientation of Egypt's informational media toward advocacy of cooperation and close economic cooperation with the West, including a public statement from Nasser to that effect." To achieve these goals, the United States would suspend aid programs, refuse arms sales, strengthen pro-American regimes in nearby countries, and work with Britain to counter Nasser's influence across the Arab world.

Shaping the public face of Omega turned out to be Foster's last major diplomatic project. Eisenhower unveiled it in a speech to a joint session of Congress on January 5, 1957, and it became known as the Eisenhower Doctrine, but it was mainly Foster's handiwork. Its core reflected his favorite theme: "Russia's desire to dominate the Middle East" was threatening freedom and American interests there.

"A greater responsibility now devolves on the United States," Eisenhower declared. "Words alone are not enough."

Eisenhower asked Congress for $200 million to support Arab governments "dedicated to the maintenance of national independence." Applause was modest, and when Foster appeared later at a congressional hearing, he found much skepticism. Senators pressed him to explain how he would spend the $200 million. He became indignant, said he would not "telegraph his punches" to the enemy, and warned that if Congress did not act, "maximum disaster" would soon envelop the Middle East. The Senate waited for two months before approving the appropriation.

Foster and Allen came up with several Omega projects they hoped would dampen the wildfire of Arab nationalism. They promoted King Saud of Saudi Arabia as a rival to Nasser; sought to foment a military coup against the pro-Nasser regime in Syria, only to be embarrassed when several Syrian officers appeared on television to reveal that they had received money from "corrupt and sinister Americans"; and even considered hiring Ugandan mercenaries to attack Upper Egypt. Nothing came of these schemes.

Allen had better luck with an old-fashioned vote-buying operation in Lebanon. The beneficiary was a Christian politician, President Camille Chamoun, who was seeking to pack Parliament so it would lift the ban on presidential re-election. Chamoun struck a deal with the Americans and soon saw results, as Allen's man in Beirut later recalled:

> Throughout the elections I traveled regularly to the presidential palace with a briefcase full of Lebanese pounds, then returned late at night to the embassy with an empty tin case I'd carried away, for [the] CIA finance-people to replenish. Soon my gold DeSoto with its stark white top was a common sight outside the palace, and I proposed to Chamoun that he use an intermediary and a more remote spot. When the President insisted that he handle each transaction by himself, I reconciled myself to the probability that anyone who really cared would have no trouble guessing precisely what I was doing.

The election-rigging project in Lebanon succeeded, but it was a modest operation by the standards to which Foster and Allen had become accustomed. They found Omega unsatisfying. It no longer aimed to destroy a regime. Nasser had stymied them. Meanwhile, half a world away, Archipelago was gaining momentum. Nasser was discouragingly strong, but Sukarno looked temptingly weak.

As Eisenhower began his second term, he and the Dulles brothers felt deep frustration at the course of events in East Asia. Shock from the "loss" of China was still reverberating through Washington. Ho Chi Minh had wrested a piece of Vietnam away from the "free world" and turned it into a Communist enclave. Now Sukarno seemed to be pulling Indonesia away from the West.

Foster and Allen fought back with a series of covert operations, including sustained campaigns against two of East Asia's most prominent neutralists, Prince Norodom Sihanouk of Cambodia and Prince Souvanna Phouma of Laos. Indonesia was many times larger, richer, and more strategically valuable than Cambodia or Laos. That made Sukarno a far more appealing target.

Sukarno did more than reject anti-Communism as a basis for foreign policy. He considered the local Communist party—known as Partai Komunis Indonesia, or PKI—as simply another faction he had to balance. It was the smallest of Indonesia's four main political parties, and he believed it deserved influence commensurate with its popular support. This completed the image that Foster and Allen saw when they beheld Indonesia.

To them this newborn and still unstable giant seemed a massive domino liable to fall with devastating force. The Indonesian islands lie within striking distance of Vietnam and China. They straddle vital sea-lanes. Several are staggeringly rich in resources. The leader of this awakening land, Sukarno, not only refused to ally himself with the United States, but openly flirted with Moscow. At home he worked freely with the PKI. He had nationalized several large Dutch businesses and was threatening the foreign-run oil industry—not just Royal Dutch Shell but American oil companies including the forerunners of Texaco, Chevron, and Mobil.

It is tempting to conclude that Foster and Allen targeted Sukarno for geopolitical reasons. They feared that he was leading a hugely important country into Moscow's orbit. Their experiences in Iran, Guatemala, and

Vietnam had honed their skill in subverting governments. Unrest in the officer corps gave them their chance to act. This confluence of motive, means, and opportunity drew them to strike against Sukarno.

Indonesia and its dazzlingly charismatic leader, however, posed a challenge that was not simply strategic but also conceptual, cultural, even spiritual. Never did Foster and Allen set out against an enemy whose worldview was so different from their own. They were shaped by missionary Calvinism and America's pioneer tradition, believed that godly and satanic forces were at war on earth, and felt called to crush the satanic ones. Sukarno emerged from an opposite tradition, one that emphasizes harmony and conciliation, finds good and evil mixed everywhere, and abhors confrontation. What Foster and Allen took as Sukarno's abandonment of the West was actually his attempt to make foreign policy according to principles that shape life in Indonesia, and especially on his home island of Java.

"It is regarded as a Javanese characteristic to avoid formulating a long-term plan of action to control the future and to provide a criterion for the making of immediate choices," one historian has written. "Rather a Javanese will allow the forces around him to work themselves out."

Although Archipelago was based on a daring use of power—clandestine war—its goal, like that of the Omega project aimed against Nasser, remained curiously ambiguous. Foster and Allen realized they had little chance of deposing Sukarno and replacing him with a submissive client, as they had done with Mossadegh and Arbenz. They did not anoint a candidate of their own for national leadership, as they had in Vietnam. Instead they decided to support dissident officers in the hope of scaring Sukarno into realizing he must make peace with Washington. If things went well, they might even secure the breakup of Indonesia. This would leave Sukarno controlling Java, where most of Indonesia's population lives, but might bring other resource-rich islands under Washington's influence.

"Don't tie yourself irrevocably to a policy of preserving the unity of Indonesia," Foster told Hugh Cumming, the Virginia-bred diplomat he chose as ambassador to Indonesia. "The territorial integrity of China became a shibboleth. We finally got a territorially integrated China—for whose benefit? The Communists. . . . As between a territorially united Indonesia which is leaning and progressing toward Communism and a breakup of that country into racial and geographical units, I would prefer the latter."

Cumming shared the sense of betrayal that coursed through official Washington after Sukarno crossed the Iron Curtain and praised Communist leaders. His anger, and Foster's, grew when Sukarno invited both the American and Soviet presidents to visit Indonesia. The Soviet president, Kliment Voroshilov—officially the chairman of the Presidium of the Supreme Soviet—accepted and made the trip. Pictures of him embracing Sukarno appeared in every Indonesian newspaper. Eisenhower never visited.

As Archipelago took shape, Foster recalled Ambassador Cumming and named him chief of the State Department's Bureau of Intelligence and Research, with responsibility for coordinating projects run jointly by the State Department and the CIA. In that role, Cumming's preoccupation with Indonesia became so intense that some called him "the assistant secretary in charge of Indonesia." He helped write an alarmist report that Foster and Allen presented to the National Security Council on March 14, 1957.

"The process of disintegration has continued in Indonesia to a point where only the island of Java remains under the control of the central government," the report asserted. This was highly exaggerated, since secessionists had emerged only on a handful of islands and did not control any. It also contradicted dispatches from the new American ambassador in Indonesia, John Allison, who portrayed the country as stable and urged a policy of "patience and understanding."

Foster had eagerly tracked the "dissident colonels" of Sumatra and Sulawesi from the moment they emerged late in 1956. When Ambassador Allison tried to arrange a meeting at which the colonels might iron out their differences with Sukarno, Foster ordered him to desist. Then, in mid-1957, a CIA officer in Sumatra was told that Colonel Maludin Simbolon, the most powerful dissident commander, wished to meet with someone from the agency. A meeting was arranged. Both sides expressed interest in a partnership.

Contacts between CIA officers and rebellious Indonesian colonels intensified over the next few months. The CIA began sending money, arms, and advisers to dissident forces. They had different but overlapping agendas. The Americans wanted to wound Sukarno because they considered him a Communist dupe. Their new Indonesian friends wanted to do it because they sought more power for themselves—Sukarno had refused to name Colonel Simbolon as chief of staff—and for the outer islands. It seemed a good fit.

During the summer of 1957, Sukarno pressed ahead with plans to shape a four-party government that would include the PKI, which had done well in a series of local elections. Vice President Mohammad Hatta, thought of as a bulwark against Communism and an advocate for the outer islands, became disaffected and ultimately resigned. American analysts concluded that construction on an island in western Indonesia was preparation for a new airport, which they warned could become a base for Soviet fighter planes. In Washington, the CIA produced a National Intelligence Estimate that predicted "a continuing increase of Communist influence" in Indonesia.

As Allen's men worked covertly, Foster applied diplomatic and political pressure. He blocked the sale of replacement parts for the Indonesian army's American-made weaponry. He directed his new deputy, Undersecretary of State Christian Herter, not to stop in Indonesia on his planned trip through East Asia. Then, rejecting strong advice from Ambassador Allison, he used American influence at the United Nations to block discussion of Indonesia's claim to western New Guinea.

Foster kept Archipelago secret from Ambassador Allison and almost everyone else involved in shaping official American policy toward Indonesia. On September 3, without consulting or notifying Allison, he asked the National Security Council to authorize "all feasible covert means" to promote military rebellion in Indonesia. Whenever he and Allen presented such a far-reaching plan, all understood that President Eisenhower had approved and that they must vote favorably. They did so without debate. Allen immediately sent $50,000 to Colonel Simbolon.

"Send more books," Simbolon wrote after receiving it.

Unaware that Archipelago was under way, Ambassador Allison suggested offering Sukarno a deal: the United States would send him generous aid in exchange for a pledge to "strictly control all Communist activity in Indonesia." Foster and Allen found themselves, as they had in Guatemala, with an ambassador who preferred diplomacy to covert intervention.

"Allison continued to raise annoying questions throughout the development of the operation," one CIA officer recalled afterward. "We handled the problem by getting Allen Dulles to have his brother relieve Allison of his post."

Once the troublesome ambassador departed—he was sent to

Czechoslovakia—Allen's men began the intense phase of their training and supply missions. They used ports, airfields, and secret bases in the Philippines, Taiwan, Singapore, Thailand, Okinawa, Guam, and Saipan. Frank Wisner later recalled that when he presented Allen with a voucher authorizing $10 million as the first payment for all this, Allen signed it "with a little flourish."

One of Allen's ideas was to use Sukarno's womanizing against him. He first approved the dissemination of news stories about a Russian airline stewardess who had apparently developed a relationship with Sukarno. Then he conceived one of his most bizarre projects, a pornographic film featuring an actor made up to look like Sukarno.

Allen reasoned that the film would seem real given what everyone knew about Sukarno's habits, and thought it could be used to undermine Sukarno's authority. The film, called *Happy Days*, featured an actor wearing a latex mask made by the CIA's Technical Services Division, with a bald head because Sukarno was supposedly sensitive about his baldness. Prints were discreetly sprinkled around East Asia, but they had no evident effect.

Far more potent were the tons of weaponry that poured onto docks and spilled from the sky in rebel-held Indonesia, courtesy of the CIA. One large shipment alone, delivered by barge in early 1958, included eighteen thousand grenades, four thousand rifles and carbines, more than two thousand land mines, and hundreds of machine guns, rockets, and mortars. Admiral Arleigh Burke, the chief of naval operations, ordered a task force led by the cruiser *Princeton*, carrying marines and twenty helicopters, to approach the Indonesian coast.

Foster watched with intense interest. He began to hope, as he told Undersecretary Herter, that conflict in Indonesia might "get to a point where we could plausibly withdraw our recognition of the Sukarno government and give it to the dissident elements in Sumatra, and land forces to protect the life and property of Americans—use this as an excuse to bring about a major shift there." In public statements he said Indonesia might soon have a new government "which reflects the real interests and desires of the Indonesian people," and that this would make him "very happy."

Washington's enthusiasm naturally flowed to CIA officers in the field and, through them, to the disaffected Indonesian colonels who had become their clients. On February 10, 1958, from their base in Sumatra, the colonels issued a public ultimatum: Sukarno must dismiss his defense minister, restore Vice President Hatta to office, and outlaw the PKI. The first two demands were their own. Their new American friends suggested the third.

The dissidents gave Sukarno five days to comply. He ignored them. They responded by declaring themselves the Revolutionary Government of Indonesia. At a press conference the next day in Washington, Foster said their "concern at growing Communist influence" had driven them to this extreme.

"We don't take any part in, or interfere with, these internal governmental problems," he hastened to add.

Sukarno, ever the juggler and conciliator, had chosen to ignore rumblings on the outer islands, and treated unhappy colonels as lost sheep rather than enemies. Once they announced their secession, however, he had no alternative other than force. Military commanders rallied to his side. The army chief of staff, General Abdul Haris Nasution, explained why.

"If a government allows several of its subordinate Commands to serve an ultimatum on it, and then fulfills their demands, we can appreciate that no future government will be able to stand," General Nasution declared in a speech. "Whatever happens, a matter of this kind must be condemned."

General Nasution swung into action more decisively than Foster or Allen had expected. He dispatched five battalions of paratroopers and marines to Sumatra, ordered naval blockades, and began planning an aerial bombing campaign. The Americans responded with more air drops and by sending a new flotilla carrying two battalions of marines to waters near Indonesia. Clashes broke out on several islands, causing hundreds of casualties.

Foster and Allen had worked to foment civil war in Indonesia. Now it was beginning.

Late one night, at an exposed government outpost in South Vietnam, two frightened Westerners were forced to take refuge when their car ran out of gas. In the darkness, their conversation turned to the growing American role in Vietnam. One of them, an idealistic young American, said the United States was intervening because the Vietnamese "don't want Communism." Then he added, "If Indochina goes . . ."

"I know that record," his older, British companion interrupted. "Siam goes. Malaya goes. Indonesia goes. What does 'go' mean?"

"They'll be forced to believe what they're told, they won't be allowed to think for themselves."

"Do you think the peasant thinks of God and Democracy when he gets inside his mud hut at night?" the older man asks incredulously. "I know the harm liberals do. . . . I've no particular desire to see you win."

This fictional scene is a fulcrum of Graham Greene's moody masterpiece *The Quiet American*, which became a best seller in 1957 and took many American readers to a place they had never known. Geographically it was Vietnam, but politically it was even stranger and harder to understand. The older man tells his young American friend that outside powers always end up oppressing the people they come to help, and being hated for it. The American, who is slowly revealed to be a CIA officer, seems truly to believe he is helping Vietnam, but in the end, his arrogance and "half-baked ideas" provoke disaster.

"I know your motives are good, they always are," the older man tells him. Later he muses: "His innocence had angered me . . . but wasn't he right too to be young and mistaken?"

The Quiet American provoked a storm of protest. One of the outraged was Allen's man in Saigon, Edward Lansdale, who some believed had been a model for the book's well-intentioned CIA blunderer. Another was Joseph L. Mankiewicz, the producer, director, and screenwriter who had made Hollywood hits like *All About Eve* and *The Philadelphia Story*. Working with the American Friends of Vietnam, a lobby group connected to the CIA, Mankiewicz bought the screen rights to *The Quiet American*. He told friends he would "completely change" the book's message, and did. His film starred the war hero Audie Murphy as the American in Vietnam, now portrayed as a selfless defender of freedom rather than a deluded imperialist. Lansdale, who helped write the screenplay, praised it as "an excellent change from Mr. Greene's novel of despair." Greene was appalled. Just as it had done with *Animal Farm* a few years earlier, the CIA helped transform a thoughtful book about the perils of power into a simpleminded Cold War fable.

The Quiet American was still on the best-seller lists when real-life violence exploded in Little Rock, Arkansas. Many Americans were shocked at graphic images of mobs seeking to prevent black children from enrolling at a public school there. The images had an even more potent effect abroad, where they were widely taken as evidence of racism in the United States and gleefully exploited by leftists. Foster saw the damage and was anguished.

"This situation is ruining our foreign policy," he told Eisenhower. "The effect of this in Asia and Africa will be worse for us than Hungary was for the Russians."

On the evening of October 4, 1957, millions of Americans sought respite from real-life turmoil by settling in front of their televisions for the premiere of a new comedy series called *Leave It to Beaver*. Just before the premiere aired, however, evening newscasters reported an astonishing development: the Soviet Union had launched a spacecraft, and it was now circling the earth. Many who were watching rushed outside. They were dumbfounded to see a small dot of light moving across the sky. It was Sputnik, the first man-made satellite to orbit the earth, and it had been launched by a nation most Americans presumed to be backward and without science.

Foster sought to downplay the launch of Sputnik, suggesting that its importance "should not be exaggerated" and assuring Americans that their government had its own space program "under orderly development." Eisenhower questioned the value of putting "one small ball up in the air." Neither man anticipated the "Sputnik panic" that swept the country. The Soviets suddenly seemed to control the sky. Many Americans feared it might be only a matter of time before the enemy used this advantage to spy, intimidate, or bomb.

"Let us not pretend that Sputnik is anything but a defeat for America," *Life* grimly concluded.

News of the Sputnik launch was taken especially hard at the CIA. One despairing officer told a colleague that despite all that their leaders had done to rouse them, Americans still underestimated the mortal danger of Communism, which he described as "like a cancer." The colleague later wrote that this officer "wasn't alone in his pessimism. The agency seemed permeated by it. We all feared that our way of life, our freedom, our religions were directly exposed to the cancer. . . . We in the agency felt that the battle for the freedom of the world was now, to a large extent, in our hands."

Fears intensified two months later when crowds assembled at Cape Canaveral to witness the launch of a Vanguard rocket that would carry

America's first satellite into space. There were repeated delays, and finally the launch was canceled. Foster was infuriated. At a meeting of the National Security Council the next day, he called the cancellation "a disaster for the United States" that had "made us the laughingstock of the free world." Worse was yet to come. When the rocket was finally launched, with millions watching on live television, it hovered above the launchpad for a few moments and then exploded.

These events set off a wave of reactions in Washington, including the creation of the National Aeronautics and Space Administration. They also reinforced a spreading sense that both the president and secretary of state had grown weak and tired. In the twenty-six months since Eisenhower's heart attack, he had suffered both an attack of ileitis—an intestinal inflammation—and a mild stroke. His speech slowed palpably. In public he sometimes seemed disconnected and adrift.

Foster also lost his glow and began to slow down. The world was entering a period of profound change, but he remained frozen in intransigence. He treated Nikita Khrushchev just as he had treated Stalin: as an enemy of humanity. At one point he publicly slapped down a feeler from Moscow about the possibility of the Soviet defense minister visiting Washington. His hostility toward "Red China" remained passionate, leading him to extremes like refusing to allow an American zoo to import a panda from China, and approving the indictment of a stamp dealer who sold Chinese stamps. He crisscrossed Europe relentlessly and focused intently on questions related to European security, but could not or would not engage with the ideals of nationalism and neutralism that were surging through the Third World. Senator Joseph Clark of Pennsylvania asserted in a widely covered speech that Foster had lost the confidence of America's allies and "many of us in Congress." Conservatives like the columnist Joseph Alsop and liberals like Senator Hubert Humphrey of Minnesota called for his resignation.

During his years in power, Foster had developed an image as prissy, forbidding, and fun-hating. In his last years he seemed sourer than ever. A rising young comedienne, Carol Burnett, seized on this image to write a song satirizing the late-fifties doo-wop hits in which girls sang about falling instantly in love with romantic, sexy boys. Since Foster was known as the opposite of romantic and sexy, Burnett's gag song grabbed the public imagination and became an offbeat hit.

The first time I saw him 'twas at the UN
Oh I never have been one to swoon over men
But I swooned and the drums started pounding and then
I made a fool of myself over John Foster Dulles.

Most Americans understood that Eisenhower's weakening was due at least in part to illness. Few knew that the same was true for Foster. At the end of 1956, after complaining of abdominal pain, he had undergone a three-hour operation. The doctors found cancer. Foster spent several weeks convalescing in Key West before returning to work. He weakened slowly over the next year.

As 1957 drew to a close, Foster joined the rest of the Dulles clan for Christmas dinner at Eleanor's home in McLean. He was in good spirits and ate heartily. His gifts for Eleanor were classic: several yellow legal pads—he bought them in bulk—and a check she could use to buy a new radio.

Foster had the usual panoply of worries. He had just returned from a NATO summit in Paris and was fighting off a new round of proposals for the neutralization of Germany. Third World leaders, meeting in Cairo, had adopted resolutions condemning nuclear tests and affirming the right of governments to nationalize foreign businesses. A highly alarming secret report produced for President Eisenhower, warning that the threat of war with the Soviet Union could "become critical" within a year or two, had been leaked to the press and sent a new shiver of fear through the country.

This fear contributed to pressure for a summit between the American and Soviet leaders. Foster had always opposed such summit meetings, and in his first speech of 1958 he repeated his view. "The great gain for the Soviets would be to have a meeting which, as I say, will utter platitudes about peace," he warned, "with the implication that there is no need any more to have this military preparation, to pay taxes in order to have a mutual security program and the like. If Khrushchev can get that, that would be the greatest triumph of his career."

Soon after making this speech, Foster flew off to visit a staunch ally, the shah of Iran, and then on to Turkey. Shortly after he arrived at the American embassy in Ankara, a building on the grounds was bombed. Hostile demonstrators jammed the streets.

Seeking a more reassuring welcome, Foster made his next trip to West Berlin, where his sister was something of a heroine and he was more popular than anywhere else on earth, including Washington. He was received warmly, as always. Janet took the chance to travel to Münster to see their son, Avery, who was studying at a Jesuit seminary there.

Foster celebrated his seventieth birthday on February 25, 1958. That year also marked the fifty-first anniversary of his first diplomatic mission, as John Watson Foster's secretary at The Hague Peace Conference. In the spring he traveled to Princeton for his fiftieth class reunion. Allen, for whom this was the forty-fourth reunion, accompanied him. He was having an easier time than his brother.

Tensions at home had eased as Allen and Clover settled into an arrangement that absolved him of most spousal responsibilities. By one account they "did not really separate; rather, they developed separate lives that came together frequently but remained on distinctly different paths." Allen lived like the flirtatious bachelor he always imagined himself to be.

He handled Congress almost as deftly. The CIA budget had grown to around $350 million, equivalent to about eight times that in the early twenty-first century. This figure was never made public. Appropriations were hidden in accounts designated for the Pentagon, the State Department, and other agencies. Congress approved them in secret hearings. According to Allen's administrative aide Lawrence White, members asked no substantial questions.

> The director always began with a summary of the world situation in the most general terms. But the way he said it, it sounded very inside and confidential. Usually that would be it. [Chairman of the House Appropriations Committee] Clarence Cannon more often than not would say, "Now there is one question I want to ask. Do you have enough money to do your business properly?" And Dulles would say, "I think, Mr. Chairman, I have asked for as much as I can spend wisely. If I get into trouble, I will come back to your committee." And Cannon would bang his gavel, "Meeting adjourned." That was that.
>
> Sometimes a congressman or senator would actually ask a question, usually something they had read in the newspaper. Just as often as not, Senator [Richard] Russell or Cannon would interrupt, "Now don't tell us about that if we don't need to know."

Occasionally Allen was able to take a break from running covert operations and playing Washington politics. One of his favorite friends, Queen
Frederika of Greece, came to the United States on a tour with her son,
the future King Constantine II, and just as her trip was about to end, she
announced without explanation that she would stay for another week. She
came to Washington, discussed "spiritual values" with President Eisenhower in the Oval Office, and then visited Allen. They had been alone in
his office for nearly an hour when an aide knocked. Hearing no response,
he entered. He found the office empty but heard noises from the adjoining
dressing room. Later Allen and the queen emerged. As she was being
driven back to the Greek embassy, the queen suggested one reason Greek-
American relations were so strong.

"We just love that man!" she exclaimed.

When fighting began in Indonesia at the beginning of 1958, Allen told
President Eisenhower and the National Security Council that the rebels had
"a reasonable chance of winning it." Sukarno had chosen to resist rather
than sue for peace. Foster and Allen dared hope they could defeat him.

The outbreak of this war riveted a nervous world. *Time* put Sukarno
on its cover, looking defiant against a dark, turbulent background. Inside
was a two-page map with icons locating Indonesia's resources, including
not just oil, coal, rubber, gold, nickel, and bauxite but also orangutans,
komodo dragons, and head hunters. The accompanying article portrayed
the rebellion just as Foster and Allen wished it to be portrayed: as a patriotic uprising against Communism, with no hint of outside involvement.

Last week Indonesia, racked by civil war, was in dire danger of splinter-
ing apart. . . . All the rebels asked was that Indonesia's President 1)
behave himself constitutionally, 2) abandon his partnership with the
Communist party . . .

Indonesia's rebellion is less a revolution against Sukarno than a last
attempt to shock the self-intoxicated President into a state of sober reason, and the hope that the appeal for a new government may lead him to
cleanse his own.

Whether Sukarno listens is of major concern for the free world. Of the
string of islands that half circle the great continent of Asia—Japan,

Okinawa, Formosa, the Philippines, Indonesia—only Indonesia is not committed to the West. If, as seems possible, Sukarno leads his nation into Communism, the Communists will have made a gigantic leap across a strategic barrier.

Over the next few weeks, Sukarno's forces pummeled the rebels with a combination of bombing, amphibious assaults, and paratroop attacks. Many rebel soldiers turned out to be poorly trained high school students. Their weaponry was not suited to local conditions, and they enjoyed only modest popular support. More crippling was the non-confrontational nature of Indonesian identity. When ordered to shoot at Indonesian soldiers, some rebels proved reluctant. Their country was newly born after bitter struggle, and fighting to break it apart seemed dishonorable. Religion also restrained them, as one CIA officer reported: "They said they would not fight their Muslim brothers."

Trouble mounted as the secrecy of Allen's arms-supply operation was slowly breached. Early in 1958, two barges loaded with weapons arrived near the Sumatran port of Padang in broad daylight and were off-loaded onto trucks as villagers watched. Then, on March 12, government paratroopers stormed onto a base where a CIA plane had just dropped supplies. They found twenty pallets loaded with machine guns, rifles, bazookas, and bundles of cash. Sukarno warned the United States not to "play with fire," and pointedly observed that if Indonesia's civil war became internationalized, he could easily raise thousands of "volunteers from outside."

Foster concluded in a private memo that with evidence of American involvement leaking out, there remained "two possibilities: (a) to give the dissidents aircraft . . . (b) to carry out bombing operations ourselves." In public he continued insisting that the conflict in Indonesia was an "internal matter" and that the United States was "not intervening in the internal affairs of this country." Eisenhower was equally disingenuous, and added a twist of his own.

"Our policy is one of careful neutrality and proper deportment all the way through, so as not to be taking sides where it is none of our business," he said at a news conference. "Now on the other hand, every rebellion that I ever heard of has its soldiers of fortune. . . . People were looking out for a good fight and getting into it, sometimes in the hope of pay and sometimes just for the heck of the thing. That is probably going to happen every time you have a rebellion."

Sukarno gleefully displayed the CIA-supplied weaponry his paratroopers had captured, but did not directly blame the United States. Instead he summoned the American ambassador and delivered a plaintive protest.

"I am called a communist by the American press, and even Secretary Dulles says Indonesia is drifting toward communism," he said. "I am not a communist. Every word I said in America I still stand by."

This plea had no effect in Washington. Allen grew concerned, however, when he learned that reporters from Knight Newspapers and *U.S. News and World Report* had filed stories about covert American intervention in Indonesia. He reacted by telephoning James Knight, the executive vice president of Knight Newspapers, and David Lawrence, the president and editor of *U.S. News and World Report*, and both agreed to have the offending stories killed or heavily edited. The *Chicago Daily News* hinted at what was happening—it said that weapons for Indonesian rebels were falling from the sky "like manna from heaven"—but no other newspaper went even that far. Many were spared the necessity of deciding what to print because their correspondents censored themselves.

"We did not write about it," an Associated Press reporter confessed years later. "Maybe it was a kind of patriotism that kept us from doing so."

Lack of honest news reporting reinforced the still-widespread presumption that American officials would not lie. This led to a burst of outrage at Sukarno for having the temerity to make charges that, as it turned out, were entirely accurate.

"It is unfortunate that high officials of the Indonesian Government have given further circulation to the false report that the United States Government was sanctioning aid to Indonesia's rebels,' the *New York Times* wrote in an editorial. "The position of the United States Government has been made plain, again and again. Our Secretary of State was emphatic in his declaration that this country would not deviate from a correct neutrality. . . . The United States is not ready . . . to step in to help overthrow a constituted government. Those are the hard facts."

As the public digested these denials that the United States was intervening in Indonesia, Foster and Allen sought ways to intensify the intervention. On a Saturday at the beginning of April, they met at Foster's home to discuss options with the Joint Chiefs of Staff and a handful of other officials. They came up with three, as Foster reported to visiting British diplomats a couple of days later: recognize the rebel force as a legitimate belligerent so it could be openly supplied with weaponry; promote "the secession of Sumatra from the Republic of Indonesia, which we would then recognize and guarantee its independence"; and/or bait the Indonesian army into attacking American businesses "so there would be so much damage to the U.S. property that U.S. troops would have to be sent in."

Before any of these tactics could be tested, the lattice of deception that supported Archipelago collapsed. Given its scope, and the sloppiness with which it was carried out, this was probably inevitable. The disaster came just weeks after Foster and his boss had made their misleading public statements, and days after the *New York Times* had pronounced its scornful verdict.

Before dawn on May 18, 1958, a Florida-born pilot named Allen Pope, who had won the Distinguished Flying Cross in Korea and then had gone to work for the CIA, strode across an airstrip at Clark Air Base in the Philippines and settled into the cockpit of his B-26 bomber. Pope had already flown several bombing missions in support of Indonesian rebels. This time, after destroying a truck and two planes at a government base, he was circling back for another pass when a warplane appeared above him. There was a dogfight, and Pope's B-26 burst into flames. It was the first and only air-to-air kill of the secret Indonesian war.

Pope ejected from the plane, breaking his foot in the process, and parachuted into a coconut grove. He was quickly captured. Interrogators discovered that instead of flying "sterile," as CIA pilots were supposed to, he was carrying no fewer than thirty compromising documents. These included an identity card granting him access to Clark Air Base, a copy of secret orders assigning him to Archipelago, and a flight log documenting his past missions. He had bombed military bases, ships, warehouses, a bridge, and even, by accident, a church—inflicting heavy casualties in the most vivid atrocity of the war.

"Tell me why!" Sukarno angrily demanded of the newly arrived American ambassador, Howard Jones. "Why did he do it?"

"Because he heard you were a Communist," Jones replied, "and he wanted to contribute in the fight against Communism."

News of the crash reached Allen within hours. According to the CIA desk officer who brought it to him, he listened while puffing on his pipe, and remained "completely calm." Then he picked up his secure phone and called his brother.

"Foster, this is the situation," he began. A few clipped sentences followed. Then Allen hung up and turned to the desk officer.

"We're pulling the plug," he said. The next day he sent the bad news to his men.

"This is the most difficult message I have ever sent," he wrote. "It is sent only under impelling necessity and in what we all view here as the highest national interest."

Allen, who had given Eisenhower optimistic reports on Archipelago, had suffered his first great defeat as director of central intelligence. The agency had not failed so utterly since its ill-fated effort to set off civil war in the Soviet Union a decade earlier. The largest covert operation the CIA had yet launched—if "covert" can describe a project embracing an army of thousands, assets in nearly a dozen countries, and everything from pornography to the Seventh Fleet—had collapsed.

Failing to topple Ho Chi Minh was not this painful, since the conflict in Vietnam was still bubbling and it was possible to hope that Ho might yet be defeated. Sukarno, by contrast, emerged triumphant. He had crushed a rebellion and preserved the unity of his young country. In doing so, he burnished his global reputation, unmasked his chief critics as agents of a foreign power, brought the army to his side, and established himself as Indonesia's savior. He quickly moved from being a weak leader, forced to conciliate among rival factions, to a strongman who ruled by command. Allen reassigned the two officers who had overseen the catastrophe, Far East division chief Al Ulmer and deputy director for plans Frank Wisner.

This failure was more directly attributable to the Dulles brothers than any other suffered by the Eisenhower administration. They could not restrain themselves from striking against Sukarno when they saw a chance to do so. In their eagerness, they oversimplified the complex political landscape of a newly independent nation, embarked on a major operation without a clear goal, underestimated the army's determination to prevent Indonesia from breaking apart, and misunderstood their clients, who despite receiving much weaponry did not want to fight.

It took less than a week after Allen Pope's plane crash for the first signs of conciliation to emerge from Washington. The United States resumed food aid to Indonesia, lifted bans on the export of small arms and airplane parts, and announced that it would help pay for several dozen diesel generating plants and a highway in Sumatra. This was a remarkable reversal: from striking against Sukarno to deciding he could be something like a partner. Foster made the new policy official by inviting the Indonesian ambassador to visit him at the State Department.

"I am definitely convinced that relations are improving," the ambassador said after their meeting.

One reason Foster and Allen were willing to concede defeat in Indonesia was that the Middle East was once again in turmoil. Nasser had shown his contempt for the rules of global commerce by nationalizing British- and French-owned industries in Egypt. He pressed ahead with his plan to merge Egypt with Syria into a new United Arab Republic, and made clear that he wished to incorporate other countries as well. Pan-Arabists in Lebanon began marching to demand that Lebanon join. Their protests escalated into civil conflict. Then, before dawn on July 14, 1958, nationalist officers in Iraq overthrew their pro-American monarchy. Soon afterward they executed the king, the crown prince, and Prime Minister Nuri as-Said, who was outspokenly pro-Western and Nasser's most potent Arab enemy.

Foster and Allen saw the coup in Iraq as a geopolitical loss for the United States, which it was, and as part of a larger plot by Nasser and the Soviets to bring the Middle East under Moscow's control, which it was not. Immediately upon learning of it, they began fearing for the fate of their client in Lebanon, President Camille Chamoun. Intervening to save Chamoun would be mildly distasteful, since he was seeking to stay in office despite a constitutional ban on re-election. A new president, however, would not be reliably pro-American and might even sympathize with Nasser—who Foster now described as an "expansionist dictator somewhat of the Hitler type."

Hours after the Iraq coup, Foster told an emergency session of the National Security Council that it must authorize armed intervention in Lebanon. "More important than Chamoun's second term is the continuous existence of a genuinely independent Lebanon with pro-Western policies," he argued. "If we were to adopt the doctrine that Nasser can whip up a civil war without our intervention, our friends will go down to defeat."

The American invasion of Lebanon—the only military operation launched to support a foreign policy doctrine Foster had shaped—was a remarkably peaceful one. It began on the morning after the coup in Iraq, with United States Marines wading ashore at beaches south of Beirut while astonished bathers watched. A few hours later, other American forces landed in Jordan, where nationalists had also clashed with police.

This operation set off anti-American protests in several Arab capitals. Khrushchev warned half-seriously that since the Americans were intervening in Lebanon, he might send "volunteers" to support the nationalist side. Finally a settlement was reached under which Chamoun was eased from office and new elections were called—a formula Foster had rejected when Nasser proposed it at the start of the crisis.

Members of Congress were unusually critical of the Lebanon invasion. Senator John F. Kennedy of Massachusetts, who was preparing a campaign for the presidency, argued that it was "sheer delusion to underestimate the cutting force of Arab nationalism," and said the United States should stop viewing the Middle East "almost exclusively in the context of East-West struggle" and begin "doing business with Nasser." Senator Wayne Morse of Oregon lamented "the mixing of American blood with Arabian oil in the Middle East." When Allen told a Senate committee that "mob action" was behind the Iraq coup, Senator William Langer of North Dakota challenged his definition of "mob."

"Do you mean the patriotic people of Iraq who were sick and tired of having those in control of Iraq bribed by the United States government?" Langer asked.

This episode also illustrated the changing image of Israel in the United States. President Truman had endorsed the creation of Israel in 1948 after overruling both his secretary of state, George Marshall, and his secretary of defense, James Forrestal, who predicted that the existence of a Jewish state would cause endless conflict in the Middle East. Many early settlers in Israel were socialists, and during its first few years of independence Israel was friendly to the Soviet Union. This kept relations between Washington and Tel Aviv cool. So did Foster's belief, shared by many in the State Department, that the existence of Israel would complicate the making of American foreign policy.

"I am aware how almost impossible it is in this country to carry out a foreign policy not approved by the Jews," he said at a press conference during the Suez crisis. "Marshall and Forrestal learned that. I am going to try to have one. . . . I am very much concerned over the fact that the Jewish influence here is completely dominating the scene and making it almost impossible to get Congress to do anything they don't approve of. . . . The Israeli Embassy is practically dictating to the Congress through influential Jewish people in this country."

The emergence of Nasser and his nationalist ideology in the mid-1950s, however, led Foster to shift his view. He considered Arab nationalism illegitimate and inherently anti-Western. Soviet leaders, sensing an opening, abandoned Israel and embraced the Arab cause. Foster, who had not previously been sympathetic to Zionism, jumped into the strategic vacuum and steered the United States steadily closer to Israel.

This made Foster and Allen midwives of both relationships that framed America's approach to the Middle East for the next half century: the one with Saudi Arabia and the one with Israel.

Omega and the wider panoply of policies Foster and Allen followed in the Arab world were based on the vain hope that they could tame Arab nationalism and shape it to fit America's Cold War needs. In Lebanon they flexed American muscle, but at the cost of inflaming Arab multitudes and giving them—many for the first time—a sense that the United States was an imperial power every bit as intrusive as the French and British had been. Nothing they did weakened Nasser. In fact, he emerged from Omega stronger than ever, reveling in his image as the triumphal defender of the Arabs against predatory foreigners.

In Egypt, Foster and Allen acted according to their deepest instincts. Chaos and disorder were the most terrifying enemies of the corporate globalism that was their creed. They saw Arab nationalism and its paladin, Nasser, as bearers of that chaotic disorder, and struck out violently against them.

Soon after Allen ordered "pulling the plug" on his anti-Sukarno plot, an official at the Indonesian foreign ministry was given a list of American diplomats who were coming for an inspection trip. One name caught his eye: Eleanor Lansing Dulles. Hers was not a popular surname in Indonesia at that moment, and when she arrived, not even a clerk appeared at the airport to greet her. She returned the slight. During a speech by Sukarno, she told an American embassy officer that he sounded "just like Hitler," and then announced that she wished to leave immediately and fly to Bali. The officer told her that her walkout would not only be noticed, but might spark an international incident.

"Listen carefully," he finally said. "Wait a minute or two, and then grab your midriff as though you are in terrible pain and make appropriate groans of distress, and I will help you out of the hall."

That resolved Eleanor's problem. There remained, however, the larger one posed by the imprisoned CIA pilot Allen Pope. He was tried and sentenced to be shot, but Sukarno proved reluctant to sign the death warrant. As he wavered, Allen ordered intensive work on a "snatch" operation in which Pope would be plucked from his prison—it was actually loose house arrest—by a low-flying aircraft. This proved unnecessary. Sukarno, who admitted that "when it comes to women I am weak," received Pope's wife and sister and could not resist their tears. He pardoned the pilot with a private message: "Lose yourself in the USA secretly. Don't show yourself publicly. Don't give out news stories. Don't issue statements. Just go home, hide yourself, get lost, and we'll forget the whole thing."

Pope kept his part of the bargain for a while. Years later, however, when the Indonesia operation became public, he became indignant at hearing Richard Bissell describe it as "a complete failure."

"We killed thousands of Communists," Pope said, "even though half of them probably didn't know what Communism meant."

Rebellions in Sumatra and Sulawesi sputtered on for several years. American support had made them possible, however, and after it was cut off, the fighting was little more than a series of skirmishes. The last members of the ill-fated Revolutionary Government of Indonesia surrendered in 1961.

Archipelago produced three winners: Sukarno, the Indonesian army, and the PKI. All believed they had won the right to more power. They fell into intensifying conflict, culminating with a failed PKI coup in 1965 and a staggeringly brutal response by the generals, who seized power and directed the massacre of hundreds of thousands of PKI members and others. They kept Sukarno in office for a couple of years as a figurehead, and then removed him. He died in 1970.

Besides stoking internal conflicts that would explode into horrific violence a few years later, American intervention shaped Indonesian politics in another decisive way. It produced what one scholar called "the prolonged exclusion from national life of some of Indonesia's most talented and capable leaders because of their association with the rebellion and the United States." Enlisting moderates for the CIA's anti-Sukarno project had seemed like a promising strategy. Once the project collapsed, however, these moderates were exposed as collaborators with the United States and were pushed from politics. Communists filled the vacuum.

The Dulles brothers struck against Mossadegh and Arbenz for reasons that stretched back to their Sullivan & Cromwell days. Their third target, Ho Chi Minh, was a lifelong Communist. Sukarno was different. Panic, ignorance, and stubbornness led Foster and Allen to attack a leader who posed no real threat to American security. Sukarno warned them not to try placing Indonesians into "neat, orderly Western pigeon holes," but their every impulse pushed them to do so. They never sought to understand Sukarno or Indonesian nationalism.

"I had great respect for Foster and Allen Dulles, but they did not know Asians well and were always inclined to judge them by Western standards," John Allison, the ambassador they removed from his post in Indonesia, observed years later. "They were both activists and insisted on doing something at once."

For his part, Sukarno never ceased lamenting the troubles he had with the United States. He saw them as fully unnecessary, the result of colossal misunderstandings. Poignantly, he accepted his share of blame.

"If there is an out-and-out question as to who began the name-calling between Sukarno and Washington, then I have to admit it was Sukarno," he wrote in his memoir. "But look here, Sukarno is a shouter. He is emotional. If he is angry, he shoots thunderbolts. But he thunders only at those he loves. I would adore to make up with the United States of America. . . . Oh, America, what is the matter with you? Why couldn't you have been my friend?"

9

THE TALL, GOATEED RADICAL

Bare-chested dancers wearing grass skirts carried a royal visitor aloft through the jammed streets of Leopoldville, the capital of the newly independent Republic of the Congo. Throngs shouted their welcome. The object of their adulation, beaming in gratitude, waved back from his red leather throne. He was no mere prince or king, but a monarch of global reach: Louis Armstrong, jazz visionary and America's premier cultural ambassador.

Jazz was a potent weapon in America's Cold War arsenal, and "Satchmo" had become arguably the most beloved musician in the world. He had played for adoring crowds across the United States and Europe, appeared in films, made hit records like "Mack the Knife," and been the first jazz musician featured on the cover of *Time*. His joyous music conveyed an image of the United States as an open, happy place. His stardom suggested that American society was free of racial prejudice. Not for nothing did the State Department sponsor his tours. The *New York Times* called him "America's secret weapon."

In 1957 Armstrong agreed to represent the United States in what would have been a groundbreaking tour of the Soviet Union, but he angrily canceled when President Eisenhower proved reluctant to support the integration of public schools in Little Rock, Arkansas. Three years later, with school integration finally proceeding in much of the South, he relented. This time the State Department wanted him to tour not the Soviet Union but Africa, where long-colonized countries were racing toward independence. It became a three-month, twenty-seven-city extravaganza.

The welcome that greeted Armstrong in Leopoldville on October 28, 1960, was one of the most jubilant. His concert, held at a packed stadium, peaked with a soulful rendition of "What a Wonderful World."

> I see skies of blue, clouds of white
> Bright blessed days, dark sacred nights,
> And I think to myself, what a wonderful world.

The world of Prime Minister Patrice Lumumba, the elected leader of the Congo, was at that moment far from wonderful. Lumumba was being held prisoner at his official residence, not far from the stadium where Armstrong performed. He was among the world's best-known prisoners, so Armstrong must have either known about his predicament and rationalized it away or kept himself willfully ignorant.

Under other circumstances, Armstrong would probably have met Lumumba. Instead he dined after his concert with a starstruck American fan named Larry Devlin, who introduced himself and, finding that the great man had no dinner plans, took him out for a night on the town.

Armstrong could not have known it, but Devlin was chief of the CIA station in Leopoldville. When the trumpeter dined with the secret agent on October 28, 1960, he was unwittingly breaking bread with a CIA officer under orders to kill one of Africa's heroes.

At the beginning of that year, almost no one outside of the Congo had heard of Lumumba. By midsummer, many powerful Americans had come to consider him a frightening new enemy. On August 18 President Eisenhower made private comments—they were not recorded—that Allen Dulles and others present interpreted as an order to kill Lumumba. A week later the Special Group, a subcommittee of the National Security Council that considered covert operations, met to discuss Lumumba, and Eisenhower's national security adviser, Gordon Gray, reported that the president had "extremely strong feelings on the necessity for very straightforward action."

Eisenhower had created the Special Group in 1955 with a decree that Allen later called "one of the most secret documents in the US government." It had just five members: the president, his national security adviser, the undersecretaries of state and defense, and the director of central intelligence. Its stated purpose was to authorize covert operations, but it also served as Eisenhower's link to covert action. "Politically and diplomatically it would have been unseemly, and inciting, for the President to order coups, assassinations, and other mischief," one historian has written. "The Special Group acted as his proxy. But in the end, its actions—its decisions, its approvals—were taken on behalf of the President, with his knowledge and approval."

Allen could not mistake the message he took from the Special Group meeting of August 18, 1960. He promised to take it "very seriously" and proceed "as vigorously as the situation permits or requires." The next day he sent Devlin a cable ordering him to strike against Lumumba.

"In high quarters here it is the clear-cut conclusion that if he continues to hold high office, the inevitable result will be at best chaos and at worst pave the way to communist takeover of the Congo with disastrous consequences for the prestige of the UN and the interests of the free world generally," Allen wrote. "Consequently we conclude that his removal must be an urgent and prime objective and that under existing conditions this should be a high priority of our covert action. You can act on your own authority if time does not permit referral here."

On September 19 Devlin received a second, more cryptic cable from CIA headquarters. It advised him to expect a courier called "Joe from Paris" who would be carrying orders so sensitive that they could only be delivered verbally. A week later, as Devlin was leaving the American embassy, where he worked under cover as a consul, a man approached him and introduced himself as "Joe from Paris." He recognized the visitor as Dr. Sidney Gottlieb, a CIA chemist who had run the MKULTRA mind-control project. Allen had named him to head a "health alteration committee," assigned to prepare toxins and incapacitating drugs for possible use in CIA operations.

The two men drove off in Devlin's car. Gottlieb came directly to the point. He was carrying lethal poison, including one dose mixed into a tube of toothpaste. Devlin was to use it to kill Lumumba.

"It's your responsibility to carry out the operation, you alone," Gottlieb said. "The details are up to you, but it's got to be clean—nothing that can be traced back to the U.S. government."

One of Devlin's Congolese agents had access to the residence where Lumumba was being held, but could not reach a bathroom where he might plant the poisoned toothpaste. CIA officers spent hours discussing other ways to carry out the killing. Meanwhile Louis Armstrong, with his mile-wide smile, gave the Congolese the idea that every American loved them.

The contrast between the idealized and real faces of power is an ancient archetype. In American and Congolese history, it has rarely been more sharply drawn than during the autumn of 1960. An American who epitomized some of his country's most appealing qualities won the hearts of the Congolese. At the same time and in the same place, a handful of other Americans were plotting to kill the Congo's most popular leader.

Allen set off against Lumumba just as passionately as he had set off against other foreign leaders he thought of as monsters. His tactics were well practiced. In one way, though, this campaign was different from the others. In the past, Allen always had Foster at his side. They attacked like a serpent: two jaws not organically connected but working in perfect harmony. This time Allen was alone.

The intimate partnership that guided Foster and Allen through their years in power was not shaken by the failure of Archipelago in Indonesia. Allen had called "pulling the plug" there his most difficult decision, but neither brother took it as an occasion for deep reflection. Their sister Eleanor found them closer than ever.

"They loved to talk into the late hours," she remembered. "Foster would call Allen for a brief telephone word, or to ask him to come to the Department or his house on any occasion when conditions presented him with a new situation or growing crisis."

One reason the brothers drew so close during this period was that their once-powerful hold on Washington was slipping. Both were increasingly seen as out of touch—Foster because he could not respond creatively to Soviet overtures or to the intensifying challenge of Third World nationalism, Allen because of his failure to manage the burgeoning CIA bureaucracy effectively. Allen was further weakened by a spate of reports that CIA officers in Indochina had abetted heroin trafficking by their tribal allies. There were new calls to split the CIA in two, separating the collection and analysis of intelligence from covert action.

On an official visit to South America in the summer of 1958, Vice President Nixon was attacked by demonstrators, and Foster and Allen were blamed for having exposed him to danger and failing to defend the image of the United States. Nixon asserted afterward that the "Communist high command in South America" had orchestrated the attacks. Allen was more realistic. In testimony to the Senate Foreign Relations Committee, he made the trenchant observation—obvious to some, but rarely spoken in Washington—that Latin Americans might have reasons to be angry at the United States. Among these reasons, he suggested, might be "our support of dictators in Cuba, the Dominican Republic, and Paraguay," and "the support of United Fruit and intervention in Guatemala."

As both brothers came under increasing public criticism, rumors of their political demise began circulating. Eisenhower was reportedly ready to name General Alfred Gruenther, the supreme allied commander in Europe, as his new secretary of state. General Mark Clark, who had commanded allied troops in Korea, was said to be his choice as the new director of central intelligence. Never before had such speculation touched Foster or Allen.

Nixon's violence-torn trip through Latin America, the collapse of Archipelago, the overthrow and murder of pro-American leaders in Iraq, and the marine landing in Lebanon were more than enough to occupy both beleaguered brothers during the spring and summer of 1958. Then, at the end of August, China resumed shelling the disputed islands of Quemoy and Matsu. Three months later, Khrushchev gave a speech asserting that it was time for all foreign powers to withdraw their troops from Berlin. He said that if the United States wished to continue occupying a sector of the city, it should negotiate with the government of East Germany, which the United States did not recognize.

Another secretary of state in another era might have played down these challenges. Foster took them both as major strategic threats, and seized on them to sharpen the sense of imminent danger that he always sought to instill in Americans. He dramatized the "offshore islands crisis" and "Berlin crisis" as threats to vital American interests. They filled front pages for months.

Foster sought momentary escape from these confrontations at a World Council of Churches conference in Cleveland. Eminent theologians and religious leaders, many of whom he had known for years, were among the delegates. He hoped for a level of spiritual as well as political solace among them, but found neither. The delegates listened politely to his speech and then, within a couple of hours, passed a resolution urging the United

States to recognize the People's Republic of China and support its entry into the United Nations. Foster was shocked.

"It was to him a real and deeply felt hurt," Eleanor wrote.

She also reported that Foster had another source of private distress: "On orders from his doctors, he had given up smoking, meaning that he was forced to sip his evening brandy without the cigar he usually enjoyed. He found this difficult, and it contributed to a recurring nightmare. In it he was sipping brandy with a group of men and was offered a cigar. As he reached for it, he would awaken drenched with sweat."

As autumn turned to winter, Foster felt intensifying abdominal pain. Despite it, he traveled to Mexico City to attend the inauguration of President Adolfo López Mateos. There he had a long talk with his son John, a mining engineer based in Monterrey, who flew in to see him. He was clearly unwell. On his way home he stopped for a few days at Smoke Tree Ranch in Palm Springs, California. He found no relief. On December 6 he entered Walter Reed Army Medical Center in Washington for a week of "rest and check-up."

At the end of that week, Foster was driven directly from Walter Reed to National Airport, from which he flew to Paris for a NATO meeting. Eisenhower, evidently sensing that the end was near, lent Foster his personal plane and pilot. The trip took a toll. Rather than return directly to Washington, Foster flew to Jamaica, where he spent two weeks at the estate of the financier Clarence Dillon.

"I feel able to carry on," he told reporters when he returned to Washington.

At the end of January 1959 Foster flew to Europe for what turned out to be his last foreign trip. His health had deteriorated to the point that he could not bathe or dress himself. In Bonn he met his old comrade Chancellor Adenauer, for what both suspected would be the last time. He could eat only porridge.

On February 10 Foster returned to Walter Reed. There he had a hernia operation, which was also a probe for cancer. After emerging, he pressed doctors for the truth about his condition. They were evasive.

"Foster was aware of certain medical facts and of his own grave physical suffering," Eleanor wrote afterward, "but he did not appear to anticipate that his work on earth was to end."

On March 30, after several days trying to relax in Florida, Foster decided he did not have the strength to continue in office. He tried writing a resignation letter on one of his ever-present yellow legal pads, but his handwriting was too unsteady. Instead he dictated it to Janet. She had it typed and passed it on to Allen, who delivered it to Eisenhower. The president replied with a letter thanking Foster for being "a staunch bulwark of our nation against the machinations of Imperialistic Communism."

Three women kept vigil outside Foster's room. Janet was quietly grief-stricken, Eleanor stoic, and Clover disarmingly cheerful, talking of miracle cures and the foolishness of doctors. As they waited, Foster underwent radiation treatments, but declined narcotic painkillers. Cancer metastasized into his bones. He died shortly after dawn on May 24, 1959. The nation mourned with an emotion few had expected.

"A few weeks before, his name had been a synonym for intransigence, rigidity, inflexibility to the point of preferring armed conflict to concession," one commentator wrote. "Now young men and women were weeping over his body."

Americans had come to view Foster the way children might view a strict old schoolmaster. At the end of his life he seemed frozen into immobility, an anachronism, a prisoner of the past. When he was gone, though, the nation felt bereft. For years he had led its resistance to what was presumed to be mortal danger. His death led many to reflect that they had survived a frightening period, and to give much of the credit to him. Virtually every American knew his name. So did most literate humans on earth. When he died, the world suddenly seemed a different place.

Allen suggested that his brother be memorialized at a small private service, but he was overruled. His fears were realized when the day of the funeral turned out to be intensely hot, a huge crowd turned out, and tributes were interminable.

"Some fellow got up and read all of the Old Testament," former secretary of state Dean Acheson groused over a drink later in the day. "Then somebody else, not to be outdone, read all of the New Testament. By that time I was so tired I could hardly bear it. The number of eulogies—you'd never believe it. . . . The greatest mistake I made was not to die in office."

Allen was naturally shaken by the death of a man to whom he had been joined, personally and professionally, for all his life. No longer was he part of a duo that could shake the world. Eisenhower invited him to the White House less often, and told aides that whenever he and Allen met he wanted at least one other person to be present.

Some thought Eisenhower might name Allen to succeed his brother, giving him the post he had long coveted, but that was never a realistic prospect. In the end Eisenhower chose Undersecretary Christian Herter, a New England patrician who had been known to wince at some of Foster's more militant turns of phrase.

"Christian Herter never really replaced Dulles," the historian Blanche Wiesen Cook wrote. "Nobody did. The tough guy who snarled was gone."

The first new figure to emerge on the world stage during Herter's tenure was one who would bedevil and obsess American leaders for decades: Fidel Castro. On January 1, 1959, Castro had seized power in Cuba after toppling the military dictator Fulgencio Batista. For years Batista had been a faithful servant of the United States, and Allen's men had trained his secret police force, which became notorious for torturing and killing revolutionaries. This alone gave Castro a threatening aura. During his first months in power he refrained from direct confrontation. Then, while Foster was dying at Walter Reed, he turned up in New York.

Castro's eleven-day visit was a sensation. Young, bearded, long-haired, and impossibly romantic, he held court at the legendary Hotel Theresa in Harlem, attended a baseball game at Yankee Stadium, visited the Central Park Zoo, ate hot dogs and hamburgers, and was kissed by a beauty queen. "He came, he saw, he conquered," the *Daily News* reported.

Eisenhower avoided meeting foreign leaders of uncertain loyalty, and assigned Vice President Nixon to meet Castro. The two men spoke for three hours. In his report, Nixon wrote that Castro "has those indefinable qualities which make him a leader of men," and worried that the United States might not be able "to orient him in the right direction."

"In his attitude toward Communism," Nixon concluded, "he sounded almost exactly like Sukarno."

That proved prescient. In the months after his return from New York, Castro decreed a sweeping land reform, forbade the ownership of property by foreigners, and signed a trade agreement with the Soviet Union. The unthinkable seemed to be happening: a country on the doorstep of the United States was slipping under Soviet influence.

Although Eisenhower was near-apoplectic at this prospect, he directed his anger at Castro, not the Soviets. In fact, as his anti-Castro fervor was rising, he decided to invite Nikita Khrushchev to Washington—something that would have been inconceivable while Foster was alive.

When Khrushchev arrived on September 15, 1959, he became the first Soviet leader to set foot on American soil and an object of immense fascination. Eisenhower had invited him to the presidential retreat at Camp David, but Khrushchev wanted to see the United States first. A horde of reporters followed his every move. One of them, Murray Kempton, later wrote that this had been "the most profoundly entertaining public experience of our lives."

In New York, Khrushchev visited the top of the Empire State Building, toured IBM headquarters, called on Eleanor Roosevelt, and sparred lustily with tycoons at Averell Harriman's town house. He visited a farm in Iowa and a supermarket in San Francisco. Photos of him were on every day's front page: embracing a live turkey, ogling chorus girls, patting a fat man's belly, even pretending to shoplift a napkin holder by slipping it under his jacket. He met Frank Sinatra, Bob Hope, and Shirley MacLaine. Newspaper headlines ranged from "Khrushchev Is a Showman on His Arrival" and "Khrushchev's US Tour Like Traveling Circus" to odd ones like "Sees K on TV, So He Murders 2" and the classic "Denied Tour of Disneyland, K Blows Top."

This visit achieved for Khrushchev just what Foster had feared. It gave him the image of a normal human being who could be at turns charming, tempestuous, irascible, threatening, and reassuring. Pictures of Eisenhower and Khrushchev together—a pair of balding grandfathers with big smiles—undermined the premise of hostility that shaped the Cold War.

At Camp David, Eisenhower screened the film *Shane* for his guest. Perhaps he wanted to send a message. Khrushchev had threatened to force Western powers out of Berlin, and the film is full of lines like, "We can't give up this valley and we ain't gonna do it." The summit produced no breakthroughs, but Khrushchev's threats over Berlin faded in what some called "the spirit of Camp David." It was something that could not have happened while Foster was alive: Khrushchev blustered, Eisenhower pretended not to notice, time passed, and both sides tacitly agreed to forget the whole episode.

Khrushchev's visit, however, did nothing to ease the fear of Castro that was coursing through Washington. In January 1960, Allen created a Cuba

Task Force and directed it to come up with a plan for covert action in Cuba. When the plan was ready, Eisenhower approved it.

As the covert war against Castro was taking shape, two things happened that distracted both Allen and his boss. On May 1, a U-2 spy plane disappeared during a high-altitude flight over the Soviet Union. Allen presumed it had exploded. He helped concoct a cover story, and Eisenhower agreed to use it. The State Department issued a statement saying the pilot of a "weather research aircraft" had "reported difficulty with his oxygen equipment," and that the plane might have "continued on automatic pilot for a considerable distance and accidentally violated Soviet airspace." Later a spokesman added, "It is ridiculous to say we are trying to kid the world about this. . . . There was absolutely no deliberate attempt to violate Soviet airspace, and there never has been." A couple of days later Khrushchev struck back.

"I must tell you a secret," he said with a smile at a press conference in Moscow. "When I made my first report, I deliberately did not say that the pilot was alive and well."

It turned out that although the pilot, Francis Gary Powers, had been given a hollowed-out silver dollar containing a lethal dose of poison, he did not use it when his plane was shot down. Even worse, the plane was hardly damaged in the crash, and all of its spy cameras were intact. Khrushchev, with evident gusto, ridiculed American leaders for the "silly things" they had said to cover up the truth.

"The whole world knows that Allen Dulles is no weatherman," he added.

Eisenhower had been caught telling Americans, and the world, a giant lie. His son John urged him to fire Allen, who had steered him into it. "I am not going to shift the blame to my underling," the president replied.

"If you gentlemen are spies and I am the government," Eisenhower mused at a press conference, "and you get caught, I can say I never heard of you or saw you before. But if you strap a U-2 to your back, it is a little more difficult, to say the least, not to admit and assume responsibility."

Eisenhower had previously agreed to meet Khrushchev in Paris on May 18, and he had told Allen to be sure nothing disrupted the summit. After the U-2 crash, just as Eisenhower had feared, Khrushchev pulled out. At an angry press conference, the Soviet leader threatened "to take the American aggressors by the scruff of the neck and give them a little shaking, and make them understand that they must not commit such acts of aggression against the Soviet Union—and that if they come again, they will receive another blow."

Although surveillance photos taken by U-2 planes had provided valuable intelligence, it was all but inevitable that at some point one would be shot down. When it happened, Cold War tensions sharpened. Eisenhower had hoped to end his term with Soviet-American relations improving. Instead they were nearly as frigid as when he took office.

"The episode humiliated Khrushchev and discredited his relatively moderate policies," George Kennan wrote. "It forced him to fall back, for the defense of his own political position, on a more strongly belligerent anti-American tone of public utterance."

As the U-2 crisis was unfolding, Patrice Lumumba suddenly emerged in the Congo and began challenging Western power. He terrified many in Washington. The war against Castro remained a priority, but in mid-1960 stopping Lumumba became even more urgent. Allen saw the chance to launch an audacious operation. At a National Security Council meeting just three weeks after Lumumba's inauguration, he grabbed everyone's attention by using a phrase calculated to strike terror into Washington's collective heart. Lumumba, he said, was "a Castro or worse."

Never was a country described with more pitiless accuracy than when the novelist Joseph Conrad called the Congo a "heart of darkness." It brings out the worst in some people. Perhaps its spectacular resource wealth is the cause. The Congo is said to be the richest piece of geography on earth. When King Leopold II of Belgium appropriated it in 1885, he called it "a splendid piece of cake." During their seventy-five-year rule, Belgians made immense fortunes in the Congo. Millions of Congolese died through massacre or in slave labor. It was the bloodiest episode in the history of European colonialism.

Foster and Allen considered themselves anti-colonialist and believed that the nations of Africa should become independent. Two of the first that did so in the late 1950s, however, produced strongly nationalist leaders: Kwame Nkrumah in Ghana and Ahmed Sékou Touré in Guinea. They considered themselves socialists and refused to ally their countries with Washington. This disconcerted both brothers.

Like all wise supporters of the status quo, Foster and Allen promoted measured, controlled change. They abhorred populist nationalism, which to them was not a response to history and indigenous conditions but a smoke screen behind which rabble-rousing demagogues could do Moscow's work. Already they had fought nationalism in Iran, Guatemala, Vietnam, Indonesia, and the Middle East. In Foster's last years it erupted in Africa. This would have been his next battleground. Instead it became Allen's.

Slaughter on an epic scale was not Belgium's only legacy to the Congo. Perhaps never has a country been granted independence with less preparation. Belgium had refused to educate its Congolese subjects; in 1960, by one count, there were just seventeen college graduates in a population of thirteen million. Not a single Congolese had substantial experience in government or public administration. There were no Congolese doctors, lawyers, or engineers. The economy was almost entirely in foreign hands. Citizens were spread out across a country the size of Western Europe, and represented a bewildering array of tribes, cultures, and languages. There was neither an educated elite nor a middle class. Since Belgian military commanders refused to promote native soldiers above the rank of sergeant, there was not even a single Congolese officer.

Even with these handicaps, the Congo might have been able to survive in peace if outsiders had left it alone. That was impossible, for two reasons. First, the Congo has too many rich resources ever to be left alone. Second, it emerged as a nation when the Cold War was raging, and could not remain apart from the global confrontation.

Belgian rule over the Congo had been well established by the time Lumumba was born in 1925. He attended religious schools and, after completing the equivalent of three years of high school, set off on a life of learning. He read voraciously, took a correspondence course to perfect his French, became a volunteer librarian, and wrote poetry. After passing a rigorous examination, he won appointment as a postal clerk, one of the few civil service jobs available to natives. Later he became a beer salesman, which gave him the chance to crisscross the Congo and hone his talents as a persuasive speaker. During this period he also developed the look that millions around the world would later recognize: tall, thin, erect, usually in a dark suit, thin tie, and starched white shirt, with a small mustache and goatee, close-cropped hair, and intense eyes behind rimmed glasses.

Independence movements blazed across Africa during the late 1950s, and in the Belgian Congo, Lumumba emerged as an indefatigable activist. Inevitably, he was arrested, and a judge sentenced him to six months of penal servitude on charges of instigating violence. He was in jail when, in January 1960, King Baudouin of Belgium summoned more than eighty Congolese citizens to a conference in Brussels to discuss ways the Congo might be granted independence. It quickly became clear that the conference could not proceed without Lumumba. Finally the Belgians agreed to release him.

In the course of barely more than a single dizzying day, Lumumba went from a prison cell in the Congo to an elegant conference hall in Brussels, from penal servitude to chief negotiator for his country's independence. Before he sat down for the first negotiating session, a Belgian doctor rubbed salve into his wrists where manacles had cut his skin, and tended to scars from flogging that laced his back.

After generations during which there had been no political change in the Congo, and indeed no politics at all, events began moving at breakneck speed. Negotiators in Brussels agreed on a formula for independence. The Congolese people were called to the polls for the first time.

"The man to beat was Patrice Lumumba, 34, the tall, goateed radical from Stanleyville, who last week was storming through the back country in a cream-colored convertible," *Time* reported.

Lumumba's party emerged victorious, defeating the "moderate" party many Belgians favored, and he prepared to take office as prime minister. Few dared to imagine what might come next. Sub-Saharan Africa had already produced two defiantly neutralist leaders. Lumumba was poised to become a world figure on a larger scale than either of them.

"Mr. Patrice Lumumba is living proof that events create men as much as men create events," wrote a correspondent for the *Times* of London. "This tall, slender young man with the little moustache and goatee beard and large gesticulating hands, glows conviction from behind his spectacles. . . . The Belgians will have to be exceedingly clever to outsmart Mr. Lumumba."

No Congolese had a better understanding of the art of governing than Lumumba. This only meant, however, that instead of no understanding at all, he had a small bit. His dream was breathtakingly ambitious: build an independent state, regulate the exploitation of natural resources, and keep his country out of the Cold War conflict. Yet his lack of experience, and lack of compatriots with experience, rendered this dream all but impossible—especially since it implied confrontation with Belgium and the United States.

Both countries had evident reasons to oppose Lumumba. Belgium feared he would cut off the rich concessions from which Belgian corporations had long benefited. The United States saw him as a Cold War enemy. Behind both of these interests, and intertwined with them, was the Congo's uniquely rich resource base. Eisenhower spoke often of the West's need to secure strategic minerals, and he realized that this need would become more acute as industrial progress accelerated. The Congo—in particular the southeastern province of Katanga—was an invaluable source of industrial diamonds and strategic metals like copper, manganese, zinc, cobalt, and chromium. It had also become the world's principal source of a suddenly precious ore: uranium. Few knew it, but the uranium used to fuel the first American nuclear reactor, built in Chicago, as well as the uranium used in the atomic bombs that had been dropped on the Japanese cities of Hiroshima and Nagasaki, had come from the Congo. Resource wealth would have made this new country a strategic prize even if the Cold War had not been raging.

Independence came to the Congo on June 30, 1960. The ceremony, held at the Palais de la Nation in Leopoldville, was supposed to be no more than a formal handover. Lumumba made it an epochal turning point.

Beside the entrance to the ornate salon stood a bronze statue of King Leopold II, whom history holds responsible for cruelties in the Congo that challenge the human imagination. Belgian dignitaries filed in. Members of the newly elected government followed. Diplomats and journalists stood by. King Baudouin began his welcoming speech by paying tribute to his genocidal grandfather, calling Congolese independence "the result of the undertaking conceived by the genius of King Leopold II." He described independence as a gift Belgium was giving the Congo. Then he addressed the country's new leaders.

"Don't compromise the future with hasty reforms, and don't replace the structures that Belgium hands over to you until you are sure you can do better," the king advised. "Don't be afraid to come to us. We will remain by your side, give you advice, train with you the technical experts and administrators you will need."

The next speaker, Joseph Kasavubu, who was about to assume the ceremonial presidency of the new Republic of the Congo, was brief and inoffensive. Then, unexpectedly, another Congolese dignitary rose to summon a speaker whose name did not appear on the official program. Patrice Lumumba, the leader of the Congo's largest political party and the incoming prime minister, strode to the microphone. Across his chest he wore the Ribbon of the Order of the Crown, a wide crimson sash the king had conferred on him.

Lumumba's first words were thunderbolts: independence was not a gift from Belgium but a triumph of "passionate, idealistic struggle" that had finally thrown off "the humiliating slavery that was imposed on us by force." By one account King Baudouin "turned a deathly pale." Lumumba continued:

> Our wounds are too fresh and too painful for us to drive them from our memory. . . . We have known sarcasm and insults, endured blows morning, noon and night because we were "niggers." . . . We have seen our lands despoiled under the terms of what was supposedly national law, but which only recognized the right of the strongest. We have seen that this law was quite different for a white than for a black: accommodating for the former, cruel and inhuman for the latter. We have seen the terrible suffering of those condemned for their political opinions or religious beliefs. . . . And finally, who can forget the massacres in which so many of our brothers perished, the cells where the authorities threw those who would not submit to a rule where "justice" meant oppression and exploitation? All of that, my brothers, we have endured. But we, who by vote of your elected representatives have been given the right to direct our dear country, we who have suffered in our body and our soul from colonial oppression, we tell you loudly: all that is now ended!

The Congolese in the hall, and thousands listening to loudspeakers outside, interrupted Lumumba no fewer than eight times with bursts of applause and cheering. Many listening on radio approached delirium. None had ever heard an African address colonial power in terms remotely like these, let alone in the presence of a reigning monarch.

In one electrifying moment, a former postal clerk and beer salesman propelled himself to mythic status.

At first it seemed that the transition might go smoothly. Eisenhower sent a veteran diplomat, Robert Murphy, to Lumumba's inauguration, bearing a bust of Lincoln and an offer to educate three hundred Congolese students at universities in the United States. "To the surprise of many whites who expected pillaging and insults from the newly independent blacks," *Time* reported, "there was universal inter-racial politeness, even open camaraderie."

Trouble began quickly. Lumumba, who had agreed to retain Belgian troops as long as they were subject to his ultimate control, appointed a commission to reorganize the military and consider the feasibility of soldiers electing their own officers. General Emile Janssens, the Belgian commander, who considered Congolese troops "a stupid rabble," sent him a curt note advising him to desist and telling him to "consider this a last and final warning." Then Janssens convened his Congolese troops, told them that "in the army the white will always remain superior to blacks," and famously wrote on a chalkboard "Before Independence = After Independence."

The soldiers, already angry that Lumumba had refused to increase their pay, rebelled at this Belgian effort to maintain control of the Congolese army. Some were propelled by tribal passions, especially in regions that felt under-represented in Lumumba's cabinet. Indiscipline and mutiny spread. Some soldiers beat, kidnapped, terrorized, and raped Europeans. Images of white families huddled into airports and packed onto ferries, fleeing violent Africans, were beamed around the world. Within a couple of days, all but a few hundred of the Congo's twenty-five thousand Belgians were gone, including nearly every doctor, civil servant, and technician in the country. On July 10, claiming the need to protect civilian lives, Belgian commandos began parachuting into remote regions of the Congo.

The first ten days of independence were an unmitigated disaster for Lumumba and his country. On the eleventh day came the crowning blow. A local figure in Katanga province, Moise Tshombe, declared Katanga independent and proclaimed himself its leader. Katanga is the center of the Congo's mineral wealth, and the powerful Belgian mining company that had exploited its wealth for generations, Union Minière du Haut Katanga, was Tshombe's sponsor. The Belgian military commander in Katanga, Colonel Lucien Champion, cashiered hundreds of soldiers loyal to Lumumba and recruited Europeans to replace them. Belgium's government sent him nine tons of ammunition. "Overnight Tshombe became the most unpopular and reviled black leader in Africa," one CIA officer reported. The London *Daily Telegraph* described him as "under the domination of Belgian officials."

As soon as the secessionist rebellion broke out, Lumumba commandeered a plane and flew to Katanga. He counted on the force of his will, and his ability to mobilize nascent Congolese patriotism, to turn the tide in his favor. His plane was not allowed to land. After returning to Leopoldville, he angrily announced that the Congo was breaking diplomatic relations with Belgium. "We accuse the Belgian government of having meticulously prepared Katanga secession in the aim of keeping a hold on our country," he wrote. Then he asked the United Nations to send troops to the Congo so that he could expel the Belgians.

Fatefully, Lumumba also took another step: he sent a cable to the Soviet leader, Nikita Khrushchev. "We ask you to follow hour by hour the evolution of the situation in the Congo," it said. "We might be forced to solicit intervention from the Soviet Union if the Western camp does not put an end to aggressive action against the sovereign Republic of the Congo."

The Soviets, like the Americans, had largely ignored the Congo. Both superpowers had presumed that the Belgians would arrange to hand power to a trusted Congolese minion, and never imagined that they would allow someone like Lumumba to emerge. Khrushchev was preoccupied with other matters: his country's intensifying relationship with Cuba, its emerging rivalry with China, the continuing U-2 crisis, and the repercussions from the shooting down of a second American reconnaissance plane on July 1. Nonetheless he could not ignore Lumumba's overture, and assured the new Congolese leader that the Soviet Union would send "whatever aid necessary for the triumph of your just cause." In case Washington missed this disturbing message, Lumumba repeated it publicly in a speech to parliament on July 15.

"We have no arms, but we shall appeal to any friendly nations that want to help us," he said. "If it is necessary, we will call on the devil."

A week later Lumumba set out for New York to present his case at the United Nations. He arrived to a storm of attention. A nineteen-gun salute greeted him at Idlewild Airport. Secretary-General Dag Hammarskjöld warmly welcomed him, and after their first meeting proclaimed himself "very optimistic, very satisfied."

Lumumba held several press conferences, in both New York and Washington, his next stop. At one of them, a reporter asked how he envisioned his personal future. He turned reflective.

"If I die tomorrow," he said, "it will be because a foreigner has armed a Congolese."

Behind closed doors, Lumumba's visit to Washington went poorly. He felt under siege—angry, suspicious, and overwhelmed by the pace of events. There was no way he could have understood the Americans' complex of fears, or learned the vocabulary he might have used to calm them. He asked Secretary of State Herter for technicians, a loan, a small plane so he could travel freely around his country, and, above all, help in forcing Belgian troops out of the Congo. Herter disingenuously replied that these were all matters for the United Nations.

Herter's deputy, Douglas Dillon, later testified that officials who met Lumumba concluded he was "just not a rational being . . . an individual whom it was impossible to deal with." Declassified transcripts suggest that the real problem may have been Lumumba's views, especially his steadfast refusal to rule out soliciting military aid from the Soviet Union. New on the world stage and unschooled in Cold War truths, he never grasped how frightened and angry the United States became when a government began flirting with Moscow. When he pronounced himself ready to invite Soviet military power into Africa's richest heartland, he may have believed he was only seeking ways to re-establish his country's unity.

By American standards, however, Lumumba seemed dangerously defiant. Eisenhower refused to see him. Washington feared that he was preparing to hand the Soviets a historic victory.

"We are being attacked because we will no longer bow down!" Lumumba declared when he returned to Leopoldville. "We are being attacked because the members of the Congolese government are honest men. . . . They have tried to buy me for millions. I refused."

Larry Devlin, the CIA station chief in Leopoldville, had been warning that Lumumba was serving "the Russian bear," and felt vindicated by the fiasco in Washington. Devlin was a classically action-oriented officer, immersed in the Cold War ethos and eager to launch covert operations. He had joined the agency the way most officers of his generation did. While he was studying at Harvard, one of his professors invited him and three other students to a genteel recruiting session conducted by McGeorge Bundy, a

Council on Foreign Relations member and the future national security adviser to President Kennedy. Bundy described the CIA's mission as "thwarting Moscow's ambitions for world domination without having to resort to open warfare." That was all Devlin needed to hear. He served in several posts in Europe, and in 1960, when he became Allen's field commander in the Congo, he considered his mission an urgently important defense of freedom. Half a century later, he was less certain.

"In retrospect, I think that Lumumba's actions and statements may well have resulted from his limited education and his total lack of experience in dealing with sophisticated leaders and governments," Devlin wrote in a memoir. "Lumumba did not act like any other government leader with whom American officials were familiar. He came across as an unpredictable loose cannon. . . . With the full backing of Headquarters, the station began work on a plan to remove Lumumba from power."

Inside the Congo, public administration had broken down, police forces had evaporated, and unemployment was skyrocketing. Lumumba proved unwilling or unable to discipline unruly soldiers, in part because he considered them a social movement and was reluctant to order them to submit themselves once again to Belgian officers. One platoon beat up a crew of Canadian and American airmen delivering a cargo of food from the UN. Secessionists remained in control of Katanga, and a second province, Kasai, center of Belgian diamond-mining interests, also seceded. Anarchy was in the air.

Eisenhower decided to summon the American ambassador in the Congo, Clare Timberlake, for a personal report. On August 1, Timberlake addressed the National Security Council. After he spoke, the council decided that the United States should be prepared "at any time to take appropriate military action to prevent or defeat Soviet military intervention in the Congo." That same day, Soviet leaders announced they were preparing "resolute measures to rebuff aggressors . . . who are in fact acting with the encouragement of the colonialist powers of NATO."

Nearly three hundred foreign journalists converged on Leopoldville to cover the "Congo disaster." They packed Lumumba's press conferences and made him, by one account, "the most talked-about man in the world." *Time* commissioned a portrait for its August 22 cover. It showed Lumumba looking intense and purposeful, against the background of a stormy forest symbolizing the turbulent Congo.

Articles about Lumumba, most with photos, had been featured in every issue of *Time* since independence, more coverage than the magazine gave to any other story during the summer of 1960. He became the focus of intense debates in the United States over race, decolonization, and the rights of emerging nations. The prospect of a *Time* cover distressed Ambassador Timberlake, who detested the man he called "Lumumbavitch." Timberlake arrived on a visit to Belgium as the magazine was going to press, and shared his frustration with his host, William Burden, the American ambassador in Brussels.

"*Time* magazine plans to do a cover story on Lumumba with his picture on the front of the magazine," Timberlake fumed. "Celebrity coverage at home will make him even more difficult to deal with. He's a first-class headache as it is."

"Then why don't you get the story killed, or at least modified?" Burden asked.

"I tried to persuade the *Time* man in Leopoldville until I was blue in the face. But he said there was nothing to do because the story had already been sent to New York."

Burden belonged to the small clique of perfectly connected aristocrats who shaped American foreign policy for the first two-thirds of the twentieth century. He had been born to wealth, attended Harvard, married a granddaughter of Cornelius Vanderbilt, joined the Council on Foreign Relations, been assistant secretary of the air force, and even served a term as president of the Museum of Modern Art, succeeding his friend Nelson Rockefeller. In the weeks before Timberlake's visit, he had sent vivid cables to Washington warning that Lumumba "threatens our vital interests in Congo and Africa generally" and that "a principal objective of our political and diplomatic action must therefore be to destroy Lumumba government."

Upon hearing Timberlake's complaint, Burden picked up his telephone, and a few minutes later had Henry Luce on the line from New York. He told Luce what the interests of the United States required: Lumumba should not appear on the cover of *Time*. Luce replied that the cover could not be changed because the magazine was going to press. Burden persisted.

"Oh, come on, Henry," he said. "You must have other cover stories in the can."

They spoke for a few more minutes. As soon as Luce hung up, he ordered that a portrait of Dag Hammarskjöld replace Lumumba's on the forthcoming cover. There was not even time to change the background. Hammarskjöld appeared before the storm-bent trees drawn originally for Lumumba.

Neither Foster nor Allen knew or cared much about Africa. The State Department had no bureau of African affairs until 1957. Allen was even slower, running Africa as a subsidiary of his Middle East division until finally creating an Africa division in mid-1959. He had no direct reporting from the Congo until Larry Devlin arrived in July 1960.

Devlin and the handful of other CIA officers Allen hurriedly dispatched to the Congo represented the best and worst of the CIA: masters of their trade, but ignorant of the country around them. They were puppeteers of power. Everything Allen and his men knew or cared to know about the Congo had to do with the Cold War. In their eyes, Lumumba was the newest incarnation of the global threat they were sworn to resist.

"None of us had any real concept of what he stood for," one of them later reflected. "He was simply an unstable former postal clerk with great political charisma, who was leaning toward the Communist bloc. In Cold War terms, he represented the other side. The fact that he was first and foremost an African nationalist who was using the East-West rivalry to advance his cause was played down by the Belgians, who greatly feared him."

Devlin first set out "to discover who the real shakers and movers were, what made them tick, and what they planned to do." Then he and his men recruited informers and provocateurs inside political parties, labor unions, youth groups, parliament, and the cabinet. One recalled "recruiting agents and running them under conditions of public disorder that would have had others fleeing for their lives." The station organized rowdy protest demonstrations, rented safe houses, planted listening devices, and provided "anti-Lumumba story lines" to friendly or suborned journalists. Politicians who had supported Lumumba began deserting him. Anonymous leaflets appeared with warnings that Lumumba "is the devil" and would soon "sell your wives to the Russians." Allen's destabilization machine was purring.

In midsummer Hammarskjöld flew to the Congo in an effort to mediate between Lumumba and the secessionists. He failed. Lumumba wanted UN troops to march into the secessionist provinces and bring them back under central government rule. That, however, would have required the UN to act against Belgian and Western interests, which was unrealistic. Lumumba was infuriated. He believed he had won a victory when the

Security Council ordered Belgian forces to leave the Congo and replaced them with fifteen thousand UN troops, but soon concluded that the UN force was simply another form of Western occupation. Seeing enemies everywhere, he decreed a nationwide state of emergency.

On August 18 Devlin cabled an urgent warning to Allen.

"Embassy and station believe Congo experiencing classic Communist effort takeover government," he wrote. "Anti-West forces rapidly increasing power Congo and therefore may be little time left in which take action to avoid another Cuba."

Later that morning—it was from 11:10 to 11:23, according to the White House log—President Eisenhower held an "off the record meeting" with Allen, Richard Bissell, and six other senior national security officials. Allen could not have failed to present Devlin's cable. Years later, congressional investigators pinpointed this as the day when Eisenhower "circumlocutiously" ordered Lumumba assassinated.

After becoming the first American president to give such an order—so far as is known—Eisenhower met briefly with the departing ambassador of Ecuador, had lunch, and then adjourned to Burning Tree Country Club in Maryland for eighteen holes of golf. Allen passed the order to Devlin.

"I was authorized to spend up to $100,000 on my own authority on any operation that appeared feasible," Devlin later recalled. "To the best of my knowledge, no other station chief had ever been given such latitude. . . . If further evidence was required that Washington supported our own conclusion about replacing Lumumba, that was it."

When plotting against a foreign leader, Allen normally worked in concert with the State Department. His relationship with Foster meant that the CIA and State Department functioned as a single agency, without any of the normal tensions or debates that might otherwise have divided them. This intimacy could not survive the death of one of the partners. Herter understood that Eisenhower wished Lumumba gone, and was willing to do what he could to help. Nonetheless he was determined to reassert the State Department's interests and positions as distinct from those of the CIA. This was a radical change.

"The moment they became aware of it, deputy assistant secretaries and foreign service officers began to maneuver for greater independence between the two agencies, feeling they could afford to hold firmer to the positions they deemed proper for their own agencies," Bissell later recalled.

"There were subtle differences of attitude as a result of this feeling that the widely presumed intimate connection at the top no longer existed."

At the end of August in Leopoldville, Ambassador Timberlake paid a discreet call on President Kasavubu. Timberlake, according to one account, "suggested that Lumumba was a dangerous man and implied that he should not continue as prime minister." Kasavubu remained impassive, as was his wont. He understood what the United States wished him to do, however, and Timberlake made clear its eagerness for his cooperation.

Lumumba and Kasavubu were rivals pushed together by politics. For a time they cooperated awkwardly, but when outside powers decided to strike against Lumumba, they found in Kasavubu a willing partner. He was one of many assets they used during those frantic summer days.

"The embassy and station were humming with activity," Devlin recalled.

Before setting out to crush the rebellions in Katanga and Kasai, Lumumba held mass rallies in Leopoldville to marshal support, attracting crowds in the tens of thousands. Then he began requisitioning transport planes from Air Congo for his attack. Tensions rose further when ten small planes from the Soviet Union turned up in Leopoldville. Each could carry twenty soldiers into battle.

Soviet leaders had paid just as little attention to sub-Saharan Africa as their American counterparts, and knew just as little about it. Their first venture in Africa had been to aid the former French colony of Guinea, which lost French support after refusing to join a Paris-centered Francophone community. In 1957 Khrushchev brought one thousand African students to schools in the Soviet Union. Then he announced the creation of Peoples' Friendship University, dedicated to educating students from Africa and the rest of the Third World. Later that year Lumumba burst onto the world scene. In a matter of weeks, he became the world's most famous African and a vivid symbol of resistance to Western power. Naturally the Soviets took notice.

Some of Lumumba's friends, notably the outspokenly neutralist President Nkrumah of Ghana, warned him that under no circumstances should he invite non-Africans to intervene in the Congo. Lumumba wavered briefly, and then, facing secessionist rebellion, took the fateful step of asking for Soviet planes. With the planes came pilots, crews, and advisers. Some of them, according to possibly exaggerated accounts in the Western press, distributed pamphlets and gave speeches about Marxism to Congolese troops. *Time* ran an alarming story headlined "Red Weeds Grow in New Soil."

Early on the evening of September 5, President Kasavubu arrived at Radio Leo, the main station in Leopoldville, and gave the station manager a tape that he said contained an urgent message for the nation. Then he prudently drove away. Twenty minutes later, an English language lesson was interrupted and Kasavubu's tape was played. He announced he was dismissing Lumumba and naming a new prime minister.

Lumumba immediately convened his cabinet and secured a unanimous vote to dismiss Kasavubu. Then he proclaimed the decision in a vivid speech on Radio Leo, blaming "Belgian and French imperialists" for fomenting the crisis. The next day, UN soldiers closed Radio Leo, depriving Lumumba of his national voice. Then they shut all airports in the Congo, making it impossible for him to tour the country and rally support.

On September 8 in Washington, the Special Group met to discuss these dramatic developments. Gordon Gray, Eisenhower's national security adviser, dropped in to convey "top-level feeling in Washington that vigorous action would not be amiss." Allen assured him that while Ambassador Timberlake was trying to arrange Lumumba's ouster through a parliamentary vote or other quasi-legal means, CIA officers were indeed taking "vigorous action."

As part of his rump regime, President Kasavubu had named a mild-mannered soldier and trained typist, Joseph Mobutu, to command the embryonic Congolese army—a post he had also held under Lumumba. Devlin immediately began passing him sums of money, then visited him and arranged a deal. Mobutu agreed to lead a coup and seize power. In exchange, Devlin promised that the United States would quickly recognize his government.

"The coup will take place within a week," Mobutu promised. "But I will need five thousand dollars to provide for my senior officers."

With that, the bargain was sealed. Mobutu struck on September 14. In a proclamation on the reopened Radio Leo, he said that he had decided to "neutralize" Lumumba and Kasavubu, close parliament, and name a College of Commissars to govern the country. He ordered the Soviet embassy closed and gave citizens of Communist countries forty-eight hours to leave. When parliament tried to assemble in defiance of his order, he sent soldiers to block the entrance.

Devlin was jubilant but could not immediately deliver American recognition for the new regime. First, he told Mobutu, a way would have to be found "to legalize the illegal," preferably by "de-neutralizing" President Kasavubu and restoring him to his position as the Congo's titular leader. Second, Mobutu should change the name of his governing council because the word *commissar* sounded "too Russian, too communist."

Mobutu resisted for a time, but before long he "de-neutralized" Kasavubu, restored him to the ceremonial presidency, and announced that the Congo's new governing council would be renamed the College of Commissioners. Both its president and vice president were on the CIA payroll.

With this accomplished, the United States recognized Mobutu's government. Leaders of many other nations howled in protest. Prime Minister Jawaharlal Nehru of India demanded that the Congolese parliament be reopened and allowed to vote on Lumumba's leadership. The powers of the world—in this case the United States, Belgium, and other Europeans with interests in Africa, acting through the United Nations—had no reason to pay heed.

Although Lumumba had been deposed, Allen remained uneasy. "Lumumba talents and dynamism appear overriding factor in reestablishing his position each time it seems half lost," one of his aides cabled to the Congo station. "In other words each time Lumumba has opportunity to have last word he can sway events to his advantage."

With that insightful message, Allen told his men in the Congo that their work was not done.

Lumumba was arrested twice in the week after the coup but talked his way free both times. He then retreated into his official residence, an elegant three-story manse where Belgian governors-general had once lived. United Nations commanders recognized danger and posted blue-helmeted guards nearby. Soon afterward, soldiers loyal to Mobutu arrived. Unable to seize their prey, they deployed nearby. Lumumba found himself surrounded by an inner ring of soldiers protecting him and a second, outer ring of others eager to capture or kill him.

Oddly, Lumumba's telephone was not cut off, and he spent many hours talking to his supporters. He planned what he would do when he returned to office. At one point he appealed to the United Nations to lend him a plane so he could fly to New York and present his case to the General Assembly, but Hammarskjöld and James Wadsworth, the new American ambassador to the UN, made sure none was provided. In an even clearer sign of American intent, Allen sent a blunt cable to his Congo station.

"We wish give every possible support in eliminating Lumumba from any possibility of resuming governmental position," he wrote.

Lumumba remained inside his residence. *Time* reported that he "prowled the balcony" to let off steam. His isolation may have saved his life, since it was during this period that CIA officers were trying to find a way to poison him. They could not penetrate the two rings of guards and cluster of friends surrounding their intended victim.

Allen encouraged officers in his Leopoldville station to think imaginatively about ways to kill Lumumba. Unable to do it with poison, they discussed other options. At one point they considered trying to lure Lumumba out of hiding and using a "commando type group" to capture him. Later they suggested hiring a sharpshooter equipped with a "high powered foreign make rifle with telescopic sight and silencer."

"Hunting good here when light's right," one officer helpfully wrote in a cable to Washington.

These ideas appealed to Allen. At his direction, Richard Bissell sent two covert operatives to the Congo with orders to concentrate full-time on the assassination plot. "[Bissell] called me in and told me he wanted me to go to the Belgian Congo, the former Belgian Congo, and to eliminate Lumumba," one of the operatives later testified. "I told him that I would absolutely not have any part of killing Lumumba. . . . What I wanted to do was to get him out, to trick him out if I could, and then turn him over . . . to the legal authorities, and let him stand trial. . . . And I am not opposed to capital punishment."

It was at this life-or-death moment—Lumumba in brooding confinement while the CIA plotted to kill him—that Louis Armstrong arrived in the Congo. Rather than playing for an audience that included Lumumba, he played for one that included Devlin and Ambassador Timberlake.

Music distracted Leopoldville only briefly. A few days after Armstrong departed, President Kasavubu traveled to New York on a crucial diplomatic mission. He asked the United Nations to strip the Congolese ambassador of his credentials and accredit a new one loyal to the Mobutu regime. Several African and Asian countries were bitterly opposed. So was the Soviet bloc. In the end, they lost to the power of Mobutu's friends: Belgium, his principal sponsor; the United States, which was paying him and saw him as a strategic bulwark; and France, always eager to prevent nationalism from spreading in Africa.

On November 22, the General Assembly voted to recognize the Mobutu regime and accredit its ambassador. Soon afterward, Lumumba's ousted ambassador, Thomas Kanza, telephoned Lumumba at his surrounded residence in Leopoldville. Kanza was the first Congolese to win a university degree, renowned for his wisdom, and he begged Lumumba to be patient.

"Wait, even indefinitely, for the resolution of the Congolese crisis," he urged.

"No," Lumumba replied. "It will be difficult for you to understand that one of us must die to save the cause of our homeland."

Lumumba rejected not only his friend's counsel, but that of the African leader he most admired, President Nkrumah of Ghana, who advised him to stay "cool as a cucumber" and wait for the situation to unfold. He also turned aside chances to escape. Supporters suggested that he seek diplomatic asylum in the embassy of Ghana or Guinea. When his wife departed to Switzerland, his Italian doctor suggested it might be possible for him to leave with her. He was not tempted. Martyrdom had become some mix of premonition and wish.

Five days after President Kasavubu won his diplomatic triumph in New York, he held a gala reception in Leopoldville to celebrate. Guests were in a festive mood. As they toasted their success, however, their nemesis, whom they believed to be safely confined, was launching a counterconspiracy. The College of Commissioners learned of it the next morning in a brief but astonishing note.

"The big rabbit has escaped," it said.

Allen enjoyed the company of wealthy people, and during his last couple of years in office, he sometimes slipped away for weekends at the Palm Beach estate of Charles Wrightsman, an oil executive and art collector who decorated his walls with paintings by Renoir and Vermeer. Among neighbors he visited regularly was retired ambassador Joseph P. Kennedy. Often other members of the Kennedy clan were around, including Senator John F. Kennedy. During one of his visits, Senator Kennedy's young wife, Jacqueline, gave him a gift.

"Here is a book you should have, Mr. Director," she said.

The book was Ian Fleming's novel *From Russia, with Love*, featuring the British secret agent James Bond, whose code number, 007, entitles him to kill in the service of the state. Senator Kennedy was already a confirmed Bond fan—he later named *From Russia, with Love* as one of his favorite books—and Allen quickly became one, too. He bought each book in the series as soon as it appeared, and often sent notes to Kennedy offering his analysis. Ian Fleming, who was himself a former intelligence officer, learned of his interest.

"As our acquaintanceship grew, Fleming condescended to include in his books references to the CIA and its people," Allen later wrote. "Occasionally CIA personnel even joined James Bond in his exploits—in a subordinate role, of course, but after all with a great by-line. . . . I would be glad to hire several James Bonds."

Allen found Bond endlessly intriguing. He even asked CIA technicians to try replicating some of the gadgets Bond used during his exploits. Most, like the homing device Bond slipped into the cars of enemies whose movements he wanted to track, proved unworkable. Allen admitted that the flamboyant Bond bore "very little resemblance" to a real spy, yet to a certain degree both he and Kennedy conflated reality with the Bond novels. Bond's triumphs strengthened their faith in covert action. It was a case of life imitating art imitating life, as when gangsters watch gangster movies for tips on how they should behave.

"Dulles liked Bond because the series was an unashamed celebration of the spy business," wrote the intelligence historian Christopher Moran. "007 projected an image of Western intelligence services as a noble band of decisive and courageous patriots, fighting an enemy in the Soviet Union that possessed a kind of wanton, undiscriminating belligerence."

Beneath the Bond novels lies a seductive assumption. In each of them, a spymaster sends an intrepid agent to a faraway land, and the agent proceeds to crush a great threat to civilization, all in secret. This was the spy trade as Allen liked to imagine it, brutal at times but essential to world peace—and always with a neat ending. Neither Bond nor his superiors ever worry about the long-term consequences of their acts, and there never are any.

One of Allen's most important real-life officers, Frank Wisner, offered a radically different narrative of the spy's life.

Wisner was one of the OSS "old boys" who formed the core of the early CIA. As deputy director for plans, he had the agency's most sensitive job. The list of places where he helped direct covert operations is an intelligence abecedarian's dream: Albania, Berlin, China, Guatemala, Hungary, Indonesia, Iran, Korea, Poland, Romania. He was never the same after Hungary.

For years Wisner had worked relentlessly on plans to liberate the "captive nations" of Eastern Europe. When his Hungarian operatives launched their uprising in 1956, he sent Allen a stream of cables demanding help. He even composed an "ultimatum" to the Soviets that he wanted Eisenhower to deliver. No one paid attention. The Soviets brutally crushed the Hungarian resistance. Wisner, not without reason, blamed himself. He felt betrayed by Allen and everyone in Washington, who, as he realized with acute pain, never intended their calls for "liberation" in Eastern Europe to be taken seriously. This tormented him.

Other failures, especially the one in Indonesia—after which Allen removed him as deputy director for plans and named Richard Bissell to succeed him—pushed Wisner further toward madness. After he received a diagnosis of "psychotic mania" and endured six months of hospitalization that included electroshock treatment, Allen gave him a new job as chief of the London station. He proved not to have recovered and had to be recalled. At home he focused his rage on Allen, who he believed had cynically sent anti-Communist partisans to their deaths.

"Frank Wisner came out to my house, and sat on my terrace and drank my liquor, and told me my brother was a no-good so-and-so!" Eleanor recalled after one of their encounters.

Wisner lost his grip on reality, or perhaps was overwhelmed by reality. Finally he left the CIA. At the age of fifty-six, he committed suicide with one of his son's shotguns. Nothing like this ever happened in James Bond novels.

If some practitioners of the spy trade are tormented by its inherent cruelties, though, Allen was not among them. Like Bond, he was untroubled by collateral damage. Failure disappointed but did not disturb him.

"He remained an actor, Mr. Chips doing intelligence," the historian Burton Hersh wrote of Allen's final years in office. "He took such obvious, boyish pleasure in all the 'side' the position entailed—the limousine pickups, the secret inks, the world-girdling inspection tours punctuated by dead-of-night takeoffs the moment he climbed aboard bundled into his custom-made jump suit. Now he was preoccupied with the overlays for the seven-story monument to civilian intelligence going up in Langley, Virginia. This was to institutionalize his work."

Allen had decided soon after taking over the agency that it needed a new headquarters to replace the scattered complex of buildings it occupied in Washington. He conceived the idea of a campus-like setting in a wooded area, found an isolated tract in northern Virginia that had once been an estate called Langley, lobbied the $65 million appropriation through Congress, and took a personal interest in the design. The 258-acre "campus" emerged as remarkably cold and forbidding, but well hidden. Eisenhower laid the ceremonial cornerstone on November 3, 1959.

Five thousand people turned out. Senators and other dignitaries mixed with CIA officers and their families. Journalists added what they already knew about the agency's budget to what they saw that day—a five-hundred-seat auditorium, a cafeteria to accommodate one thousand people, a three-thousand-car parking garage—and concluded that the CIA probably had about thirty thousand employees worldwide.

"By its very nature, the work of this agency demands of its members the highest order of dedication, ability, trustworthiness, and selflessness—to say nothing of the finest type of courage, whenever needed," Eisenhower said in his speech. "Success cannot be advertised: failure cannot be explained. In the work of intelligence, heroes are undecorated and unsung, often even among their own fraternity. . . . The reputation of your organization for quality and excellence of performance, under the leadership of your director, Mr. Allen Dulles, is a proud one."

This tribute was no doubt sincere, but, with Foster gone, Allen's influence in Washington had palpably declined. The same was true for Eleanor. She had a last hurrah in her beloved Berlin, dedicating an avenue that Mayor Willy Brandt named John-Foster-Dulles-Allee, and then was eased out of her job. Herter sent her on a forty-nation tour to assess the impact of Soviet aid in the Third World.

On a flight between Saigon and Phnom Penh, which she shared with chickens and livestock, Eleanor was struck by an intestinal attack. Despite obvious pain, and not wishing to be seen as proof that women could not handle strenuous assignments, she pressed on through Bangkok, Rangoon, New Delhi, Karachi, Tehran, Ankara, and the rest of her scheduled stops.

Upon her return to Washington she checked into a clinic, underwent a month of treatment and recuperation, and then began writing her report. She was sixty-four and could have retired, but was determined to make the best of her career and leave a strong example for women to follow.

Allen's best hope to regain Eisenhower's favor was to rid the world of troublesome Lumumba, and during the second half of 1960 he worked intently to accomplish it. Nonetheless he was always alert for any chance to wound the Communist giants. In late 1960, the Sino-Soviet split burst into public view when Khrushchev abruptly withdrew all Soviet advisers from China, which had emerged as the more radical of the two countries. This development intensified interest in covert action there. Allen welcomed it. His plan to foment civil war in China by attacking from Burma had failed but, undaunted, he decided to try again a thousand miles away, in Tibet.

The Tibetans had resisted Chinese efforts to subject and assimilate them in the 1950s, and some had turned to rebellion. The CIA, always alert for chances to make trouble inside the Communist heartland, began working with Tibetan rebels in 1957 and ultimately brought more than 250 of them to Fort Hale, Colorado, for secret mountain-warfare training. CIA planes dropped weaponry to hideouts nestled in the Himalayas— much of it from stockpiles that had been designated for Indonesia before Archipelago collapsed. At the peak of this "war for the roof of the world," the CIA was supporting an army of fourteen thousand men. Ultimately and inevitably, their rebellion was crushed by overwhelming Chinese power. Tens of thousands were killed. The Dalai Lama, Tibet's principal leader, who fled the repression in 1959, later observed that Americans' help for his cause had been "a reflection of their anti-Communist policies, rather than genuine support for the re-establishment of Tibetan independence." Allen said the operation was worthwhile because it baited the Chinese into brutal repression and therefore produced "propaganda value."

A tropical rainstorm engulfed Leopoldville on the night of November 27, 1960, as the Congolese drama entered its final phase. Both groups of guards surrounding Lumumba's residence took refuge in a small shelter. Only a couple of them stirred when Lumumba's Chevrolet station wagon appeared out of the darkness at around nine o'clock. The chauffeur said he was going for cigarettes. He was waved through. Curled on the floor of the car, behind the front seat, was Lumumba.

Lumumba began planning this breakout immediately after learning that the United Nations had ratified the ouster of his government. He contacted a handful of close friends and enlisted them in a plan that was as simple as it was mad. He would sneak out of the residence that had become his prison, flee Leopoldville, reconnect with his supporters in the countryside, travel 750 miles to his home base in Stanleyville, and from there lead a movement that would restore his power.

After stopping briefly at the Guinean embassy, Lumumba set off in a convoy of three cars and a truck. His trip was an odyssey of arrests, escapes, roadblocks on rain-slicked roads, and river crossings by ferry and canoe. At several points, local people demanded that he speak to them. News of these impromptu rallies gave the authorities an idea of where he was. Devlin, by his own account, was "working closely" with Congolese police "to get roads blocked" and to cut off "possible escape routes."

On November 29, Lumumba's pursuers pinpointed his location through the use of a spotter plane. It was provided by what one report called "a European airline company," complete with "the European pilot, a specialist in low altitude reconnaissance flights."

Soldiers loyal to Mobutu moved in and stopped the convoy. They pulled Lumumba from his car and subjected him to what one European witness called "a very bad fifteen minutes." After hurried consultation, they placed him on an Air Congo DC-3 bound to Leopoldville. There, his hands tied behind his back, he was led through a jeering crowd and driven to a military base.

"Colonel Mobutu, with folded arms, calmly watched the soldiers slap and abuse the prisoner," the Associated Press reported.

After Lumumba was thrown onto the back of a pickup truck, one soldier produced a copy of a statement in which he had declared that he was still the Congo's legitimate prime minister. The soldier read it aloud, then crumpled the paper and stuffed it into the prisoner's mouth. Lumumba, his hands bound behind him, remained impassive. Television cameras recorded the scene. Millions of Americans saw it that evening.

At his military prison, Lumumba was regularly beaten. News of his ordeal leaked out, and calls for his release echoed around the world. The leaders of Morocco, Ghana, and Mali demanded that the "illegal Mobutu bands" free him.

Mobutu and his foreign sponsors—represented by the CIA and its Belgian counterpart, the Sûreté de l'État—wished Lumumba dead, but also wanted to avoid the opprobrium of killing him. As they pondered their options, time began to press on them. President Kasavubu suggested convening roundtable talks among all political factions, presumably including Lumumba's. The United Nations voted to form a "conciliation commission" to consider the possibility of a new Congolese government African leaders who sympathized with Lumumba held an emergency summit in Casablanca, and there were rumors they might try to foment an uprising to free him. Worst of all, John F. Kennedy had been elected president of the United States and would take office soon. Kennedy's younger brother Edward had accompanied a fact-finding mission to the Congo that heard pleas on Lumumba's behalf. It seemed plausible that the new president might revoke the death sentence Eisenhower had pronounced.

"Present government may fall within a few days," Devlin wrote to Allen on January 15, 1961. "Such conditions would almost certainly insure [Lumumba] victory in Parliament. . . . Refusal take drastic steps at this time will lead to defeat of policy in Congo."

Lumumba's enemies came up with an elegant solution. They decided to turn him over to the secessionists in Katanga, tools of Western power who were also his most violent tribal and political enemies.

Early on the morning of January 17, Lumumba and two of his comrades were hustled onto a plane. All three were handcuffed to their seats and pummeled steadily during the six-hour flight. The pilot, who was Belgian, locked himself in the cockpit to avoid the spectacle. His radio operator, also Belgian, vomited.

As the plane approached Elisabethville, the capital of Katanga, its pilot radioed, "I have three precious packages aboard." The prisoners were near death. A CIA officer on the scene cabled to Devlin in Leopoldville, "Thanks for Patrice. If we had known he was coming we would have baked a snake." Half a century later Brian Urquhart, a United Nations official, gave this account of what happened next:

After Lumumba and his two companions were dumped, bloody and disheveled, in a remote corner of the Elisabethville airfield, they were beaten again with rifle butts, and thrown onto a jeep and driven two miles from the airport to an empty house in the bush, where a veteran Belgian officer, Captain Julien Gat, took charge. A series of visitors—the notorious Katangese interior minister Godefroid Munongo and other ministers, Tshombe himself, and various high-ranking Belgians—came to the house to gloat over the prisoners, who were again beaten. . . .

[T]he prisoners were stuffed into a car with Captain Gat and police commissioner Frans Verscheure, and, in a convoy that also carried Tshombe, Munongo, and four other "ministers," were driven at high speed to a remote clearing fifty kilometers out in the wooded savanna. Joseph Okito, the former vice-president of the Senate, was the first to face the firing squad; next came Maurice Mpolo, the first commander of the Congolese National Army; and finally Patrice Lumumba. Their corpses were thrown into hastily dug graves. . . .

The Belgians also decided that the corpses must disappear once and for all. Two Belgians and their African assistants, in a truck carrying demijohns of sulphuric acid, an empty two-hundred-liter barrel, and a hacksaw, dug up the corpses, cut them into pieces, and threw them into the barrel of sulphuric acid. When the supply of acid ran out, they tried burning the remains. The skulls were ground up and the bones and teeth scattered during the return journey. The task proved so disgusting and so arduous that both Belgians had to get drunk in order to complete it, but in the end no trace was left of Patrice Lumumba and his companions. Lumumba was thirty-six years old. . . .

Patrice Lumumba's assassination was an unpardonable, cowardly, and disgustingly brutal act. Belgium, Kasavubu and Mobutu, and Moise Tshombe bear the main responsibility for this atrocity. The United States, and possibly other Western powers as well, tacitly favored it and did nothing to stop it.

Three days later, John F. Kennedy was inaugurated. He had spoken repeatedly about the need to support change in Africa, and on February 9 he publicly raised a possibility that Eisenhower would never have considered: Lumumba should be freed and integrated into a new Congolese government. It was a remarkable change of heart for the United States, but it came too late.

Hours after Kennedy made his appeal, secessionists in Katanga announced that Lumumba had escaped. A couple of days later they said that hostile villagers had killed him. By then he had been dead for a month. Kennedy received the news with what his press secretary called "great shock."

The shock extended far beyond Washington. Angry crowds carried portraits of Lumumba through the streets of London, Paris, Vienna, Warsaw, Moscow, Damascus, Lagos, and New Delhi. Half a million marched in Shanghai. In Belgrade, Marshal Tito said the killing had "no precedent in modern history," and a mob stormed the Belgian embassy. The same thing happened in Cairo, where after tearing down a portrait of King Baudouin inside the embassy and replacing it with one of Lumumba, rioters set the building afire. French and American embassies, as well as UN offices, were attacked in several cities. A protester outside UN headquarters in New York carried a sign reading THE MURDER OF LUMUMBA EXPOSES TRUE NATURE OF COLONIALISM.

Jean-Paul Sartre lamented the loss of "a meteor in the African firmament." Malcolm X called Lumumba "the greatest black man who ever walked the African continent." Aimé Césaire, the leading dark-skinned voice of French culture, wrote that Lumumba was "invincible—like the hope of a people, like a prairie fire, like pollen in the wind, like roots in the blind earth." In Africa, streets, hospitals, and schools were named for him, stamps were issued in his honor, and parents christened newborn children "Lumumba." Khrushchev announced that Peoples' Friendship University in Moscow would henceforth be known as Patrice Lumumba University.

The oddest leader of the Lumumba cult was the new strongman, Joseph Mobutu. Rather than seek to tarnish Lumumba's image in order to justify his own seizure of power, Mobutu did the opposite. Acting as if he were as grieved as anyone in the Congo, he pronounced Lumumba a national hero, ordered a statue of him, and even renamed the capital of Katanga, where he was killed, in his honor. Elisabethville became Lumumbashi.

"I have nothing against him," Mobutu shrugged when asked about his professed admiration for the man he had delivered to death.

Larry Devlin later came to believe that America's fears of Lumumba were "far-fetched," but placed them in the context of the era.

"In those days, when everything was seen in Cold War terms, we were convinced that we were observing the beginning of a major Soviet effort to gain control of a key country in Central Africa as a springboard to the rest of the continent," Devlin wrote. "There was little doubt in our minds that the Congo was a strategic linchpin in that epic struggle."

If this was a misjudgment, it was a colossal one. Lumumba's murder stunned the world and set off a wave of anti-Western passion in Africa and beyond. In the decades that followed, the Congo became a hell of repression, poverty, corruption, and violence. There is much to support the view that this killing was, as the Belgian scholar Ludo De Witte has suggested, "one of the twentieth century's most important political assassinations."

Lumumba, it is now clear, had no long-term geopolitical strategy. He spent the two hundred days between his inauguration and his death frantically improvising, reacting to onrushing events. Khrushchev did the same.

The first Soviet aid project in Africa was a shipment of snowplows for Guinea, where no flake of snow has ever fallen. Next was a cargo of wheat for the Congo's "oppressed workers and peasants," which could not be used since the Congo had no flour mill. Propaganda leaflets that Soviet advisers distributed to Congolese soldiers were written in English, which few Congolese could read. All of this, as Devlin later conceded, "made clear that our Cold War adversaries were not ten feet tall." At the time, though, they seemed to be.

If Lumumba's greatest error was believing he could choose his own allies while the Cold War raged, his other important one was trusting the United Nations. He fully misunderstood its mission. In his imagination, it was a supranational body with the will and power to crush all who sought to break nations apart. Too late, he recognized it as a tool that powerful countries could use to impose their will.

Once in the Congo, UN forces effectively protected the secessionists in Katanga. They helped ensure Lumumba's downfall by preventing him from using radio networks or flying to cities where he might rally his supporters. Belgium also bears heavy responsibility for the crime. Belgian officers were present at his execution. The fatal shots were fired by Congolese, so they and their superiors, especially Mobutu and Tshombe, share the guilt.

The CIA worked intently to force Lumumba from power and was authorized by Eisenhower to kill him. Yet in the end its officers were only junior partners to the more decisive and resourceful Belgians. The result was what both Belgium and the United States wanted.

Less than two years later, Allen casually admitted that he might have exaggerated the danger Lumumba posed to the West. A television interviewer, Eric Sevareid, asked him if he had come to believe that any of his covert operations were unnecessary. He named just one.

"I think that we overrated the danger in, let's say, the Congo," Allen said. "It looked as though they were going to make a serious attempt at takeover in the Belgian Congo. Well, it didn't work out that way at all. Now maybe they intended to do it, but they didn't find the situation ripe and they beat a pretty hasty retreat."

10

THE BEARDED STRONGMAN

Less than forty-eight hours after narrowly winning the presidency on November 8, 1960, John F. Kennedy emerged from his waterfront home in Hyannis Port, Massachusetts, to meet reporters. More than a hundred had descended on the little village, and the only place big enough to hold them all was the National Guard armory. They waited on folding chairs to hear what the president-elect would say.

Kennedy won the election in part because of his image of dynamic vigor, and he used this press conference to announce that he had already chosen key members of his new team. One reporter wrote that he reeled off names "in rapid-fire succession." The first one was familiar.

"I have asked Mr. Allen Dulles to stay on as director of central intelligence, and he has acceded to that request," Kennedy said. "He has served every president since Wilson, in a variety of capacities, and a continuity of stability and direction in this particular post is imperative."

Allen's decision to accept reappointment would decisively reshape his place in history. He had emerged from eight years as Eisenhower's spymaster with a powerful reputation. His triumphs were widely rumored, his failures little known, and his lack of interest in managing the sprawling CIA apparent only to Washington insiders. To all appearances he was both a brilliantly successful intelligence officer and an honorable gentleman. Had he retired at this point, he might have basked in admiration for the rest of his life.

Clover urged him to step down. In the end, though, he could not bring himself to leave the life he loved. There was still more to do. He wanted to be in office to dedicate the new CIA headquarters at Langley. His Laos station was opening a new front in the war against Ho Chi Minh. Most important, he was plotting to bring down another "monster."

Allen had just helped crush Lumumba, but could not consider it a true CIA victory because Belgian agents had struck the decisive blow. His operations in Tibet and Laos were faltering. Eager for a decisive triumph, he went forth against Fidel Castro, the young radical who had seized power in Cuba.

Castro's rise had set off a surge of controlled panic in Washington. Eisenhower had directed Allen to design a plan for covert action against him. Rather than produce one, Allen did something entirely new. He turned the operation over to a subordinate and withdrew into a private cocoon. As the CIA planned this far-reaching and highly complex operation, its director was almost entirely detached. He never focused on the plot. At times he even seemed to disassociate himself from it, as if it were none of his business. By sleepwalking through this history, Allen helped guide the United States to a devastating defeat that forever tarnished his legacy.

Cuba holds a unique place in the American imagination. It lies so close to the United States and offers such rich resources and strategic advantage that it long seemed a natural candidate for annexation to the United States. Presidents since Thomas Jefferson have coveted it.

"I candidly confess that I have ever looked on Cuba as the most interesting addition which could ever be made to our system of States," Jefferson wrote. "The control which, with Florida, this island would give us over the Gulf of Mexico, and the countries and isthmus bordering on it, as well as all those whose waters flow into it, would fill up the measure of our political well-being."

In 1898 President William McKinley sent American troops to Cuba to help rebels overthrow Spanish rule. They succeeded. Immediately afterward, the United States Congress voted to renege on its pledge, enshrined in law as the Teller Amendment, to withdraw the troops after victory and respect Cuban independence. McKinley named an American military governor. Later the United States granted Cuba limited self-rule but landed troops whenever American interests seemed threatened. That happened in

1906, 1912, and 1917—when Secretary of State Robert Lansing dispatched an occupation force at the suggestion of his nephew John Foster Dulles, whose Sullivan & Cromwell clients wished to ensure the continuance in power of a regime that respected their investments.

For much of the twentieth century Cuba remained a quasi-colony of the United States. During the 1950s, the last of its pliant dictators, Fulgencio Batista, struck lucrative deals with American gangsters, who built lavish hotels and casinos, filled them with American tourists, and turned Havana into the most garishly sinful city in the hemisphere. American businesses, including Sullivan & Cromwell clients, dominated the country. They owned most of its sugar plantations—two of the largest belonged to United Fruit— and were heavily invested in oil, railroads, utilities, mining, and cattle ranching. Eighty percent of Cuban imports came from the United States. When International Telephone & Telegraph asked Batista to approve a steep rate hike in 1957, Foster sent a message advising him that the increase would serve "the interests of Cuba." Batista approved it. In a vivid display of gratitude—the scene became a centerpiece of the film *The Godfather, Part II*—executives from ITT presented him with a golden telephone.

Although most Americans could not or would not see it, Cuba's corrupt tyranny was increasingly unpopular. During 1958 Castro's guerrillas won a series of victories. On the last day of the year, Batista resigned. Before dawn on January 1, 1959, he fled to the Dominican Republic, taking several hundred million dollars with him. A week later, after a jubilant trip across the island, Castro arrived in Havana and began a political career that would shape world history.

Foster was convalescing in nearby Jamaica when Castro seized power. "I don't know whether this is good or bad for us," he mused after hearing the news.

Three months later Castro made his tumultuous trip to the United States. The nascent counterculture embraced him. Allen Ginsberg and Malcolm X came to his hotel in Harlem. Supporters cheered outside. One carried a sign reading MAN, LIKE US CATS DIG FIDEL THE MOST—HE KNOWS WHAT'S HIP AND WHAT BUGS THE SQUARES.

After returning home, Castro gave a speech scorning Vice President Nixon, the highest-ranking American he met, as "an impenitent disciple of the gloomy and obstinate Foster Dulles." Soon afterward he confiscated hundreds of millions of dollars in American investments, grievously wounding Sullivan & Cromwell clients as well as gangsters like Lucky Luciano and Meyer Lansky. He imprisoned thousands of suspected counter-revolutionaries, including some with close ties to the United States, and executed several hundred.

Time charged that "the bearded strongman" was consolidating his "chaotic dictatorship" with help from foreign Communists and money seized from wealthy Cubans. "Vilification of the US broke all bounds of diplomacy—and even sanity," the magazine reported after one of his speeches. "No one knows where Castro's madness will lead him next."

Anti-Castro terror began soon after the revolution. A large department store in Havana went up in flames, a ship in the harbor was blown up with the loss of more than one hundred lives, sugar plantations were burned, and planes from Florida dropped bombs and mysteriously disappeared. Some of the first attacks may have been carried out by freelance exiles, but soon Allen took control of the campaign. His first decision was to turn it over to Richard Bissell, his deputy director for plans.

"There was considerable discussion of the situation in Cuba," a note taker wrote after a meeting at CIA headquarters on January 8, 1960. "The Director requested Dick Bissell to organize a special task force to insure that we were attacking this situation from all possible angles."

"Dickie" Bissell was one of the restless sons of privilege Allen had recruited to help him run the CIA. He came from a wealthy Connecticut family, graduated from Groton and Yale, worked for the Marshall Plan and the Ford Foundation—both of which collaborated closely with the CIA—and ran with Allen's stylish "Georgetown Set." As deputy director for plans, he supervised one of history's farthest-flung intelligence networks, with thousands of officers working out of fifty stations around the world. Bissell not only embraced the CIA ethos of constant action, but physically embodied it. He paced incessantly and charged down hallways. When forced to sit, he channeled his nervous energy into shuffling his feet, wringing his hands, twisting paper clips, and throwing pencils.

"Bissell spent little time before Congress, but lots of time with the President in off-the-record meetings," one historian has written. "What happened in those meetings no one knew, but it was likely to be interesting. Many believed that next to President Eisenhower, Richard Bissell had more raw power—power to make things happen, power to change the shape of the world—than any man in Washington."

On January 15 Allen asked the Special Group—the secret body that reviewed covert operations—for authorization to begin plotting against Castro. Eisenhower said he would favor any plot to "throw Castro out" because he was a "madman." By mid-January, the CIA had eighteen officers in Washington and another twenty-two in Cuba designing "proposed Cuba operations."

A lifetime of military command had given Eisenhower the habit of denying covert operations, and he maintained it as president. Less than two weeks after he authorized plotting against Castro, he told reporters that although he was "concerned and perplexed" by Castro's anti-American statements, the United States would take no action against him. At a Special Group meeting on February 17, he brushed aside a proposal from Allen under which the CIA would sabotage Cuban sugar mills and directed him to come up with more audacious ideas, "including even possibly things that might be drastic." Yet when asked about Cuba during a trip through Latin America in March, he insisted that the United States had "no thought of intervention."

Eisenhower launched the anti-Castro operation with determination and focused enthusiasm. He gave his orders directly to Allen and Bissell. "There was an informal but understood short cut in the chain of command," an internal CIA history later concluded. "Basic decisions were made at the DDP, DCI, or Presidential level."

Allen presented "A Program of Covert Action Against the Castro Regime," written by Bissell, to a combined meeting of the Special Group and the National Security Council on March 17, 1960. It proposed a multi-stage operation "to bring about the replacement of the Castro regime with one more devoted to the interests of the Cuban people and more acceptable to the US, in such a manner as to avoid any appearance of US intervention." The CIA would build a covert network inside Cuba, saturate the island with anti-Castro propaganda, infiltrate small teams of guerrilla fighters, use them to set off a domestic uprising, and provide a "responsible, appealing, and unified" new regime.

Eisenhower asked several questions, then said he could imagine "no better plan" and approved. He insisted on one condition: American involvement must be kept strictly secret.

"The great problem is leakage and breach of security," he said. "Everyone must be prepared to swear he has not heard of it."

With that, Eisenhower made the overthrow of Castro an official though secret U.S. policy goal. Something else, almost as momentous, emerged from that meeting. Allen spoke first, but when there were questions, he deferred to Bissell. It was an early sign that Allen would not supervise this operation.

The anti-Castro plot was as ambitious a project as the CIA had ever undertaken. Much hung on the outcome. Allen, however, floated above it. Each time he and Bissell came to the White House to brief Eisenhower on its progress, Bissell took the lead while Allen listened. When Bissell briefed the Joint Chiefs of Staff on April 8, Allen did not even attend.

Allen had once played the role of clandestine world shaper and suspected second-most-powerful-man-in-Washington. In the late 1950s he ceded it to Bissell. This was a remarkable fade, a deepening of character traits—distraction, inability to focus, lack of attention to detail, aversion to rigorous debate—that people around him had long observed.

Stories of Allen's behavior circulated quietly. One day in 1958, an analyst brought him a new batch of U-2 photos but found him unwilling to switch off his radio, which was broadcasting a Washington Senators game. He paid little attention to the photos and remained absorbed in the game, muttering comments like, "He couldn't hit a bull in the ass with a banjo." With this same extreme inattention, he absented himself from planning the Bay of Pigs invasion.

"He had turned the whole thing over to Dick Bissell three quarters of the time," William Bundy, a Kennedy adviser, said afterward. "I had the feeling that by then he was slowing down a little. Thinking about it, after the whole thing was over, I came to the conclusion that he hadn't been quite the man I had known. All through, he hadn't been as much on top of the operation as I had expected."

Bissell had overseen development of the U-2 spy plane, but his more relevant experience was running the theatrical "rebel air force" that had helped push Jacobo Arbenz from power in Guatemala in 1954. Most of the officers he assembled for his anti-Castro operation were also veterans of the Guatemala campaign. Tracy Barnes, David Atlee Phillips, J. C. King, and E. Howard Hunt were given roles approximating those they had played during PB/Success. Their team leader, Jacob Esterline, had directed the Washington end of the Guatemala coup and afterward became CIA station chief in Guatemala.

All had enough experience to recognize the considerable differences between Guatemala in 1954 and Cuba in 1960.

One of Castro's closest comrades, the Argentine-born guerrilla Che Guevara, had been in Guatemala in 1954 and witnessed the coup against Arbenz. Later he told Castro why it succeeded. He said Arbenz had foolishly tolerated an open society, which the CIA penetrated and subverted, and also preserved the existing army, which the CIA turned into its instrument. Castro agreed that a revolutionary regime in Cuba must avoid those mistakes. Upon taking power, he cracked down on dissent and purged the army. Many Cubans supported his regime and were ready to defend it. All of this made the prospect of deposing him daunting indeed.

Yet most of the CIA's "best men" emerged from backgrounds where all things were possible, nothing ever went seriously wrong, and catastrophic reversals of fortune happened only to others. World leaders had fallen to their power. They never believed that deposing Castro would be easy, but they relished the challenge. This was why they had joined the CIA.

Quietly, but watched closely by Castro's spies, CIA officers fanned out through the Cuban sections of Miami, where anti-Castro fervor ran hot. They recruited a handful of exiles to serve as the political front for a counterrevolutionary movement, and dozens more who wanted to fight. The would-be guerrillas were brought to camps in Florida, Puerto Rico, Guatemala, and the Panama Canal Zone and trained in tactics ranging from air assault to underwater demolition.

Tensions between Havana and Washington rose steadily. Cuba recognized the People's Republic of China and signed a trade agreement with the Soviet Union. Tankers carrying Soviet petroleum arrived in Cuba. American oil companies refused to refine it. Castro nationalized the recalcitrant companies. The United States stopped buying most Cuban sugar. Cuba began selling sugar to the Soviets.

In mid-1960 this hostility broke beyond politics and economics and into the Cuban soul. The Eisenhower administration pressed the International League, one of professional baseball's top minor leagues, to announce that it was pulling its baseball team, the Sugar Kings, out of Havana. Love of baseball is deeply ingrained in the Cuban psyche. Castro, an avid fan who had been known to suspend cabinet meetings so he could watch the Sugar Kings play, protested that this blow violated "all codes of sportsmanship." He even offered to pay the team's debts. It was to no avail. The Sugar Kings became the Jersey City Jerseys, who went bankrupt the next year. The Cuban people lost one of their strongest sentimental ties to the United States.

"The thing we should never do in dealing with revolutionary countries, in which the world abounds, is to push them behind an iron curtain raised by ourselves," Walter Lippmann warned in a column after the withdrawal of the Sugar Kings. "On the contrary, even when they have been seduced and subverted and are drawn across the line, the right thing to do is to keep the way open for their return."

Fears of the threat from Cuba gripped Washington. So did fears of raging nationalism in the Congo. Allen, however, was most steadily preoccupied with a third country: Laos.

History is littered with the names of small places that suddenly flash to the center of world attention. So it was with Laos in the late 1950s. Some Americans came to see it as a vulnerable outpost of freedom, threatened by Communist aggression. Allen was one of them. In the jungles of Laos, he and his men launched the largest paramilitary operation the CIA had yet conceived.

Laotian leaders sought to keep their country out of the East-West conflict, and the American ambassador, Horace Smith, advised Washington to accept a neutral Laos. Eisenhower, however, rejected neutralism because it implied cooperation with Communists. Ambassador Smith was removed. CIA officers forged several thousand tribesmen into a secret army, and supported royalist factions in a civil war against neutralists and Communists. Ho Chi Minh sent units from the North Vietnamese army to fight in Laos. American and Soviet weaponry poured in. Pitched battles foreshadowed the carnage to come in Vietnam.

"We must not allow Laos to fall to Communism," Eisenhower told aides at the White House, "even if it involves war."

Although Allen never spoke afterward about this "secret war," his right-hand man, Bissell, came to believe it might have been misconceived. "Our failure to support [neutralism] reflected Washington's inability to understand the ground situation in Laos," he later wrote. "Had we shown more open-mindedness (which is not always compatible with crisis management), the advice and perceptions of experts on Laotian politics, history, and culture might have received more attention."

Allen stepped out of a courier plane on July 23, 1960, and into a car that took him to Hyannis Port, where he had come to brief Senator Kennedy. This was part of a traditional effort to maintain a modicum of comity between presidential candidates on national security issues. Allen knew Kennedy from their days relaxing in Florida, and their shared fascination with covert action gave them a special bond. On that summer day, the director of central intelligence spent two hours with the Democratic presidential nominee. By his own account he mentioned Cuba, but said nothing about "our own government's plans or programs for action." Outside, the two men bantered with reporters.

"I just told Kennedy what he could read in the morning *Times*," Allen told them.

Much debate surrounds this briefing. Kennedy's opponent, Vice President Richard Nixon, later suggested that it might have cost him the presidency. Within the Eisenhower administration, Nixon was actively promoting the plot against Castro, but he was sworn to secrecy. He suspected that Kennedy realized this after Allen's briefing. In campaign speeches, Kennedy boldly vowed never to tolerate "a hostile and militant Communist satellite" or "a potential enemy missile or submarine base only ninety miles from our shores." Nixon could not reply.

"Are they falling dead over there?" Nixon asked an aide in frustration over what he saw as the CIA's failure to act. "What in the world are they doing that takes months?"

American newspapers closely covered the presidential campaign. They also had plenty of foreign news to report, including the startling split between China and the Soviet Union, new rumblings of war in Indochina, and reverberations from the U-2 spy plane crisis. One historic story, however, went unreported and remained secret for decades.

This was the summer when Eisenhower did twice what no previous American president is known ever to have done: approve plans to assassinate a foreign leader.

In accordance with ancient principles of statecraft, Eisenhower never explicitly decreed anyone's death. Understandings of his intent emerged from private conversations he had with Allen, and from his veiled comments at small meetings. Castro was the first he seemed to sentence. On May 13, 1960, after a briefing from Allen, Eisenhower told the Special Group he wanted the Cuban leader "sawed off." His second target, Lumumba, had not yet risen to power.

Years later Richard Bissell, who set both assassination plots in motion, testified that Allen ordered him to do so. Both times, he said, Allen told him the orders had been approved "at the highest level."

"In that period of history, its meaning would have been clear," Bissell recalled. "Eisenhower was a tough man behind that smile."

Since no American intelligence officer had ever been sent to kill a foreign leader, Bissell had to conjure a way to strike at Castro. His idea was either brilliant or ridiculous: hire the Mafia.

American gangsters had forged a rewarding partnership with Batista and lost everything when Castro swept to power. Bissell saw what he wanted: men angry enough at Castro to want him dead, and experienced enough to know how to kill him. He dispatched a middleman to meet with "Handsome" Johnny Roselli, a dapper Mafia figure whom the FBI had connected to thirteen murders. Roselli brought other gangsters into the plot. At one point the CIA passed them six poison pills compounded by Dr. Sidney Gottlieb, chief of the agency's "health alteration committee." Allen did not monitor this project. Bissell mentioned it to him once, and he "only nodded."

On August 18, 1960, as the plot to kill Castro was unfolding, Eisenhower decreed his second death sentence. Lumumba's meteoric rise in the Congo terrified Washington. It temporarily distracted Eisenhower. He found himself juggling two regime change operations, both involving murder.

After Kennedy won the presidential election in November, Eisenhower might have frozen the anti-Castro operation, or at least asked Allen to test Kennedy's interest. Instead he expanded it. He approved what Bissell later called a "change in concept"; rather than smuggle small teams of infiltrators into Cuba, the CIA would launch a full-scale invasion, perhaps with support from the U.S. military. Eisenhower's national security adviser, Gordon Gray, suggested staging a phony Cuban attack on the American base at Guantánamo Bay to use as a pretext for war.

Against this background, Allen and Bissell flew to Palm Beach on

November 18 to brief President-elect Kennedy on CIA operations around the world. They sat near the pool, hunched over a map. Precisely what was said remains uncertain. By most accounts the CIA men referred to the anti-Castro plot but did not impress Kennedy with its scope.

On November 29, Eisenhower awoke to the good news that Lumumba had been arrested. Years later, a CIA reconstruction of the anti-Castro plot included this passage: "On November 29, 1960, the level of interest of the US Government escalated sharply with the sudden resurgence of interest on the part of President Dwight David Eisenhower. In contrast to the period from July 1960 through the presidential election of early November—when, as noted earlier, there was, at most, minimal attention to the developing anti-Castro program at the White House level—suddenly the President emerged as one of the principal decision makers. . . . When asked for an explanation of this sudden resurgence, Jake Esterline, then chief [of the CIA Cuba task force], stated, 'I can't explain it.'"

One explanation lies in what only a handful of people could then have known. Eisenhower approved covert action against Castro early in 1960, but Lumumba's sudden emergence in the Congo distracted him. When he received news that Lumumba had been captured, he realized he had won his African battle. Immediately he turned back to Cuba. He summoned Allen and Bissell to the White House and ordered them to repeat in Cuba what the CIA had just achieved in the Congo. "Take more chances and be aggressive," he told them.

On that day—November 29, 1960—one Dulles "monster" fell into the hands of mortal enemies and President Eisenhower ordered redoubled covert action against another.

Preparations for the invasion of Cuba steadily intensified. Bissell and his men consolidated their exile army at a secret training camp in Guatemala. They borrowed several vintage B-26 bombers from the Alabama Air National Guard, repainted them with Cuban insignia, and prepared to use them for air raids that would be portrayed as the work of defecting Cuban pilots. As the base for their clandestine "air force" and embarkation point for their exile army, they chose a bluff near Puerto Cabezas, a sleepy town on the Caribbean coast of Nicaragua. They code-named it Happy Valley.

Allen understood that all of this was happening, but none of it was the result of his decisions or directives. He watched from the sidelines. Only once during the months of planning for the invasion of Cuba did he present an independent report to the Special Group. It had nothing to do with the operation itself, but reflected how close he remained to his old friends on Wall Street.

"During the 21 December 1960 meeting of the Special Group, Allen Dulles briefed the attendees on a meeting that he had participated in the previous day in New York with a group of American businessmen," according to a CIA account that remained secret for nearly half a century. "In attendance at this meeting were the vice president for Latin America of Standard Oil of New Jersey, the chairman of the Cuban-American Sugar Company, the president of the American Sugar Domino Refining Company, the president of the American & Foreign Power Company, the chairman of the Freeport Sulphur Company and representatives from Texaco, International Telephone and Telegraph, and other American companies with business interests in Cuba. The tenor of the conversation was that it was time for the US to get off dead center and take some direct action against Castro."

At the next Special Group meeting, on December 28, discussion turned to military requirements for the exile invasion. This time Allen deferred not to Bissell, but to Colonel Jack Hawkins, a Marine Corps amphibious warfare expert who had been detailed to organize the landing. Hawkins was forceful—and chillingly prophetic.

"It is axiomatic in amphibious operations that control of air and sea in the objective area is required," he said. "The Cuban air force and naval vessels capable of opposing our landing must be knocked out or neutralized before our amphibious shipping makes its final run to the beach. If this is not done, we will be courting disaster. . . . The operation [should] be abandoned if policy does not provide for use of adequate tactical air support."

Events moved quickly as 1960 turned to 1961. Arms from Communist countries were unloaded in Havana. The American aircraft carrier *Franklin D. Roosevelt*, carrying marines and accompanied by destroyers, began maneuvers off Cuba's coast. A talkative exile leader in Miami bragged to reporters that his fighters were "ready to invade." Cubans built barricades along the shoreline.

On New Year's Day a powerful bomb exploded in Havana. "It is the American Embassy that is paying the terrorists to place bombs in Cuba!"

Castro told a cheering crowd the next night. Then he said he would no longer allow the United States to station more than eleven diplomats at its embassy in Havana. Eisenhower responded by shutting the embassy entirely and breaking diplomatic relations with Cuba. Castro warned Cubans that this meant an invasion was imminent.

"We don't know what they're talking about," Eisenhower's press secretary told reporters in Washington.

At a Special Group meeting on January 4, the CIA circulated a memo outlining "preparations for the conduct of an amphibious/airborne and tactical air operation against the Government of Cuba."

"The initial mission of the invasion force will be to seize and defend a small area," the memo said. "It is expected that these operations will precipitate a general uprising throughout Cuba and cause the revolt of a large segment of the Cuban army and militia. . . . The way will then be paved for United States military intervention aimed at pacification of Cuba, and this will result in the prompt overthrow of the Castro government."

Six days later the *New York Times* carried a startling headline: "US Helps Train an Anti-Castro Force at Secret Guatemalan Air-Ground Base." The story was accompanied by a map pinpointing the CIA camp, where it said "commando-like forces are being drilled in guerrilla warfare tactics by foreign personnel, mostly from the United States."

This was not the first sign that operational security had been breached. The *Miami Herald* had prepared a similar story, but withheld it after Allen warned editors that publication "would be most harmful to the national interest." Allen also managed to have a *Washington Post* story killed. Much of the material in those suppressed stories, however, surfaced elsewhere. The *Nation* ran a report headlined "Are We Training Cuban Guerrillas?" A Guatemalan newspaper, *La Hora*, sent reporters to the CIA camp and published a host of details. Rumors about the planned invasion coursed through Miami. Allen persuaded the *New York Times* to downplay its story—it took up one column at the center of the front page, rather than four columns at the top—but so much was already known about the operation that *Times* editors felt justified publishing what they had.

"I decided that we should say nothing at all about this article," Eisenhower later wrote.

It was an odd decision. Eisenhower had repeatedly warned that the anti-Castro operation could succeed only if American involvement remained secret. Now any hope of secrecy was gone. Upon realizing this, Eisenhower or Allen—or both—might have stepped back and reconsidered the plot. Instead they pressed ahead, determined to fight and reassured by a diffuse, supra-rational assumption that American power must always prevail in the end.

"The desire to contain the spread of Communism in our hemisphere had grown in the light of ongoing incursions in Africa and Asia," Bissell wrote later. "Propelled by the momentum of our planning, the operation had been transformed from a guerrilla movement to a full-scale invasion. . . . Kennedy inherited certain policy decisions of the previous administration and was under pressure to carry them out."

At nine o'clock on the morning of January 19, 1961, Eisenhower's last full day in office, he welcomed Kennedy to the White House. The incoming and outgoing presidents spent nearly three hours together. The first foreign crisis they discussed was the one in Laos. Kennedy brought up the obvious next one.

"Should we support guerrilla operations in Cuba?" he asked.

"To the utmost," Eisenhower replied. "We cannot have the present government there go on."

During the first days of his presidency, Kennedy learned details of the plot against Castro. So did attentive Americans. *Time* reported "guerrilla training camps in Florida and Guatemala, arms-carrying PT boats that average a trip a week to Cuba, [and] an air group of some 80 flyers who reportedly fly out of the mystery field at Retalhuleu in Guatemala and the inoperative US Marine Corps Opa Locka airbase in Florida."

Kennedy faced a no-win situation. He was young, inexperienced in world affairs, and new in office. During his campaign he had vowed to confront Castro. Many Americans wished him to do so. Now Allen—with Bissell always at his side—was giving him a plan.

Allen pointedly reminded Kennedy that canceling the operation would give him a "disposal" problem. Cuban exiles at the Guatemala camp would have to be discharged. Many would return to Miami. Their story would be, "We were about to overthrow Castro, but Kennedy lost his nerve and wouldn't let us try." This narrative would become part of Kennedy's permanent legacy.

"We made it very clear to the President that to call off the operation would have resulted in a very unpleasant situation," Allen later said.

Kennedy came into office determined to reshape relations between the United States and Latin America. On March 1 he signed an executive order creating the Peace Corps, and called for volunteers "anxious to sacrifice their energies and time and toil to the cause of world peace and human progress." Two weeks later, at a glittering White House reception for 250 guests, he unveiled the Alliance for Progress, an ambitious new aid program that aimed to transform Latin America while proving that "liberty and progress walk hand in hand." As Kennedy imagined a new era of hemispheric cooperation, however, the plan to invade Cuba gathered momentum.

"Allen and Dick didn't just brief us on the Cuban operation, they sold us on it," one of Kennedy's aides groused afterward. Another said the two CIA men "fell in love with the plan and ceased to think critically about it." Allen conceded their point.

"You present a plan, and it isn't your job to say, 'Well, that's a rotten plan I've presented,'" he reasoned. "In presenting the merits of the plan, the tendency is always—because you're meeting a position, you're meeting this criticism and that criticism—to be drawn into more of a salesmanship job than you should."

None of Kennedy's security advisers raised serious doubts about the plan, but some on the fringes of power did. One White House aide, Arthur Schlesinger Jr., sent Kennedy a memo warning that the United States would certainly be blamed for any invasion of Cuba, and that this would "fix a malevolent image of the new Administration in the minds of millions." Senator J. William Fulbright of Arkansas, the chairman of the Senate Foreign Relations Committee, counseled him to treat Castro as "a thorn in the flesh, but not as a dagger in the heart." When former secretary of state Dean Acheson visited the White House, Kennedy told him that the CIA was preparing an invasion of Cuba and sketched out the plan. Acheson was incredulous.

"Are you serious?" he asked. "It doesn't take Price Waterhouse to figure out that fifteen hundred Cubans aren't as good as twenty-five thousand."

Kennedy had doubts about the invasion plan, and Bissell accommodated each of them. The plan called for exiles to land near a town below the rugged Escambray Mountains, but Kennedy feared this would be too "noisy." Bissell satisfied him by choosing a remote beach one hundred miles eastward, at the Bay of Pigs. When Kennedy worried that using sixteen disguised planes for the first wave of air strikes would increase the odds that the CIA's role would become clear, Bissell agreed to cut the fleet to eight. Kennedy insisted that the United States military must not be involved; Bissell assured him this would not be necessary.

Historians have long wondered why Bissell allowed the operation to proceed despite these major changes, rather than telling Kennedy that they greatly reduced the chances for success.

"[He] still thought it would succeed, even as modified," one historian has written. "Personal pride and ambition, too, may have encouraged Bissell to accept mounting changes and risks. His reputation in the CIA and the Kennedy administration was riding on this operation, as was his position as Allen Dulles's heir-apparent. To cancel would have been equivalent to a forfeit. Nothing in Bissell's character suggests this would have been an acceptable outcome to him. Another possible reason . . . was that Bissell assumed President Kennedy would not let it fail—would do, that is, whatever was necessary to make it succeed, even if that meant sending US military forces to the rescue. Yet another possibility: Bissell assumed the Mafia would finally get its act together and take out Castro before, or coincident with, the invasion."

Bissell ignored one last, poignant warning. It came on Sunday morning, April 9, just eight days before the exile army was supposed to storm ashore at the Bay of Pigs. Bissell was at his home in the Cleveland Park section of Washington when his doorbell rang. Outside were Jacob Esterline, the CIA officer he had put in day-to-day charge of the operation, and Colonel Jack Hawkins, its senior military planner. They were evidently overwrought after a night of agonizing. Bissell ushered them in, and they poured out their hearts. They told him what he already knew: the new landing beach was isolated, with no local population to support the invaders and few escape routes; there would not be enough air cover to prevent Castro from counterattacking; the secrecy that was an essential part of the original plan had evaporated. Given these new conditions, they told Bissell, the invasion was certain to end in "terrible disaster." If Bissell did not cancel it, they would resign.

Not even this appeal from the operation's two most important planners moved Bissell. He told them the plot was too advanced to be called off and, as Hawkins later put it, "earnestly asked us not to abandon him at this late date." His appeal to their patriotism and *esprit de corps* finally prevailed. As they drove away from his house, a last chance vanished with them.

"We made a bad mistake by not sticking to our guns and staying resigned," Hawkins later lamented.

Equally striking is that the two officers considered Bissell the only target for their plea. Allen had so fully distanced himself from the operation's planning that they never considered appealing to him.

At a news conference on April 12, Kennedy asserted that "there will not be, under any conditions, an intervention in Cuba by United States armed forces." The next morning, CIA planes began transporting Cuban exiles from their training camp in Guatemala to the Happy Valley base on Nicaragua's Caribbean coast. Before dawn on April 17, the exile force, about fourteen hundred strong, waded ashore at the Bay of Pigs. Thousands of Cuban troops counterattacked. Castro himself arrived to take command.

As this news was flashed back to Washington, Colonel Hawkins made a frantic call, awakening his boss, General David Shoup, the commandant of the Marine Corps. He told Shoup that all would be lost unless American planes were quickly ordered to strike against Castro's troops.

"You've got to get ahold of the President," Hawkins pleaded. "We're going to fail."

"Christ knows I can't do anything," Shoup replied.

Kennedy had made clear that he would not use American military power to support the invasion. When the crucial moment came, he refused to change his mind. News of his resolution was radioed from Washington to the base at Happy Valley. The senior military officer there, Colonel Stanley Beerli, commander of the Alabama Air National Guard, threw his cap to the ground in disgust.

"There goes the whole fucking war!" he swore.

On that excruciating day, the invasion force was scattered by Cuban artillery, attacked by Cuban bombers, and overwhelmed by Cuban troops. Allen was nearby. He was not in a spotter plane or aboard one of the many American warships poised near the Cuban coast. Instead he was in San Juan, Puerto Rico, joining Margaret Mead and Dr. Benjamin Spock as speakers at a convention of young businessmen. Radio Moscow reported that he had traveled to San Juan to "command in person the aggressive actions against Cuba." That was the logical assumption; what else would the chief of a covert service be doing while his service launched its least covert operation ever? The truth was more prosaic. Allen was doing just what he seemed to be doing: delivering a bland speech while men he had helped send to war were dying on a beach not far away.

"Well, how is it going?" he asked an aide who met his plane late that night in Baltimore.

"Not very well, sir," came the reply.

"Oh, is that so?"

The two men chatted on the ride to Allen's home in Georgetown. When they arrived, Allen invited his aide in for a drink. Over whiskey, he shifted the subject away from Cuba and began rambling aimlessly. The aide later used a single word to describe this moment: "unreal."

At White House meetings the next day, Kennedy fended off more pleas that he send U.S. forces to support the Bay of Pigs invaders. The strongest came from his chief of naval operations, Admiral Arleigh Burke, who came to the Oval Office late in the evening with an equally agitated Bissell.

"Let me take two jets and shoot down those enemy aircraft," Burke pleaded.

"No," Kennedy replied. "I don't want to get the United States involved in this."

"Can I not send in an air strike?"

"No."

"Can we send in a few planes?"

"No, because they could be identified as United States."

"Can we paint out their numbers?"

"No."

Grasping for options, Burke asked if Kennedy would authorize artillery attacks on Cuban forces from American destroyers. The answer was the same: "No."

Later that day Kennedy told an aide, "I probably made a mistake keeping Allen Dulles." By then Allen had also recognized the scope of the disaster. He made his way to the home of one of his old friends, Richard Nixon. Nixon saw immediately that Allen was under "great emotional stress" and offered him a drink.

"I really need one," Allen replied. "This is the worst day of my life."

"What's wrong?"

"Everything is lost."

So it was. More than one hundred of the invaders died. Most of the rest were rounded up and imprisoned. For Castro it was a supreme, ecstatic triumph. Kennedy was staggered.

"How could I have been so stupid?" he wondered aloud.

Others were equally stunned. Criticism of the CIA, in both the press and Congress, rose to unprecedented intensity. Allen was not spared. The cover story in *Time*, headlined "The Cuba Disaster," questioned his very concept of intelligence.

"Last week the CIA was back in the news in a big way—and will probably stay there for some time, while a basic question that has been long and heatedly debated is argued out," *Time* wrote. "Should any intelligence-gathering organization also have an operational responsibility? The British have long said no, arguing that a combination of the functions gives such an organization a vested operational interest in proving its intelligence correct. That dual function seems to have been one of the causes of the Cuban tragedy."

Standing before reporters in the White House, Kennedy took "sole responsibility" for the failure. "Victory has a hundred fathers and defeat is an orphan," he mused.

Allen fell into a period of shock. Robert Kennedy later wrote that he "looked like living death . . . had the gout and had trouble walking, and he was always putting his head in his hands." In the weeks that followed, however, he was invited to White House meetings as usual. No harsh words were spoken.

On May 1 the Senate Foreign Relations Committee held closed hearings into the Bay of Pigs debacle. Allen insisted that the military, not the CIA, was to blame. "We took the highest, the best military advice we could get," he testified. "This included, of course, the military officers who helped formulate the plans, and also the Joint Chiefs of Staff."

The top U.S. military commanders were outraged. Admiral Burke was withering in his judgment of Allen.

"The fact is that he just wasn't involved in that operation," Burke said. "He showed up at meetings and sat there smoking his pipe. . . . I blame him for not being there."

Passions cooled as spring unfolded over Washington. Allen believed he had weathered the storm. He began hovering around the construction site at Langley where the new CIA headquarters was being built. Retirement, he told friends, would come in two years, when he turned seventy.

If Allen had not yet confronted the implications of the Bay of Pigs disaster, Kennedy had. In private he cursed "CIA bastards" for luring him into it, and wished he could "splinter the CIA into a thousand pieces and scatter it into the winds." One day in August, deciding that a decent interval had passed, he summoned Allen to the White House.

"Under a parliamentary system of government, it is I who would be leaving office," he told Allen. "But under our system it is you who must go."

Kennedy allowed Allen to remain in office until a dedication ceremony could be held at the new Langley headquarters. It was set for November 28, 1961. Hundreds of CIA officers attended. Kennedy gave a lighthearted speech.

"Your successes are unheralded, your failures are trumpeted," he told the crowd. "I sometimes have that feeling myself."

The incoming CIA director, John McCone, a former chairman of the Atomic Energy Commission, was seated beside Kennedy. Richard Bissell, whom Kennedy had removed from the agency along with Allen, was nearby. It was a moment to heal family wounds.

"Would you step forward, Allen?" Kennedy asked after finishing his speech.

When Allen reached the podium, Kennedy produced a National Security Medal, the highest award for an American intelligence officer. He pinned it to Allen's lapel and said, "I know of no man who brings a greater sense of personal commitment to his work, who has less pride in office than he has."

Then a curtain was drawn back to reveal a Bible verse chiseled into granite. It graces the entrance wall to this day: "And ye shall know the truth, and the truth shall make you free."

A year later, Castro released the Bay of Pigs prisoners in exchange for $52 million in donated food and medicine. That hardly closed the episode, however. Its effects have reverberated through history. This was the first time the CIA was fully unmasked seeking to depose the leader of a small country whose crime was defying the United States. It became a reviled symbol of imperialist intervention. A new wave of anti-Americanism began coursing around the world.

In 1965 two former Kennedy aides, Theodore Sorensen and Arthur Schlesinger Jr., published articles that held Allen largely to blame for the Bay of Pigs fiasco. Sorensen wrote that Kennedy had asked Allen if he was sure the invasion would succeed and that Allen had replied: "I stood right here at Ike's desk and told him I was certain the Guatemala operation would succeed. And Mr. President, the prospects for this plan are even better than they were for that one."

Allen set to work on a sharp rebuttal called "My Answer to the Bay of Pigs." "The myth that President Kennedy was advised that the Cuban operation was sure to succeed [is] diametrically opposed to the facts," he wrote. "We had a fighting chance and no more. That was the position I took with regard to Cuba in the highest counsels of our government."

Allen's sister Eleanor believed that he "had already begun to lose his command over his memory and ideas" and persuaded him not to publish this article. It survives—a jumble of typescript and handwritten notes— only in his personal archive. One of the notes suggests an answer to the question of why he allowed the Bay of Pigs invasion to proceed despite clear signs that it would fail.

"We felt that when the chips were down—when the crisis arose in reality—any action required for success would be authorized, rather than permit the enterprise to fail," Allen wrote. "We believed that in a time of crisis, we would gain what we might lose if we had provoked an argument."

Eight years of experience under Eisenhower led Allen to believe this. He presumed that Kennedy, like Eisenhower, would do whatever was necessary to ensure victory once a covert operation was under way. Apparently he never took seriously Kennedy's vow to keep the United States out of war in Cuba.

Eleanor was another casualty of changing times in Washington. Secretary of State Dean Rusk called her into his office early in 1962 and told her, "The White House has asked me to get rid of you." Part of the impetus may have come from Attorney General Robert Kennedy, who had been outraged at the Bay of Pigs failure and, by one account, "didn't want any more of the Dulles family around." Eleanor unwillingly left the State Department after fifteen years. She went on to teach at Duke and Georgetown, wrote several books, and traveled widely, most often to Germany, including with President Lyndon Johnson to attend Konrad Adenauer's funeral in 1967. Her constitution proved hardier than those of her brothers; she remained active until near the end of her life, which came in 1996, when she was 101 years old.

In retirement, Allen found himself in demand as an after-dinner speaker. He also devoted himself halfheartedly to writing. His book *The Craft of Intelligence* was unspectacular—several chapters were ghost-written by a CIA comrade, E. Howard Hunt—but two collections of spy stories he assembled from history and fiction sold well. He spent time in Switzerland, where his son was in a sanatorium, and in the Bahamas. Clover traveled with him. He took pleasure in grandchildren. Twice, most unexpectedly, President Johnson gave him delicate assignments that brought him back to public life.

Allen was at his home at Lloyd Neck when he received news of John F. Kennedy's assassination on November 22, 1963. A week later, Johnson called. He wanted Allen to serve on a high-level panel that would investigate the assassination—the Warren Commission.

Johnson told friends in Congress that the Kennedy assassination had "some foreign complications, CIA and other things." Placing Allen on the Warren Commission ensured that these "complications" would remain secret. Allen never told the other members of the Warren Commission that the CIA had plotted to kill Castro, or revealed what it knew about Kennedy's accused assassin, Lee Harvey Oswald. He advised other members of the commission about ways to question CIA officers, while at the same time advising the officers how to reply. By one account he "systematically used his influence to keep the commission safely within bounds, the importance of which only he could appreciate. . . . From the start, before any evidence was reviewed, he pressed for the final verdict that Oswald had been a crazed gunman, not the agent of a national and international conspiracy."

Allen was in a unique position: the former director of central intelligence, dismissed by President Kennedy, helping to investigate Kennedy's murder while guarding the CIA's own murder plots. Some have found this suspicious.

As the Warren Commission was completing its work, Johnson asked Allen to take on a very different mission. On June 20, 1964, three civil rights workers disappeared in Mississippi. Johnson wanted to send an envoy and settled on Allen because he was not identified with any side in the civil rights debate. Allen protested his ignorance—he did not even know the name of Mississippi's governor—but accepted. He spent two days in Mississippi, met with black and white leaders, and submitted a bland report warning about polarization between segregationists and a "new breed of Negro agitators." It had no apparent effect and was quickly forgotten.

Once these projects were behind him, Allen made a sentimental trip back to Ascona in southern Switzerland, where he had helped broker the "secret surrender" of Nazi forces twenty years before. Other veterans of the operation met him there for a reunion. One was Karl Wolff, the former "second man of the SS." Wolff had reason for gratitude. Documents released decades later show that Allen played a key role in shielding him from prosecution at the Nuremberg tribunal after World War II; keeping him free for more than a decade, until a West German court convicted him of complicity in genocide; and, after he was released, ensuring that he was not banned from employment as a convicted war criminal.

Allen weakened during the late 1960s. His body ached. A torrent of anti-CIA books, articles, and investigations disoriented him. He began losing his way on the streets of Georgetown. "Perhaps it was what we call Alzheimer's disease today," a relative who cared for him suggested later.

When Allen came to CIA headquarters one morning in 1967 for a final honor, he was pale and overweight, had trouble walking, and looked all of his seventy-four years. Richard Helms, the director of central intelligence, welcomed him warmly and then unveiled a new memorial. It was a profile of Allen, chiseled in bas-relief, above a simple inscription:

ALLEN WELSH DULLES
Director of Central Intelligence 1953–1961
His Monument Is Around Us

Allen talked of writing a memoir but never did. "I am too old, I have forgotten so much," he told historians who approached him in his later years. He had several strokes. After the last one, he was admitted to Walter Reed Army Medical Center. His room was near the one in which his brother had drawn a final breath ten years before. He died there just before midnight on January 29, 1969, of influenza complicated by pneumonia.

Allen's memorial service, as he wished, was small. Only a few dignitaries attended, led by Vice President Spiro Agnew, representing President

Nixon. Tributes were warm but brief. The *Washington Post* called Allen "the most creative, powerful, and eminent American intelligence officer of recent times."

"He possessed a zest for the romance of cloak-and-dagger work which is rarely found at the top of intelligence bureaucracies," the *Post* concluded. "On the other hand, the Bay of Pigs—another product of the Dulles CIA—is generally considered the greatest US intelligence blunder."

PART III

ONE CENTURY

11

A FACE OF GOD

One of the most compelling works of twentieth-century political art is *Glorious Victory*, a spectacular mural by the Mexican master Diego Rivera. It is a sprawling panorama on linen, sixteen feet long, depicting the 1954 coup in Guatemala. In the foreground are biting caricatures of the men who carried it out.

John Foster Dulles is at the center, dressed in a flak jacket and grinning cruelly. Allen Dulles sneers from behind, his chin resting on Foster's shoulder. A satchel of cash hangs from his waist. Dwight Eisenhower's smiling face decorates a bomb planted in front of them. Dead Guatemalan children lie at their feet. In the background, laborers bend under the weight of bags of bananas they are carrying toward a freighter decorated with an American flag.

Rivera was one of countless Latin Americans who were outraged when the United States engineered the overthrow of Guatemala's government. On July 2, 1954, he and his wife, Frida Kahlo, joined a protest march in Mexico City despite Kahlo's severe illness. She died eleven days later. Soon afterward, he set out to paint *Glorious Victory*.

Allen found the mural delightful. Rivera may have believed he was documenting a historic crime, but he was a Communist, so Allen reveled in his enmity. He even ordered small-format copies of *Glorious Victory* and proudly handed them out to friends.

Rivera sent his mural to be exhibited in Warsaw, and it was later taken to the Soviet Union. It was never shown there, however, because Rivera's freewheeling brand of Communism did not fit with the Kremlin's tastes and he was considered unsuitable. For half a century its whereabouts were unknown. Finally, after the Cold War ended, Mexican art historians discovered it in a warehouse of the Pushkin Museum in Moscow. They arranged for it to be shown in Mexico in 2007, and then in Guatemala.

After these showings, the mural was returned to Moscow. Having gazed intently at reproductions, I wanted to see the original, and contacted the Pushkin Museum to arrange a visit.

"I have to communicate to you that the big tableau by Diego Rivera, *Glorious Victory*, is not available to see, because it is kept as a huge roll, wound on the shaft," the museum's deputy director replied. "We could manage that you will be able to see this roll, but we can't open it, because we haven't enough space to expand it."

At the beginning of my quest into the lives of these extraordinary brothers, I had searched for the bust of John Foster Dulles at the airport that bears his name, and found that it had been relegated to a closed room near baggage claim. As my quest ended, I learned that a similar fate had befallen *Glorious Victory*. The Pushkin Museum is reputed to take good care of works in its warehouses, so this masterpiece is not likely to be lost. No one can say, however, when or whether it will again be shown in public.

Both of these works—the bust and *Glorious Victory*—were intended to give a measure of immortality, for better or worse, to the Dulles brothers. Now both are locked away and forgotten. They deserve better.

John Foster Dulles and Allen Dulles guided their country through the world during an era of extremes. The passage of time, and the end of the Cold War, make it difficult to grasp the depth of fear that gripped many Americans during the 1950s. Foster and Allen were chief promoters of that fear. They did as much as anyone to shape America's confrontation with the Soviet Union. Their actions helped set off some of the world's most profound long-term crises.

The brothers' lives uniquely suited them to the roles they played. From their remarkable family they absorbed the belief that Providence had ordained a special global role for the United States. They were also immersed in missionary Calvinism, which holds that the world is an eternal battleground between saintly and demonic forces. Finally, both brothers spent decades serving the global interests of America's richest corporations, and fully absorbed Wall Street's view of the world.

"Once you touch the biographies of human beings," Walter Lippmann observed while the Dulles brothers were in power, "the notion that political beliefs are logically determined collapses like a pricked balloon."

Foster and Allen took a ruthlessly confrontational view of the world. They saw it as a theater of conflict between two mighty empires, one of which must ultimately vanquish the other. This paradigm began gaining currency in the years after World War II. By the time Foster and Allen rose to power, it was close to a national consensus.

There had been no similar rush toward global engagement after World War I. Many Americans were content to return to life at peace and allow other countries to shape their own destinies. For a brief period after World War II, it seemed the same might happen. Senator Robert Taft ran for the Republican presidential nomination in 1952 urging a foreign policy closer to isolationism than imperialism. His defeat marked the end of serious dissent from the spreading consensus. Foster and Allen's brand of liberal internationalism, aggressive engagement, and corporate globalism emerged triumphant.

Soon after they became secretary of state and director of central intelligence, Foster and Allen failed their first conceptual test. Stalin died in Moscow on March 5, 1953, and in the months and years that followed, his successors made periodic overtures to the West. Foster and Allen categorically rejected them. They considered each Soviet call for "peaceful coexistence" a ruse designed to lull Americans into a false sense of security. By failing to explore possibilities for a new superpower relationship in the period after Stalin's death, the Dulles brothers may have sharpened and lengthened the Cold War.

Their next great failure of imagination was their inability to understand Third World nationalism. They were too quick to see Moscow's hand behind cries for independence and social reform in Latin America, Asia, and Africa. These continents were to them little more than a vast Cold War battleground. They never sought to engage creatively with the aspirations of hundreds of millions of people who were emerging from colonialism and looking for their place in a tumultuous world. Instead they waged destructive campaigns against foreign "monsters" who never truly threatened the United States.

Historians have recognized these two far-reaching lapses in judgment. A third has become clear with the passage of time. Foster and Allen never imagined that their intervention in foreign countries would have such devastating long-term effects—that Vietnam would be plunged into a war costing more than one million lives, for example, or that Iran would fall to violently anti-American zealots, or that the Congo would descend into decades of horrific conflict. They had no notion of "blowback." Their lack of foresight led them to pursue reckless adventures that, over the course of decades, palpably weakened American security.

One reason Foster and Allen never re-examined their assumptions was that the two men so fully reinforced each other. Their worldviews and operational codes were identical. Deeply intimate since childhood, they turned the State Department and the CIA into a reverberating echo chamber for their shared certainties.

"I have always felt it was a great mistake that the two men should have had these two offices at the same time," John Allison, the ambassador Foster removed from Indonesia in 1957, mused after retiring. "Because while I had a high regard for both of them, it was only human that Foster would listen to Allen before he would listen to anyone else. And he would take Allen's views in preference to those of anyone else."

One of Eisenhower's most intriguing private thoughts about the Dulles brothers emerged in a memoir by the American diplomat David Bruce. He recalled a conversation with Sir Kenneth Strong, who had been Eisenhower's chief intelligence officer during World War II and remained close to him. "[Strong] told me President Eisenhower once said to him that he wished he could have appointed Allen Dulles secretary of state, instead of Foster," Bruce wrote. "I have always thought Allen would have, because of his far superior skill in dealing with individuals, been preferable in that position, but the possibility was never really in the cards, since Foster, as the senior, had always coveted the job."

During Foster's term as secretary of state and for decades afterward, many historians and journalists considered him the true conceptualizer of American foreign policy during the 1950s. "Dulles, not Eisenhower, was the prime mover of American foreign policy," concluded a biography published the year after his death. "It was he who generated it. It was he who persuaded the President. It was he who carried it forward. That made

Dulles the effective commander of American power for the six years of his Secretaryship. And the world recognized him as such."

This view has shifted decisively. The consensus of twenty-first-century scholars is that Eisenhower shaped his own foreign policy, guiding Foster with a "hidden hand" and shrewdly using him as a "global attack dog."

"There is no longer any question that Eisenhower rather than Dulles was the key figure in making American policy in the 1950s," asserts a college textbook published in 2012.

Another text published around the same time reports a second consensus: besides being less powerful than he seemed, Foster was also less wise and successful. "Inspired by a Manichean conception of good and evil and a messianic devotion to advance the boundaries of what he called the 'free world,' the new Secretary of State challenged all foreign nations to choose between enlisting in the American campaign for global righteousness or submitting to Soviet domination," this text says. It dates the easing of global tensions to the Eisenhower-Khrushchev summit of September 1959—and points out that the summit took place soon after "the death in May 1959 of John Foster Dulles, the preeminent symbol of the Cold War mentality in the American government."

The narrative of permanent threat that Foster relentlessly promoted was not fabricated, since Soviet ambition was quite real. He and others in Washington, however, exaggerated the danger and allowed private prejudices to distort their view of Soviet intentions. The period when Soviet power descended over Eastern Europe, and when Communist forces invaded South Korea, was also the period when the United States turned back Soviet challenges in Iran, Turkey, Greece, and Berlin. Each side feared the other. It is a classic security dilemma: states feel threatened; they act to defend themselves; rivals see their actions as aggressive and respond in kind. The Cold War was a product of this spiral. During the 1950s, Foster fell into it.

The end of the Cold War allowed scholars to study long-secret archives in formerly Communist countries. In 1996 the historian Melvyn Leffler summarized their first wave of research. His review depicts a world quite different from the one Foster and Allen saw.

Soviet leaders were not focused on promoting worldwide revolution. They were concerned mostly with configurations of power, with protecting their country's immediate periphery, ensuring its security, and preserving their rule. Governing a land devastated by two world wars, they feared a resurgence of German and Japanese strength. They felt threatened by the United States, that alone among the combatants emerged from the war wealthier and armed with the atomic bomb. Soviet officials did not have pre-conceived plans to make Eastern Europe communist, to support the Chinese communists, or to wage war in Korea. . . .

US words and deeds greatly heightened ambient anxieties and subsequently contributed to the arms race and the expansion of the Cold War into the Third World. . . . US officials acted prudently in the early years of the Cold War, but their actions increased distrust, exacerbated frictions, and raised the stakes. Subsequently, their relentless pursuit of a policy of strength and counterrevolutionary warfare may have done more harm than good to Russians and the other peoples of the former Soviet Union, as well as East Europeans, Koreans, and Vietnamese. Quite a few of the new books and articles suggest that American policies made it difficult for reformers inside the Kremlin to gain the high ground. . . . Stalin's successors might have liked to stabilize the relationship and curtail the competition with the West, but the perceived threat emanating from the United States held them back.

Documents from foreign archives, according to this review, suggest that "rather than congratulate themselves on the Cold War's outcome, Americans must confront the negative as well as the positive consequences of U.S. actions and inquire more searchingly into the implications of their nation's foreign policies." Foster was America's preeminent Cold Warrior of that age. If American leaders made misjudgments that helped intensify global tension, none was more responsible than he.

"Mr. Dulles' moral universe makes everything quite clear, too clear," Reinhold Niebuhr wrote in 1958. "For self-righteousness is the inevitable fruit of simple moral judgments, placed in the service of moral complacency."

Foster spoke regularly to the American people, often from a collapsible podium he carried on his plane so he could make "departure statements" and "arrival statements," and he periodically appealed to Europeans, but his communication efforts stopped there. When he addressed the rest of the world, he used a stern preacher's tone. His message was usually dark, bellicose, and vaguely threatening, rarely uplifting or inspirational.

"So long as our foreign broadcasts, diplomatic pronouncements, and overt acts in the international arena give one-sided emphasis to our nuclear prowess, our readiness for massive retaliation, and our determination to defend American interests wherever they may be," the social psychologist Urie Bronfenbrenner warned after visiting the Soviet Union in 1960, "we only confirm the image of aggressive intransigence in the eyes not only of the communist world, but—what is perhaps more important—the non-committed nations as well."

Foster's inability to empathize with masses of people in a changing world robbed the United States of a historic chance. He conveyed a harsh, snarling image that alienated millions and contributed to generations of anti-Americanism.

Although Foster did not live to see his reputation decline, Allen did. His last and best-known operation, the Bay of Pigs invasion, was an epic disaster that humiliated him and his country before the world. He lost his job and dropped from public life. Few missed him.

Allen may have been a master case officer, but his broader legacy is clouded. He shared his brother's closed-mindedness. It led him, like Foster, to dismiss the possibility of accommodation with the Soviets and to refuse to reach out to the rising Third World. Nor is he known ever to have reflected on the possible long-term consequences of his covert operations.

Even before the CIA was created, Allen developed a sweeping concept of what it should be and do. In 1947, driven by his fascination with operations, he helped persuade Congress to give the new agency a covert capability. That allowed him, when he became director, to transform the CIA from an intelligence agency that carried out occasional clandestine plots into a global force ceaselessly engaged in paramilitary and regime-change campaigns.

At Allen's urging, CIA officers around the world adopted an activist mentality in which, as one of them later recalled, "you had to develop operations or you would fade away." At home he demanded analysis that confirmed his view of an ever-aggressive Soviet Union. "We had constructed for ourselves a picture of the USSR, and whatever happened had to be made to fit into that picture," said one of his analysts, Abbot Smith, who later became director of the Office of National Estimates. "Intelligence estimates can hardly commit a more abominable sin."

By the time Allen retired, the Bay of Pigs fiasco had shattered the reputation of his beloved CIA. It never returned to the peak of power and influence it enjoyed during his term as director. For this he bears considerable responsibility.

Under Allen's lackadaisical leadership, the agency endlessly tolerated misfits. Even in high positions it was not unusual to find men who were evidently lazy, alcoholic, or simply incompetent. Allen never imposed discipline on the agency. He hated to fire people. "We carried our walking wounded much too far," a CIA inspector general later wrote.

The passage of years also revealed Allen's partial responsibility for the epic "mole hunt" that shook the CIA for more than a decade. It was during the last months of his directorship, in 1961, that his counterintelligence chief, James Jesus Angleton, launched what became an obsessive search for Soviet agents inside the CIA. This drama unfolded out of public view, but it unhinged the agency and, according to one officer, "caused havoc" for years.

Allen's reputation eroded further as some of his unsavory operations became public. His involvement in plots to assassinate foreign leaders was slowly documented, and President Johnson complained privately that the CIA had been running "a goddamn Murder Inc. in the Caribbean." Investigators also uncovered MKULTRA, the operation in which psychoactive drugs were administered to unknowing victims. The family of Frank Olsen, the CIA officer reported to have jumped to his death during one of these tests in 1953, filed a lawsuit alleging that he had not jumped but was murdered after returning from a trip to Europe disturbed by what he had seen in secret prisons.

A Senate report in the 1970s described Allen's years running the CIA as "a lost opportunity."

"Jolly, gregarious, and extroverted in the extreme, Dulles disliked and avoided confrontations at every level," the report concluded. "He failed to provide even minimal direction over the departmental intelligence components at a time when intelligence capabilities were undergoing dramatic changes."

Allen had the cold-bloodedness an intelligence director needs, but not enough intellectual rigor or curiosity. Carried away by his love of the cloak-and-dagger game, he lost sight of the limits to what covert action can achieve.

His own record suggests how severe those limits are. He was not the brilliant spymaster many believed him to be. In fact, the opposite is true. Nearly every one of his major covert operations failed or nearly failed. His plot in Guatemala was on the brink of collapse from the loss of CIA planes, only to succeed when Eisenhower agreed to send replacement planes and President Arbenz suffered a providential failure of nerve. In Iran, only a fatal misjudgment by nationalists allowed a second CIA coup to succeed after the first collapsed. From there, the geography of Allen's operational failure spreads across the world: Berlin, Eastern Europe, the Soviet Union, China and Taiwan, Vietnam, Laos, Burma, Indonesia, Tibet, Egypt, Syria, Iraq, Cuba, and beyond.

Allen imagined himself as a modern incarnation of Sir Francis Walsingham, the chief of Queen Elizabeth's feared spy network in the sixteenth century, who promoted English power through deft combinations of intrigue and violence. The truth was more prosaic. Allen spent much time in a world of self-reinforcing fantasy. He created an image for himself and came to believe it.

"Allen Dulles was a frivolous man," Arthur Schlesinger Jr. concluded. "He was most intelligent and a man of great charm, unlike his brother. But he was frivolous in the sense that he would make these decisions which involved people's lives, and never would really think them through. He always left that to someone else."

In the end, Foster and Allen depended on Eisenhower for all they did. They could not have waged their secret war without his approval. Nonetheless they decisively shaped the way the United States used power at the height of the Cold War. Their inability to adapt to a changing world, or even to see that it was changing, reinforced Eisenhower's instincts. So did their faith in covert action.

Foster and Allen were born into privilege and steeped in the ethos of pioneers and missionaries. They spent decades promoting the business and strategic interests of the United States. More than any other figures of their age, they were vessels of American history. No other secretary of state and director of central intelligence could have done what they did. Only brothers could have achieved it—and only these two.

———

Unique biographies are part of what led Foster and Allen to misjudge the world. Human psychology is a second factor. During the 1950s, the United States was gripped by a diffuse but intense complex of terrors. When Foster warned Americans that an enemy with "slimy, octopus-like tentacles" was threatening them with the "black plague of Soviet communism," they heard and were afraid.

Foster and Allen believed that most challenges to the United States were part of a master plan orchestrated from Moscow. A foreign ambassador once asked Foster how he knew that the Soviets were tied to land reform in Guatemala. He admitted that it was "impossible to produce evidence" but said evidence was unnecessary because of "our deep conviction that such a tie must exist." This was how he saw Third World nationalism.

"It is all part of a single pattern," he insisted.

From this assumption flowed a second one: since the leaders in the Kremlin were plotting world domination, they would never negotiate in good faith. "It is inevitable that orthodox communism should reject peaceful ways, except as a matter of temporary expediency, because it rejects the moral premises that alone make possible the permanent organization of peace," Foster once reasoned.

Foster often contrasted Soviet cynicism with American virtue. "It is the policy of the United States not to intervene in the internal affairs of other nations," he had his spokesman assert when he was at the peak of his interventionist campaign. Whether he was simply keeping secrets or had actually convinced himself that this was true cannot be known. When provoked, though, he became impatient.

During one of his meetings with religious leaders, a prominent Methodist, Bishop Bromley Oxnam, observed that the United States had itself been guilty of intolerance and aggression. Foster was indignant.

"Why do we have to run that down?" he asked. "Why present ourselves as such a terrible species of being?"

The Dulles brothers were not adept at synthesizing, compromising, listening, adapting, or evolving. Political nuance rarely clouded their worldview. Neither did moral ambiguity.

"For us there are two kinds of people in the world," Foster once said.

"There are those who are Christians and support free enterprise, and there are the others."

Historians describe this approach to global politics as a Cold War trope that the Dulles brothers embraced with special fervor. Science is providing another explanation. Neurophysiologists, evolutionary biologists, and social and cognitive psychologists have made remarkable discoveries about the working of the brain that are highly relevant to Cold War history. They also provide intriguing insights into how the Dulles brothers perceived reality.

Researchers have learned that people's brains are programmed to favor information that confirms what they already believe. Contradictory information threatens cognitive dissonance. The brain rebels against it.

Social scientists have long used examples from the Cold War to illustrate the syndromes of groupthink, thought suppression, denial projection, structural blindness, and even mass hysteria. In 1960 the psychologist Charles Osgood wrote that the pull toward consistency "can plague big minds as well as little, in high places as well as low." He called his first piece of evidence "Specimen 1: International Affairs."

"Before the delegates to the United Nations, Khrushchev makes sweeping proposals for world disarmament," Osgood postulated. "A large segment of the American press editorializes about the deceptive nature of these proposals—that rather than sincere overtures toward peaceful solution of problems, his proposals are carefully planned moves in the Cold War. It is cognitively inconsistent for us to think of people we dislike and distrust making honest, conciliatory moves. . . . We strive to maintain internal consistency among our attitudes and beliefs, often at the price of doctoring reality."

In the twenty-first century, discoveries about how the brain works set off a mini-boom of books seeking to convey these discoveries to lay readers. They comprise a leap in understanding—not simply of psychology and human behavior, but of a force that, at times, influences world history. The Cold War was one of those times. All of these observations, made by scientists and researchers, are strongly applicable to the Dulles brothers.

- People are motivated to accept accounts that fit with their preexisting convictions; acceptance of those accounts makes them feel better, and acceptance of competing claims makes them feel worse.

- Dissonance is eliminated when we blind ourselves to contradictory propositions. And we are prepared to pay a very high price to preserve our most cherished ideas.
- Moral hypocrisy is a deep part of our nature: the tendency to judge others more harshly for some moral infraction than we judge ourselves.
- Groupthink leads to many problems of defective decision making, including incomplete survey of alternatives and objectives, failure to examine the risks of the preferred choice, poor information search, selective bias in processing information, and failure to assess alternatives.
- We are often confident even when we are wrong. . . . Declarations of high confidence mainly tell you that an individual has constructed a coherent story in his mind, not necessarily that the story is true.
- Certain beliefs are so important for a society or group that they become part of how you prove your identity. . . . The truth is that our minds just aren't set up to be changed by mere evidence.

None of this absolves the Dulles brothers from the responsibilities of rational decision making. Like most adults, they had the ability to balance their emotional responses with cognition and adjust their behavior according to circumstance. Nonetheless both suffered acutely from what psychologists call confirmation bias—the tendency to reject discordant information. When their own envoys advised them to tolerate Mossadegh and Arbenz, or to accept neutralist regimes in Indonesia and Laos, they could not hear. Instead they replaced the envoys with others who gave them the reports they wanted.

Experience shaped the Dulles brothers, but so did private psychology. People can be deaf when their deeply held beliefs are challenged. The Dulles brothers had this quality to excess.

An American political scientist, Ole Holsti, studied the way Foster made decisions, and found that he dealt with "discrepant information" by "discrediting the source of the new information; reinterpreting the new information so as to be consistent with his belief system; [or] searching for other information consistent with preexisting attitudes."

"Dulles was the archetype of the inner-directed person," Holsti wrote. "The advice of subordinates was neither actively sought nor, when tendered, was it often of great weight."

Early astronomers found the chaos of stars overwhelming, and came up with the idea of constellations as a way of imposing a design on the firmament. Like them, Foster and Allen were drawn to structure, order, and predictability. Their deepest impulses drove them to find patterns in a kaleidoscopic world.

A fictional product of the Dulles era, Rabbit Angstrom, is the central character in a series of novels by John Updike. In *Rabbit Redux*, Angstrom marvels at America's role in the world.

"America is beyond power, it acts as in a dream, as a face of God," he reflects. "Wherever America is, there is freedom, and wherever America is not, madness rules with chains and darkness strangles millions."

Foster and Allen saw the world this way. Their radiant self-image was ultimate justification for everything they did. Why did they do it? Part of the answer lies in their personal backgrounds, part in the realm of psychology. The most important explanation, however, may be: they did it because they are us. If they were shortsighted, open to violence, and blind to the subtle realities of the world, it was because those qualities help define American foreign policy and the United States itself.

The Dulles brothers personified ideals and traits that many Americans shared during the 1950s, and still share. They did not colonize America's mind or hijack United States foreign policy. On the contrary, they embodied the national ethos. What they wanted, Americans wanted.

Foster and Allen believed they knew what was best for all people. They considered the United States an instrument of destiny, blessed by Providence. This gave them deep self-confidence and a sense of infinite possibility. When they treated other nations cruelly, they comforted themselves with the thought that it was all for good in the end. They felt a noble, civilizing call. "Exceptionalism"—the view that the United States has a right to impose its will because it knows more, sees farther, and lives on a higher moral plane than other nations—was to them not a platitude, but the organizing principle of daily life and global politics.

In all of this, the Dulles brothers were one with their fellow Americans. Their attitudes were rooted in the American character. They were pure products of the United States.

Nor was the Dulles brothers' exaggeration of threats something new in

American history. Conspiracy theories are as old as the Republic. Most of them posit a secret cabal—Catholics, Jews, Muslims, Masons, anarchists, bankers—that plots world revolution. Foster and Allen saw such a cabal during the 1950s.

"International communism is a conspiracy composed of a certain number of people, all of whose names I do not know, and many of whom I suppose are secret," Foster once told a congressional committee. "They have gotten control of one government after another."

No secret group hovered above and manipulated nations during the 1950s. Believing it, however, comforted Americans. Foster helped persuade them that their troubles in the world did not reflect the frustration of millions—or the conceptual failures of their leaders—but the blind hatred of a few obscure fanatics.

One historian has called the Cold War paradigm "one of the most powerfully developed national narratives in recorded history." It gripped Americans in a frightening age, another has written, because it offered "a comprehensive way of understanding the world. . . . Fear served as the emotional glue that held this world together: fear of Soviet expansionism, of communist subversion at home, of nuclear war."

Theorists in various eras have suggested that nations need enemies in order to maintain cohesiveness and inner strength. Foster deeply believed this. He encouraged "preparedness" projects like building bomb shelters and holding air raid drills, and conveyed the scope of the threat by authorizing live television broadcast of nuclear weapons tests in the Nevada desert. America's state of fear during the 1950s was to him not a regrettable by-product of the Cold War but a prerequisite for victory.

"If there's no evident menace from the Soviet Union," he reasoned, "our will to maintain unity and strength may weaken."

Even after lifetimes serving the cause of economic colonialism, Foster and Allen considered themselves anti-colonial. They rationalized their use of violence with the conviction that their cause—the once-in-a-millennium confrontation between civilization and barbarism—was so transcendent that it justified any extreme. Many Americans agreed.

Foster and Allen brought the United States into partnership with dictators in several parts of the world, and in some countries they intervened to replace democratic governments with tyrannies. Nonetheless they considered themselves paladins of liberty. By some standards, this leap of logic made them hypocrites. They justified it by applying a particular definition of freedom. It had little to do with civil rights or social welfare. Their view of freedom was above all economic: a country whose leaders respected private enterprise and welcomed multinational business was a free country.

This too reflected a widely shared American belief.

"Depriving the individual of his right to possession in favor of the collective, even in the name of social justice as communism in the abstract would do, seems inherently wrong to Americans—and this is understandable, given the American experience," Paul Kattenburg, the State Department desk officer for Indochina during the 1950s, wrote after retiring. "That it does not seem wrong to millions of human beings in the world who have not shared the American bounty or the American experience and have never owned property or anything else, does not obviously strike many Americans."

There was one other component to freedom as Foster and Allen saw it: religion. Countries that encouraged religious devotion, and that were led by men on good terms with Christian clerics, were to them free countries. Using these two criteria—attitude toward business and attitude toward religion—they conjured an explanation of why they condemned some dictatorships but not others.

Senator Fulbright once complained that Foster "misleads public opinion, confuses it, [and] feeds it pap." Yet many Americans devoured his narrative. It fit with how they saw their own lives and history.

The world seemed threatened by malefactors. Someone had to crush them. Foster told Americans that Providence had given the United States this mission. With this discourse he plucked chords of collective memory that bind Americans to Indian wars, range wars, frontier marshals, shoot-outs, marine landings on foreign shores, and the richness of manifest destiny. His world was much like the untamed valley in *Shane* or the terrorized town in *High Noon*: a once-peaceful place threatened by evil, in need of a savior.

Americans are not patient by nature. When faced with a challenge or problem, our impulse is to act. We like to *do* things, not understand things. Reality does not limit our ambition. In fact, we are sometimes tempted to believe we can reshape reality to fit our needs. This is another national trait that Foster and Allen perfectly embodied.

Their approach to Vietnam was one example. In the mid-1950s Winston Churchill advised his American friends to recognize that Ho Chi Minh was unbeatable, accept his victory, and try to make the best of it. This the Dulles brothers could not do—because they were Americans. Churchill had on his side only negative, depressive, defeatist Old World reality. Foster and Allen counted on something they considered more powerful: the genius of America. They believed that their country's vast resources, focused energy, endless ingenuity, and sheer material power would allow it to achieve what others could not. This optimism, somewhere between creative and delusional, was not simply a peculiar product of summers with "Grandfather Foster" and decades at Sullivan & Cromwell. It was and is central to the idea of America.

In some countries, American impatience had a strong political overlay. Foster and Allen found President Arbenz of Guatemala abhorrent, for example, but his term was ending and he was likely to be succeeded by a more pro-American figure. Yet Foster and Allen could not wait. An orderly transfer of power in Guatemala would show that it was possible for a country's voters to choose socialism and then freely return to traditional capitalism. This would undermine the Cold War model, which rested on the premise that socialist influence must be resisted because socialist gains are always irreversible.

Foster and Allen could not allow history to prove them wrong, so they set out to change it. Lashing out against real or imagined enemies, as they did, is typically American. Quietly watching history unfold is not.

"By the late 1950s the United States had established an interventionist policy with a global reach," the historian Odd Arne Westad has written. "Only regimes that accepted the American hegemony in foreign policy and in development strategy were seen as viable, and some of the 'unviable' states were condemned for voluntarily or involuntarily opening up for Communism, and thereby provoking a U.S. intervention. Even in cases such as Indonesia, where Washington's strategy did not work out, there were few regrets. To the Eisenhower administration it was more important to spoil the chances for a successful left-wing development strategy than it was to impose its own version of development on newly independent countries."

Americans often find it difficult to imagine how other people see the United States, the world, or life itself. Foster and Allen exemplified this national egoism. Empathy was beyond their emotional range. Sympathizing with the enormous complexities facing leaders of emerging nations would have required them to consider those leaders independent agents, rather than instruments of Soviet power. Their compulsive oversimplification of the world prevented them from seeing its rich diversity. In this, too, they were quintessentially American.

Their worldview fit the age. Americans were only a few years past the trauma of World War II, which taught them the horrors of global conflict. Urged on by Foster, Allen, and others in Washington and beyond, they projected the crimes of their World War II enemies onto the Soviet Union. Since Japan had attacked the United States without warning, they presumed the Soviets were liable to do the same; since Hitler had used negotiation as a tactic to give him room for war, they scorned diplomacy.

The half century of history that has unfolded since Foster and Allen passed from the scene suggests that they share responsibility for much that has gone wrong in the world. The blame, however, does not end with them. To gaze at their portraits and think, "They did it," would be reassuring. It would also be unfair. Americans who seek to understand the roots of their country's trouble in the world should look not at Foster and Allen's portraits but in a mirror.

Foster and Allen exemplified the nation that produced them. A different kind of leader would require a different kind of United States.

The story of the Dulles brothers is the story of America. Their determination to project power was the same impulse that pushed settlers across prairies and over mountains, wrested rich territories from Mexico, crushed Native American resistance, and drew the United States into wars from Central America to Siberia. It remains potent. As long as Americans believe their country has vital interests everywhere on earth, they will be led by people who believe the same.

Foster and Allen tell Americans much about ourselves. Not all of it is comforting. Perhaps that is part of the reason they have faded into such obscurity. Forgetting their geopolitical sins allows the United States to forget its own.

One way to bring Americans to reflect on their past—and future—would be to revive memory of the Dulles brothers. Their actions frame the grand debate over America's role in the world that has never been truly joined in the United States. Fundamental assumptions that guide

American foreign policy have not changed substantially since the era when they were in power. Many Americans still celebrate their country's providential "exceptionalism." The Dulles brothers embraced this paradigm. Understanding what they did, and why they did it, is a step toward understanding why the United States acts as it does in the world.

Restoring Foster and Allen to their deserved place in America's national consciousness would require an affirmative act. Two would be better.

The bust of John Foster Dulles that was once the centerpiece of Dulles International Airport should be the centerpiece again. It could be a mini-memorial, with texts explaining Foster's career in ways that suggest questions Americans might ask themselves about their country's identity and global role.

Behind it, on a wall, should be the brilliantly colorful Diego Rivera mural *Glorious Victory*. Rivera wanted it displayed in the Soviet Union, but the audience that needs to see it is in the United States. It serves no purpose rolled up in the basement of the Pushkin Museum. At the bustling international airport that serves Washington, it would be a provocative history lesson.

Keeping these two objects out of public view allows Americans to ignore realities that many wish to ignore. It encourages the childlike belief that since bad things are done by bad people, they will stop happening when the bad people are gone. Restoring Foster's bust to its original place, and enhancing it with *Glorious Victory*, would be a blow against the amnesia that has allowed a nation to forget two men who helped guide it at a crucial moment.

The Dulles brothers' approach to the world did not work out well for the United States. As a result, they have faded from national memory. Rather than forget or vilify them, however, Americans should embrace them. Their stories are full of deep meaning for the United States. They are us. We are them.

NOTES

INTRODUCTION

1   a bereft nation mourned: Richard Goold-Adams, *John Foster Dulles: A Reappraisal* (New York: Appleton-Century-Crofts, 1962), p. 12.

1   "one of the truly great men": *New York Times*, May 25, 1959.

1   Chantilly International: *New York Times*, Jan. 19, 1961, Nov. 18, 1962; *Washington Post*, Dec. 1, 2012.

2   "How appropriate": http://www.presidency.ucsb.edu/ws/index.php?pid=9017 #axzz1cHFJ9RI1.

2   "mixture of veneration and hatred": Goold-Adams, *John Foster Dulles*, p. 4.

3   "most of the *éclat*": Leonard Mosley, *Dulles: A Biography of Eleanor, Allen, and John Foster Dulles and Their Family Network* (New York: Dial, 1978), p. 4.

3   "so powerful and implacable": Ibid., p. 5.

3   "greatest intelligence officer": James Srodes, *Allen Dulles: Master of Spies* (Washington, D.C.: Regnery, 1999), p. 6.

3   "Do you realize": Mosley, *Dulles*, p. 7.

1: UNMENTIONABLE HAPPENINGS

7   Early every summer: Richard H. Immerman, *John Foster Dulles: Piety, Pragmatism, and Power in U.S. Foreign Policy* (Wilmington, Del.: Scholarly Resources, 1999), p. 2; Mosley, *Dulles*, p. 21; Ronald W. Pruessen, *John Foster Dulles: The Road to Power* (New York: Free Press, 1982), p. 4; Mark G. Toulouse, *The Transformation of John Foster Dulles: From Prophet of Realism to High Priest of Nationalism* (Macon, Ga.: Mercer University Press, 1985), p. 5.

7   "finding the fish": Mosley, *Dulles*, p. 23.

8   "Here in delightful surroundings": Allen Dulles, *The Craft of Intelligence* (New York: Harper & Row, 1963), pp. 2–3.

8   The first American member: Eleanor Lansing Dulles, *Chances of a Lifetime* (Englewood Cliffs, N.J.: Prentice-Hall, 1980), pp. xi, 15–17; Toulouse, *Transformation of John Foster Dulles*, p. 4; Peter Grose, *Gentleman Spy: The Life of Allen Dulles* (New York: Houghton Mifflin, 1994), p. 7.

8   His family was pious: Toulouse, *Transformation of John Foster Dulles*, p. 4; Edwin Wilbur Rice, *The Sunday-School Movement, 1780–1917, and the American Sunday-School Union* (Philadelphia: American Sunday-School Union, 1917), pp. 98, 187.

8   One of the most cosmopolitan: Srodes, *Allen Dulles*, p. 14; Grose, *Gentleman Spy*, pp. 6–7.

9   The boys grew up: Mosley, *Dulles*, pp. 13–14; Eleanor Lansing Dulles, *John Foster Dulles: The Last Year* (New York: Harcourt, Brace & World, 1963), p. 27; Srodes, *Allen Dulles*, p. 12; Grose, *Gentleman Spy*, p. 9.

9   Relgiosity permeated: John Robinson Beal, *John Foster Dulles: A Biography* (New York: Harper & Brothers, 1957), p. 28.

9   Foster . . . felt the impact: Immerman, *John Foster Dulles*, p. 2; Frederick Marks, *Power and Peace: The Diplomacy of John Foster Dulles* (Westport, Conn.: Praeger, 1995), p. 124; Pruessen, *John Foster Dulles*, p. 4.

10   "We did not think": Eleanor Lansing Dulles, *John Foster Dulles*, pp. 62, 128.

10   Edith considered her boys: Michael A. Guhin, *John Foster Dulles: A Statesman and His Times* (New York: Columbia University Press, 1972), pp. 10, 19; Immerman, *John Foster Dulles*, p. 4; Pruessen, *John Foster Dulles*, pp. 6–7; Srodes, *Allen Dulles*, p. 17.

10   "Its strengths": Toulouse, *Transformation of John Foster Dulles*, p. 8.

11   "The native inhabitants": John Watson Foster, *American Diplomacy in the Orient* (Boston: Houghton Mifflin, 1904), p. 366.

11   After leaving office: Pruessen, *John Foster Dulles*, pp. 5–8; "John W. Foster (1892–1893): Secretary of State," http://millercenter.org/president/bharrison /essays/cabinet/381.

12   "Grandfather Foster" was infatuated: Eleanor Lansing Dulles, *John Foster Dulles*, pp. 61–62; Pruessen, *John Foster Dulles*, p. 8.

13   "women with their sequins": Eleanor Lansing Dulles, *John Foster Dulles*, p. 62.

13   "I was an avid listener": Allen Dulles, *Craft of Intelligence*, p. vii.

13   During that first winter: Mosley, *Dulles*, p. 16; Grose, *Gentleman Spy*, p. 13; Srodes, *Allen Dulles*, p. 26.

13   That view: Mosley, *Dulles*, pp. 23–24; Goold-Adams, *John Foster Dulles*, p. 16; Grose, *Gentleman Spy*, p. 13; Srodes, *Allen Dulles*, p. 26.

14   Already the two brothers: Eleanor Lansing Dulles, *Chances of a Lifetime*, pp. 12–13; Mosley, *Dulles*, p. 15.

14   The passage of time: Srodes, *Allen Dulles*, p. 19; Mosley, *Dulles*, pp. 5–6.

14   Two of the boys' three sisters: Mosley, *Dulles*, pp. 40–41, 66–67.

15   "He developed a schoolboy 'crush'": Ibid., pp. 24–25.

15   "nearly broke my mother's heart": Goold-Adams, *John Foster Dulles*, p. 17.

15   Not every student: Mark F. Bernstein, "An American Hero in Iran," *Princeton Alumni Weekly*, May 9, 2007; Robert D. Burgener, "Iran's American Martyr," *The Iranian*, Aug. 31, 1998; S. R. Shafagh, *Howard Baskerville 1885–1909, Fiftieth Anniversary: The Story of an American Who Died in the Cause of Iranian Freedom and Independence* (Tabriz, Iran: Keyhan, 1959).

16   Foster graduated second: Mosley, *Dulles*, p. 26.

16   Allie arrived at Princeton: Ibid., p. 27.

16   Among the many girls: Ibid., pp. 14, 26; Pruessen, *John Foster Dulles*, pp. 12–13.

17   As Foster had guessed: Pruessen, *John Foster Dulles*, p. 15.

17   "Isn't the memory": Beal, *John Foster Dulles*, p. 55.

17   His starting salary: Ibid., p. 56; Nancy Lisagor and Frank Lipsius, *A Law Unto Itself: The Untold Story of the Law Firm of Sullivan & Cromwell* (New York: William Morrow, 1988), p. 61.

17   "Just you wait": Mosley, *Dulles*, p. 30.

17   The two were married: Townsend Hoopes, *The Devil and John Foster Dulles* (Boston: Little, Brown, 1973), p. 26.

18   "What warts": Mosley, *Dulles*, p. 30.

18   in 1879: Lisagor and Lipsius, *Law Unto Itself*, pp. 34–37.

19   "the man whose masterful mind": Pruessen, *John Foster Dulles*, p. 16.

19   Clients favored Sullivan & Cromwell: Ibid., pp. 15–16.

19   His first clients: Ibid., pp. 17–18.

19   Allie was also setting out: Srodes, *Allen Dulles*, p. 36.

19   *Kim*: Rudyard Kipling, *Kim* (Hollywood, Fla.: Simon & Brown, 2011), pp. 141, 115.

20   He never parted with his copy: Grose, *Gentleman Spy*, p. 18.

20   During his stay in India: Srodes, *Allen Dulles*, p. 38; Mosley, *Dulles*, p. 34.

20   "It is a great thing": Grose, *Gentleman Spy*, p. 19.

21   Few in Washington: Srodes, *Allen Dulles*, p. 45; Grose, *Gentleman Spy*, p. 36.

22   Of all that Lansing did: Srodes, *Allen Dulles*, p. 45.

22   "He thought Gaunt": Mosley, *Dulles*, p. 38.

22   His first post: Grose, *Gentleman Spy*, p. 23.

23   The war years: Ibid., pp. 27–28, 32; Srodes, *Allen Dulles*, pp. 84–85; Douglas C. Waller, *Wild Bill Donovan: The Spymaster Who Created the OSS and Modern American Espionage* (New York: Free Press, 2011), pp. 267–70.

23   "made the most of the area's recreational facilities": Srodes, *Allen Dulles*, p. 78.

23   tennis balls: Grose, *Gentleman Spy*, p. 29.

23   In one letter home: Srodes, *Allen Dulles*, p. 72.

24   "spectacularly buxom . . . sisters": Ibid.

24   Years afterward he learned: Grose, *Gentleman Spy*, p. 26; Mosley, *Dulles*, pp. 47–48.

24   Around the same time: Srodes, *Allen Dulles*, pp. 81–82; Mosley, *Dulles*, pp. 45–46.

24   By the time: Srodes, *Allen Dulles*, p. 76.

24 A pro-American regime in Cuba: Pruessen, *John Foster Dulles*, pp. 21–22; Lisagor and Lipsius, *Law Unto Itself*, p. 67.

25 "Uncle Bert" was impressed: Beal, *John Foster Dulles*, pp. 59–60; Pruessen, *John Foster Dulles*, pp. 22–23.

25 Costa Rica at this time: Jason Colby, *The Business of Empire: United Fruit, Race, and U.S. Expansion in Central America* (Ithaca, N.Y.: Cornell University Press, 2011), p. 131.

25 "sincere friendliness": Dulles to the Secretary of State, May 21, 1917, Dulles Papers, box 1.

25 By the time Foster returned: Lisagor and Lipsius, *Law Unto Itself*, p. 66; Grose, *Gentleman Spy*, p. 26.

26 Foster found his uncle: Mosley, *Dulles*, p. 55.

27 This news: Srodes, *Allen Dulles*, p. 90; Goold-Adams, *John Foster Dulles*, p. 17.

27 Foster's nine months: Mosley, *Dulles*, p. 56.

27 In between negotiating sessions: Lisagor and Lipsius, *Law Unto Itself*, pp. 171–73.

28 "an art of living": *The Independent*, Nov. 6, 2009.

28 she became pregnant: Mosley, *Dulles*, pp. 60–61.

28 Their sister Eleanor: Ibid., p. 40.

29 "Thousands of fine young men": Eleanor Lansing Dulles, *Chances of a Lifetime*, p. 71.

29 Vietnamese nationalist: Jean Lacouture, *Ho Chi Minh: A Political Biography* (New York: Random House, 1968), p. 24; A. J. Langguth, *Our Vietnam: The War 1954–1975* (New York: Touchstone, 2000), p. 35.

29 Wilson argued ceaselessly: Mosley, *Dulles*, pp. 31, 47; David A. Andelman, *A Shattered Peace: Versailles 1919 and the Price We Pay Today* (Hoboken, N.J.: Wiley, 2007) pp. 120–29.

30 "how completely they had been deceived": Mosley, *Dulles*, p. 216.

30 "If the United States delegation": Andelman, *Shattered Peace*, p. 125.

30 "a banana lying across the face of Europe": Grose, *Gentleman Spy*, p. 60.

31 It was the destiny of the United States: Pruessen, *John Foster Dulles*, p. 216.

31 Allie wrote home: Grose, *Gentleman Spy*, p. 65.

31 "the major benefit I got from Princeton": Pruessen, *John Foster Dulles*, p. 10.

32 "Our industrial fortunes": Woodrow Wilson, *Addresses of President Woodrow Wilson* (Washington, D.C.: U.S. Government Printing Office, 1919), p. 32.

32 "not humiliating but a benefit": Karen L. Stanford, *If We Must Die: African American Voices on War and Peace* (Lanham, Md.: Rowman & Littlefield, 2008), p. 106.

32 "the poison of Bolshevism": Pruessen, *John Foster Dulles*, p. 26.

32 "the criminal, the depraved, and the mentally unfit": John M. Thompson, *Russia, Bolshevism, and the Versailles Peace* (Princeton: Princeton University Press, 1967), p. 15.

33 Hoover . . . "true social ends": Markku Ruotsila, *British and American Anticommunism Before the Cold War* (London: Routledge, 2001), p. 82.

33   "on a certain day": Anne Hagedorn, *Savage Peace: Hope and Fear in America, 1919* (New York: Simon and Schuster, 2008), p. 229.

33   Cromwell made him a partner: Hoopes, *Devil and John Foster Dulles*, p. 33; Mosley, *Dulles*, pp. 59–63.

34   ghostwriting assignment: https://www.kirkusreviews.com/book-reviews/jordan-a-schwarz-3/the-speculator-bernard-m-baruch-in-washington-1.

34   not a happy match: Grose, *Gentleman Spy*, pp. 73–75, 86; Srodes, *Allen Dulles*, p. 10; Mosley, *Dulles*, pp. 73–74.

35   Rather than send Allen back: Srodes, *Allen Dulles*, pp. 124–25; Grose, *Gentleman Spy*, pp. 77, 84; Mosley, *Dulles*, p. 71.

35   Meeting with remarkable men: Srodes, *Allen Dulles*, pp. 121–22, 136.

35   learned of his relationship: Mosley, *Dulles*, p. 74.

2: THE TAINT OF MY ENVIRONMENT

37   On a breezy day: Lisagor and Lipsius, *Law Unto Itself*, pp. 99–100.

38   In the 1920s: Pruessen, *John Foster Dulles*, pp. 67–72.

38   "A Bavarian hamlet": Ibid., p. 72.

38   "I saw John Foster Dulles": Mosley, *Dulles*, p. 76.

39   "with humility": William O. Douglas, "An Understanding of Asia," *The Rotarian*, Dec. 1956.

39   "I'm not sure": Author's interview with Cathleen Douglas Stone, 2012.

39   Not long after: Srodes, *Allen Dulles*, p. 142.

39   "I want to keep": Grose, *Gentleman Spy*, pp. 93–94.

39   "the little minister": Lisagor and Lipsius, *Law Unto Itself*, p. 129.

40   The first important new client: Grose, *Gentleman Spy*, p. 96.

40   accused Allen of fixing . . . a candidate: Lisagor and Lipsius, *Law Unto Itself*, pp. 129–30.

40   In recognition: Grose, *Gentleman Spy*, p. 100.

40   While Allen was in Paris: Grose, *Gentleman Spy*, p. 10; Lisagor and Lipsius, *Law Unto Itself*, p. 130.

40   "lived it to the hilt": Grose, *Gentleman Spy*, p. 101.

41   Poland's electric system: Lisagor and Lipsius, *Law Unto Itself*, p. 130.

41   "He never bothered": Grose, *Gentleman Spy*, pp. 102–3.

41   Ivar Kreuger: Lisagor and Lipsius, *Law Unto Itself*, p. 131.

42   No fewer than fifteen of these companies: Pruessen, *John Foster Dulles*, pp. 119–20; Beal, *John Foster Dulles*, p. 86.

42   Neither brother lacked for money: Srodes, *Allen Dulles*, pp. 190–91.

42   Allen . . . and United Fruit: Hoopes, *Devil and John Foster Dulles*, p. 52.

42   "Where he was an asset": Mosley, *Dulles*, p. 77.

43   Third Avenue elevated train: Hoopes, *Devil and John Foster Dulles*, p. 39; Mosley, *Dulles*, pp. 80, 125; Grose, *Gentleman Spy*, pp. 103, 129.

43   "My father was . . . extroverted": Srodes, *Allen Dulles*, p. 452.

43   eleven extended foreign trips: Grose, *Gentleman Spy*, p. 100.

43   Letters he wrote home: Ibid., p. 106; Srodes, *Allen Dulles*, p. 165; Mosley, *Dulles*, p. 125.

44   "at least a hundred women": Mosley, *Dulles*, p. 125.

44   never to pick up a napkin: Grose, *Gentleman Spy*, p. 107.

44   Soon after returning: Ibid., pp. 106–7; Srodes, *Allen Dulles*, p. 192.

44   "Sex . . . was . . . a form of physical therapy: Srodes, *Allen Dulles*, p. 165.

45   John Watson Foster Dulles: Mosley, *Dulles*, pp. 80–81.

45   "He called Dean": Marquis Childs, oral history, Dulles Papers.

46   one of his last public pronouncements: *New York Times*, Dec. 13, 2008.

46   Foster's middle child: Mosley, *Dulles*, p. 82.

46   Allen Macy Dulles: Grose, *Gentleman Spy*, pp. 104, 332–38; Srodes, *Allen Dulles*, pp. 181, 193, 446–49; Eleanor Lansing Dulles, *Chances of a Lifetime*, pp. 233–34.

46   Both of Allen's daughters: Srodes, *Allen Dulles*, p. 181; Grose, *Gentleman Spy*, p. 104.

46   Her older sister: Srodes, *Allen Dulles*, pp. 120, 161, 193; Grose, *Gentleman Spy*, pp. 104–5.

47   their independent-minded sister: Mosely, *Dulles*, pp. 84–88, 93–95, 105–6; Hoopes, *Devil and John Foster Dulles*, p. 42.

47   Roosevelt . . . invited Allen: Grose, *Gentleman Spy*, pp. 108–10.

48   Adolf Hitler: Ibid., pp. 114–15; Srodes, *Allen Dulles*, pp. 170–72.

48   "sinister impression": Grose, *Gentleman Spy*, p. 121.

49   devoted himself . . . to Germany: Pruessen, *John Foster Dulles*, pp. 67–70.

49   From his course: Mosley, *Dulles*, pp. 90, 99.

49   "These dynamic peoples": Grose, *Gentleman Spy*, p. 131.

49   loans to Germany: Ibid., p. 92.

50   He sharply rejected critics: Pruessen, *John Foster Dulles*, pp. 74–75.

50   International Nickel: Lisagor and Lipsius, *Law Unto Itself*, p. 126; Pruessen, *John Foster Dulles*, pp. 127–28.

50   chemical cartel: Pruessen, *John Foster Dulles*, pp. 124–28.

50   loan of nearly $500 million: Ibid., pp. 110, 126.

51   "several provincial governments": Mosley, *Dulles*, p. 88.

51   it "thrived on its cartels": Lisagor and Lipsius, *Law Unto Itself*, p. 125.

51   Drew Pearson: Pruessen, *John Foster Dulles*, p. 123.

51   "facade of starched respectability": Robert E. Conot, *Justice at Nuremberg* (New York: Basic Books, 1983), p. 470.

52   Germany effectively defaulted: Adam Klug, *The German Buybacks, 1932–1939: A Cure for Overhang?* (Princeton: Princeton University International Economics, 1993), pp. 5–54.

52   "cost Americans a billion dollars": Lisagor and Lipsius, *Law Unto Itself*, p. 83.

52   Sullivan & Cromwell had "permitted debt to pile up": Ibid., p. 135.

52   "dynamic" countries . . . "potentialities": Ibid., p. 132.

53   Hotel Esplanade: Ibid., p. 119.

53   "rationalizing this Hitler movement": Mosley, *Dulles*, p. 90.

53 "great harm to our prestige": Ibid., p. 91.

53 "closing down . . . in Germany: Ibid., p. 92; Lisagor and Lipsius, *Law Unto Itself*, pp. 133–34.

53 By some accounts, Foster wept: Srodes, *Allen Dulles*, p. 183; Hoopes, *Devil and John Foster Dulles*, p. 47.

53 he backdated the announcement: Mosley, *Dulles*, p. 92; Lisagor and Lipsius, *Law Unto Itself*, p. 134.

53 He and Janet . . . continued to visit Germany: Pruessen, *John Foster Dulles*, p. 125; Lisagor and Lipsius, *Law Unto Itself*, p. 134; Srodes, *Allen Dulles*, p. 183.

54 Churchill, Roosevelt . . . "warmongers": Mosley, *Dulles*, p. 111.

54 Hitler impressed him: Grose, *Gentleman Spy*, p. 125.

54 "Only hysteria entertains the idea": Ibid., p. 133.

54 "neither in the underlying causes": Mosley, *Dulles*, p. 99.

54 "How can you call yourself a Christian": Ibid., p. 96.

54 "I regret very much": Grose, *Gentleman Spy*, p. 133.

55 to run for a seat in Congress: Srodes, *Allen Dulles*, pp. 189–90; Grose, *Gentleman Spy*, pp. 128–29.

55 Foster wrote a letter: *New York Times*, Mar. 8, 1933.

55 Roosevelt . . . "class feeling": Dulles to Dr. Stanley High, September 11, 1936, Dulles Papers, box 15.

55 testified against . . . Securities Act: Lisagor and Lipsius, *Law Unto Itself*, pp. 113–15.

56 Council on Foreign Relations: Laurence H. Shoup and William Minter, *Imperial Brain Trust: The Council on Foreign Relations and United States Foreign Policy* (Thornton, Ontario: Author's Choice, 2004), pp. 11–56.

57 "No nation can reach the position": Grose, *Gentleman Spy*, p. 125.

57 classified policy memos: Pruessen, *John Foster Dulles*, p. 186.

57 Grose may have been closer: Grose, *Gentleman Spy*, pp. 98, 123.

57 "well ordered domestic economy": Pruessen, *John Foster Dulles*, p. 170.

58 "strategic nexus of international finance": Grose, *Gentleman Spy*, p. 90.

58 "What a difference between them": Ibid., p. 95.

58 relationship with Thomas Dewey: Mosley, *Dulles*, p. 108; Hoopes, *Devil and John Foster Dulles*, pp. 53–54, 70–74; David M. Jordan, *FDR, Dewey, and the Election of 1944* (Bloomington: Indiana University Press, 2011), pp. 100, 217–20, 224.

59 rising to the presidency: Mosley, *Dulles*, p. 79.

59 imagined becoming secretary of state: Grose, *Gentleman Spy*, pp. 82, 97, 109, 128.

59 "Uncle Bert" . . . to do favors: Pruessen, *John Foster Dulles*, pp. 20–23, 61.

59 Pearson . . . "rounds of golf": Grose, *Gentleman Spy*, p. 96.

60 "operator for the bankers": Ibid., p. 110.

60 "Possibly I shouldn't have done it": Ibid., p. 93.

60 "the room": Ibid., pp. 152–53; Srodes, *Allen Dulles*, pp. 152–53, 185–87, 194.

61 Foster . . . was disgusted: Mosley, *Dulles*, p. 107.

61   William Donovan: Anthony Cave Brown, *Wild Bill Donovan: The Last Hero* (New York: Times Books, 1982), pp. 127–43; Richard Dunlop, *Donovan: America's Master Spy* (New York: Rand McNally, 1982), pp. 184–202; Waller, *Wild Bill Donovan*, pp. 50–68.

61   "While in Britain": Allen Dulles, *Craft of Intelligence*, pp. 6–7.

62   "began to beat on Roosevelt": Srodes, *Allen Dulles*, p. 195.

62   Allen . . . an obvious recruit: Dunlop, *Donovan*, p. 203.

3: DULL, DULLER, DULLES

63   Ian Fleming: Srodes, *Allen Dulles*, p. 204.

63   "Donovan was a born leader of men": Allen Dulles, *Craft of Intelligence*, pp. 4, 42.

64   Coordinator of Information: Srodes, *Allen Dulles*, pp. 204–5; Grose, *Gentleman Spy*, pp. 111–12; Rhodri Jeffreys-Jones, *The CIA and American Democracy* (New Haven: Yale University Press, 1989), pp. 16–18.

64   job . . . required "absolute discretion": Grose, *Gentleman Spy*, p. 141.

64   By some accounts he was already working: Srodes, *Allen Dulles*, p. 207.

64   "New York was the logical first place": Ibid., p. 210.

65   two principal assignments: Grose, *Gentleman Spy*, p. 146.

65   Mohawk Trading Corporation: Ibid., p. 146.

65   Allen had chosen his suite: Srodes, *Allen Dulles*, p. 201.

65   "He had much to teach me": Mosley, *Dulles*, p. 114.

66   "Donovan's blueprint": Allen Dulles, *The Secret Surrender* (New York: Harper & Row, 1966), p. 9.

66   Allen hired many of them: Ibid., p. 10.

67   Donovan . . . sent President Roosevelt notice: William J. Donovan, Memorandum for the President no. 537, May 27, 1942, PSF box 166, OSS Files, Roosevelt Presidential Library, Hyde Park, N.Y.

67   "my past experience would serve me": Grose, *Gentleman Spy*, p. 149.

67   Allen had to reach Bern: Allen Dulles, *Secret Surrender*, pp. 13–14.

68   "While my train made its way": Ibid., pp. 13–15.

69   apartment at Herrengasse 23: Srodes, *Allen Dulles*, p. 228.

69   "I had been in Switzerland": Allen Dulles, *Secret Surrender*, p. 15.

70   Nazi agents, who also read the newspapers: Srodes, *Allen Dulles*, p. 236.

70   a quick series of successes: Allen Dulles, *Secret Surrender*, pp. 17, 22–23; Srodes, *Allen Dulles*, pp. 237–38, 302; Grose, *Gentleman Spy*, p. 245.

70   "a tall, burly, sporting type": Grose, *Gentleman Spy*, p. 155.

70   Bancroft was a dynamic woman: Mary Bancroft, *Autobiography of a Spy* (New York: William Morrow, 1983), pp. 8–81.

71   "let the work cover the romance": Ibid., p. 137.

71   Every morning: Ibid., p. 138.

71   "We settled onto the living room couch": Ibid., pp. 152–61.

71   Mary . . . submitted herself to Jung's analysis: Ibid., pp. 91–96.

72   "all news . . . is being discounted": Brown, *Wild Bill Donovan*, pp. 277–78.

72   wildly wrong predictions: Ibid., p. 566.

72   Two began when strangers knocked: Mosley, *Dulles*, p. 137; Srodes, *Allen Dulles*, pp. 177–97, 256–57.

73   "dramatic event may take place": Grose, *Gentleman Spy*, p. 198.

73   Operation Sunrise: Mosley, *Dulles*, pp. 243–44; R. Harris Smith, *OSS: The Secret History of America's First Central Intelligence Agency* (Berkeley: University of California Press, 1972), pp. 105–11; Allen Dulles, *Secret Surrender*, pp. 28–247.

73   emissaries: Mosley, *Dulles*, pp. 143–44.

73   "German armies . . . have surrendered": *Stars and Stripes*, May 3, 1945.

74   Clover . . . formed a remarkably strong bond: Srodes, *Allen Dulles*, pp. 129, 338–41; Mosley, *Dulles*, p. 246; Bancroft, *Autobiography of a Spy*, pp. 290–92.

75   "What had been gained": *New York Review of Books*, Sept. 8, 1966.

75   With the war over: Mosley, *Dulles*, pp. 230–36, 249; Srodes, *Allen Dulles*, p. 400; Waller, *Wild Bill Donovan*, p. 270.

75   transferred the OSS research unit: Mark M. Lowenthal, *U.S. Intelligence: Evolution and Anatomy* (New York: Praeger, 1992), p. 13.

76   Commission . . . Just and Durable Peace: Pruessen, *John Foster Dulles*, p. 190.

76   The society of nation-states: Ibid., pp. 191–92, 205, 208; Toulouse, *Transformation of John Foster Dulles*, pp. 57, 98, 101, 105.

77   "Lunched with A.": Hoopes, *Devil and John Foster Dulles*, p. 53.

77   "To look at him": *Life*, Aug. 21, 1944.

78   Republicans proposed Foster: Toulouse, *Transformation of John Foster Dulles*, p. 133; Hoopes, *Devil and John Foster Dulles*, p. 58; Pruessen, *John Foster Dulles*, pp. 236–37.

78   Foster had become the only major figure: Pruessen, *John Foster Dulles*, pp. 178–79, 187–89, 205–6; William A. Inboden III, *Religion and American Foreign Policy, 1945–1960: The Soul of Containment* (Cambridge: Cambridge University Press, 2010), pp. 41–42.

79   "at least a third": T. Jeremy Gunn, *Spiritual Weapons: The Cold War and the Forging of an American National Religion* (Westport, Conn.: Praeger, 2008), p. 214.

79   "The two Presbyterians": Ibid., pp. 316–17.

80   picture of the Soviet threat: *Life*, June 3 and 10, 1946.

81   Kennan's words, "a great political force": William Nester, *International Relations: Politics and Economics in the 21st Century* (Independence, Ky.: Wadsworth, 2000), p. 234.

81   "scare the hell out of the country": Dean Acheson, *Present at the Creation: My Years in the State Department* (New York: W.W. Norton, 1969), pp. 219–25; James Chace, *Acheson: The Secretary of State Who Created the American World* (New York: Simon and Schuster, 1998), pp. 162–65.

81   "American commitment to individual liberty": Hoopes, *Devil and John Foster Dulles*, p. 116.

81   Foster traveled to Amsterdam: Toulouse, *Transformation of John Foster Dulles*, pp. 198–200.

82   America's refusal to recognize: Pruessen, *John Foster Dulles*, p. 268.

82   "proceed on the assumption": Ibid., p. 279.

83   What led Foster to this turnaround: Imboden, *Religion and American Foreign Policy*, pp. 226–37; Toulouse, *Transformation of John Foster Dulles*, pp. 170–80.

83   "clear understanding of the fundamentals": Toulouse, *Transformation of John Foster Dulles*, p. 170.

83   obsessively reading . . . *Problems of Leninism*: Hoopes, *Devil and John Foster Dulles*, p. 64; Eleanor Lansing Dulles, *John Foster Dulles*, p. 99.

83   In speeches and articles: Toulouse, *Transformation of John Foster Dulles*, pp. 171, 175, 210, 212.

84   "a challenge to established civilization": Pruessen, *John Foster Dulles*, p. 286.

84   "The outlook for world peace": *New York Post*, July 28, 1947.

84   "We are the only great nation": Robert Wuthnow, *The Restructuring of American Religion: Society and Faith Since World War II* (Princeton: Princeton University Press, 1990), p. 38.

85   "the similarity between our sin and the guilt of others": *Christianity and Crisis*, Oct. 19, 1942.

85   "If we should perish": Reinhold Niebuhr, *The Irony of American History* (Chicago: University of Chicago Press, 2008), p. 174.

85   "a streak of lightning": Toulouse, *Transformation of John Foster Dulles*, p. 88.

85   "no doubt about it": Mosley, *Dulles*, p. 194.

4: THAT FELLA FROM WALL STREET

86   "We'll clean up!": Grose, *Gentleman Spy*, p. 247.

86   "Much of the sparkle . . . went out": Bancroft, *Autobiography of a Spy*, p. 139.

86   Allen's . . . favorite companions: Mosley, *Dulles*, pp. 218–20, 225, 258.

87   Central Intelligence Group: Evan Thomas, *The Very Best Men: The Daring Early Years of the CIA* (New York: Simon and Schuster, 1995), p. 28; Joseph J. Trento, *The Secret History of the CIA* (New York: MJF, 2001), p. 45; John Prados, *Safe for Democracy: The Secret Wars of the CIA* (Chicago: Ivan R. Dee, 2006), pp. 32–33; Tim Weiner, *Legacy of Ashes: The History of the CIA* (New York: Doubleday, 2007), pp. 14–19.

87   "The collection of secret intelligence": Srodes, *Allen Dulles*, p. 425.

88   Marshall . . . did not want his department to be involved: Lowenthal, *U.S. Intelligence*, p. 19.

88   "There were strong objections": David M. Barrett, *The CIA and Congress: The Untold Story from Truman to Kennedy* (Lawrence: University Press of Kansas, 2005), pp. 20–24.

88   "The fear generated by competition": Robert Dallek, *The Lost Peace: Leadership in a Time of Horror and Hope, 1945–1953* (New York: Harper, 2010), p. 249.

89   Truman did offer to make him ambassador: Grose, *Gentleman Spy*, p. 281.

89   "not intended to be a 'Cloak and Dagger Outfit'!": Weiner, *Legacy of Ashes*, p. 3.

89   upcoming elections in Italy: Burton Hersh, *The Old Boys: The American Elite and the Origins of the CIA* (New York: Charles Scribner's Sons, 1992), pp. 223–32; James E. Miller, "Taking Off the Gloves: The United States and the Italian Elections of 1948," in *Diplomatic History* 7, no. 1 (Winter 1983), pp. 33–55; Weiner, *Legacy of Ashes*, pp. 29–31; Robin Winks, *Cloak and Gown: Scholars in the Secret War, 1939–1961* (New York: William Morrow, 1987), pp. 383–86.

90   Corsican gangsters: Rhodri Jeffreys-Jones, *Cloak and Dollar: A History of American Secret Intelligence* (New Haven: Yale University Press, 2003), p. 156.

90   *Bogotazo*: Ibid., pp. 53–55.

90   "with dramatic suddenness": Frank Kofsky, *Harry S. Truman and the War Scare of 1948: A Successful Campaign to Deceive the Nation* (New York: Palgrave Macmillan, 1995), p. 93.

90   "near-hysteria": Mosley, *Dulles*, p. 242.

90   NSC 10/2: http://www.voltairenet.org/article163480.html; Sarah-Jane Corke, *US Covert Operations and Cold War Strategy: Truman, Secret Warfare and the CIA, 1945–53* (London: Routledge, 2008), pp. 59–62; William Daugherty, *Executive Secrets: Covert Action and the Presidency* (Lexington: University of Kentucky Press, 2006), pp. 122–24.

91   "that shirt salesman": Mosley, *Dulles*, p. 189.

91   "It is based on the theory": James L. Baughman, *Henry R. Luce and the Rise of the American News Media* (Baltimore: Johns Hopkins University Press, 2001), p. 135.

91   Foster was Dewey's foreign policy adviser: Pruessen, *John Foster Dulles*, p. 359.

92   Foster began making plans: David Pietrusza, *1948: Harry Truman's Improbable Victory and the Year that Transformed America* (New York: Union Square Press, 2011), pp. 189, 196, 340.

92   "You see before you": Mosley, *Dulles*, p. 215.

92   "quite a bombshell": Pruessen, *John Foster Dulles*, p. 387

92   wrote a private proposal: Grose, *Gentleman Spy*, pp. 283–84, 290–92; Pruessen, *John Foster Dulles*, p. 359.

93   he wound up paying a somber call: Grose, *Gentleman Spy*, p. 290.

93   Duck Island: Beal, *John Foster Dulles*, p. 37.

93   lighthouse keeper who had a radio: Ibid., pp. 106–7.

93   "a living instrument for righteousness": Pruessen, *John Foster Dulles*, p. 395.

94   "They even cut your hair": Mosley, *Dulles*, p. 218.

94   "modern-day equivalents of the founders of the Church": Hoopes, *Devil and John Foster Dulles*, p. 78.

94   campaign brochure: Dulles Papers, box 16.

95   The special election was set: Pruessen, *John Foster Dulles*, pp. 395–403; Hoopes, *Devil and John Foster Dulles*, p. 56; Mosley, *Dulles*, pp. 216–21; Grose, *Gentleman Spy*, pp. 298–99; Beal, *John Foster Dulles*, p. 114.

95   "glad that duck lost": Grose, *Gentleman Spy*, p. 299.

95   "What, that bastard": Mosley, *Dulles*, p. 251.

96   "no point in being at the end": Pruessen, *John Foster Dulles*, p. 499.

96   policy decree called NSC-68: NSC-68: United States Objectives and Programs for National Security, http://www.fas.org/irp/offdocs/nsc-hst/nsc-68.htm.

97   "I know nothing": Grose, *Gentleman Spy*, p. 306.

98   "deputy director for plans": Ibid., p. 307; Srodes, *Allen Dulles*, pp. 428–30.

98   Ehrenburg took note: *Washington Post*, Jan. 31, 1969.

98   Smith "did not trust Allen's capacity": Grose, *Gentleman Spy*, pp. 309–10.

98   "Once one gets a taste for it": Hersh, *Old Boys*, p. 95.

99   Congress approved . . . $100 million: Grose, *Gentleman Spy*, p. 332; Barrett, *CIA and Congress*, pp. 103–12.

99   hundreds in Europe, thousands in Asia: Weiner, *Legacy of Ashes*, pp. 46, 54.

99   "At least we're getting experience": Thomas, *Very Best Men*, p. 73.

99   Philby . . . less impressed with Allen: Mosley, *Dulles*, p. 283.

100   "All were gregarious": Thomas Powers, *Intelligence Wars: American Secret History from Hitler to Al-Qaeda* (New York: New York Review of Books, 2002), p. 44.

100   "They were pining to get back": Thomas, *Very Best Men*, p. 24.

101   "Lansdale operated with very little money": Jonathan Nashel, *Edward Lansdale's Cold War* (Amherst: University of Massachusetts Press, 2005), pp. 34–35.

101   American newspapers ran articles: Grose, *Gentleman Spy*, p. 227.

102   officials . . . "hit the ceiling": Ibid., pp. 230–31.

102   "The Director explained": U.S. Department of State, *Foreign Relations of the United States, 1952–1954: Guatemala* (Washington, D.C.: U.S. Government Printing Office, 2003), p. 36.

103   "I didn't feel like raising the matter": *Los Angeles Times*, Mar. 26, 1979.

103   Foster left the general with the manuscript: Grose, *Gentleman Spy*, p. 332.

103   "A Policy of Boldness": *Life*, May 19, 1952.

104   condemned the "containment": Stephen E. Ambrose and Douglas G. Brinkley, *Rise to Globalism: American Foreign Policy Since 1938* (New York: Penguin, 1988), p. 133.

104   "lost the peace": Beal, *John Foster Dulles*, p. 131.

104   Ambrose has written: Stephen E. Ambrose, *Nixon: The Education of a Politician, 1913–1962* (New York: Simon and Schuster, 1988), p. 226.

105   "We were all hysterical": Harry Rositzke, *The CIA's Secret Operations: Espionage, Counterespionage, and Covert Action* (New York: Reader's Digest, 1977), pp. 13–15.

106   leaning toward . . . McCloy: Grose, *Gentleman Spy*, p. 333.

106   also considered Paul Hoffman . . . and Walter Judd: Weiner, *Legacy of Ashes*, p. 28, 32.

106   "a lot of opposition": Mosley, *Dulles*, p. 292.

106   surprising move to block Foster: Gunn, *Spiritual Weapons*, p. 334.

106   confirmation   hearing: http://alvaradohistory.com/yahoo_site_admin/
       assets/docs/3ContainmentorLiberationbyDulles.362195419.pdf.

107   "Smooth is an inadequate word": I. F. Stone, *The Haunted Fifties, 1953–1963: A
       Nonconformist History of Our Times* (Boston: Little, Brown, 1963), pp. 14–16.

107   Smith "made no secret of his concern": Grose, *Gentleman Spy*, p. 335.

107   Donovan, warned Eisenhower: Waller, *Wild Bill Donovan*, pp. 360–64.

108   Ford Foundation: Grose, *Gentleman Spy*, p. 336.

108   "incompatible with democracy": *Washington Post*, Jan. 9, 1953.

108   "left hand of the king": Srodes, *Allen Dulles*, pp. 431–32.

108   she had "the best brain": Mosley, *Dulles*, p. 293.

108   Attitudes . . . still outraged Eleanor: Eleanor Lansing Dulles, *Chances of a
       Lifetime*, pp. 228, 240.

109   Eisenhower . . . inaugural: http://avalon.law.yale.edu/20th_century/eisen1.asp.

110   "It has always surprised me": Bancroft, *Autobiography of a Spy*, p. 139.

5: A WHIRLING DERVISH WITH A COLLEGE EDUCATION

120   OCI proposal: Overseas Consultants Inc., *Report on Seven Year Develop-
       ment Plan for the Plan Organization of the Imperial Government of Iran*
       (New York: OCI, 1949).

120   "OCI provided the King of Kings": *Time*, Oct. 24, 1949.

120   "My government and people are eager": Council on Foreign Relations
       papers, Princeton University, series 4, box 442; James A. Bill, *The Eagle and
       the Lion: The Tragedy of American-Iranian Relations* (New Haven: Yale Uni-
       versity Press, 1988), p. 40.

122   "We were, perhaps, slow": Acheson, *Present at the Creation*, p. 504.

122   "He talked and corresponded": Homa Katouzian, *Mussadiq and the Struggle
       for Power in Iran* (London: I. B. Tauris, 1999), p. 13.

123   "a grandiose plan": Acheson, *Present at the Creation*, p. 501.

123   "break the back of future generations": Center for Documents of the Islamic
       Consultative Assembly, July 29, 1949, http://www.ical.ir/index.php?option=
       com_content& view=article&id=2377&Itemid=12.

123   "Iran should not blindly follow": Center for Documents of the Islamic Consul-
       tative Assembly, Nov. 23, 1948, http://www.ical.ir/index.php?option=com
       _mashrooh&view=session&id=6514&page=122342&Itemid=38.

123   parliament . . . effectively killed it: Acheson, *Present at the Creation*, p.
       502.

123   Foster, who was then seeking business: Geoffrey Wawro, *Quicksand: Ameri-
       ca's Pursuit of Power in the Middle East* (New York: Penguin, 2010), p. 139.

124   Mossadegh's opposition to Western privilege: Bill, *Eagle and the Lion*, pp.
       54–57; James A. Goode, *The United States and Iran: In the Shadow of Musad-
       diq* (New York: Palgrave Macmillan, 1997), p. 13.

124   He rarely ventured out: Immerman, *John Foster Dulles*, p. 10.

124   "I scold my children": Hoopes, *Devil and John Foster Dulles*, p. 144.

124   "clicking noises": Beal, *John Foster Dulles*, p. 10.

125   "His speech was slow": *Times Literary Supplement*, July 19, 1974.

125   "In an Ancient Game": *Time*, Aug. 3, 1953.

125   Foster followed: *Time*, Oct. 12, 1953.

125   dense network of media contacts: Hugh Wilford, *The Mighty Wurlitzer: How the CIA Played America* (Cambridge, Mass.: Harvard University Press, 2008), pp. 225–27; Carl Bernstein, "The CIA and the Media," *Rolling Stone*, Oct. 20, 1977.

125   he could "pick up the phone": Weiner, *Legacy of Ashes*, p. 77.

125   "notoriously thin skin": Barrett, *CIA and Congress*, p. 202.

125   Operation Mockingbird: Deborah Davis, *Katharine the Great: Katharine Graham and the Washington Post* (New York: Harcourt Brace Jovanovich, 1979), pp. 137–38; Mary Louise, "Operation Mockingbird: CIA Media Manipulation," http://www.prisonplanet.com/analysis_louise_01_03_03 _mockingbird.html; Clint Symons, *In Bad Company* (n.p.: CreateSpace, 2009), pp. 44–48, 58–64; "Project Mockingbird," http://www.thedailybell .com/printerVersion.cfm?id=2719.

126   Wisner . . . called it: Wilford, *Mighty Wurlitzer*, p. 226.

126   Home life remained as complicated: Srodes, *Allen Dulles*, p. 450.

126   In his first speech: Hoopes, *Devil and John Foster Dulles*, p. 161; Richard H. Immerman (ed.), *John Foster Dulles and the Diplomacy of the Cold War* (Princeton: Princeton University Press, 1990), pp. 58–59.

127   Mossadegh sent Eisenhower a message: Yonah Alexander and Allen Nanes (eds.), *The United States and Iran: A Documentary History* (Frederick, Md.: Aletheia, 1980), pp. 230–32.

127   a secret trip to Washington: Bill, *Eagle and the Lion*, p. 86; Weiner, *Legacy of Ashes*, p. 655.

127   "When we knew what the prejudices": Christopher Montague Woodhouse, *Something Ventured* (London: Granada, 1982), p. 117.

127   "initially took little interest": Jean Edward Smith, *Eisenhower in War and Peace* (New York: Random House, 2012), p. 623.

127   "newly installed chief": Weiner, *Legacy of Ashes*, p. 83.

128   vivid dispatches: Goode, *United States and Iran*, p. 116.

128   wanted his country "to avoid entanglement": B. R. Nanda, *Indian Foreign Policy: The Nehru Years* (Delhi: Vikas, 1976), p. 134.

128   "we've never had trouble": H. W. Brands, *The Devil We Knew: Americans and the Cold War* (New York: Oxford University Press, 1994), p. 53.

128   "They might be more or less invisible": David Halberstam, *The Fifties* (New York: Villard, 1993), pp. 373–74.

129   "United States clearly had an interest": Bill, *Eagle and the Lion*, p. 81.

130   "If disorders flare up": *Life*, June 4, 1951.

130   "driven back to our island": Wawro, *Quicksand*, p. 132.

130   Truman to "gallop together": Mostafa Elm, *Oil, Power, and Principle: Iran's*

Oil Natioralization and Its Aftermath (Syracuse, N.Y.: Syracuse University Press, 1992), pp. 250–52.

131   "distinct cleavage": Acheson, *Present at the Creation*, p. 505.

131   Eisenhower came into office believing: Blanche Wiesen Cook, *The Declassified Eisenhower: A Divided Legacy of Peace and Political Warfare* (Garden City, N.Y.: Doubleday, 1981), p. 106.

131   "If it weren't for the Cold War": Wawro, *Quicksand*, p. 139.

131   as many as ten times: Dwight Eisenhower, oral history, Dulles Papers.

131   Foster and Allen: Mosley, *Dulles*, p. 344; Immerman, *John Foster Dulles*, p. 134; Grose, *Gentleman Spy*, p. 339.

131   "The line between intelligence and policy": Grose, *Gentleman Spy*, p. 341.

132   "Many of the liberals": Jeffreys-Jones, *CIA and American Democracy*, p. 76.

132   "if I could not be where I had grown up": Grose, *Gentleman Spy*, p. 342.

132   truly global organization: Ted Gup, *The Book of Honor: Covert Lives and Classified Deaths at the CIA* (New York: Doubleday, 2000), p. 74.

132   fifteen thousand employees in fifty countries: Weiner, *Legacy of Ashes*, p. 68; Barrett, *CIA and Congress*, p. 149.

132   operations in Eastern Europe: Rositzke, *CIA's Secret Operations*, pp. 169–71; Prados, *Safe for Democracy*, pp. 59–64, 70–77.

132   did not foresee Stalin's death: Trento, *Secret History of the CIA*, pp. 106–7.

132   Burma was an early example: Prados, *Safe for Democracy*, pp. 134–37; David Wise and Thomas B. Ross, *The Invisible Government* (New York: Random House, 1964), pp. 129–32.

133   National Security Council: Grose, *Gentleman Spy*, p. 500; Karl F. Inderfurth and Loch K. Johnson (eds.), *Fateful Decisions: Inside the National Security Council* (New York: Oxford University Press, 2004), pp. 17–62.

133   March 4, 1953: *FRUS*, Iran, pp. 692–99.

134   exploded in frustration: Goode, *United States and Iran*, p. 111.

134   "Moscow's involvement in Iran was negligible": Immerman, *John Foster Dulles*, p. 65.

134   "Eisenhower participated in none of the meetings": Stephen E. Ambrose, *Eisenhower: Soldier and President* (New York: Simon and Schuster, 1991), p. 333.

134   Allen signed an order: Prados, *Safe for Democracy*, p. 102.

135   MKULTRA: "Declassified MK-Ultra Project Documents." http://www.michael-robinett.com/declass/c000.htm; *Project MKUltra, the CIA's Program of Research into Behavioral Modification. Joint Hearing before the Select Committee on Intelligence and the Subcommittee on Health and Scientific Research of the Committee on Human Resources, United States Senate, Ninety-fifth Congress, First Session, August 3, 1977* (Government Printing Office, 1977); *New York Times*, Sept. 3, 1977; *Final Report of the Select Committee to Study Governmental Operations with Respect to Intelligence Activities, United States Senate, Together with Additional, Supplemental, and Separate Views, April 26, 1976* (Washington: U.S. Senate, 1976), pp. 385–420.

135   One prisoner who participated: Dick Lehr and Gerard O'Neill, *Whitey: The Life of America's Most Notorious Mob Boss* (New York: Crown, 2013), p. 121.

135   secret prisons: Weiner, *Legacy of Ashes*, p. 64.

135   farthest-reaching projects: Daniele Ganser, "Terrorism in Western Europe: An Approach to NATO's Secret Stay-Behind Armies," *Whitehead Journal of Diplomacy and International Relations* 6, no. 1 (Winter/Spring 2005); *New York Times*, Nov. 16, 1990; *Guardian*, Mar. 26, 2001; *Nation*, Apr. 6, 1992; John Prados, *William Colby and the CIA: The Secret Wars of a Controversial Spymaster* (Lawrence: University Press of Kansas, 2009), pp. 53–56.

136   House Appropriations Committee: Barrett, *CIA and Congress*, pp. 150–52.

137   withheld "no secrets": Ibid., pp. 238–39.

137   "We cannot defend the nation": Richard A. Melanson and David Mayers (eds.), *Reevaluating Eisenhower: American Foreign Policy in the Fifties* (Urbana: University of Illinois Press, 1989), p. 54.

138   "disturbing revelation": *New York Times*, Apr. 24, 1953.

138   Eisenhower's favorite: *High Noon: New York Review of Books*, Apr. 26, 2012.

138   "In their recognition": Stanley Corkin, *Cowboys as Cold Warriors: The Western and U.S. History* (Philadelphia: Temple University Press, 2004), pp. 130, 151, 153.

138   "no disposition to meddle": *New York Times*, May 25, 1953.

139   "Although it was hoped": Alexander and Nanes, *United States and Iran*, pp. 232–33.

139   "how we get rid of that madman": Wawro, *Quicksand*, pp. 142–43.

139   "anything but assent would be ill-received": Kermit Roosevelt, *Countercoup: The Struggle for Control of Iran* (New York: McGraw-Hill, 1979), pp. 1–19.

140   calling the president: Wawro, *Quicksand*, p. 143.

140   Eisenhower sent a tart answer: Alexander and Nanes, *United States and Iran*, pp. 234–35.

140   Eleanor had been given this post: Eleanor Lansing Dulles, *Chances of a Lifetime*, p. 243.

141   "Riddleberger went to see Foster": Srodes, *Allen Dulles*, p. 406.

141   the morning of June 16: Eleanor Lansing Dulles, *Chances of a Lifetime*, pp. 253–55.

141   "fascist putsch was staged": Grose, *Gentleman Spy*, p. 357.

141   "Some of the provocateurs": Andrew Tully, *Central Intelligence Agency: The Inside Story* (New York: Corgi, 1963), p. 64.

142   "woefully lacks any prospect": Goode, *United States and Iran*, p. 116.

142   Goiran . . . wrote himself out of the script: Stephen Dorril, *MI6: Inside the Covert World of Her Majesty's Secret Intelligence Service* (New York: Free Press, 2000), p. 584.

143   Douglas . . . championed Mossadegh: William O. Douglas, *Strange Lands and Friendly People* (New York, Harper, 1951), p. 119.

143   "If you and I were in Persia": *New Republic*, Apr. 28, 1952.

143   Foster never forgot the trauma: Eleanor Lansing Dulles, *John Foster Dulles*, p. 129.

143   "find a basis for cooperation": Laura A. Belmonte, *Selling the American Way: U.S. Propaganda and the Cold War* (Philadelphia: University of Pennsylvania Press, 2010), p. 52.

143   singled out John Carter Vincent . . . and John Paton Davies: Hoopes, *Devil and John Foster Dulles*, pp. 153–55.

144   "positive loyalty": Ibid., p. 158.

144   called the CIA: Ted Morgan, *Reds: McCarthyism in Twentieth-Century America* (New York: Random House, 2004) pp. 448–54; Grose, *Gentleman Spy*, pp. 344–46; Weiner, *Legacy of Ashes*, p. 106.

145   Roosevelt crossed into Iran: Stephen E. Ambrose, *Ike's Spies: Eisenhower and the Espionage Establishment* (Jackson: University of Mississippi Press, 1981), pp. 206–14; Bill, *Eagle and the Lion*, pp. 86–94; Central Intelligence Agency, *Overthrow of Premier Mossadeq of Iran, November 1952–August 1953*, http://www.nytimes.com/library/world/mideast/041600iran-cia-index.html; Richard W. Cottam, *Iran and the United States: A Cold War Case Study* (Pittsburgh: University of Pittsburgh Press, 1988), pp. 103–9; Dorril, *MI6*, pp. 558–600; Goode, *United States and Iran*, pp. 109–37; Stephen Kinzer, *All the Shah's Men: An American Coup and the Roots of Middle East Terror* (Hoboken, N.J.: John Wiley & Sons, 2003), pp. 1–16, 165–88; Prados, *Safe for Democracy*, pp. 99–107; Roosevelt, *Countercoup*, pp. 140–203; Weiner, *Legacy of Ashes*, pp. 81–92.

146   "serious defeat": Robert A. Divine, *Eisenhower and the Cold War* (Oxford: Oxford University Press, 1981), p. 76.

6: THE MOST FORTHRIGHT PRO-COMMUNIST

147   Guatemalan figurines decorated: Grose, *Gentleman Spy*, p. 370; photos of Allen's home in Dulles Papers, box 127.

147   "Some paradox": Lionel Trilling, *The Liberal Imagination* (New York: New York Review of Books, 2008), p. 221.

148   "If the finance minister were to overdraw": *Fortune*, Mar. 1933.

148   Sullivan & Cromwell also represented: Author's interview with Thomas McCann, 2013.

148   signed in 1936: Richard H. Immerman, *The CIA in Guatemala: The Foreign Policy of Intervention* (Austin: University of Texas Press, 1982), p. 71.

148   "Dulles . . . reputed to be the author": Thomas McCann, *An American Company: The Tragedy of United Fruit* (New York: Random House, 1988), p. 56; Immerman, *CIA in Guatemala*, p. 124.

149   "legal and pseudo-legal assaults": *New York Times*, Feb. 26, 1949.

149   "Guatemala's government": McCann, *American Company*, p. 45.

149   inaugural address: Juan José Arévalo and Jacobo Arbenz. *Discursos del Doctor Juan José Arévalo y del Teniente Coronel Jacobo Arbenz Guzmán en el*

Acto de Transmisión de la Presidencia de la República (Guatemala: Tipografía Nacional, 1951), p. 26.

150 "I reported at the White House": Roosevelt, *Countercoup* pp. 209–10.

151 Eisenhower offered Foster his job: Eleanor Lansing Dulles, *Chances of a Lifetime*, p. 314.

152 "This fellow preaches": John Lukacs, *Churchill: Visionary. Statesman. Historian.* (New Haven: Yale University Press, 2004), p. 80.

152 European Defense Community: Mosley, *Dulles*, p. 324; Hoopes, *Devil and John Foster Dulles*, pp. 162–165; Immerman (ed.), *John Foster Dulles and the Diplomacy of the Cold War*, pp. 79–98.

152 "Employed to inspire the allies": Chris Tudda, *Truth Is Our Weapon: The Rhetorical Diplomacy of Dwight D. Eisenhower and John Foster Dulles* (Baton Rouge: Louisiana State University Press, 2006), pp. 72–73.

153 "different packages" tied together: Kenneth Osgood, *Total Cold War: Eisenhower's Secret Propaganda Battle at Home and Abroad* (Lawrence: University Press of Kansas, 2008), pp. 198–99.

153 "perception that the USSR was using negotiations": Ibid., pp. 212–13.

154 "Adenauer wanted to know": Eleanor Lansing Dulles, *Chances of a Lifetime*, pp. 245–46.

155 "cataclysmic powers": Immerman (ed.), *John Foster Dulles and the Diplomacy of the Cold War*, p. 111.

155 "shortcomings of a serious nature": Ibid., p. 272.

155 The first spy . . . second was quickly: Weiner, *Legacy of Ashes*, p. 110.

155 A team that he assembled: Grose, *Gentleman Spy*, pp. 402–4.

156 "This law has affected United Fruit Company land": Guillermo Toriello, *La Batalla de Guatemala* (Santiago de Chile: Editorial Universitaria, 1955), pp. 249–53.

156 ties to United Fruit: Immerman, *CIA in Guatemala*, pp. 116–18, 124–25; McCann, *American Company*, p. 56; Peter Chapman, *Bananas: How the United Fruit Company Shaped the World* (Edinburgh: Canongate, 2009), p. 98; Toriello, *Batalla de Guatemala*, p. 501.

157 *Why the Kremlin Hates Bananas*: Gunn, *Spiritual Weapons*, p. 141.

157 "In Czechoslovakia": Author's interview with Arthur Hulnick, 2012.

157 first proposal: *FRUS*, Guatemala, pp. 102–8.

158 "most vitally important": Prados, *Safe for Democracy*, p. 116.

158 "Dulles became the executive agent": Ibid., pp. 109–10.

158 Arbenz . . . speak defiantly: *Time,* Mar. 15, 1954.

158 overthrowing Figueres: Wise and Ross, *Invisible Government*, pp. 127–28.

159 "Our main enemy": Immerman (ed.), *John Foster Dulles and the Diplomacy of the Cold War*, p. 171.

159 the official position: Kenneth Lehman, "Revolutions and Attributions: Making Sense of Eisenhower Administration Policies in Bolivia and Guatemala," *Diplomatic History* 21, no. 2 (Spring 1997), pp. 185–213.

159 "Marxist rather than communist": Ibid., p. 193.

159 "Bolivia was far from the United States": Bryce Wood, *The Dismantling of the Good Neighbor Policy* (Austin: University of Texas Press, 1985), p. 151.

160 "You don't know what you're talking about": Halberstam, *Fifties*, p. 373.

160 "The CIA recruiter asked my college president": Author's interview with retired CIA officer, 2012.

162 "You've just joined the Cold War arm": Joseph B. Smith, *Portrait of a Cold Warrior: Second Thoughts of a Top CIA Agent* (New York: Ballantine, 1976), p. 55.

163 Mansfield delivered the sharpest public critique: Barrett, *CIA and Congress*, p. 173.

163 "aggressive and suspicious nature": Ibid., pp. 172–75.

163 managed to derail the bill: Jeffreys-Jones, *CIA and American Democracy*, p. 78.

163 "Never before or since": Mosley, *Dulles*, pp. 364–65.

164 "State Department for unfriendly countries": Ambrose, *Ike's Spies*, p. 178.

164 "phenomenal" quantities: Srodes, *Allen Dulles*, p. 345.

165 "too cautious": Prados, *Safe for Democracy*, p. 110.

165 situation "very ticklish": John Moors Cabot, oral history, Dulles Papers.

165 gave a dramatic speech: U.S. Department of State, *Tenth Inter-American Conference: Report of the Delegation of the United States of America with Related Documents* (Washington, D.C.: U.S. Government Printing Office, 1955), p. 9.

166 "conspirators and the foreign monopolies": Toriello, *Batalla de Guatemala*, p. 91.

166 One delegate: *Time*, Mar. 15, 1954.

166 It declared that: http://avalon.law.yale.edu/20th_century/intam10.asp.

166 Toriello later marveled: Toriello, *Batalla de Guatemala*, p. 77.

166 "striking victory for freedom": *Washington Post*, Mar. 15, 1954.

166 "triumph for Secretary Dulles": *New York Times*, Mar. 14, 1954.

167 one of the largest bases: Nick Cullather, *Secret History: The CIA's Classified Account of Its Operations in Guatemala, 1952–1954* (Stanford: Stanford University Press, 1999), p. 46; Immerman, *CIA in Guatemala*, p. 138.

167 "Continue the good work": Prados, *Safe for Democracy*, p. 116.

167 had Gruson recalled: Cullather, *Secret History*, p. 94.

167 had rarely appeared in print: Barrett, *CIA and Congress*, pp. 166–67.

168 one of every fifty: Cullather, *Secret History*, p. 41.

168 "inspired . . . by the devil": David Aikman, *Billy Graham: His Life and Influence* (Nashville: Thomas Nelson, 2007), p. 68.

169 admired Francisco Franco: Greg Grandin, *The Last Colonial Massacre: Latin America in the Cold War* (Chicago: University of Chicago Press, 2011), pp. 80, 236.

169 "approached Spellman in 1954": John Cooney, *The American Pope: The Life and Times of Francis Cardinal Spellman* (New York: Dell, 1986), p. 297.

169 pastoral letter: *El Calvario de Guatemala* (Guatemala: Comité de Estudiantes Universitarias Anticomunistas, 1955), pp. 319–24.

170 directed their Guatemala team: *FRUS*, Guatemala, pp. 267–68.

170   "considered himself a communist": Piero Gleijeses, *Shattered Hope: The Guatemalan Revolution and the United States, 1944–1954* (Princeton: Princeton University Press, 1991), p. 147.

170   constitution required: Ibid., p. 205.

171   "Guatemalan aggression": *New York Times*, May 25, 1954.

171   "be damn good and sure": W. Thomas Smith, *Encyclopedia of the Central Intelligence Agency* (New York: Facts on File, 2003), p. 115.

171   "With the Dulles Brothers": *New York Times*, June 20, 1954.

172   "If at any time": Stephen G. Rabe, *Eisenhower and Latin America: The Foreign Policy of Anticommunism* (Chapel Hill: University of North Carolina Press, 1988), p. 60.

173   "Heartiest congratulations": *FRUS*, Guatemala, p. 409.

173   "Thanks, Allen": Rabe, *Eisenhower and Latin America*, p. 81.

173   Some were dubious: *FRUS*, Guatemala, p. 377.

173   "Tonight I should like to talk": United States Department of State, *Intervention of International Communism in the Americas*, Publication 5556 (Washington, D.C.: Department of State, 1954), pp. 30–34.

174   A few months later: Toriello, *Batalla de Guatemala*, p. 9.

7: A MATCHLESS INTERPLAY OF RUTHLESSNESS AND GUILE

175   "Mysterious Doings of the CIA": *Saturday Evening Post*, Oct. 30, Nov. 6, and Nov. 13, 1954.

176   "Man of the Year": *Time*, Jan. 3, 1955.

177   he quoted American scripture: Paul M. Kattenburg, *The Vietnam Trauma in American Foreign Policy, 1945–75* (New Brunswick, N.J.: Transaction, 1980), p. 119; Fredrik Logevall, *Embers of War: The Fall of an Empire and the Making of America's Vietnam* (New York: Random House, 2012), pp. 642–45.

178   American diplomats in Vietnam reported: Michael H. Hunt, *Lyndon Johnson's War: America's Cold War Crusade in Vietnam, 1945–1968* (New York: Hill & Wang, 1997), p. 9.

178   Douglas wrote: William O. Douglas, *North from Malaya* (New York: Doubleday, 1953), pp. 150, 153, 165.

178   Washington press conference: Hoopes, *Devil and John Foster Dulles*, p. 209.

179   "Not unless our automobiles collide": Langguth, *Our Vietnam*, p. 72.

179   "Question whether Ho": *FRUS*, Vietnam, vol. 7, pp. 29–30.

179   "To lose those countries": Hunt, *Lyndon Johnson's War*, p. 11.

179   subsidizing France's war: *The Pentagon Papers, Gravel Edition* (Boston: Beacon Press, 1971), volume 1, chapter 4, "U.S. and France in Indochina, 1950–56," https://www.mtholyoke.edu/acad/intrel/pentagon/pent9.htm.

180   One mid-level figure: Kattenburg, *Vietnam Trauma*, p. 40.

181   "just no sense in talking about": Blema S. Steinberg, *Shame and Humiliation: Presidential Decision Making on Vietnam* (Montreal: McGill Queens University Press, 1996), p. 257.

181 "Nothing could hold Dulles back": David Halberstam, *The Best and the Brightest* (New York: Penguin, 1972), p. 180.

181 "from a scratch on the map": *Time*, Mar. 29, 1954.

181 "a matchless interplay": *Time*, Nov. 22, 1954.

181 "immediate armed intervention": Robert D. Schulzinger, *A Time for War: The United States and Vietnam, 1941–1975* (New York: Oxford University Press, 1999), p. 67.

181 Eisenhower appealed to Prime Minister Churchill: John Prados, *Vietnam: The History of an Unwinnable War, 1945–1975* (Lawrence: University Press of Kansas, 2009), p. 29.

182 "loss of the fortress": Logevall, *Embers of War*, p. 506.

182 Hagerty, warned that: James C. Hagerty Papers, Hagerty Diary, July 11, 1954, Dwight D. Eisenhower Presidential Library.

182 "In certain areas at least": Robert Mann, *A Grand Delusion: America's Descent into Vietnam* (New York: Basic Books, 2001), p. 152.

182 "against sending American GI's into the mud": Gerald Astor, *Presidents at War: From Truman to Bush, the Gathering of Military Power to Our Commanders in Chief* (Hoboken, N.J.: John Wiley & Sons, 2006), p. 54.

182 only "intervention on a Korean scale": Arthur M. Schlesinger Jr., *A Thousand Days: John F. Kennedy in the White House* (New York: Mariner, 2002), p. 322.

183 "wishful thinking": Kathryn Statler, *Replacing France: The Origins of American Intervention in Vietnam* (Lexington: University Press of Kentucky, 2009), p. 110.

183 "Far Eastern Munich": Herbert S. Parmet, *Eisenhower and the American Crusades* (New York: Macmillan, 1972), p. 303.

183 "develop plans . . . for certain contingencies": John P. Burke and Fred I. Greenstein, *How Presidents Test Reality: Decisions on Vietnam 1954 and 1965* (New York: Russell Sage Foundation, 1989), p. 36.

183 Foster launched his part: Address to Overseas Press Club, Dulles Papers, box 87.

184 claimed to have cabinet-level sources: Mosley, *Dulles*, p. 324.

185 John . . . defected: Tully, *Central Intelligence Agency*, pp. 57–58.

185 Liberal Democratic Party: Weiner, *Legacy of Ashes*, pp. 119–20.

185 "We ran Japan": Ibid., p. 121.

185 propaganda and mass psychology: Osgood, *Total Cold War*, p. 303.

186 "These covertly sponsored activities": Rositzke, *CIA's Secret Operations*, p. 162.

186 *Animal Farm*: Frances Stonor Saunders, *The Cultural Cold War: The CIA and the World of Arts and Letters* (New York: New Press, 2001), pp. 293–95.

186 "a child's enjoyment": Srodes, *Allen Dulles*, p. 453.

186 "Dulles was enthralled": Trento, *Secret History of the CIA*, p. 168.

187 Doolittle's conclusions: http://cryptome.org/cia-doolittle.pdf.

187 fire Allen Dulles: George C. Herring, *America's Longest War: The United States and Vietnam, 1950–1975* (New York: McGraw-Hill, 1986), p. 356; Weiner, *Legacy of Ashes*, p. 108.

188   A senior British agent: Ambrose, *Ike's Spies*, p. 174.

188   phone-tapping tunnel: Trento, *Secret History of the CIA*, pp. 144–46, 161; Weiner, *Legacy of Ashes*, pp. 110–12.

188   "one of the major coups": Prados, *Safe for Democracy*, pp. 153–55; Weiner, *Legacy of Ashes*, pp. 123–25.

189   Buraimi Oasis: Wawro, *Quicksand*, pp. 228–29; Mosley, *Dulles*, pp. 348–49; Tore T. Peterson, "Anglo-American Rivalry in the Middle East: The Struggle for the Buraimi Oasis, 1952–1957," *International History Review* 14, no. 1 (Feb. 1992), pp. 71–91.

189   More successful: Mosley, *Dulles*, pp. 350–51.

190   "The process of delegation": Eugene McCarthy, *Up 'Til Now: A Memoir* (New York: Harcourt, 1987), p. 128.

191   "pathological rage and gloom": Immerman, *John Foster Dulles*, p. 93.

191   "pinched distaste of a puritan": Hoopes, *Devil and John Foster Dulles*, p. 222.

191   "At the first meeting": U. Alexis Johnson, oral history, Dulles Papers.

191   "governments or rulers that do not respect": *New York Times*, Jan. 19, 1954.

192   "Dull, unimaginative, uncomprehending": Logevall, *Embers of War*, p. 557.

192   "leave it to the Communists": Maurice Couve de Murville, oral history, Dulles Papers.

192   "French blood will no longer flow": Logevall, *Embers of War*, p. 612.

192   "refrain from the threat or use of force": William J. Duiker, *U.S. Containment Policy and the Conflict in Indochina* (Stanford: Stanford University Press, 1994), pp. 188–89.

192   He believed the United States had a duty: Richard H. Immerman, *Empire for Liberty: A History of American Imperialism from Benjamin Franklin to Paul Wolfowitz* (Princeton: Princeton University Press, 2010), pp. 192–93.

193   "extremely pig-headed": Gunn, *Spiritual Weapons*, p. 169.

193   "a psychopath": Ibid., p. 162.

193   "I had said to Foster Dulles": Maurice Couve de Murville, oral history, Dulles Papers.

194   "I want you to do": Nashel, *Edward Lansdale's Cold War*, p. 136.

194   Lansdale saved him twice: Stanley Karnow, *Vietnam: A History* (New York: Viking, 1983), pp. 221–22; Logevall, *Embers of War*, pp. 642–45.

195   "Up to now": Ho Chi Minh, *Down with Colonialism!* (London: Verso, 2007), p. 134.

195   every Vietnamese agent: Cook, *Declassified Eisenhower*, p. 246.

195   more than 150 different books: Osgood, *Total Cold War*, p. 118.

195   "extremely intensive . . . operation": Bernard Fall, *The Two Vietnams: A Political and Military Analysis* (Westport, Conn.: Greenwood, 1967), pp. 153–54.

196   In his best-selling book: Tom Dooley, *Deliver Us from Evil* (New York: Signet, 1981), pp. 55, 139.

197   "The American press reported": Gunn, *Spiritual Weapons*, p. 171.

197   "As a key agent": Peter Brush, "Doctor Tom Dooley," http://www.library
       .vanderbilt.edu/central/Brush/Tom-Dooley.htm.

197   "A remarkable lack of psychology": Statler, *Replacing France*, p. 108.

199   "more likely to promote mistrust": Lubna Saif, "Pakistan and SEATO," *Pakistan Journal of History and Culture* 28, no. 2 (2007), p. 84.

199   "When military aid comes in": L. Natarajan, *American Shadow over India* (New Delhi: People's Publishing House, 1956), p. 147.

199   "nothing . . . has so exercised India: *New York Times*, Jan. 10, 1953.

199   "sharp deterioration": *New York Times*, Jan. 25, 1953.

199   Foster was sympathetic: Hoopes, *Devil and John Foster Dulles*, pp. 277–78.

200   "We're not talking now": Ibid., p. 266.

200   "One must look to . . . Dulles": Daniel Aaron Rubin, "Pawns of the Cold War: John Foster Dulles, the PRC, and the Imprisonments of John Downey and Richard Fecteau," http://drum.lib.umd.edu/bitstream/1903/1839/1/umi-umd-1832.pdf.

201   "absolutely no regard": Mosley, *Dulles*, pp. 353–54.

201   "always ready to go on the rampage": James Cable, *The Geneva Conference of 1954 on Indochina* (New York: St. Martin's, 1986), p. 38.

201   "Dulles is the only case I know": Mosley, *Dulles*, p. 361.

202   "My Power Is the Love of the People": *Time*, Oct. 26, 1953.

202   "When you figure": Mosley, *Dulles*, p. 380.

202   "heavy opaqueness": Hoopes, *Devil and John Foster Dulles*, p. 142.

203   "department has gone too far": Ibid., p. 144.

203   "How terrifically dynamic": Richard Wright, *The Color Curtain* (Oxford: University Press of Mississippi, 1995), p. 136.

203   "communist road show": *Time*, Apr. 18, 1955.

203   "so-called Afro-Asian conference": Wright, *Color Curtain*, p. 88.

203   In private his aides scorned it: Herring, *America's Longest War*, p. 395.

203   They cheered Nehru : George McTurnan Kahin, *Asian-African Conference: Bandung, Indonesia* (Ithaca, N.Y.: Cornell University Press, 1956), p. 65.

203   Nasser insisted: The Asian African Conference, *Vital Speeches of the Day*, June 1, 1955, p. 1258.

204   "affable of manner": Carlos Romulo, *The Meaning of Bandung* (Chapel Hill: University of North Carolina Press, 1956), p. 11.

204   "He behaved very humbly": Goold-Adams, *John Foster Dulles*, p. 168.

204   Powell wrote in his memoir: Adam Clayton Powell III, *Adam by Adam: The Autobiography of Adam Clayton Powell, Jr.* (New York: Kensington, 2001), pp. 107–9.

205   "There was something extra-political": Wright, *Color Curtain*, p. 14.

205   Malcolm X did not attend: George Breitman (ed.), *Malcolm X Speaks: Selected Speeches and Statements* (New York: Merit, 1965), p. 5.

206   "pactomania": Hoopes, *Devil and John Foster Dulles*, p. 241.

207   "possibly eighty percent": Gunn, *Spiritual Weapons*, p. 175.

207   "gentleman's agreement": Daniel P. O'C. Greene, "John Foster Dulles and the End of the Franco-American Entente in Indochina," *Diplomatic History* 16, no. 4 (Oct. 1992), p. 551.

207   "suppression of alternatives": Pentagon Papers, Section 1, pp. 179–214, https://www.mtholyoke.edu/acad/intrel/pentagon/pent9.htm.

207   an interview he gave: *Life,* Jan. 30, 1956.

207   "edgy gambler": Hoopes, *Devil and John Foster Dulles*, p. 311.

208   "He doesn't just stumble": *New York Times*, Jan. 15, 1956.

208   "We will not be tied down": Jessica Chapman, "Staging Democracy: South Vietnam's 1955 Referendum to Depose Bao Dai," *Diplomatic History* 30, no. 4 (Sept. 2006), p. 694.

208   a "dung beetle": Ibid.

208   claimed more than 600,000 votes: Anthony Best et al., *International History of the Twentieth Century and Beyond* (London: Routledge, 2008), p. 298.

208   put aside their doubts: Jessica Chapman, "Staging Democracy," pp. 698–99.

209   "No systematic or serious examination": *New York Review of Books*, Dec. 2, 1971.

209   Foster considered the possibility: John R. Lampe et al., *Yugoslav-American Economic Relations Since World War II* (Durham, N.C.: Duke University Press, 1990), p. 57; Lorraine M. Lees, *Keeping Tito Afloat: The United States, Yugoslavia, and the Cold War* (University Park: Pennsylvania State University Press, 1997), pp. 144–46, 155.

210   "We have been exploring ways": Arthur J. Dommen, *The Indochinese Experience of the French and the Americans: Nationalism and Communism in Cambodia, Laos, and Vietnam* (Bloomington: Indiana University Press, 2002), p. 275.

210   "long-range program": Pentagon Papers, Part IV, A, 3, http://en.wikisource .org/wiki/United_States_%E2%80%93_Vietnam_Relations,_1945%E2%80 %931967:_A_Study_Prepated_by_the_Department_of_Defense/IV._A._3 ._U.S._and_France%27s_Withdrawal_from_Vietnam,_1954%E2%80 %9356.

210   "None of [Foster] Dulles's actions": Hoopes, *Devil and John Foster Dulles*, p. 202.

211   set out to circle the globe: Grose, *Gentleman Spy*, p. 432.

211   Soviets "have never occupied": John Lewis Gaddis, *We Now Know: Rethinking Cold War History* (Oxford: Clarendon, 1997), p. 168.

211   Allen sent Kermit Roosevelt: Wawro, *Quicksand*, p. 169.

212   "Remember Guatemala": Mosley, *Dulles*, p. 388.

212   "choke on your fury": Tully, *Central Intelligence Agency*, p. 108.

214   "administrative inadequacies of Allen Dulles": Jeffreys-Jones, *CIA and American Democracy*, p. 108.

214   prepare a report on the CIA: http://cryptome.org/0001/bruce-lovett.htm.

215   second inaugural address: http://www.pagebypagebooks.com/Dwight_D
       _Eisenhower/Second_Inaugural_Address/Second_Inaugural_Address_p1
       .html.

8: THE SELF-INTOXICATED PRESIDENT

216   "today is a famous anniversary": *Vital Speeches of the Day* 21, no. 16, June 1,
       1955, pp. 1250–51.
216   "As the leader and personification": *FRUS*, Indonesia, p. 236.
217   Their meeting was pleasant: Cindy Adams and Sukarno, *Sukarno: An Auto-
       biography* (New York: Bobbs-Merrill, 1965), p. 227.
217   "I am a brown man": *Baltimore Evening Sun*, May 17, 1956.
217   "Sukarno Captivates Washington": *New York Times*, May 16, 1956.
217   "President Wows Capital": *St. Louis Globe Democrat*, May 17, 1956.
217   "sensitive Asian nationalist": *New York Times*, May 17, 1956.
217   "Understand that, and you have the key": *New York Herald Tribune*, May 17,
       1956.
218   two-week tour: Paul F. Gardner, *Shared Hopes, Separate Fears: Fifty Years of
       U.S.-Indonesian Relations* (Boulder, Colo.: Westview, 1997), p. 126; Brian May,
       The Indonesian Tragedy (n.p.: Non Basic Stock Line, 2000), p. 126; *Washington
       Post*, May 18, 1956.
218   "I find only one fault": Adams and Sukarno, *Sukarno*, p. 275.
218   "tried to explain": May, *Indonesian Tragedy*, p. 128.
219   loan "will place Soviet 'technicians'": *Time*, Sept. 24, 1956.
219   Sukarno felt insulted: Adams and Sukarno, *Sukarno*, p. 294.
220   "I think it's time": Smith, *Portrait of a Cold Warrior*, p. 197.
220   one of the largest-scale covert operations: Prados, *Safe for Democracy*,
       p. 140.
220   "During the late 1950s": Audrey R. Kahin and George McT. Kahin, *Subver-
       sion as Foreign Policy: The Secret Eisenhower and Dulles Debacle in Indone-
       sia* (Seattle: University of Washington Press, 1995), pp. 3, 106.
221   "three gorgeous . . . stewardesses": John Ranelagh, *The Agency: The Rise and
       Decline of the CIA* (London: Sceptre, 1988), p. 334.
222   Khrushchev changed course: Odd Arne Westad, *The Global Cold War: Third
       World Interventions and the Making of Our Times* (Cambridge: Cambridge
       University Press, 2007), p. 68.
222   softer line was "a strategy": Osgood, *Total Cold War*, p. 70.
222   "Far from seeing": Ibid., p. 68.
223   tourism in the Soviet Union: Ibid., p. 217; Rositzke, *CIA's Secret Operations*,
       pp. 59–60.
223   begin obtaining the weaponry: Rositzke, *CIA's Secret Operations*, p. 61.
224   "If that colonel of yours": Hoopes, *Devil and John Foster Dulles*, p. 373.
224   "even drastic ones": Ray Takeyh, *The Origins of the Eisenhower Doctrine: The*

US, Britain and Nasser's Egypt, 1953–57 (New York: Palgrave Macmillan, 2000), p. 108.

224   "Given the conception": Ibid., p. xiii.

224   campaign of escalating coercion: Ibid., pp. 111–12.

224   Eisenhower unveiled it: C. Philip Skardon, *A Lesson for Our Times: How America Kept the Peace in the Hungary-Suez Crisis of 1956* (n.p.: Authorhouse, 2010), p. 625; Irene L. Gendzier, *Notes from the Minefield: United States Intervention in Lebanon and the Middle East, 1945–1958* (New York: Columbia University Press, 2006), pp. 215–16.

225   He became indignant: Patrick Tyler, *A World of Trouble: The White House and the Middle East—From the Cold War to the War on Terror* (New York: Farrar, Straus & Giroux, 2009), p. 59.

225   several Omega projects: Prados, *Safe for Democracy*, pp. 125–26; Tully, *Central Intelligence Agency*, p. 113; Wawro, *Quicksand*, pp. 139, 235.

225   "Throughout the elections": Gendzier, *Notes from the Minefield*, p. 222.

226   sustained campaigns against two . . . neutralists: Kahin and Kahin, *Subversion as Foreign Policy*, pp. 10–14.

226   nationalized several . . . businesses: Geoff Simons, *Indonesia: The Long Oppression* (New York: Palgrave Macmillan, 2000), p. 152.

227   "a Javanese characteristic": John D. Legge, *Sukarno: A Political Biography* (Singapore: Didier Millet, 2007), p. 22.

227   "Don't tie yourself irrevocably": Kahin and Kahin, *Subversion as Foreign Policy*, p. 75.

228   Foster recalled Ambassador Cumming: Ibid., p. 83.

228   Simbolon . . . wished to meet: Ibid., pp. 70, 101–2; Kenneth Conboy and James Morrison, *Feet to the Fire: CIA Covert Operations in Indonesia, 1957–1958* (Annapolis: Naval Institute Press, 1999), p. 33.

229   four-party government: Kahin and Kahin, *Subversion as Foreign Policy*, p. 77.

229   National Security Council to authorize: *FRUS*, Indonesia, p. 2.

229   Allen immediately sent $50,000: Gardner, *Shared Hopes, Separate Fears*, p. 145.

229   "Send more books": Conboy and Morrison, *Feet to the Fire*, p. 29.

229   "raise annoying questions": Smith, *Portrait of a Cold Warrior*, p. 221.

230   "with a little flourish": Thomas, *Very Best Men*, p. 158.

230   one of his most bizarre projects: Srodes, *Allen Dulles*, p. 169; Smith, *Portrait of a Cold Warrior*, p. 169; Thomas, *Very Best Men*, p. 159.

230   One large shipment alone: Conboy and Morrison, *Feet to the Fire*, p. 180.

230   "get to a point": Kahin and Kahin, *Subversion as Foreign Policy*, p. 124.

230   In public statements: Ibid., p. 142.

231   public ultimatum: May, *Indonesian Tragedy*, p. 79.

231   "We don't take any part": Ibid., p. 149.

231   "If a government allows": Kahin and Kahin, *Subversion as Foreign Policy*, p. 148.

231   Late one night: Graham Greene, *The Quiet American* (New York: Penguin, 2004), p. 119.

232   "your motives are good": Ibid., p. 172.

232   "completely change" the book's message: Wilford, *Mighty Wurlitzer*, pp. 176–77.

233   "ruining our foreign policy": Cary Fraser, "Crossing the Color Line in Little Rock: The Eisenhower Administration and the Dilemma of Race for U.S. Foreign Policy," *Diplomatic History* 24, no. 2 (Jan. 2000), p. 247.

233   "Let us not pretend": *Life*, Oct. 7, 1957.

233   "like a cancer": Ralph W. McGhee, *Deadly Deceits: My 25 Years in the CIA* (Melbourne: Ocean Press, 1999), p. 42.

234   "disaster for the United States": "Discussion at the 347th Meeting of the National Security Council, Thursday, December 5, 1957," http://history.nasa .gov/sputnik/dec57.html.

234   had grown weak and tired: Hoopes, *Devil and John Foster Dulles*, pp. 338, 429.

234   widely covered speech: *New York Times*, Nov. 12, 1958.

234   Alsop and . . . Humphrey: Hoopes, *Devil and John Foster Dulles*, p. 403.

234   Burnett's gag song: http://www.youtube.com/watch?v=IgTN13_bfXQ.

235   Christmas dinner: Eleanor Lansing Dulles, *John Foster Dulles*, p. 18.

235   "great gain for the Soviets": Ibid., pp. 100–101.

236   traveled to Princeton: Ibid., p. 124.

236   they "did not really separate": Srodes, *Allen Dulles*, p. 451.

236   "The director always began": Ibid., p. 485.

237   One of his favorite friends: Ibid., p. 451.

237   "a reasonable chance": Conboy and Morrison, *Feet to the Fire*, p. 60.

237   "Indonesia, racked by civil war": *Time*, Mar. 10, 1958.

238   "would not fight their Muslim brothers": Conboy and Morrison, *Feet to the Fire*, pp. 51, 92.

238   barges loaded with weapons: Ibid., p. 34; Weiner, *Legacy of Ashes*, p. 148.

238   "play with fire": Kahin and Kahin, *Subversion as Foreign Policy*, p. 186.

238   Foster concluded: Ibid., p. 156.

238   "Our policy is one of careful neutrality": Wise and Ross, *Invisible Government*, p. 145.

239   "I am called a communist": *FRUS*, Indonesia, p. 76.

239   reacted by telephoning: Gardner, *Shared Hopes, Separate Fears*, p. 52.

239   "We did not write about it": Kahin and Kahin, *Subversion as Foreign Policy*, p. 158.

239   "It is unfortunate": *New York Times*, May 9, 1957.

239   they met at Foster's home: *FRUS*, Indonesia, p. 99.

240   Pope's B-26 burst into flames: Kahin and Kahin, *Subversion as Foreign Policy*, pp. 179–81; Conboy and Morrison, *Feet to the Fire*, pp. 132–40.

240   He had bombed military bases: Conboy and Morrison, *Feet to the Fire*, pp. 118, 122.

240   "Tell me why": Adams and Sukarno, *Sukarno*, p. 269.

241   "pulling the plug": Grose, *Gentleman Spy*, pp. 453–54; Conboy and Morrison, *Feet to the Fire*, pp. 145–46.

242   "I am definitely convinced": Wise and Ross, *Invisible Government*, p. 152.

242   "dictator somewhat of the Hitler type": Wawro, *Quicksand*, p. 235.

242   "More important than Chamoun's second term: Ibid., pp. 234, 238.

243   Chamoun was eased from office: Hoopes, *Devil and John Foster Dulles*, p. 437.

243   "sheer delusion": Wawro, *Quicksand*, p. 240.

243   lamented the "mixing of American blood": Gendzier, *Notes from the Minefield*, p. 329.

243   "patriotic people of Iraq": Ibid., p. 333.

245   "Listen carefully": Gardner, *Shared Hopes, Separate Fears*, pp. 161–62.

245   Allen ordered intensive work: Conboy and Morrison, *Feet to the Fire*, pp. 162–65.

245   "when it comes to women": Adams and Sukarno, *Sukarno*, p. 271.

245   "We killed thousands": Weiner, *Legacy of Ashes*, p. 153.

245   Rebellions . . . sputtered on: Kahin and Kahin, *Subversion as Foreign Policy*, p. 216.

246   "prolonged exclusion": May, *Indonesian Tragedy*, p. 162.

246   "neat, orderly Western pigeon holes": Ibid., p. 66.

246   "I had great respect": Weiner, *Legacy of Ashes*, p. 146.

246   "If there is an out-and-out question": Adams and Sukarno, *Sukarno*, p. 300.

9: THE TALL, GOATEED RADICAL

247   carried a royal visitor aloft: *New York Times*, Oct. 29, 1960; Penny von Eschen, *Satchmo Blows Up the World: Jazz Ambassadors Play the Cold War* (Cambridge, Mass.: Harvard University Press, 2006), pp. 58, 66–68, 71, 77; video is at http://www.youtube.com/watch?v=hXWy0NvzlCA.

247   "America's secret weapon": *New York Times*, Nov. 6. 1955.

248   "extremely strong feelings": Ambrose, *Ike's Spies*, p. 196; Brands, *Devil We Knew*, p. 63.

248   "one of the most secret documents": Jim Rasenberger, *The Brilliant Disaster: JFK, Castro, and America's Doomed Invasion of Cuba's Bay of Pigs* (New York: Scribner, 2011), p. 49.

249   "it would have been unseemly": Rasenberger, *Brilliant Disaster*, p. 50.

249   Allen could not mistake the message: Madeleine G. Kalb, *The Congo Cables: The Cold War in Africa—from Eisenhower to Kennedy* (New York: Macmillan, 1982), p. 64.

249   "In high quarters": Larry Devlin, *Chief of Station, Congo: Fighting the Cold War in a Hot Zone* (New York: PublicAffairs, 2007), p. 62.

249   Devlin received a second . . . cable: Ibid., p. 20; Kalb, *Congo Cables*, p. 66.

249   "It's your responsibility": Devlin, *Chief of Station, Congo*, p. 95.

250   "They loved to talk": Eleanor Lansing Dulles, *John Foster Dulles*, p. 124.

250   a spate of reports: Mosley, *Dulles*, p. 457.

250   new calls to split the CIA in two: Grose, *Gentleman Spy*, p. 478.

251   "Communist high command": Barrett, *CIA and Congress*, p. 285.

251   Allen was more realistic: Ibid., p. 286.

251   Eisenhower was reportedly ready to name: Hoopes, *Devil and John Foster Dulles*, p. 428.

251   Clark . . . was said to be his choice: Devlin, *Chief of Station, Congo*, p. 47.

252   "a real and deeply felt hurt": Eleanor Lansing Dulles, *John Foster Dulles*, p. 197.

252   "a recurring nightmare": Ibid., p. 28.

252   His health had deteriorated: Ibid., pp. 226–29; Mosley, *Dulles*, 444–45.

252   "Foster was aware of certain medical facts": Eleanor Lansing Dulles, *John Foster Dulles*, p. 230.

253   resignation letter . . . president replied: Hoopes, *Devil and John Foster Dulles*, p. 485.

253   outside Foster's room: Mosley, *Dulles*, p. 447; Eleanor Lansing Dulles, *John Foster Dulles*, pp. 225–31; Grose, *Gentleman Spy*, pp. 457–62.

253   "A few weeks before": Mosley, *Dulles*, p. 448.

253   "Some fellow got up": Ibid., p. 449.

254   Eisenhower invited him: Grose, *Gentleman Spy*, p. 463.

254   "Herter never really replaced Dulles": Cook, *Declassified Eisenhower*, p. 211.

254   trained his secret police force: Thomas G. Paterson, *Contesting Castro: The United States and the Triumph of the Cuban Revolution* (New York: Oxford University Press, 1995), pp. 63, 74, 192, 279.

254   *Daily News* reported: http://www.nydailynews.com/new-york/fidel-new -york-gallery-1.48730.

254   Nixon to meet Castro: Carl Mydans, *The Violent Peace* (New York: Scribner, 1968), p. 313; Jeffrey J. Stafford, "The Nixon-Castro Meeting of 19 April 1959," *Diplomatic History* 4, no. 4 (October 1980), pp. 425–31.

255   Kempton, later wrote: Peter Carlson, *K Blows Top: A Cold War Comic Interlude Starring Nikita Khrushchev, America's Most Unlikely Tourist* (New York: PublicAffairs, 2009), p. xiii.

255   Khrushchev visited: Ibid., pp. 49–250.

256   U-2 spy plane disappeared: Thomas Charles Fensch (ed.), *Top Secret: The CIA and the U-2 Program, 1954–1974* (The Woodlands, Tex.: New Century, 2001), pp. 161–98; Michael R. Beschloss, *May Day: Eisenhower, Khrushchev, and the U-2 Affair* (New York: Harper and Row, 1988), pp. 27–30; Alex von Tunzelmann, *Red Heat: Conspiracy, Murder, and the Cold War in the Caribbean* (New York: Henry Holt, 2011), pp. 173–74.

256   "Allen Dulles is no weatherman": Tunzelmann, *Red Heat*, p. 174.

256   "I am not going to shift the blame": Grose, *Gentleman Spy*, p. 488.

256   "If you gentlemen are spies: Tully, *Central Intelligence Agency*, p. 128.

256   an angry press conference: http://www.upi.com/Audio/Year_in_Review/
       Events-of-1960/The-Paris-Summit-Falls-Apart/12295509435928-2/#ixzz23
       cwtISFB.

257   "The episode humiliated Khrushchev": *New York Times*, Oct. 28, 1982.

257   calculated to strike terror: Westad, *Global Cold War*, p. 138; Ludo De Witte,
       The Assassination of Lumumba (London: Verso, 2001), p. 78.

258   seventeen college graduates: *New York Review of Books*, Oct. 4, 2001.

258   attended religious schools: Robin McKown, *Lumumba: A Biography* (Gar-
       den City, N.Y.: Doubleday, 1969), pp. 11–53; Jean Omassombo Tshonda,
       "Patrice Lumumba's Youth," in Bogumil Jewsiewicki et al., *A Congo Chroni-
       cle: Patrice Lumumba in Urban Art* (New York: Museum for African Art,
       1999), pp. 29–37.

259   In the course of barely more than a . . . day: McKown, *Lumumba*, pp. 75–78.

259   "The man to beat": *Time,* May 30, 1960.

259   "Lumumba is living proof": *Times* (London), July 15, 1960.

260   uranium used to fuel: McKown, *Lumumba*, p. 21.

260   Baudouin began his welcoming speech: De Witte, *Assassination of Lumumba*,
       p. 1.

261   "turned a deathly pale": *Time*, July 11, 1960.

261   "Our wounds are too fresh": McKown, *Lumumba*, pp. 101–4.

262   "inter-racial politeness": *Time*, July 11, 1960.

262   "consider this a . . . final warning": *Time*, July 25, 1960.

262   Janssens convened his Congolese troops: McKown, *Lumumba*, pp. 109–10;
       De Witte, *Assassination of Lumumba*, p. 6.

262   soldiers, already angry: *Time*, July 18, 1960.

262   Belgians were gone: McKown, *Lumumba*, 114.

262   Belgian commandos began parachuting: Ibid., pp. 112–13.

262   Union Minière du Haut: Ibid., p. 81; David W. Doyle, *True Men and Traitors*
       (New York: John Wiley, 2001), p. 135.

262   Champion, cashiered hundreds: Doyle, *True Men and Traitors*, pp. 138–39;
       McKown, *Lumumba*, p. 133; G. Heinz and H. Donnay, *Lumumba: The Last
       Fifty Days* (New York: Grove, 1969), pp. 97–98.

263   sent him nine tons: *Time*, Sept. 19, 1960.

263   "Tshombe became the most unpopular . . . leader": Doyle, *True Men and
       Traitors*, p. 135.

263   "under the domination of Belgian officials": *Daily Telegraph*, July 27, 1960.

263   "We accuse the Belgian government": McKown, *Lumumba*, p. 126.

263   Lumumba also took another step: Ibid., p. 127.

263   "We have no arms": Ibid., p. 129.

263   Hammarskjöld . . . "very optimistic": Kalb, *Congo Cables*, p. 34.

264   "If I die tomorrow": McKown, *Lumumba*, p. 170.

264   "not rational being": Kalb, *Congo Cables*, p. 37.

264   real problem may have been: Ibid.; *New York Review of Books*, Oct. 4, 2001.

264   "We are being attacked": Heinz and Donnay, *Lumumba*, p. 163.

264   Devlin . . . had been warning: Devlin, *Chief of Station, Congo*, p. 54.

264   genteel recruiting session: Ibid., pp. 1–2.

265   "In retrospect": Ibid. pp. 54, 66.

265   Lumumba proved unwilling or unable: Leo Zeilig, *Patrice Lumumba: Africa's Lost Leader* (London: Haus, 2008), p. 104.

265   the council decided: Kalb, *Congo Cables*, p. 38.

265   preparing "resolute measures": Ibid., p. 41.

265   foreign journalists converged: McKown, *Lumumba*, pp. 135–37.

266   detested the man he called "Lumumbavitch": Kalb, *Congo Cables*, p. 92.

266   vivid cables to Washington: Ibid., p. 27.

266   Burden picked up his telephone: Devlin, *Chief of Station, Congo*, pp. 45–46.

267   State Department had no bureau of African affairs: Kalb, *Congo Cables*, p. xxvi.

267   "None of us had any real concept": Doyle, *True Men and Traitors*, p. 129.

267   "recruiting agents and running them": Ibid., pp. 128–29.

267   The station organized: Devlin, *Chief of Station, Congo*, pp. 57–61, 68–69.

267   Anonymous leaflets: McKown, *Lumumba*, pp. 142–43.

268   On August 18 Devlin cabled: William H. Worger et al., *Africa and the West: A Documentary History*, vol. 2, *From Colonialism to Independence, 1875 to the Present* (New York: Oxford University Press, 2010), p. 136.

268   "off the record meeting": The President's Appointments, July–December, 1960, *President's Daily Appointments Schedules: Dwight D. Eisenhower: Records as President, 1953–1961*, Dwight D. Eisenhower Library.

268   "I was authorized": Devlin, *Chief of Station, Congo*, p. 63.

268   "The moment they became aware": Mosley, *Dulles*, p. 450.

269   "The embassy and station were humming": Devlin, *Chief of Station, Congo*, p. 68.

269   Lumumba held mass rallies: Zeilig, *Patrice Lumumba*, p. 113.

269   Lumumba's friends . . . warned him: Kalb, *Congo Cables*, pp. 69, 86; Zeilig, *Patrice Lumumba*, p. 116; Devlin, *Chief of Station, Congo*, p. 77.

270   "Red Weeds Grow": *Time*, Sept. 12, 1960.

270   Kasavubu's tape was played: *Time*, Sept. 19, 1960.

270   proclaimed the decision: Devlin, *Chief of Station, Congo*, p. 67.

270   UN soldiers closed: McKown, *Lumumba*, pp. 149–50.

270   convey "top-level feeling": Kalb, *Congo Cables*, p. 79.

270   Mobutu agreed to lead a coup: Devlin, *Chief of Station, Congo*, p. 87; *Time*, Sept. 26, 1960.

271   Both . . . were on the CIA payroll: Godfrey Mwakikagile, *Africa 1960–1970: Chronicle and Analysis* (Dar es Salaam: New Africa Press, 2009), p. 82; Stephen R. Weissman, "Congo-Kinshasa: U.S. Role in Lumumba Murder Revealed," http://allafrica.com/stories/200207220024.html?viewall=1.

271   Nehru of India demanded: McKown, *Lumumba*, p. 157.

271   "Lumumba talents and dynamism": Devlin, *Chief of Station, Congo*, p. 17; Kalb, *Congo Cables*, p. 87.

271   Lumumba was arrested twice: Heinz and Donnay, *Lumumba*, pp. 22–23.

271   Wadsworth . . . made sure: Kalb, *Congo Cables*, p. 99.

272   "give every possible support": Ibid., p. 102.

272   "prowled the balcony": *Time*, Oct. 24, 1960.

272   CIA officers were trying . . . to poison him: http://www.gwu.edu/~nsarchiv
        /NSAEBB/NSAEBB222/top06.pdf.

272   "Hunting good here": United States Senate, *Alleged Assassination Plots
        Involving Foreign Leaders* (Washington, D.C.: U.S. Government Printing
        Office, 1975), p. 57.

272   "[Bissell] called me in": Kalb, *Congo Cables*, p. 151; Loch K. Johnson and
        James J. Wirtz (eds.), *Strategic Intelligence: Windows into a Secret World*
        (Cary, N.C.: Roxbury, 2004), pp. 224–30.

273   "Wait, even indefinitely": Heinz and Donnay, *Lumumba*, p. 10.

273   "cool as a cucumber": Zeilig, *Patrice Lumumba*, p. 130.

273   wife departed to Switzerland: Heinz and Donnay, *Lumumba*, p. 31.

273   "The big rabbit": Ibid., p. 41.

274   book was Ian Fleming's novel: Grose, *Gentleman Spy*, p. 491.

274   "Dulles liked Bond": Christopher Moran, "Ian Fleming and CIA Director
        Allen Dulles: The Very Best of Friends," in James G. Wiener et al. (eds.),
        James Bond in World and Popular Culture: The Films Are Not Enough (New-
        castle upon Tyne: Cambridge Scholars, 2011), p. 209.

275   "Wisner came out to my house": Hersh, *Old Boys*, p. 402.

275   Wisner lost his grip: Ibid., pp. 435–41; Weiner, *Legacy of Ashes*, pp. 153, 262–
        64; Powers, *Intelligence Wars*, p. 96.

275   "He remained an actor": Hersh, *Old Boys*, pp. 420–21.

276   Five thousand people turned out: Rasenberger, *Brilliant Disaster*, p. 41.

276   sent her on a forty-nation tour: Mosley, *Dulles*, pp. 452–53.

277   working with Tibetan rebels: Prados, *Safe for Democracy*, pp. 184–203; Bar-
        rett, *CIA and Congress*, pp. 346–51.

278   Lumumba began planning this breakout: Zeilig, *Patrice Lumumba*, p. 120;
        Heinz and Donnay, *Lumumba*, pp. 3–5; McKown, *Lumumba*, p. 162; De
        Witte, *Assassination of Lumumba*, pp. 52–55.

278   "working closely" with Congolese police: Kalb, *Congo Cables*, p. 158.

278   Lumumba's pursuers pinpointed his location: De Witte, *Assassination of
        Lumumba*, pp. 52–57; Heinz and Donnay, *Lumumba*, pp. 42–43.

278   "very bad fifteen minutes": Heinz and Donnay, *Lumumba*, p. 43.

278   "Mobutu . . . calmly watched": Ibid., p. 46.

278   thrown onto the back of a pickup truck: McKown, *Lumumba*, p. 171; video is
        at http://www.youtube.com/watch?v=JGnGFaJqmzU.

279   "illegal Mobutu bands": Heinz and Donnay, *Lumumba*, p. 70.

279   emergency summit in Casablanca: Kalb, *Congo Cables*, p. 189.

279   "Present government may fall": Johnson and Wirtz (eds.), *Strategic Intelli-
        gence*, p. 237.

279   hustled onto a plane: De Witte, *Assassination of Lumumba*, pp. 90–94; Heinz and Donnay, *Lumumba*, p. 93.

279   "we would have baked a snake": Kalb, *Congo Cables*, p. 192.

279   Urquhart . . . gave this account: *New York Review of Books*, Oct. 4, 2001.

280   Lumumba should be freed: McKown, *Lumumba*, p. 185.

281   "great shock": *Lewiston Daily Sun*, Feb. 14, 1961.

281   shock extended far beyond Washington: Zeilig, *Patrice Lumumba*, p. 133; Nyunda ya Rubango, "Patrice Lumumba at the Crossroads of History and Myth," in Jewsiewicki, *Congo Chronicle*, pp. 56–57.

281   Sartre lamented the loss: De Witte, *Assassination of Lumumba*, p. xxiv.

281   Malcolm X called Lumumba: http://congolese.blogspot.com/2008/09 /lumumba.html.

281   Lumumba was "invincible": Aimé Césaire, *A Season in the Congo* (New York: Seagull, 2010), p. 124.

281   oddest leader of the . . . cult: McKown, *Lumumba*, pp. 178, 187–88, 193; De Witte, *Assassination of Lumumba*, pp. 148, 165, 174; Zeilig, *Patrice Lumumba*, pp. 131–33.

281   "I have nothing against him": McKown, *Lumumba*, p. 193.

281   Devlin later came to believe: Devlin, *Chief of Station, Congo*, pp. 54, 56.

282   "one of the . . . most important political assassinations": De Witte, *Assassination of Lumumba*, p. xviii.

282   Soviet aid project: Devlin, *Chief of Station, Congo*, pp. 26, 77.

283   "we overrated the danger": Stephen R. Weissman, *American Foreign Policy in the Congo 1960–1964* (Ithaca, N.Y.: Cornell University Press, 1974), p. 280.

10: THE BEARDED STRONGMAN

284   "rapid-fire succession": *Montana Standard*, Nov. 11, 1960.

284   "I have asked Mr. Allen Dulles": http://www.youtube.com/watch?v=Wa -rbVCMvG0.

285   "I candidly confess": Lars Schoultz, *That Infernal Little Cuban Republic: The United States and the Cuban Revolution* (Chapel Hill: University of North Carolina Press, 2011), p. 19.

286   Castro made his tumultuous trip: Tunzelmann, *Red Heat*, p. 183; Rasenberger, *Brilliant Disaster*, pp. 86–89.

286   "an impenitent disciple": *Pittsburgh Press*, Jan. 18, 1960.

287   imprisoned thousands . . . and executed several hundred: Tunzelmann, *Red Heat*, p. 129.

287   "bearded strongman": *Time*, Feb. 8, 1960.

287   "Vilification of the US broke all bounds": *Time*, Mar. 21, 1960.

287   "There was considerable discussion": Peter Kornbluh (ed.), *Bay of Pigs Declassified: The Secret CIA Report on the Invasion of Cuba* (New York: New Press, 1988), p. 32.

287   restless sons of privilege: Rasenberger, *Brilliant Disaster* pp. 57–64; Thomas, *Very Best Men*, pp. 87–97; Peter Wyden, *Bay of Pigs: The Untold Story* (New York: Simon and Schuster, 1979), p. 13.

287   "Bissell spent little time": Rasenberger, *Brilliant Disaster*, p. 65.

288   Eisenhower . . . would favor any plot: Richard M. Bissell Jr., *Reflections of a Cold Warrior: From Yalta to the Bay of Pigs* (New Haven: Yale University Press, 1996), p. 153.

288   "concerned and perplexed": Robert E. Quirk, *Fidel Castro* (New York: W.W. Norton, 1995), p. 289.

288   "things that might be drastic": Jack Pfeiffer, *Official History of the Bay of Pigs Operation*, p. 50, http://www.gwu.edu/~nsarchiv/NSAEBB/NSAEBB355/bop-vol1-part1.pdf.

288   "no thought of intervention": Daniel F. Solomon, *Breaking Up with Cuba: The Dissolution of Friendly Relations Between Washington and Havana, 1956–1961* (Jefferson, N.C.: McFarland, 2011), p. 175.

288   "informal . . . short cut": Pfeiffer, *Official History*, p. 34.

288   Allen presented "A Program": Kornbluh (ed.), *Bay of Pigs Declassified*, p. 269; Bissell, *Reflections of a Cold Warrior*, p. 153; Howard Jones, *The Bay of Pigs* (New York: Oxford University Press, 2010), p. 19.

288   could imagine "no better plan": Kornbluh (ed.), *Bay of Pigs Declassified*, p. 269.

288   "great problem is leakage": Rasenberger, *Brilliant Disaster*, p. 56; Barrett, *CIA and Congress*, p. 431.

289   Allen did not even attend: Rasenberger, *Brilliant Disaster*, p. 76.

289   "couldn't hit a bull": Thomas, *Very Best Men*, p. 304.

289   "He had turned the whole thing over": Mosley, *Dulles*, p. 470.

290   told Castro why it succeeded: Simon Reid-Henry, *Fidel and Che: A Revolutionary Friendship* (New York: Walker, 2009), p. 229; Cullather, *Secret History*, p. 110.

290   would-be guerrillas were brought to camps: Kornbluh (ed.), *Bay of Pigs Declassified*, p. 273.

290   Tensions . . . rose steadily: Rasenberger, *Brilliant Disaster*, pp. 76–77.

290   pulling its baseball team: Solomon, *Breaking Up with Cuba*, pp. 187, 217.

291   "The thing we should never do": Schoultz, *That Infernal Little Cuban Republic*, p. 100.

291   "We must not allow Laos to fall": David E. Kaiser, *American Tragedy: Kennedy, Johnson, and the Origins of the Vietnam War* (Cambridge, Mass.: Belknap, 2002), p. 31.

291   "Had we shown more open-mindedness": Bissell, *Reflections of a Cold Warrior*, pp. 141–42.

292   By his own account: Rasenberger, *Brilliant Disaster*, p. 94.

292   "I just told Kennedy": Ibid., p. 79.

292   In campaign speeches: Wyden, *Bay of Pigs*, pp. 66–67; Grose, *Gentleman Spy*, p. 507.

292   "Are they falling dead": Rasenberger, *Brilliant Disaster*, p. 80.

293 wanted the Cuban leader "sawed off": Ibid., p. 83.

293 "In that period": Ibid.; Jones, *Bay of Pigs*, pp. 27–28; Bissell, *Reflections of a Cold Warrior*, p. 144.

293 CIA passed them six poison pills: Jones, *Bay of Pigs*, pp. 22–27; Rasenberger, *Brilliant Disaster*, pp. 81–83, 142–43; Solomon, *Breaking Up with Cuba*, p. 188; Wyden, *Bay of Pigs*, pp. 40–43; Tunzelmann, *Red Heat*, p. 205.

293 suggested staging a phony Cuban attack: Rasenberger, *Brilliant Disaster*, p. 101.

293 Allen and Bissell flew to Palm Beach: Bissell, *Reflections of a Cold Warrior*, p. 160; Kornbluh (ed.), *Bay of Pigs Declassified*, p. 278; Prados, *Safe for Democracy*, p. 241; Rasenberger, *Brilliant Disaster*, pp. 99–100.

294 "level of interest . . . escalated": Pfeiffer, *Official History*, pp. 165–66.

294 "Take more chances": Kornbluh (ed.), *Bay of Pigs Declassified*, p. 278.

294 Preparations for the invasion: Rasenberger, *Brilliant Disaster*, p. 6.

295 "Dulles briefed the attendees": Pfeiffer, *Official History*, p. 182.

295 "It is axiomatic": *FRUS*, Cuba, p. 14.

295 Arms . . . were unloaded in Havana: Rasenberger, *Brilliant Disaster*, pp. 132–35.

295 fighters were "ready to invade": Solomon, *Breaking Up with Cuba*, p. 196.

295 "American Embassy that is paying the terrorists": Solomon, *Breaking Up with Cuba*, p. 194.

296 "don't know what they're talking about": Ibid., p. 196.

296 CIA circulated a memo: Ibid., p. 195; Kornbluh (ed.), *Bay of Pigs Declassified*, pp. 281–82.

296 startling headline: *New York Times*, Jan. 10, 1961.

296 Allen warned editors: Solomon, *Breaking Up with Cuba*, p. 188; Wyden, *Bay of Pigs*, pp. 45–46; Kornbluh (ed.), *Bay of Pigs Declassified*, p. 274.

296 "Are We Training Cuban Guerrillas": *Nation*, Nov. 19, 1960.

296 A Guatemalan newspaper: Wyden, *Bay of Pigs*, p. 46; Kornbluh (ed.), *Bay of Pigs Declassified*, pp. 277–78.

296 Allen persuaded the *New York Times*: Kornbluh (ed.), *Bay of Pigs Declassified*, p. 301.

296 "I decided that we should say nothing": Dwight D. Eisenhower, *Waging Peace, 1956–1961: The White House Years* (New York: Doubleday, 1965), p. 614.

297 Bissell wrote later: Bissell, *Reflections of a Cold Warrior*, p. 163.

297 "To the utmost": Solomon, *Breaking Up with Cuba*, p. 109; Rasenberger, *Brilliant Disaster*, p. 109.

297 *Time* reported "guerrilla training camps": *Time*, Jan. 27, 1961.

297 "disposal" problem: Rasenberger, *Brilliant Disaster*, p. 130; Wyden, *Bay of Pigs*, p. 100; Prados, *Safe for Democracy*, p. 246.

298 "We made it very clear": Lucien S. Vandenbroucke, "Anatomy of a Failure: The Decision to Land at the Bay of Pigs," *Political Science Quarterly* 99, no. 3 (Fall 1998), p. 476.

298   Peace Corps . . . Alliance for Progress: Tunzelmann, *Red Heat*, p. 208.

298   "sold us on it": Rasenberger, *Brilliant Disaster*, p. 127.

298   "You present a plan": Ibid.

298   "fix a malevolent image": Ibid., p. 129.

298   "thorn in the flesh": Ibid., p. 152; Jones, *Bay of Pigs*, p. 65.

298   "doesn't take Price Waterhouse": Rasenberger, *Brilliant Disaster*, p. 147.

298   too "noisy": Ibid., p. 185; Bissell, *Reflections of a Cold Warrior*, p. 170; Prados, *Safe for Democracy*, p. 270.

299   "still thought it would succeed": Rasenberger, *Brilliant Disaster*, p. 141.

299   last, poignant warning: Ibid., pp. 173–76.

300   "We made a bad mistake": Don Bohning, "A Remembrance of Jake Esterline," *Intelligencer: Journal of U.S. Intelligence Studies* 19, no. 2 (Summer/Fall 2012), p. 42.

300   "there will not be . . . an intervention": Jones, *Bay of Pigs*, p. 69.

300   "get ahold of the President": Rasenberger, *Brilliant Disaster*, p. 235.

300   Radio Moscow reported: Ibid., p. 249.

301   "how is it going": Ibid., p. 259.

301   Burke . . . came to the Oval Office: Ibid., pp. 282–83.

301   "I probably made a mistake": Ibid., p. 272; Grose, *Gentleman Spy*, p. 531.

302   "Everything is lost": Solomon, *Breaking Up with Cuba*, p. 205; Rasenberger, *Brilliant Disaster*, p. 307; Prados, *Safe for Democracy*, p. 264.

302   "How could I have been so stupid": Rasenberger, *Brilliant Disaster*, p. 314.

302   "Cuba Disaster": *Time*, Apr. 28, 1961.

302   "Victory has a hundred fathers": Jeffreys-Jones, *CIA and American Democracy*, p. 127.

302   "looked like living death": Grose, *Gentleman Spy*, p. 525.

302   No harsh words: Ibid., p. 530.

302   "We took the . . . best military advice": Barrett, *CIA and Congress*, p. 452.

302   "he just wasn't involved": Srodes, *Allen Dulles*, p. 520.

303   Retirement . . . would come in two years: Grose, *Gentleman Spy*, p. 534.

303   wished he could "splinter the CIA": Jones, *Bay of Pigs*, p. 131; *New York Times*, Apr. 25, 1966.

303   dedication ceremony: Grose, *Gentleman Spy*, p. 538.

304   "I stood right here": *Look*, Aug. 10, 1965.

304   sharp rebuttal: Srodes, *Allen Dulles*, pp. 556–58; Allen Dulles, "My Answer to the Bay of Pigs," unpublished, Allen Dulles Papers, box 224.

304   "had already begun to lose": Mosley, *Dulles*, p. 479.

304   "when the chips were down": Higgins Trumble, *The Perfect Failure: Kennedy, Eisenhower, and the CIA at the Bay of Pigs* (New York: W.W. Norton, 1989), p. 103.

304   Eleanor was another casualty: Mosley, *Dulles*, pp. 473–74; Eleanor Lansing Dulles, *Chances of a Lifetime*, p. 305.

305   In retirement: Grose, *Gentleman Spy*, pp. 538–39.

305   "some foreign complications": Ibid., p. 542.

305   "systematically used his influence": Ibid., p. 544; Jones, *Bay of Pigs*, pp. 168–69.

306   bland report: Grose, *Gentleman Spy*, p. 558.

306   sentimental trip: Mosley, *Dulles*, p. 480.

306   Wolff had reason for gratitude: Ibid.; Grose, *Gentleman Spy*, pp. 253–54; *New York Review of Books*, Dec. 29, 1966, and Mar. 9, 1967.

306   "Perhaps it was what we call": Srodes, *Allen Dulles*, p. 580.

306   looked all of his . . . years: Grose, *Gentleman Spy*, p. 564; Srodes, *Allen Dulles*, p. 560.

306   "I am too old": Grose, *Gentleman Spy*, p. 560.

307   "creative, powerful, and eminent": *Washington Post*, Jan. 31, 1969.

11: A FACE OF GOD

311   ordered small-format copies: Beal, *John Foster Dulles*, pp. 235–36.

313   "Once you touch the biographies": Walter Lippmann, *A Preface to Politics* (n.p.: CreateSpace, 2012) p. 86.

314   "I have always felt": May, *Indonesian Tragedy*, p. 113.

314   One of Eisenhower's . . . thoughts: Raj Roy and John W. Young, *Ambassador to Sixties London: The Diaries of David Bruce, 1961–1969* (Dordrecht, Netherlands: Republic of Letters, 2009).

314   "Dulles, not Eisenhower": Roscoe Drummond and Gaston Coblentz, *Duel at the Brink: John Foster Dulles' Command of American Power* (Garden City, N.Y.: Doubleday, 1960), p. 25.

315   This view has shifted: Prados, *Safe for Democracy*, p. 459; Divine, *Eisenhower and the Cold War*, p. 23; Fred I. Greenstein, *The Hidden-Hand Presidency: Eisenhower as Leader* (Baltimore: Johns Hopkins University Press, 1994), pp. 6, 62, 137, 213, 228.

315   "no longer any question": Jerald A. Combs, *The History of American Foreign Policy from 1895* (London: M.E. Sharpe, 2012), p. 256.

315   "Inspired by a Manichean conception": William R. Keylor, *The Twentieth-Century World and Beyond: An International History Since 1900* (New York: Oxford University Press, 2011), pp. 287, 308.

315   Leffler summarized: Melvyn P. Leffler, "Inside Enemy Archives: The Cold War Reopened," *Foreign Affairs* 75, no. 4 (July/Aug. 1996), pp. 120–35.

316   "Dulles' moral universe": *New Republic*, Dec. 1, 1958.

317   "So long as our foreign broadcasts": Urie Bronfenbrenner, "The Mirror Image in Soviet-American Relations," in Edwin P. Hollander and Raymond G. Hunt (eds.), *Current Perspectives in Social Psychology* (New York: Oxford University Press, 1969), p. 622.

317   "you had to develop operations": Jeffreys-Jones, *CIA and American Democracy*, p. 98.

317   "We had constructed for ourselves": Weiner, *Legacy of Ashes*, p. 154.

318   "We carried our walking wounded": Doyle, *True Men and Traitors*, p. 248.

318   "caused havoc": Ibid., p. 227.

318   filed a lawsuit alleging: *New York Times*, Nov. 26, 2012.

318   "a lost opportunity": U.S. Senate, *Final Report on Intelligence Activities*, pp. 44–45.

319   Allen imagined himself as . . . Walsingham: Smith, *Portrait of a Cold Warrior*, p. 139.

319   "a frivolous man": Srodes, *Allen Dulles*, p. 522.

320   "slimy, octopus-like tentacles": Guhin, *John Foster Dulles*, p. 129.

320   "impossible to produce evidence": Stephen G. Rabe, *Eisenhower and Latin America: The Foreign Policy of Anticommunism* (Chapel Hill: University of North Carolina Press, 1988), p. 57.

320   "a single pattern": Guhin, *John Foster Dulles*, p. 129.

320   "It is inevitable": *Spokane Daily Chronicle*, Aug. 24, 1948.

320   "policy . . . not to intervene": William Blum, *Killing Hope: U.S. Military and C.I.A. Interventions Since World War II* (Monroe, Me.: Common Courage, 2008), p. 78.

320   During one of his meetings: Andrew Preston, *Sword of the Spirit, Shield of Faith: Religion in American War and Diplomacy* (New York: Alfred A. Knopf, 2012), pp. 454–55.

320   "two kinds of people": Christian Pineau, oral history, Dulles Papers.

321   "Specimen 1": Charles E. Osgood, "Cognitive Dynamics in the Conduct of Human Affairs," in Hollander and Hunt (eds.), *Current Perspectives in Social Psychology*, pp. 358, 360.

321   People are motivated: Cass M. Sunstein, *Going to Extremes: How Like Minds Unite and Divide* (New York: Oxford University Press, 2011), p. 110.

322   Dissonance is eliminated: Margaret Heffernan, *Willful Blindness: Why We Ignore the Obvious at Our Peril* (New York: Walker, 2011), pp. 24, 51.

322   Moral hypocrisy: Robert Trivers, *The Folly of Fools: The Logic of Deceit and Self-Deception in Human Life* (New York: Basic Books, 2011), pp. 22–23.

322   Groupthink leads: Irving L. Janis, *Groupthink: Psychological Studies of Policy Decisions and Fiascoes* (Independence, Ky.: Cengage Learning, 1982), p. 86.

322   We are often confident: Daniel Kahneman, *Thinking, Fast and Slow* (New York: Farrar, Straus & Giroux, 2011), pp. 4, 212.

322   Certain beliefs are so important: Jonathan Haidt, *New York Times*, Aug. 19, 2012.

322   An American political scientist: Ole Holsti, "Cognitive Dynamics and Images of the Enemy: Dulles and Russia," in David J. Finlay et al., *Enemies in Politics* (Chicago: Rand McNally, 1967).

323   "America is beyond power": John Updike, *Rabbit Redux* (New York: Random House, 1996), p. 49.

324   "International communism is a conspiracy": Beal, *John Foster Dulles*, p. 232.

324   "one of the most powerfully developed narratives": Christina Klein, *Cold War Orientalism: Asia in the Middlebrow Imagination 1945–1961* (Berkeley: University of California Press, 2003), p. 36.

324 "If there's no evident menace": Stanley E. Spangler, *Force and Accommodation in World Politics* (Washington, D.C.: U.S. Government Printing Office, 1991), p. 88.

325 "Depriving the individual of his right": Kattenburg, *Vietnam Trauma*, p. 37.

325 Foster "misleads public opinion": *Ocala Star Banner*, Feb. 3, 1959.

326 "By the late 1950s": Westad, *Global Cold War*, p. 130.

BIBLIOGRAPHY

Acheson, Dean. *Present at the Creation: My Years in the State Department*. New York: W.W. Norton, 1969.

Adams, Cindy, and Sukarno. *Sukarno: An Autobiography*. New York: Bobbs-Merrill, 1965.

Aikman, David. *Billy Graham: His Life and Influence*. Nashville: Thomas Nelson, 2007.

Alexander, Charles C. *Holding the Line: The Eisenhower Era, 1952–1961*. Bloomington: University of Indiana Press, 1975.

Alexander, Yonah, and Allen Nanes (eds.). *The United States and Iran: A Documentary History*. Frederick, Md.: Aletheia, 1980.

Aliano, Richard A. *American Defense Policy from Eisenhower to Kennedy: The Politics of Changing Military Requirements, 1957–1961*. Athens: Ohio University Press, 1975.

Allen, Craig. *Eisenhower and the Mass Media: Peace, Prosperity, and Prime-Time TV*. Chapel Hill: University of North Carolina Press, 1993.

Allison, Graham T. *Essence of Decision: Explaining the Cuban Missile Crisis*. Boston: Little, Brown, 1971.

Alsop, Stewart, and Tom Braden. *Sub Rosa: The OSS and American Espionage*. New York: Reynal and Hitchcock, 1948.

Ambrose, Stephen E. *Eisenhower: Soldier and President*. New York: Simon and Schuster, 1991.

———. *Eisenhower: The President*. New York: Simon and Schuster, 1984.

———. *Ike's Spies: Eisenhower and the Espionage Establishment*. Jackson: University of Mississippi Press, 1981.

———. *Nixon: The Education of a Politician 1913–1962*. New York: Simon and Schuster, 1988.

———. *Rise to Globalism: American Foreign Policy Since 1938*. New York: Penguin, 1988.

Ameringer, Charles D. *U.S. Foreign Intelligence: The Secret Side of American History.* Lexington, Mass.: D. C. Heath, 1990.

Andelman, David A. *A Shattered Peace: Versailles 1919 and the Price We Pay Today.* Hoboken, N.J.: John Wiley & Sons, 2007.

Anderson, David L. *Trapped by Success: The Eisenhower Administration and Vietnam, 1953–1961.* New York: Columbia University Press, 1991.

Andrew, Christopher. *For the President's Eyes Only: Secret Intelligence and the American Presidency from Washington to Bush.* New York: Harper Perennial, 1995.

Arévalo, Juan José, and Jacobo Arbenz. *Discursos del Doctor Juan José Arévalo y del Teniente Coronel Jacobo Arbenz Guzmán en el Acto de Transmisión de la Presidencia de la República.* Guatemala: Tipografía Nacional, 1951.

Arnold, James. *The First Domino: Eisenhower, the Military, and America's Intervention in Vietnam.* New York: William Morrow, 1991.

Astor, Gerald. *Presidents at War: From Truman to Bush, the Gathering of Military Power to Our Commanders in Chief.* Hoboken, N.J.: John Wiley & Sons, 2006.

Ball, Simon J. *The Cold War: An International History, 1947–1991.* London: Arnold, 1998.

Bancroft, Mary. *Autobiography of a Spy.* New York: William Morrow, 1983.

Barnard, Ellsworth. *Wendell Willkie: Fighter for Freedom.* Amherst: University of Massachusetts Press, 1971.

Barrett, David M. *The CIA and Congress: The Untold Story from Truman to Kennedy.* Lawrence: University Press of Kansas, 2005.

Beal, John Robinson. *John Foster Dulles: A Biography.* New York: Harper & Brothers, 1957.

Belmonte, Laura A. *Selling the American Way: U.S. Propaganda and the Cold War.* Philadelphia: University of Pennsylvania Press, 2010.

Berding, Andrew. *Dulles on Diplomacy.* Princeton: D. Van Nostrand, 1965.

Bernstein, Carl. "The CIA and the Media," *Rolling Stone*, Oct. 20, 1977.

Beschloss, Michael R. *May Day: Eisenhower, Khrushchev, and the U-2 Affair.* New York: Harper and Row, 1988.

Best, Anthony, et al. *International History of the Twentieth Century and Beyond.* London: Routledge, 2008.

Bill, James A. *The Eagle and the Lion: The Tragedy of American-Iranian Relations.* New Haven: Yale University Press, 1988.

—— and William Roger Louis (eds.). *Mussadiq, Iranian Nationalism, and Oil.* London: I. B. Tauris, 1988.

Billings-Yun, Melanie. *Decision Against War: Eisenhower and Dien Bien Phu, 1954.* New York: Columbia University Press, 1988.

Bissell, Richard M., Jr. *Reflections of a Cold Warrior: From Yalta to the Bay of Pigs.* New Haven: Yale University Press, 1996.

Blight, James G., and Peter Kornbluh (eds.). *Politics of Illusion: The Bay of Pigs Invasion Reexamined.* Boulder: Lynne Rienner, 1998.

Blight, James G., and David A. Welch (eds.). *Intelligence and the Cuban Missile Crisis.* London: Frank Cass, 1998.

Bogle, Lori Lyn. *The Cold War: National Security Policy Planning from Truman to Reagan and from Stalin to Gorbachev*. London: Routledge, 2001.

Bohning, Don. *The Castro Obsession: U.S. Covert Operations Against Cuba, 1959–1965*. Washington, D.C.: Potomac, 2005.

———. "A Remembrance of Jake Esterline," *Intelligencer: Journal of U.S. Intelligence Studies* 19, no. 2 (Summer/Fall 2012), pp. 41–47.

Bowie, Robert R., and Richard H. Immerman. *Waging Peace: How Eisenhower Shaped an Enduring Cold War Strategy*. New York: Oxford University Press, 1998.

Brands, H. W. *The Devil We Knew: Americans and the Cold War*. New York: Oxford University Press, 1994.

———. *Inside the Cold War: Loy Henderson and the Rise of the American Empire, 1918–1961*. New York: Oxford University Press, 1991.

Breitman, George (ed.). *Malcolm X Speaks: Selected Speeches and Statements*. New York: Merit, 1965.

Brown, Anthony Cave. *Wild Bill Donovan: The Last Hero*. New York: Times Books, 1982.

Brush, Peter, "Doctor Tom Dooley," http://www.library.vanderbilt.edu/central/Brush/Tom-Dooley.htm.

Burke, John P., and Fred I. Greenstein. *How Presidents Test Reality: Decisions on Vietnam 1954 and 1965*. New York: Russell Sage Foundation, 1989.

Burton, Robert. *On Being Certain: Believing You Are Right Even When You Are Not*. New York: St. Martin's Griffin, 2008.

Cable, James. *The Geneva Conference of 1954 on Indochina*. New York: St. Martin's, 1986.

Carlson, Peter. *K Blows Top: A Cold War Comic Interlude Starring Nikita Khrushchev, America's Most Unlikely Tourist*. New York: PublicAffairs, 2009.

Central Intelligence Agency. *Overthrow of Premier Mossadeq of Iran, November 1952–August 1953*. http://www.nytimes.com/library/world/mideast/041600iran-cia-index.html.

Chace, James. *Acheson: The Secretary of State Who Created the American World*. New York: Simon and Schuster, 1998.

Chapman, Jessica. "Staging Democracy: South Vietnam's 1955 Referendum to Depose Bao Dai," *Diplomatic History* 30, no. 4 (Sept. 2006), pp. 671–703.

Chapman, Peter. *Bananas: How the United Fruit Company Shaped the World*. Edinburgh: Canongate, 2009.

Chernus, Ira. *General Eisenhower: Ideology and Discourse*. East Lansing: Michigan State University Press, 2002.

Colby, Jacob. *The Business of Empire: United Fruit, Race, and U.S. Expansion in Central America*. Ithaca, N.Y.: Cornell University Press, 2011.

Colby, William. *Honorable Men: My Life in the CIA*. London: Hutchinson, 1978.

Combs, Jerald A. *The History of American Foreign Policy from 1895*. Armonk, N.Y.: M. E. Sharpe, 2012.

Conboy, Kenneth, and James Morrison. *The CIA's Secret War in Tibet*. Lawrence: University Press of Kansas, 2011.

——. *Feet to the Fire: CIA Covert Operations in Indonesia, 1957–1958*. Annapolis: Naval Institute Press, 1999.

Conot, Robert E. *Justice at Nuremberg*. New York: Basic Books, 1983.

Cook, Blanche Wiesen. *The Declassified Eisenhower: A Divided Legacy of Peace and Political Warfare*. Garden City, N.Y.: Doubleday, 1981.

Cooney, John. *The American Pope: The Life and Times of Francis Cardinal Spellman*. New York: Dell, 1986.

Corkin, Stanley. *Cowboys as Cold Warriors: The Western and U.S. History*. Philadelphia: Temple University Press, 2004.

Corson, William R. *The Armies of Ignorance: The Rise of the American Intelligence Empire*. New York: Dial, 1977.

Cottam, Richard W. *Iran and the United States: A Cold War Case Study*. Pittsburgh: University of Pittsburgh Press, 1988.

Cullather, Nick. *Secret History: The CIA's Classified Account of Its Operations in Guatemala, 1952–1954*. Stanford: Stanford University Press, 1999.

Currey, Cecil B. *Edward Lansdale: The Unquiet American*. Boston: Houghton Mifflin, 1988.

Dallek, Robert. *The American Style of Foreign Policy: Cultural Politics and Foreign Affairs*. New York: Alfred A. Knopf, 1983.

——. *The Lost Peace: Leadership in a Time of Horror and Hope, 1945–1953*. New York: Harper, 2010.

Davis, Deborah. *Katharine the Great: Katharine Graham and the Washington Post*. New York: Harcourt Brace Jovanovich, 1979.

Devlin, Larry. *Chief of Station, Congo: Fighting the Cold War in a Hot Zone*. New York: PublicAffairs, 2007.

De Witte, Ludo. *The Assassination of Lumumba*. London: Verso, 2001.

Diggins, John Patrick. *Why Niebuhr Now*. Chicago: University of Chicago, 2011.

Divine, Robert A. *Eisenhower and the Cold War*. Oxford: Oxford University Press, 1981.

Dockrill, Saki. *Eisenhower's New-Look National Security Policy, 1953–1961*. New York: St. Martin's, 1996.

Dommen, Arthur J. *The Indochinese Experience of the French and the Americans: Nationalism and Communism in Cambodia, Laos, and Vietnam*. Bloomington: Indiana University Press, 2002.

Donovan, John C. *The Cold Warriors: A Policy-Making Elite*. Lexington, Mass.: D. C. Heath, 1974.

——. *Conflict and Crisis: The Presidency of Harry S. Truman 1948–1953*. New York: W.W. Norton, 1982.

Dooley, Tom. *Deliver Us from Evil*. New York: Signet, 1981.

Dorril, Stephen. *MI6: Inside the Covert World of Her Majesty's Secret Intelligence Service*. London: Fourth Estate, 2000.

Douglas, William O. *North from Malaya*. New York: Doubleday, 1953.

——. *Strange Lands and Friendly People*. New York: Harper, 1951.

Doyle, David W. *True Men and Traitors*. New York: John Wiley & Sons, 2001.

Drummond, Roscoe, and Gaston Coblentz. *Duel at the Brink: John Foster Dulles' Command of American Power*. Garden City, N.Y.: Doubleday, 1960.

Duiker, William J. *U.S. Containment Policy and the Conflict in Indochina*. Stanford: Stanford University Press, 1994.

Dulles, Allen. *The Craft of Intelligence*. New York: Harper & Row, 1963.

———. *Great Spy Stories from Fiction*. New York: Harper & Row, 1969.

———. *Great True Spy Stories*. New York: Ballantine, 1987.

———. *The Secret Surrender*. New York: Harper & Row, 1966.

Dulles, Eleanor Lansing. *Chances of a Lifetime*. Englewood Cliffs, N.J.: Prentice-Hall, 1980.

———. *John Foster Dulles: The Last Year*. New York: Harcourt, Brace & World, 1963.

Dulles, John Foster. *American Unity*. Washington, D.C.: U.S. Government Printing Office, 1948.

———. *America's Role in World Affairs*. Washington, D.C.: Carnegie Endowment, 1939.

———. *Peaceful Change Within the Society of Nations*. Washington, D.C.: Carnegie Endowment, 1936.

———. *A Righteous Faith for a Just and Durable Peace*. Washington, D.C.: Carnegie Endowment, 1942.

———. *War or Peace*. Edinburgh: Harrap, 1950.

———. *War, Peace and Change*. New York: Harper & Brothers, 1939.

Dunlop, Richard. *Donovan: America's Master Spy*. New York: Rand McNally, 1982.

Eisenhower, Dwight D. *Mandate for Change, 1953–1956: The White House Years*. Garden City, N.Y.: Doubleday, 1963.

Elm, Mostafa. *Oil, Power, and Principle: Iran's Oil Nationalization and Its Aftermath*. Syracuse, N.Y.: Syracuse University Press, 1992.

Elson, R. E. *The Idea of Indonesia*. Cambridge: Cambridge University Press, 2008.

Eveland, Wilbur Crane. *Ropes of Sand: America's Failure in the Middle East*. New York: W.W. Norton, 1980.

Fall, Bernard. *The Two Vietnams: A Political and Military Analysis*. Westport, Conn.: Greenwood, 1967.

———. *Viet-Nam Witness, 1953–1966*. New York: Praeger, 1966.

Fensch, Thomas Charles (ed.). *Top Secret: The CIA and the U-2 Program, 1954–1974*. The Woodlands, Tex.: New Century, 2001.

Firth, Noel E., and James H. Noren. *Soviet Defense Spending: A History of CIA Estimates, 1950–1990*. College Station: Texas A&M Press, 1998.

Fitzgerald, Frances. *Fire in the Lake: The Vietnamese and the Americans in Vietnam*. New York: Vintage, 1972.

Foster, John Watson. *American Diplomacy in the Orient*. Boston: Houghton Mifflin, 1904.

Freeman, Joshua B. *American Empire: The Rise of a Global Power, the Democratic Revolution at Home 1945–2000*. New York: Viking, 2012.

Fursenko, Aleksandr, and Timothy Naftali. *Khrushchev's Cold War: The Inside Story of an American Adversary*. New York: W.W. Norton, 2007.

Gaddis, John Lewis. *George F. Kennan: An American Life*. New York: Penguin, 2012.

———. *The Long Peace: Inquiries into the History of the Cold War*. New York: Oxford University Press, 1989.

———. *Strategies of Containment: A Critical Appraisal of Postwar American National Security Policy*. New York: Oxford University Press, 1982.

———. *The United States and the Origins of the Cold War, 1941–1947*. New York: Columbia University Press, 2000.

———. *We Now Know: Rethinking Cold War History*. Oxford: Clarendon, 1997.

Ganser, Daniele. "Terrorism in Western Europe: An Approach to NATO's Secret Stay-Behind Armies," *Whitehead Journal of Diplomacy and International Relations* 6, no. 1 (Winter/Spring 2005).

Gardner, Paul F. *Shared Hopes, Separate Fears: Fifty Years of U.S.-Indonesian Relations*. Boulder, Colo.: Westview, 1997.

Gasiorowski, Mark J., and Malcolm Byrne (eds.). *Mohammad Mossadeq and the 1953 Coup in Iran*. Syracuse, N.Y.: Syracuse University Press, 2003.

Gendzier, Irene L. *Notes from the Minefield: United States Intervention in Lebanon and the Middle East, 1945–1958*. New York: Columbia University Press, 2006.

Gibbs, David M. *The Political Economy of Third World Intervention: Mines, Money, and U.S. Policy in the Congo Crisis*. Chicago: University of Chicago Press, 1991.

Gleijeses, Piero. *Shattered Hope: The Guatemalan Revolution and the United States, 1944–1954*. Princeton: Princeton University Press, 1991.

Goode, James A. *The United States and Iran: In the Shadow of Musaddiq*. New York: Palgrave Macmillan, 1997.

Goold-Adams, Richard. *John Foster Dulles: A Reappraisal*. New York: Appleton-Century-Crofts, 1962.

Graebner, Norman A. *An Uncertain Tradition: American Secretaries of State in the Twentieth Century*. New York: McGraw-Hill, 1961.

Grandin, Greg. *Empire's Workshop: Latin America, the United States, and the Rise of the New Imperialism*. New York: Owl Books, 2006.

———. *The Last Colonial Massacre: Latin America in the Cold War*. Chicago: University of Chicago Press, 2011.

Granville, Johanna C. *The First Domino: International Decision Making During the Hungarian Crisis of 1956*. College Station: Texas A&M University Press, 2004.

Greene, Daniel P. O'C. "John Foster Dulles and the End of the Franco-American Entente in Indochina," *Diplomatic History* 16, no. 4 (Oct. 1992), pp. 551–72.

Greene, Graham. *The Quiet American*. New York: Penguin, 2004.

Greenstein, Fred I. *The Hidden-Hand Presidency: Eisenhower as Leader*. Baltimore: Johns Hopkins University Press, 1994.

Grose, Peter. *Gentleman Spy: The Life of Allen Dulles*. New York: Houghton Mifflin, 1994.

———. *Operation Rollback: America's Secret War Behind the Iron Curtain*. Boston: Houghton Mifflin, 2000.

Guhin, Michael A. *John Foster Dulles: A Statesman and His Times*. New York: Columbia University Press, 1972.

Gunn, T. Jeremy. *Spiritual Weapons: The Cold War and the Forging of an American National Religion*. Westport, Conn.: Praeger, 2009.

Gup, Ted. *The Book of Honor: Covert Lives and Classified Deaths at the CIA*. New York: Doubleday, 2000.

Hagedorn, Anne. *Savage Peace: Hope and Fear in America, 1919*. New York: Simon and Schuster, 2008.

Halberstam, David. *The Best and the Brightest*. New York: Penguin, 1972.

———. *The Fifties*. New York: Villard, 1993.

Halle, Louis J. *The Cold War as History*. New York: Harper and Row, 1967.

Heffernan, Margaret. *Willful Blindness: Why We Ignore the Obvious at Our Peril*. New York: Walker, 2011.

Heinz. G., and H. Donnay. *Lumumba: The Last Fifty Days*. New York: Grove, 1969.

Herring, George C. *America's Longest War: The United States and Vietnam, 1950–1975*. New York: McGraw-Hill, 1986.

Hersh, Burton. *The Old Boys: The American Elite and the Origins of the CIA*. New York: Charles Scribner's Sons, 1992.

Heuer, Richard J., Jr. *Psychology of Intelligence Analysis*. Washington, D.C.: Center for the Study of Intelligence, Central Intelligence Agency, 1999.

Higgins, Trumbull. *The Perfect Failure: Kennedy, Eisenhower, and the C.I.A. at the Bay of Pigs*. New York: W.W. Norton, 1989.

Hinds, Lynn Boyd, and Theodore Otto Windt Jr. *The Cold War as Rhetoric: The Beginnings, 1945–1950*. New York: Praeger, 1991.

Ho Chin Minh. *Down with Colonialism!* London: Verso, 2007.

Hogan, Michael J. *A Cross of Iron: Harry S. Truman and the Origins of the National Security State, 1945–1954*. Cambridge: Cambridge University Press, 1992.

Hollander, Edwin P., and Raymond G. Hunt (eds.). *Current Perspectives in Social Psychology*. New York: Oxford University Press, 1968.

Hoopes, Townsend. *The Devil and John Foster Dulles*. Boston: Little, Brown, 1973.

Hunt, E. Howard. *Undercover: Memoirs of an American Secret Agent*. New York: Berkley/Putnam, 1974.

Hunt, Michael H. *Lyndon Johnson's War: America's Cold War Crusade in Vietnam, 1945–1968*. New York: Hill & Wang, 1997.

Immerman, Richard H. *The CIA in Guatemala: The Foreign Policy of Intervention*. Austin: University of Texas Press, 1982.

———. *Empire for Liberty: A History of American Imperialism from Benjamin Franklin to Paul Wolfowitz*. Princeton: Princeton University Press, 2010.

———. *John Foster Dulles: Piety, Pragmatism, and Power in U.S. Foreign Policy*. Wilmington, Del.: Scholarly Resources, 1999.

———. (ed.) *John Foster Dulles and the Diplomacy of the Cold War*. Princeton: Princeton University Press, 1990.

Inboden, William. *Religion and American Foreign Policy, 1945–1960: The Soul of Containment*. Cambridge: Cambridge University Press, 2008.

Inderfurth, Karl F., and Loch K. Johnson (eds.). *Fateful Decisions: Inside the National Security Council*. New York: Oxford University Press, 2004.

Jacobs, Seth. *America's Miracle Man in Vietnam: Ngo Dinh Diem, Religion, Race, and U.S. Intervention in Southeast Asia, 1950–1957.* Durham, N.C.: Duke University Press, 2004.

———. *Cold War Mandarin: Ngo Dinh Diem and the Origins of America's War in Vietnam.* Lanham, Md.: Rowman & Littlefield, 2006.

Janis, Irving L. *Groupthink: Psychological Studies of Policy Decisions and Fiascoes.* Independence, Ky.: Cengage Learning, 1982.

Jefferson, Louis. *The John Foster Dulles Book of Humor.* New York: St. Martin's, 1986.

Jeffreys-Jones, Rhodri. *The CIA and American Democracy.* New Haven: Yale University Press, 1989.

———. *Cloak and Dollar: A History of American Secret Intelligence.* New Haven: Yale University Press, 2003.

Johnson, Loch K., and James J. Wirtz (eds.). *Strategic Intelligence: Windows into a Secret World.* Cary, N.C.: Roxbury, 2004.

Jones, Howard. *The Bay of Pigs.* New York: Oxford University Press, 2010.

Kahin, Audrey R., and George McT. Kahin. *Subversion as Foreign Policy: The Secret Eisenhower and Dulles Debacle in Indonesia.* Seattle: University of Washington Press, 1997.

Kahin, George McTurnan. *Asian-African Conference: Bandung, Indonesia, April 1955.* Ithaca, N.Y.: Cornell University Press, 1956.

Kahneman, Daniel. *Thinking, Fast and Slow.* New York: Farrar, Straus & Giroux, 2011.

Kaiser, David E. *American Tragedy: Kennedy, Johnson, and the Origins of the Vietnam War.* Cambridge, Mass.: Belknap, 2002.

Kalb, Madeleine G. *The Congo Cables: The Cold War in Africa—from Eisenhower to Kennedy.* New York: Macmillan, 1982.

Karnow, Stanley. *Vietnam: A History.* New York: Viking, 1983.

Katouzian, Homa. *Mussadiq and the Struggle for Power in Iran.* London: I. B. Tauris, 1999.

Kattenburg, Paul M. *The Vietnam Trauma in American Foreign Policy, 1945–75.* New Brunswick, N.J.: Transaction, 1980.

Katz, Barry M. *Foreign Intelligence: Research and Analysis in the Office of Strategic Services, 1942–1945.* Cambridge, Mass.: Harvard University Press, 1989.

Kennedy, Paul. *The Rise and Fall of the Great Powers: Economic Change and Military Conflict from 1500 to 2000.* New York: Random House, 1987.

Kessler, Ronald. *Inside the CIA: Revealing the Secrets of the World's Most Powerful Spy Agency.* New York: Pocket, 1994.

Keylor, William R. *The Twentieth Century World and Beyond: An International History Since 1900.* New York: Oxford University Press, 2011.

Kinzer, Stephen. *All the Shah's Men: An American Coup and the Roots of Middle East Terror.* Hoboken, N.J.: John Wiley & Sons, 2003.

———. *Bitter Fruit: The Story of the American Coup in Guatemala.* Cambridge, Mass.: Harvard University Press, 2005.

Kipling, Rudyard. *Kim.* Hollywood, Fla.: Simon & Brown, 2011.

Klein, Christina. *Cold War Orientalism: Asia in the Middlebrow Imagination, 1945–1961.* Berkeley: University of California Press, 2003.

Knott, Stephen F. *Secret and Sanctioned: Covert Operations and the American Presidency*. New York: Oxford University Press, 1996.

Kofsky, Frank. *Harry S. Truman and the War Scare of 1948: A Successful Campaign to Deceive the Nation*. New York: Palgrave Macmillan, 1995.

Kornbluh, Peter (ed.). *Bay of Pigs Declassified: The Secret CIA Report on the Invasion of Cuba*. New York: New Press, 1988.

Kowert, Paul A. *Groupthink of Deadlock: When Do Leaders Learn from Their Advisors?* Albany: State University of New York Press, 2002.

Kwitny, Jonathan. *Endless Enemies: The Making of an Unfriendly World*. New York: Congdon and Weed, 1984.

Lacouture, Jean. *Ho Chi Minh: A Political Biography*. New York: Random House, 1968.

Lampe, John R., et al. *Yugoslav-American Economic Relations Since World War II*. Durham, N.C.: Duke University Press, 1990.

Langguth, A. J. *Our Vietnam: The War 1954–1975*. New York: Touchstone, 2000.

Leary, William M. (ed.). *The Central Intelligence Agency: History and Documents*. Tuscaloosa: University of Alabama Press, 1984.

Lederer, William J., and Eugene Burdick. *The Ugly American*. New York: Crest, 1958.

Legge, John D. *Sukarno: A Political Biography*. Singapore: Didier Millet, 2007.

Lees, Lorraine M. *Keeping Tito Afloat: The United States, Yugoslavia, and the Cold War*. University Park: Pennsylvania State University Press, 1997.

Lefever, Ernest. *Crisis in the Congo: A United Nations Force in Action*. Washington, D.C.: Brookings Institution, 1965.

Leffler, Melvyn P. *A Preponderance of Power: National Security, the Truman Administration, and the Cold War*. Stanford: Stanford University Press, 1992.

Lehman, Kenneth. "Revolutions and Attributions: Making Sense of Eisenhower Administration Policies in Bolivia and Guatemala," *Diplomatic History* 21, no. 2 (Spring 1997), pp. 185–213.

Lehr, Dick, and Gerard O'Neill. *Whitey: The Life of America's Most Notorious Mob Boss*. New York: Crown, 2013.

Lisagor, Nancy, and Frank Lipsius. *A Law Unto Itself: The Untold Story of the Law Firm of Sullivan & Cromwell*. New York: William Morrow, 1988.

Logevall, Fredrik. *Embers of War: The Fall of an Empire and the Making of America's Vietnam*. New York: Random House, 2012.

Longhurst, Henry. *Adventure in Oil: The Story of British Petroleum*. London: Sidgwick and Jackson, 1959.

Louise, Mary. "Operation Mockingbird: CIA Media Manipulation," http://www .prisonplanet.com/analysis_louise_01_03_03_mockingbird.html.

Lovell, Stanley P. *Of Spies & Stratagems*. New York: Pocket Books, 1964.

Lukacs, John. *Churchill: Visionary. Statesman. Historian*. New Haven: Yale University Press, 2004.

Lynch, Grayston L. *Decision for Disaster: Betrayal at the Bay of Pigs*. Dulles, Va.: Potomac, 2000.

Mackenzie, Angus. *Secrets: The CIA's War at Home*. Berkeley: University of California Press, 1997.

Mangold, Tom. *Cold Warrior: James Jesus Angleton, the CIA's Master Spy Hunter.* London: Simon and Schuster, 1991.

Mann, Robert. *A Grand Delusion: America's Descent into Vietnam.* New York: Basic Books, 2001.

Marks, Frederick W., III. *Power and Peace: The Diplomacy of John Foster Dulles.* Westport, Conn.: Praeger, 1993.

Matthews, John P. C. *Explosion: The Hungarian Revolution of 1956.* New York: Hippocrene, 2007.

————. *Tinderbox: East-Central Europe in the Spring, Summer, and Early Fall of 1956.* Tucson, Ariz.: Fenestra, 2003.

May, Brian. *The Indonesian Tragedy.* N.p.: Non Basic Stock Line, 2000.

McCann, Thomas. *An American Company: The Tragedy of United Fruit.* New York: Random House, 1988.

McCarthy, Eugene J. *Up 'Til Now: A Memoir.* New York: Harcourt, 1987.

McCoy, Alfred W. *The Politics of Heroin in Southeast Asia.* New York: Harper & Row, 1973.

McGhee, George. *Envoy to the Middle World: Adventures in Diplomacy.* New York: Harper & Row, 1983.

McGhee, Ralph W. *Deadly Deceits: My 25 Years in the CIA.* Melbourne: Ocean Press, 1999.

McKown, Robin. *Lumumba: A Biography.* Garden City, N.Y.: Doubleday, 1969.

McLellan, David S. *Dean Acheson: The State Department Years.* New York: Dodd Mead, 1976.

Melanson, Richard A., and David Mayers (eds.). *Reevaluating Eisenhower: American Foreign Policy in the Fifties.* Urbana: University of Illinois Press, 1989.

Miller, James E. "Taking Off the Gloves: The United States and the Italian Elections of 1948," in *Diplomatic History 7*, no. 1 (Winter 1983).

Morgan, Joseph G. *The Vietnam Lobby: The American Friends of Vietnam, 1955–1975.* Chapel Hill: University of North Carolina Press, 1997.

Morgan, Ted. *Reds: McCarthyism in Twentieth-Century America.* New York: Random House, 2004.

Morley, Jefferson. *Our Man in Mexico: Winston Scott and the Hidden History of the CIA.* Lawrence: University Press of Kansas, 2008.

Mosley, Leonard. *Dulles: A Biography of Eleanor, Allen, and John Foster Dulles and Their Family Network.* New York: Dial, 1978.

Mydans, Carl. *The Violent Peace.* New York: Scribner, 1968.

Nashel, Jonathan. *Edward Lansdale's Cold War.* Amherst: University of Massachusetts Press, 2005.

Natarajan, L. *American Shadow Over India.* Delhi: People's Publishing House, 1956.

Nester, William. *International Relations: Politics and Economics in the 21st Century.* Independence, Ky.: Wadsworth, 2000.

Niebuhr, Reinhold. *The Irony of American History.* Chicago: University of Chicago Press, 2008.

————. *Moral Man and Immoral Society.* New York: Charles Scribner's Sons, 1932.

Okumu, Washington. *Lumumba's Congo: Roots of Conflict*. New York: Ivan Obolensky, 1963.

Olmsted, Kathryn S. *Challenging the Secret Government: The Post-Watergate Investigations of the CIA and FBI*. Chapel Hill: University of North Carolina Press, 1996.

Osgood, Kenneth. *Total Cold War: Eisenhower's Secret Propaganda Battle at Home and Abroad*. Lawrence: University Press of Kansas, 2008.

Overseas Consultants, Inc. *Report on Seven Year Development Plan for the Plan Organization of the Imperial Government of Iran*. New York: OCI, 1949.

Parmet, Herbert S. *Eisenhower and the American Crusades*. New York: Macmillan, 1972.

Paterson, Thomas G. *Contesting Castro: The United States and the Triumph of the Cuban Revolution*. New York: Oxford University Press, 1995.

Pearson, John. *The Life of Ian Fleming*. London: Jonathan Cape, 1996.

Pender, C. L. M. *The Life and Times of Sukarno*. Cranbury, N.J.: Associated University Press, 1974.

Pentagon Papers, Gravel Edition, https://www.mtholyoke.edu/acad/intrel/pentagon/pent9.htm.

Persons, Albert C. *Bay of Pigs: A Firsthand Account of the Mission by a U.S. Pilot in Support of the Cuban Invasion Force in 1961*. Jefferson, N.C.: McFarland, 2011.

Peterson, Tore T. "Anglo-American Rivalry in the Middle East: The Struggle for the Buraimi Oasis, 1952–1957," *International History Review* 14, no. 1 (Feb. 1992), pp. 71–91.

Pfeiffer, Jack. *Official History of the Bay of Pigs Operation*. www.gwu.edu/~nsarchiv/NSAEBB/NSAEBB355/.

Phillips, David Atlee. *The Night Watch*. New York: Atheneum, 1977.

Pietrusza, David. *1948: Harry Truman's Improbable Victory and the Year that Transformed America*. New York: Union Square Press, 2011.

Pisani, Sallie. *Lumumba Lost*. N.p.: Xlibris, 2003.

Powell, Adam Clayton III. *Adam by Adam: The Autobiography of Adam Clayton Powell, Jr.* New York: Kensington, 2001.

Powers, Thomas. *Intelligence Wars: American Secret History from Hitler to Al-Qaeda*. New York: New York Review of Books, 2002.

———. *The Man Who Kept the Secrets: Richard Helms and the CIA*. New York: Pocket Books, 1979.

Prados, John. *The Hidden History of the Vietnam War*. Chicago: Ivan R. Dee, 1988.

———. *Safe for Democracy: The Secret Wars of the CIA*. Chicago: Ivan R. Dee, 2006.

———. *The Sky Would Fall: Operation Vulture: The Secret U.S. Bombing Mission to Vietnam, 1954*. New York: Dial, 1983.

———. *Vietnam: The History of an Unwinnable War, 1945–1975*. Lawrence: University Press of Kansas, 2009.

———. *William Colby and the CIA: The Secret Wars of a Controversial Spymaster*. Lawrence: University Press of Kansas, 2009.

Preston, Andrew. *Sword of the Spirit, Shield of Faith: Religion in American War and Diplomacy*. New York: Alfred A. Knopf, 2012.

Pruessen, Ronald W. *John Foster Dulles: The Road to Power*. New York: Free Press, 1982.

Quirk, E. Robert. *Fidel Castro*. New York: W.W. Norton, 1995.

Rabe, Stephen G. *Eisenhower and Latin America: The Foreign Policy of Anticommunism*. Chapel Hill: University of North Carolina Press, 1988.

———. *The Killing Zone: The United States Wages Cold War in Latin America*. New York: Oxford University Press, 2012.

Ranelagh, John. *The Agency: The Rise and Decline of the CIA*. London: Sceptre, 1988.

Rasenberger, Jim. *The Brilliant Disaster: JFK, Castro, and America's Doomed Invasion of Cuba's Bay of Pigs*. New York: Scribner, 2011.

Reid-Henry, Simon. *Fidel and Che: A Revolutionary Friendship*. New York: Walker, 2009.

Rice, Edwin Wilbur. *The Sunday-School Movement, 1780–1917, and the American Sunday-School Union*. Philadelphia: American Sunday-School Union, 1917.

Romulo, Carlos. *The Meaning of Bandung*. Chapel Hill: University of North Carolina Press, 1956.

Roosevelt, Kermit. *Countercoup: The Struggle for the Control of Iran*. New York: McGraw-Hill, 1979.

Root, Hilton L. *Alliance Curse: How America Lost the Third World*. Washington, D.C.: Brookings Institution, 2008.

Rositzke, Harry. *The CIA's Secret Operations: Espionage, Counterespionage, and Covert Action*. New York: Reader's Digest, 1977.

Roy, Raj, and John W. Young. *Ambassador to Sixties London: The Diaries of David Bruce, 1961–1969*. Dordrecht, Netherlands: Republic of Letters, 2009.

Rubin, Daniel Aaron. "Pawns of the Cold War: John Foster Dulles, the PRC, and the Imprisonments of John Downey and Richard Fecteau," http://drum.lib.umd.edu/bitstream/1903/1839/1/umi-umd-1832.pdf.

Rudgers, David F. *Creating the Secret State: The Origins of the Central Intelligence Agency, 1943–1947*. Lawrence: University Press of Kansas, 2000.

Ruotsila, Markku. *British and American Anticommunism Before the Cold War*. London: Routledge, 2001.

Saif, Lubna. "Pakistan and SEATO." *Pakistan Journal of History and Culture* 28, no. 2 (2007).

Saunders, Frances Stonor. *The Cultural Cold War: The CIA and the World of Arts and Letters*. New York: New Press, 2001.

Schlesinger, Arthur M., Jr. *A Thousand Days: John F. Kennedy in the White House*. New York: Mariner, 2002.

Schoultz, Lars. *That Infernal Little Cuban Republic: The United States and the Cuban Revolution*. Chapel Hill: University of North Carolina Press, 2011.

Schulzinger, Robert D. *A Time for War: The United States and Vietnam, 1941–1975*. New York: Oxford University Press, 1999.

Sheehan, Neil. *A Bright Shining Lie: John Paul Vann and America in Vietnam*. New York: Modern Library, 2009.

———. *A Fierce Peace in a Cold War: Bernard Schreiver and the Ultimate Weapon*. New York: Random House, 2009.

Simons, Geoff. *Indonesia: The Long Oppression*. New York: St. Martin's, 2000.

Skardon, C. Philip. *A Lesson for Our Times: How America Kept the Peace in the Hungary-Suez Crisis of 1956*. N.p.: Authorhouse, 2010.

Slotkin, Richard. *Gunfighter Nation: The Myth of the Frontier in Twentieth-Century America*. Norman: University of Oklahoma Press, 1998.

Smith, Bradley F. *The Shadow Warriors: OSS and the Origins of the CIA*. New York: Basic Books, 1983.

Smith, Jean Edward. *Eisenhower in War and Peace*. New York: Random House, 2012.

Smith, Joseph B. *Portrait of a Cold Warrior: Second Thoughts of a Top CIA Agent*. New York: Ballantine, 1976.

Smith, Richard Harris. *OSS: The Secret History of America's First Central Intelligence Agency*. Guilford, Conn.: Lyons, 2005.

Smith, W. Thomas. *Encyclopedia of the Central Intelligence Agency*. New York: Facts on File, 2003.

Solomon, Daniel F. *Breaking Up with Cuba: The Dissolution of Friendly Relations Between Washington and Havana, 1956–1961*. Jefferson, N.C.: McFarland, 2011.

Srodes, James. *Allen Dulles: Master of Spies*. Washington, D.C.: Regnery, 1999.

Stanford, Karen L. *If We Must Die: African American Voices on War and Peace*. Lanham, Md.: Rowman & Littlefield, 2008.

Statler, Kathryn. *Replacing France: The Origins of American Intervention in Vietnam*. Lexington: University Press of Kentucky, 2009.

Steinberg, Blema S. *Shame and Humiliation: Presidential Decision Making on Vietnam*. Montreal: McGill Queens University Press, 1996.

Stockwell, John. *In Search of Enemies: A CIA Story*. New York: W.W. Norton, 1978.

Sunstein, Cass M. *Going to Extremes: How Like Minds Unite and Divide*. New York: Oxford University Press, 2011.

Takeyh, Ray. *The Origins of the Eisenhower Doctrine: The US, Britain and Nasser's Egypt, 1953–57*. New York: Palgrave Macmillan, 2000.

Tavris, Carol, and Elliot Aronson. *Mistakes Were Made (But Not by Me): Why We Justify Foolish Beliefs, Bad Decisions, and Hurtful Acts*. New York: Harvest, 2007.

Thomas, Evan. *Ike's Bluff: President Eisenhower's Secret Battle to Save the World*. New York: Little, Brown, 2012.

———. *The Very Best Men: The Daring Early Years of the CIA*. New York: Simon and Schuster, 1995.

Thompson, John M. *Russia, Bolshevism, and the Versailles Peace*. Princeton: Princeton University Press, 1967.

Toriello, Guillermo. *La Batalla de Guatemala*. Santiago de Chile: Editorial Universitaria, 1955.

Toulouse, Mark G. *The Transformation of John Foster Dulles: From Prophet of Realism to High Priest of Nationalism*. Macon, Ga.: Mercer University Press, 1985.

Trento, Joseph J. *The Secret History of the CIA*. New York: MJF, 2001.

Trilling, Lionel. *The Liberal Imagination*. New York: NYRB Classics, 2008.

Trivers, Robert. *The Folly of Fools: The Logic of Deceit and Self-Deception in Human Life*. New York: Basic Books, 2011.

Troy, Thomas F. *Donovan and the CIA: A History of the Establishment of the Central Intelligence Agency.* Westport, Conn.: Praeger, 1981.

Trumbull, Higgins. *The Perfect Failure: Kennedy, Eisenhower, and the CIA at the Bay of Pigs.* New York: W.W. Norton, 1989.

Tshonda, Jean Omassombo. "Patrice Lumumba's Youth," in Bogumil Jewsiewicki et al., *A Congo Chronicle: Patrice Lumumba in Urban Art.* New York: Museum for African Art, 1999.

Tudda, Chris. *Truth Is Our Weapon: The Rhetorical Diplomacy of Dwight D. Eisenhower and John Foster Dulles.* Baton Rouge: Louisiana State University Press, 2006.

Tully, Andrew. *Central Intelligence Agency: The Inside Story.* New York: Corgi, 1963.

Tunzelmann, Alex von. *Red Heat: Conspiracy, Murder, and the Cold War in the Caribbean.* New York: Henry Holt, 2011.

Twing, Stephen W. *Myths, Models, and U.S. Foreign Policy: The Cultural Shaping of Three Cold Warriors.* Boulder, Colo.: Lynn Rienner, 1998.

Tyler, Patrick. *A World of Trouble: The White House and the Middle East—From the Cold War to the War on Terror.* New York: Farrar, Straus & Giroux, 2009.

United States Department of State. *Foreign Relations of the United States.* Washington, D.C.: U.S. Government Printing Office.

1952–1954. Guatemala. Publication 11026.

1952–1954. Vol. IV, the American Republics.

1952–1954. Vol. IX, the Near and Middle East.

1952–1954. Vol. X, Iran.

1952–1954. Vol. XIII, Indochina.

1955–1957. Vol. I, Vietnam.

1955–1957. Vol. XVI, Suez Crisis, July 26–December 31, 1956.

1955–1957. Vol. XXI, East Asian security; Cambodia; Laos.

1955–1957. Vol. XXII, Southeast Asia.

1958–1960. Vol. I, Vietnam.

1958–1960. Vol. VI, Cuba.

1958–1960. Vol. VII, Berlin Crisis.

1958–1960. Vol. XI, Lebanon and Jordan.

1958–1960. Vol. XIV, Africa.

1961–1963. Vol. XI, Cuba.

———. *Intervention of International Communism in Guatemala.* Westport, Conn.: Greenwood, 1954.

———. *Intervention of International Communism in the Americas.* Washington, D.C.: Department of State, 1954.

———. *Tenth Inter-American Conference: Report of the Delegation of the United States of America with Related Documents.* Washington, D.C.: Department of State, 1955.

United States Senate. *Alleged Assassination Plots Against Foreign Leaders: An Interim Report.* Washington, D.C.: U.S. Government Printing Office, 1975.

———. *Final Report of the Select Committee to Study Governmental Operations with Respect to Intelligence Activities, United States Senate: Together with Additional,*

Supplemental, and Separate Views. Washington, D.C.: U.S. Government Printing Office, 1976.

———. *Project MKUltra, the CIA's Program of Research into Behavioral Modification. Joint Hearing before the Select Committee on Intelligence and the Subcommittee on Health and Scientific Research of the Committee on Human Resources, United States Senate, Ninety-fifth Congress, First Session.* Washington, D.C.: U.S. Government Printing Office, 1977.

Vandenbroucke, Lucien S. "Anatomy of a Failure: The Decision to Land at the Bay of Pigs," *Political Science Quarterly* 99, no. 3 (Fall 1998), p. 476.

Vickers, Adrian. *A History of Modern Indonesia.* Cambridge: Cambridge University Press, 2005.

Von Eschen, Penny M. *Satchmo Blows Up the World: Jazz Ambassadors Play the Cold War.* Cambridge, Mass.: Harvard University Press, 2006.

Waller, Douglas C. *Wild Bill Donovan: The Spymaster Who Created the OSS and Modern American Espionage.* New York: Free Press, 2011.

Warner, Roger. *Back Fire: The CIA's Secret War in Laos and Its Link to the War in Vietnam.* New York: Simon and Schuster, 1995.

Wawro, Geoffrey. *Quicksand: America's Pursuit of Power in the Middle East.* New York: Penguin, 2010.

Weiner, Tim. *Legacy of Ashes: The History of the CIA.* New York: Doubleday, 2007.

Weissman, Stephen R. *American Foreign Policy in the Congo, 1960–1964.* Ithaca, N.Y.: Cornell University Press, 1974.

Welch, Richard E., Jr. *Response to Revolution: The United States and the Cuban Revolution, 1959–1961.* Chapel Hill: University of North Carolina Press, 1985.

Whitfield, Stephen J. *The Culture of the Cold War.* Baltimore: Johns Hopkins, 1991.

Wilford, Hugh. *The Mighty Wurlitzer: How the CIA Played America.* Cambridge, Mass.: Harvard University Press, 2008.

Wilson, Woodrow. *Addresses of President Woodrow Wilson.* Washington, D.C.: U.S. Government Printing Office, 1919.

Winks, Robin. *Cloak and Gown: Scholars in the Secret War, 1939–1961.* New York: William Morrow, 1987.

Wise, David, and Thomas B. Ross. *The Invisible Government.* New York: Random House, 1964.

Wood, Bryce. *The Dismantling of the Good Neighbor Policy.* Austin: University of Texas Press, 1985.

Woodhouse, Christopher Montague. *Something Ventured.* London: Granada, 1982.

Wright, Richard. *The Color Curtain.* Oxford: University Press of Mississippi, 1995.

Wyden, Peter. *Bay of Pigs: The Untold Story.* New York: Simon and Schuster, 1979.

Zabih, Sepehr. *The Mossadegh Era: Roots of the Iranian Revolution.* Chicago: Lake View, 1982.

Zeilig, Leo. *Patrice Lumumba: Africa's Lost Leader.* London: Haus, 2008.

ACKNOWLEDGMENTS

This book ranges widely over politics, history, and geography—so widely that no individual could master all the themes and episodes with which it deals. Regional specialists, historians, and other experts decisively deepened my understanding of this material. By agreeing to read and comment on sections of the manuscript, they enriched the story this book presents. I owe a great debt to them: Kenneth Conboy, Nick Cullather, Ludo De Witte, Farhad Diba, H. D. S. Greenway, Peter Kornbluh, Steven Pinker, John Prados, Stephen Rabe, and Jim Rasenberger.

William Keylor shared his deep expertise in matters related to the Paris peace conference and Versailles treaty. Tom McCann provided important details about the Dulles brothers' role in Guatemala. Ksenya Khinchuk helped me track down the *Glorious Victory* mural. María Soledad Cervantes Ramírez located its copyright owners in Mexico. Sophiya Shahla did enterprising work in Iranian archives that produced valuable new material.

One of my outstanding students at Northwestern University, Benjamin Armstrong, did research that allowed me to shape this project in its early stage. Two equally remarkable students at Boston University, Justine States and Matthew Seaton, also devoted many hours to productive research.

Sharon Sullivan and other librarians at the Truro Public Library in Massachusetts obtained a series of obscure books for me. Daniel Linke, Amanda Pike, and their colleagues at the Seeley G. Mudd Manuscript

Library at Princeton University, which houses the papers of John Foster Dulles and Allen Dulles, were unfailingly helpful. Archivists at the National Archives in College Park, Maryland, guided me to valuable material.

Three sharp-eyed readers, Jane Kinzer, David Shuman, and James M. Stone, read large sections of the manuscript and made highly valuable suggestions.

None of these people reviewed the final manuscript, so I alone am responsible for any errors of fact or interpretation. Without their help, however, this book would be considerably less than it is.

I would also like to thank my wise and insightful editor, Paul Golob, who skillfully guided this project from beginning to end.

INDEX

ABOUT THE AUTHOR

STEPHEN KINZER has written about U.S. foreign intervention in books including *All the Shah's Men*, *Overthrow*, and *Bitter Fruit*. An award-winning foreign correspondent, he served as the *New York Times*'s bureau chief in Turkey, Germany, and Nicaragua and as the *Boston Globe*'s Latin America correspondent. He is a visiting fellow at the Watson Institute for International Studies at Brown University, where he teaches in the International Relations program. He contributes to *The New York Review of Books* and is a columnist for *The Guardian*. He lives in Boston.